INHABITANTS
OF *the* DEEP

BLACK OUTDOORS: INNOVATIONS IN THE POETICS OF STUDY

A series edited by J. Kameron Carter and Sarah Jane Cervenak

INHABITANTS OF *the* DEEP

the BLUENESS OF BLACKNESS

JONATHAN HOWARD

Duke University Press *Durham and London* 2025

© 2025 DUKE UNIVERSITY PRESS
All rights reserved
Printed in the United States of America on acid-free paper ∞
Project Editor: Lisa Lawley
Designed by Courtney Leigh Richardson
Typeset in Garamond Premier Pro by Westchester Publishing Services

Library of Congress Cataloging-in-Publication Data
Names: Howard, Jonathan, [date] author.
Title: Inhabitants of the deep : the blueness of blackness / Jonathan Howard.
Other titles: Black outdoors.
Description: Durham : Duke University Press, 2025. | Series: Black outdoors: innovations in the poetics of study | Includes bibliographical references and index.
Identifiers: LCCN 2025013300 (print)
LCCN 2025013301 (ebook)
ISBN 9781478032618 (paperback)
ISBN 9781478029281 (hardcover)
ISBN 9781478061489 (ebook)
Subjects: LCSH: American fiction—African American authors—History and criticism. | Ecocriticism. | African Americans in literature. | African diaspora in literature. | Water in literature. | Sea in literature.
Classification: LCC PS153.B53 H693 2025 (print) | LCC PS153.B53 (ebook) | DDC 813.009/352996073—dc23/eng/20250627
LC record available at https://lccn.loc.gov/2025013300
LC ebook record available at https://lccn.loc.gov/2025013301

Cover art: Calida Rawles, *Echo My Moonlight* (detail), 2020. Acrylic on canvas, 30 × 24 in. © Calida Rawles. Courtesy of the artist and Lehmann Maupin, New York, Seoul, and London. Photo by Marten Elder.

Publication of this book has been aided by a grant from the Frederick W. Hilles Publication Fund of Yale University and supported by Duke University Press's Scholars of Color First Book Fund.

for the jumpers and the jettisoned
and my shipmate, alese

Often did I think many of the inhabitants
of the deep much more happy than myself;
I envied them the freedom they enjoyed, and as often wished
I could change my condition for theirs.

—OLAUDAH EQUIANO,
The Interesting Narrative of the Life of Olaudah Equiano

Contents

Prologue

THE BLUENESS OF BLACKNESS

I came into this world anxious to uncover the meaning of things, my soul desirous to be at the origin of the world, and here I am an object among other objects.
—FRANTZ FANON, *Black Skin, White Masks*

Before all of this, there was a deep Black dream that woke as us.
—ALEXIS PAULINE GUMBS, *Undrowned*

IN THE BEGINNING, black was blue. Not the ocean of lamentation poured out from the souls of blues people that Amiri Baraka spoke of (though not *not* this). But the literal ocean. The "In 1492, Columbus sailed the ocean blue" blue. The other hue playing midwife to our births in the centuries when our skin learned speech and started talking to the world behind our backs. The water that there was in the beginning.

The history exhibit of the National Museum of African American History and Culture (NMAAHC) in Washington, DC, begins at this beginning. Visitors, however, do not. Instead, your escort to the beginning is a glass-walled elevator which looks out onto a black shaft that doubles as a timeline. White year markers roll by, subtitling your backward trek through time, as you make your one-way descent into the depths of black history:

1877
1808
1776
1565
1400

The museum will not remember for you. Will not spare you the formality of having to actually work your way back through time—its thickness, its accumulation, its depth. You do not enter the museum on the ground floor. To get to the beginning, you've got to plunge. Like the unnamed narrator in the prologue of Ralph Ellison's *Invisible Man*, you don't just enter history as he did music; you descend into its depths, the centuries closing in over your head, until you arrive at the lowest level, where someone can be heard beginning a sermon about the "blackness of blackness." *In the beginning, there was blackness*, you almost hear them say. *And that blackness was blue.*

Our preacher, in this instance, is Olaudah Equiano, and his text is *The Interesting Narrative of the Life of Olaudah Equiano, or Gustavus Vassa, the African, Written by Himself* (1789). Soon after exiting the elevator, following a brief survey of precolonial African history, you encounter perhaps the narrative's most famous sentence printed gravely on a wall:

> The first object which saluted my eyes when I arrived on the coast, was . . . a slave ship . . . waiting for its cargo.[1]

Invoked by the museum as part of the introductory apparatus of a history exhibit spanning three floors and progressing vertically "*up* from slavery," as Booker T. Washington might describe it, Equiano's words bespeak blackness's beginnings (figure P.1).[2] They name what, in the curatorial imagination of the museum, is supposed to have come "first": namely, the original and originating hail of the slave ship. And in this, the NMAAHC is hardly alone. Black history, which the playwright August Wilson has suggestively characterized as the "black American odyssey," for many begins with the transatlantic slave trade, or what is otherwise known as the *Middle Passage*.[3] And Equiano's narrative in particular—as history's only firsthand account of Middle Passage written by and from the perspective of the enslaved and one of the earliest works of African Diaspora literature—is often regarded as a point of entry for African Diaspora history and literature.[4] Recently, however, this status of black history's single narrative tether to Middle Passage has been thrown into question. Archival evidence discovered by notable Equiano biographer Vincent Carretta suggests that Equiano actually may have been born in South Carolina and not

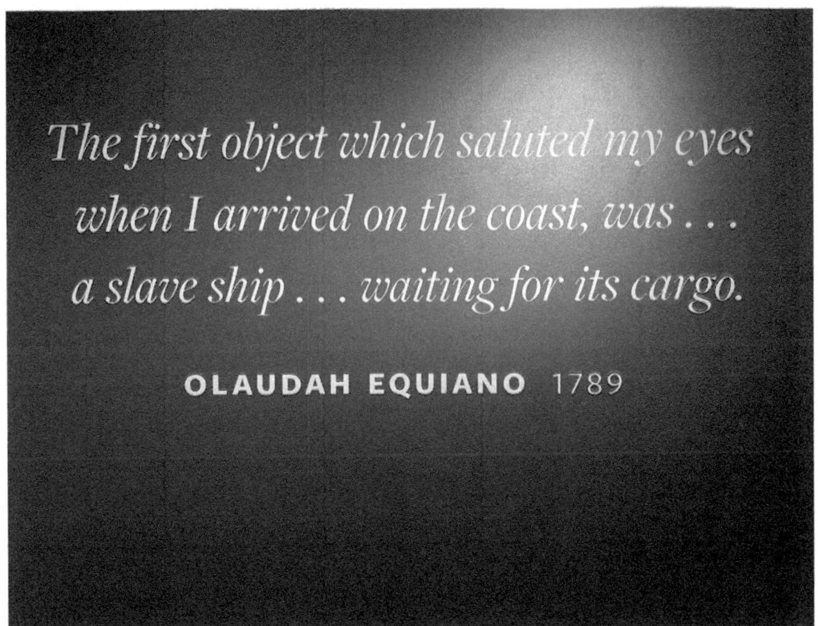

FIGURE P.1. Excerpt from *The Interesting Narrative of Olaudah Equiano* displayed on a wall in the National Museum of African American History and Culture, Washington, DC.

in an Igbo village as his narrative claims.[5] If so, Carretta argues, Equiano likely "invented his African childhood and the much-quoted account of the Middle Passage on a slave ship." Although Carretta cautions that we can never know for sure, he insists that "anyone who still contends that Equiano's account of the early years of his life is *authentic* is obligated to account for the powerful conflicting evidence."[6]

So one of history's most authenticated slave narratives—in and after its time, including by Carretta himself—has succumbed to the genre's birthright of suspicion: the then oxymoronic prospect of a black author that necessitated the tautological assurance that the author's narrative was "Written by Himself" in the first place.[7] Or the thorny questions of authenticity that scholars have since raised about the slave narrative genre because of the explicitly political context of its creation and its subjection to varying degrees of mediation by publishers or amanuenses.[8] What, then, are we to make of the presence of Equiano's words on a load-bearing wall on the ground floor of the NMAAHC? Of African American history's seeming false start? Achilles' heel? If some have gone so far as to dismiss Equiano entirely as a "liar," and his narrative by extension as unreliable, then what of the history that invokes Equiano's words in and as the beginning?[9]

Part of what is so unwelcome about Carretta's discovery, despite his efforts to redeem Equiano's alleged dishonesty as a genius enactment of self-fashioning, is its reification of blackness's already uncertain relationship to history owing to the historical rupture of Middle Passage. What might be gleaned from DNA testing notwithstanding, the precise when and where of history and origins are as open a question as they are a wound for those belonging to what Saidiya Hartman has called "the tribe of Middle Passage."[10] If we did not know any better, the anonymous vacuum of the specific peoples and places from which we hail might even force us to conclude, with Hegel and others, that the scattered children of the Dark Continent have no history. That to be black is to be ahistorical. Having to "say goodbye" to Equiano, as one scholar argues we must in the wake of Carretta's explosive discovery, only adds insult to this injury by cutting the children of Middle Passage off from the one historical tether to a beginning that we do have:

> Although we would love to have a firsthand account such as that in the *Interesting Narrative* that brings alive the Middle Passage and New World slavery, we have to say goodbye to Equiano as a guide to that experience. He may remain important as an example of black self-fashioning but in the great scheme of things such importance is of limited and specialized interest. We may have to accept that, as Primo Levi argued for understanding the Holocaust, "the survivors are not the true witnesses" because the "true witnesses" are the "drowned, the submerged, the annihilated." In my opinion, Equiano cannot remain a central figure in the reconstruction of the Atlantic world unless the doubt that Carretta has cast upon his *authenticity* as an African disappears.[11]

Without Equiano, the Middle Passage beginnings of blackness threaten to slip into utter inarticulacy and join the chorus of the archive's deafening silence. But here, just as for Carretta, the doubt surrounding Equiano's narrative has specifically to do with its "authenticity." The horizon of this study, however, is *not* authenticity, and happily so. Consequently, I feel no such obligation to account for Equiano's possible South Carolinian birth, which, as far as I'm concerned, either is beside or helps to make my point. Far more than the narrative's authenticity, which was already in question to the degree that the authenticity of every slave narrative is in question, I'm concerned with the "truth" of Equiano's witness. And with respect to the experiences of black folk in particular, I've known fiction to tell the truth just as often as I've known history to lie. For my purposes, it matters little whether Equiano got his knowledge of Middle Passage first- or secondhand. In fact, I mean to trouble that distinction altogether by suggesting that black life has yet to witness the end of the beginning it claims in Middle Passage. Notwithstanding the linear, vertical climb we perform as we make our way through the museum's history exhibit and the implicit suggestion that the beginning is safely in our historical rearview, Middle Passage is still with us. It persists, if not quite first*hand*, then perhaps in the trouble still visited upon the *soles* of black folk, who can no more stand their ground today than the steps they blinked on the face of the Atlantic yesterday. Far from saying goodbye to Equiano, then, this book goes decisively in the other direction—continuing to consult *The Interesting Narrative* as a faithful guide not only to the Middle Passage beginnings of blackness but also to black life more broadly. The "true witnesses" of Middle Passage are indeed the "drowned" and "submerged"; but perhaps they are also those Alexis Pauline Gumbs has dubbed the "undrowned"—the survivors and their descendants who nevertheless struggle to breathe in a world inimical to their breath.[12] If so, the truth of their witness inheres not just in the testimony of the deaths we die, for which the dead indeed have the inside track, but also in the testimony of the lives we live.

But let's for the moment imagine that we could resurrect the drowned and hear the whole of their annihilation. It'd be no less devastating, but at least we'd be expecting to hear how desperately lungs full of water still can thirst. But would we be ready to answer their questions about the terrible pressure? These questions first occurred to me while I was learning to scuba dive. My instructor emphasized the importance of equalizing frequently—pinching and blowing my nose, the way we often do on airplanes—to relieve the painful pressure that builds in your ears as you descend. Even with careful instruction, I was not prepared for how quickly the pain sneaks up on you and how quickly it becomes unbearable. Still, I at least understood my pain and how to remedy it: stop, hold my nose, and blow. Eventually, to stay ahead of the pain, I had to learn to equalize every few feet. But what of the drowned and their untutored dives? What of the ones who could not stop or control the pace of their descent because they were weighed down with ball and chain? What of those who descended so many more feet than I? To be troubled by history during a scuba diving lesson, to be haunted by an underwater revelation and eventually succumb to writing it down, I hope is the extension and practice of a kind of care. A defense, and not a disturbance, of the dead.[13] But I'm not sure it brings me any closer to the "truth" of Middle Passage. Offloading the obligation to bear witness exclusively onto the dead in this way may even reify the narrow sense of truth that notoriously constrained early historiography of the transatlantic slave trade. History's earliest efforts to tell the truth about Middle Passage worried extensively over the precise number of Africans who embarked, perished at sea, and disembarked in the New World—facts and figures we cannot know for certain but which, nevertheless, enjoy a privileged relationship to truth.[14] Yet I've never felt closer to whatever a "true witness" of Middle Passage might be than when reading these speculative lines from Dionne Brand's *Land to Light On*:

> This those slaves must have known who were my mothers, skin
> falling from their eyes, they moving toward their own bone,
> "so thank god for the ocean and the sky all implicated, all
> unconcerned," they must have said, "or there'd be nothing
> to love."[15]

Could there really have been love? And could there really have been love for the more-than-human world? If it's possible to sit with and be stunned by the "true witness" of a poem, then perhaps you'll understand why I'm uninclined to say goodbye to Equiano and his possible experiments with fiction—except perhaps as the historical foundation of a people's climb *up*, from slavery or anywhere. I'm not sure that *The Interesting Narrative* was ever cut out as a launching pad for a vertical telling of history that, in the case of the NMAAHC, starts with Middle Passage and ends triumphantly with the inauguration of the first black president of the United States. Before its authenticity could be called into question, *The Interesting Narrative* already told of a people thrown into question. A "Negro Question" for which history still has no satisfactory answer. Good thing, then, that the animating velocity of this book is not up but down. And whatever our assessments of its historical authenticity, I've found *The Interesting Narrative* to be an excellent guide to getting down.[16]

But you wouldn't know it from the elided way in which Equiano's writing appears on the wall—the not inconsequential ellipsis we find between *was* and *a slave ship*. It is an elision we often see fit to make, within and without black studies, but one perhaps we can no longer afford in our age of ecological crisis. I'd like to turn, then, to a consideration of the unelided account of Equiano's famous words. To peek behind the veil of the ellipsis and explore what more, beyond the slave ship, there is to apprehend in the Middle Passage beginnings of blackness.

I. the missing sea

On the day Equiano became "black," he stood at the threshold of a "world" that was going to kill him and bore witness to its and his own creation. There, on the coast of West Africa, he saw both astonishing and terrible things. But the water, we must always remember, was first:

> The first object which saluted my eyes when I arrived on the coast was *the sea*, and a slave ship, which was then riding at anchor and waiting for its cargo. These filled me with astonishment which was soon converted to terror when I was carried on board. I was immediately handled and tossed up to see if I were sound by some of the crew; and I was now persuaded that I had gotten into a world of bad spirits and that they were going to kill me.[17]

What goes elided in the museum's invocation of Equiano's famous words, then, is "the sea," which, we discover, is not only missing but first: "The *first* object which saluted my eyes when I arrived on the coast was *the sea*," and then "a slave ship." This elision of "the sea" may seem inconsequential, especially to the extent that the slave ship already implies the ocean. The grammar of Equiano's phrasing, which conflates "the sea, and a slave ship" as a single "object," even invites this reading. If the slave ship represents only a part of the whole of Middle Passage, perhaps it makes for a suitable metonym as the only part capable of distinguishing Middle Passage from a day at the beach. But this word that I have—about blackness and the blueness of blackness—queries this elision by nevertheless distinguishing "the sea" as first among "the first object" to catch Equiano's eye and, what's more, as an aspect of Middle Passage we cannot neglect without neglecting crucial dimensions of blackness itself.

Far from unique to the NMAAHC, however, this elision of "the sea" arguably evidences a broader neglect of the ocean inside and outside of black studies.[18] Something like the museum's elision of the sea and emphasis instead on the slave ship, for instance, can also be witnessed in conceptions of blackness that center the subjection and abjection of the slave ship and its hold. Perhaps the most influential expression of this tendency in black study is Frank Wilderson's now famous exhortation to "stay in the hold of the ship."[19] In this way, Wilderson advocates for a practice of black study that does not flinch from the recognition that black abjection ballasts the world no less today than when enslaved Africans brimmed the holds of slave ships. As a pioneering scholar of an influential school of black thought known as Afropessimism, Wilderson forwards the iconoclastic argument that slavery—abolition, emancipation, and Civil Rights notwithstanding—never ended. Because more than a coerced laborer or property the slave, following Orlando Patterson's classic redefinition, is a "socially dead person."[20] Afropessimism extends Patterson's redefinition of slavery by further arguing that *blackness* is "social death." If, according to Hartman, slavery inaugurated a "measure of man and a ranking of life and worth that has yet to be undone," then within this unelapsed measure of man and life, Afropessimism contends that blackness not only originates but persists irrevocably as "social death" in a constitutively antiblack world.[21] And when it comes specifically to Wilderson's critique of the antiblack world, I hope not to flinch. I want all the smoke of the "pyrotechnics" that Wilderson argues are necessary to bring about the end of the antiblack world.[22] There are too many thousands gone and gone on to want anything else. But I also wonder if, in the critical triage of attending to the emergency of the hold and its manifold afterlives along with the regime of Humanity they support, we sometimes, unwittingly, miss "the sea," along with whatever implications for our study of blackness might inhere in the recognition that, at least for Equiano, the sea was first.

The possibility of black study's neglect of the sea has previously been raised by Omise'eke Natasha Tinsley in the "writing out of materiality" she observes in two of the field's most influential conceptions of diasporic blackness: Paul Gilroy's "black Atlantic" and Antonio Benítez-Rojo's "Peoples of the Sea."[23] Tinsley writes, "These tropes of the black Atlantic, of Peoples of the Sea, do call to me as powerful enunciations of crosscurrents of African diaspora identity, and I evoke them in respect and solidarity. And yet as [they] call on maritime metaphors without maritime histories . . . their writing out of materiality stops short of the most radical potential of such oceanic imaginations. There are other Atlantic and Caribbean histories that these scholars could have evoked to make sense of the present, *other material details* of maritime crossings they could have drawn on to make their metaphors richer conceptual tools."[24] What "other material details" have we neglected in our understanding of Middle Passage? What might constitute their "radical potential"? And how might an openness to these "other material details" apply a generative pressure to a black study that stays in the hold, not unto the hold's disavowal, but toward an extension of our attention to the ocean that also captivated Equiano in the beginning? Especially if, as Tinsley suggests, "diving into this water stands to transform African diaspora scholarship in ways as surprising as Equiano's first glimpse of the sea."[25]

Beyond the "writing out of [oceanic] materiality" sometimes witnessed in black study, the museum's elision of "the sea" arguably exemplifies an even broader regard for the environment as little more than background for the real goings-on of human history. With growing awareness of climate change and global ecological crisis, however, such neglect of the more-than-human natural world has come under increasing scrutiny. This growing ecological consciousness has led to the emergence of what—in critique of the general *anthropocentrism*, or human-centeredness, of the humanities—has otherwise come to be known as the *environmental* humanities. Within the effort of this interdisciplinary field of study to recuperate a neglected and degraded environment, several environmental humanities scholars have remarked upon a still more specific neglect of, if not outright antagonism toward, the ocean, which is especially at issue in the museum's elision of "the sea." In *Shakespeare's Ocean*, for example, ecocritical scholar Dan Brayton surveys the long-standing cultural status of the ocean in the West as a "void lying eternally outside—or on the margins—of human social constructs."[26] Perhaps, in this way, the ocean, too, is socially dead. Indeed, its position "eternally outside" the western world and its social constructs strikingly resembles what is generally meant by Afropessimism's elaboration of blackness as "social death." It is not for nothing that Herman Melville characterizes the ocean in *Moby-Dick* as "unspeakably unsocial and repelling."[27] In many respects, such a characterization of the sea is unremarkable. Humans are, after all, land creatures. Although we make occasional visits to the sea, as air-breathing bipeds our stomping grounds are undeniably terra firma. Nevertheless, it is the strange contention of a growing cohort of scholars that we humans are perhaps more amphibious than we let on.[28] These scholars argue that western humanism is animated by an uninterrogated "terrestrial bias," or "terracentrism": an organizing fetishization of land at the expense of a profound neglect of the ocean.[29] Thus, beyond the environmental humanities' general recuperation of the biophysical environment, Steve Mentz has argued even more specifically for a "blue humanities" that would grant the ocean a critical attention proportional to our overwhelmingly blue planet.[30]

Intriguingly, the recent developments in black studies and the environmental humanities surveyed above share a mutual turn to the ocean and a mutual critique of the exclusionary logics of western humanism. Yet they have largely been elaborated independently of each other. The fact that these seemingly disparate fields have arrived, albeit in different ways and with different stakes, at a similar object of critique (the Human) and study (the ocean) suggests an interrelation far beyond their extant dialogue. Their confluence constitutes the organizing curiosity of this book, inspiring not only its attempt at a writing *in* of the oceanic materiality of Middle Passage and a blue recalibration of human being but the conviction that these endeavors are critical kin, long-lost but ready-made collaborators. Taking up the intersection of black and blue in this way, this book's black study not only stays in the hold but also wades in the water, awaiting the trouble blue might bring to our thinking about black and human life on earth. Yet if, in this way, this book *blues* black, it also *blackens* blue (and green, for that matter) by privileging the black maritime experiences of middle passing Africans in the blue humanities' effort to think the human inhabitant of our blue planet. As far as I know, only that black cohort of humans who, like the famous castaway Pip, could be sold in Alabama have ever made their home in the ocean and lived to tell about it. Their souls took the measure of our immeasurably blue planet not as an isolated or individual experience but as the experiential crucible that birthed a people. Any environmental or blue humanities that merely or uncritically appends a concern for the environment to western humanism fails to speak adequately to the experiences of these non-Human humans or apprehend a modern humanism that is not just anti-ecological but also antiblack.[31] Or rather, both these things, together and irreducibly. We've read too much Sylvia Wynter to remain optimistic about the "genre" of Human behind the rise of the Anthropocene, which arguably took its first steps not in the Industrial Revolution's factory but on the deck of a slave ship, ballasted by *all* of its non-Human cargo, human and nonhuman alike. Since humans have also been reckoned nonhuman, and none more paradigmatically than the Black, this book pursues an intercalation of the critiques of the Human arising out of both the environmental humanities and black studies. More specifically, it takes up the environmental or, even more precisely, *blue* humanity elaborated by the non-Human human, or the Black, in blackness's primordial encounter with our blue planet.

II. "ancient waters"

I come, again and again, to these words by Equiano in the devoted way I've been coming since boyhood to the words that famously open the book of Genesis, which, incidentally, also speak of the water that there was in the beginning: "In the beginning God created the heavens and the earth. The earth was without form, and void; and darkness was on the face of the deep. And the Spirit of God was hovering over the face of the waters."[32] Equiano's words, in comparison, aren't canon, and no doubt some would bristle at the suggestion, but I come to his dramatic encounter with the ocean, like Frantz Fanon, "desirous to be at the origin of the world." Which is to say that I believe Equiano's words to be a sacred, even holy, record of the beginning. That anyone desiring to be at the origin of *this* world had sooner come here than to Genesis. And I believe this in spite of how I discover myself in Equiano, black *adam* of humans who are not Human, as, again to invoke Fanon, "an object among other objects."[33]

In the Genesis account of creation, we read of darkness and the spirit of God hovering over the face of the deep (*tehom*) in prelude to a creation repeatedly consummated as "good." Yet in what I propose might be alternatively read as the genesis of our world, we find blackness over the face of the Atlantic and "*bad* spirits" hovering over the face of its waters. We might locate the creation of what I am asking us to apprehend as a "world," the precise moment of its Big Bang, so to speak, in the instant Equiano is "carried on board." That is, the moment Equiano recognizes that the ship "waiting for its cargo" was waiting for him. That he *is* the cargo for which the slave ship waits. The entire passage pivots on this moment. All in the accelerated time and space warp of *soon*, we witness not just the end of Equiano's old world but the creation of a new one. A terrible zeroing and terrific expansion simultaneously elapse in the fissioning of humanity that inheres, with all of the worlding energy of a Big Bang, in Equiano's transformation into mere cargo. It's this redoubled conversion, of astonishment into terror, of people into cargo, all in the elapsing interval of *soon*, that I propose catalyzes the creation of the "world" Equiano "had gotten into." Incidentally, a world is precisely the scale at which black studies has challenged us to think the nature of antiblackness as neither merely interpersonal nor structural but ultimately constitutive of an "antiblack world." To what else, if not the creation of this antiblack world, does Equiano bear witness in his recognition that he had "gotten into a world" whose most immediate identifying trait was that it was "going to kill [him]." The problem of being black, then, is nothing short of a world. Our world. The antiblack world. Or, for those whose constitutions can only admit the euphemism, the modern world. What dawns with Middle Passage is nothing short of a world aimed with now crushing historical momentum at the genre of Human indexed by whiteness and made possible by the accumulation and death of those coming to be hailed as black, cargo among other cargo.

Whatever parallel with Genesis may be recognized in Equiano's encounter with "the sea, and a slave ship," is made even more explicit in Richard Wright's *Native Son* (1940). In the novel's final chapter, poignantly entitled "FATE," we find the novel's famed protagonist, Bigger Thomas, resigning himself to his impending execution for the unintentional murder of a white woman. It is a resignation that brings him face-to-face with not only the same "ancient waters" that confronted Equiano but also, more ancient still, *tehom*:

> Having felt in his heart some obscure need to be at home with people . . . and failed, he chose not to struggle any more. With a supreme act of will springing from the essence of his being, he turned away from his life and the long train of disastrous consequences that had flowed from it and looked wistfully upon the dark face of the ancient waters upon which some spirit had breathed and created him, the dark face of the waters from which he had been first made in the image of a man with a man's obscure need and urge; feeling that he wanted to sink back into those waters and rest eternally.[34]

Behind Wright's invocation of "the dark face of the ancient waters" and "some spirit" loom not only Equiano's "the first object . . . was the sea, and a slave ship," and "I had gotten into a world of bad spirits" but also, more ancient still, Genesis's "darkness on the face of the deep" and "the spirit of God hovering over the face of the waters." These waters flow in and out of each other to the point of palimpsestic indistinction. Given the immediate context of Wright's effort to imagine the origins of antiblackness, "ancient waters" arguably alludes most immediately to the Atlantic Ocean. Yet by casting these waters in the familiar language of Genesis, Wright also ascribes to them cosmological import, similar to what we've observed in Equiano. Above even *tehom*, Wright signals to his readers that the beginnings of our world may be found here, on the face of this deep.

Yet for all the ways he invokes the language of Genesis, Wright's rendering of the beginning differs in one conspicuous way: Whereas in Genesis God "formed man of the dust of the *ground*, and breathed into his nostrils the breath of life," Wright informs us that it was directly upon the water that "some *spirit* had breathed and created" Bigger.[35] And what better culprit for Bigger's differentiated creation than those "bad spirits" we find pushing wind with their sails across the face of the deep in Equiano's narrative? So distinguishing the creation of blackness from the universal creation of humanity, Wright imagines black being as cosmologically excluded from the ontological property that the Human otherwise claims in the ground. Here, black being takes the specific form of an ontological disinheritance of ground and a corresponding consignment to the water, while Humanness inheres in an ontological claim to and in the ground, in a way reminiscent of the evolutionary narration of the human as a biped—distinguished from the rest of nonhuman nature by the ability to stand on our own two feet. To stand our ontological ground, as it were, atop a hierarchization of nature. Moreover, as the space *back* into which Bigger sinks in his racialized inability "to be at home with people," these "ancient waters" further index the radical exclusion from Human society that has come to be theorized in black studies as "social death." If blackness indeed is social death, as Wilderson argues, and if the Black is "an anti-Human, a position against which Humanity establishes, maintains, and renews its coherence, its corporeal integrity," then in Bigger this non-Humanity inheres specifically in an extrahuman identification with the ocean.[36] And what better symbol for the "social death" of blackness, when humans are otherwise paradigmatically recognized as land creatures?[37] The intervening years between Equiano's *Interesting Narrative* and Wright's *Native Son* notwithstanding, according to the testimony of Bigger, the world into which Equiano had gotten remains intact and continues to rotate on the axis of black (social) death.

III. "desirous to be at the origin of the world"

As a Sunday school mainstay, I was oriented during childhood by the knowledge of a single, universal beginning in which we all share. So imagine the vertigo of falling upon Equiano's words as a college freshman and discovering myself among the number of those whom history has made to begin again. Imagine the vertigo of learning of the genesis that is Middle Passage, or what Wilderson has provocatively labeled the "dawning of Blackness" and "the Black's first ontological instance."[38] It's not just the dizzying matter of claiming your beginning in two moments at once, and so being born again into a kind of cosmological double consciousness. It's also the ontological stretching of discovering yourself in Equiano as modernity's "cargo." Such a beginning yields no suitable anchor for (Human) ontology. Rather, it is the bottom falling out of ontology altogether, the ontological equivalent of the physical danger facing Equiano in all that water. It is we who are called black falling into and in with the nonhuman company of the hold, as the "handled" kin of a handled earth.

But perhaps such talk of the beginning has fallen out of favor. If so, it is not without good reason. Often, the first order of operations in the justification of all manner of violent exclusions inheres in what we have come to believe or think about the beginning. In enormously consequential interpretations of the book of Genesis alone, we can identify the groundwork of nearly every ism under the sun. The anthropocentrism behind global ecological crisis, for example, has historically found reliable ideological cover in a humanity that alone is created in the image of God and granted dominion over the earth. Patriarchy too has found cover in the creation of Eve from Adam's rib and her ignoble status as the first sinner. And heterosexism in the first marriage between a man and woman. And racism in the curse of Noah's son Ham. And in a book as preoccupied with the deep as this one, I take note that each of these hermeneutical incidents follows in the wake of a despised *tehom*, yielding in the traditional Christian doctrine of creation ex nihilo not a second sex but a second geography, a maligned primordial ocean signifying chaos, disorder, and nothingness.[39]

In a similar way, the beginning that blackness traditionally locates in Middle Passage has also fallen out of critical favor, either to the critical promotion of alternative beginnings, whose principal significance inheres in their circumvention of the blighted timeline of slavery, or to the effort to think blackness more flexibly and inclusively. Perhaps the most notable example of the former impulse is Ivan Van Sertima's *They Came Before Columbus*, which explores the African presence in ancient America. More than the important claims and critiques of Van Sertima's classic, however, I'm interested in its popular appeal as a redemption of blackness's American origins from the scourge of enslavement. Just as the appeal to ancient African civilizations has historically warded off claims of black inferiority by recalling a time when "we were kings," arriving before Christopher Columbus similarly allows us to take solace in the fact that "we were explorers." Aside from securing a beginning beyond enslavement, the Middle Passage beginnings of blackness have also been challenged on account of their exclusiveness. In *Physics of Blackness*, for example, Michelle Wright critiques what she theorizes as an overdetermining "Middle Passage epistemology" in black study, which "negotiates the complexity of the origins of Blackness in the West by stressing the process of being ripped from one existence and brutally thrust into another" and in this way fails to reflect the full diversity of black diasporic identity.[40] Wright observes:

> Most discourses on Blackness in the United States and the Caribbean locate themselves in the history of the Middle Passage, linking our cultural practices and expressions, our politics and social sensibilities, to the historical experience of slavery in the Americas and the struggle to achieve full human suffrage in the West. These histories are both constructed and phenomenological: they are a chosen arrangement of historical events (spaces and times) perceived to be the defining moments of collective Blackness.[41]

Citing the example of contemporary African migrants, whose black experiences are more defined by colonialism and capitalism than Middle Passage and slavery, Wright argues that this "linear progress narrative," which proceeds from the fixed origin of Middle Passage, often works to exclude "others who do not share in this origin but appear elsewhere in the narrative."[42] Opening up, rather than completely disavowing, what John Hope Franklin famously described as the journey "from slavery to freedom," Wright calls for a more inclusive "model for defining Blackness across the Diaspora"[43] that eschews the sense of blackness as a monolithic *what* for a more expansive understanding of various "Blacknesses" performed across multiple *whens* and *wheres*.[44]

Furthermore, in her critique of the assumption of Middle Passage as the fixed beginning of blackness, Wright specifically references the controversy surrounding the authenticity of Equiano's narrative: "This ambiguity about Equiano makes it difficult to locate him in the linear spacetime of the Middle Passage epistemology, because we can no longer be sure about the truth of his *Narrative*. If we cannot know where Equiano was born or exactly where he traveled before arriving in England, we cannot be sure that his life reflects a heroic drive for freedom rather than a compromised and self-interested career in pseudoheroics (perhaps hiding yet more deception)—or something in between. The meaning of his *Narrative* now escapes us."[45] Indeed, the doubt surrounding the authenticity of *The Interesting Narrative* troubles its status as what historian Nell Irvin Painter has labeled "a kind of founding myth of African American history."[46] Do I return, again and again, then, to a grifter? Is it quite right that Equiano's possibly fabricated record of what came first begins a national exhibit of African American *history*?

Yet as much as "we can no longer be sure about the truth" of Equiano's narrative, I am also compelled by Jon Sensbach's assertion that "a South Carolinian birth does not necessarily invalidate Equiano's story but recasts it with a different kind of *authenticity*. If he did not endure the Middle Passage himself, how else should he have learned about it and reported on it so persuasively from the perspective of the captives themselves but by listening, at some point, somewhere, to those who had?"[47] If Equiano's account of the beginning is not historical, in the strict sense of recording actual past events, perhaps it possesses "a different kind of authenticity" as historiography or, alternatively, what Hartman has called "critical fabulation," informed by the primary source testimonies of those who did endure Middle Passage.[48] Even if Equiano delivers such history under the pretense of autobiography, it's not as if New World Africans had much license or opportunity to practice history straight in the eighteenth century. If Equiano's narrative is unreliable as a witness of the experiences of an individual, perhaps we might reimagine its reliability as the collective witness of a people. But even if we decide that Equiano's record of the beginning is too compromised to qualify as history, I'm much more invested in reimagining its validity as a kind of liturgy—performing liturgy's good work by hosting and facilitating the wonder and wondering of a people. Insofar as Equiano's narrative has served as a "founding myth," liturgy is what becomes of myth or scripture when it is repeatedly, devotionally, and collectively read and recited, just as visitors do nearly every day on the ground floor of the NMAAHC.

Such liturgy need not lay the groundwork for an exclusionary linear progress narrative, even if the museum's journey from the slave ship to the White House yields just that. Instead, it can be invoked as sacred speech capable of transporting those who are, like Fanon, "desirous to be at the origin of the world." All the aforementioned problems with talk of the beginning notwithstanding, I would not discourage such desire and, in fact, think that the origin of the world is a place we need to visit. The problem with the beginning, as I see it, inheres not in itself but rather in what we ask or want from it: a rigid ordering of the world or fixed origins we invoke to justify exclusions and separations. But as I understand it, Middle Passage (or Genesis, for that matter) is not that kind of beginning, and it may only function as such precisely to the degree that it disavows or neglects an ocean that is, in many ways, the enemy of both fixity and linearity. While I agree with Michelle Wright that blackness is a performance as much as a construction, since Middle Passage those varied performances have also shared the common stage of the antiblack world. And perhaps the most remarkable aspect of this stage is how uniquely unsuited it is for standing—or at least standing *your* ground. From the steps middle passing Africans blinked upon the face of the Atlantic to Trayvon Martin felled on a Florida sidewalk, this bottomless stage attends black life everywhere. In fact, we might recognize contemporary African migrants perishing at sea as foundering in the same antiblack world that claimed the lives of those who jumped, or else were thrown, over the side during Middle Passage. Although I think it's important to hold open a distinction between the antiblack world and the Earth, the former, being a world, is more suggestive of a sphere than the line in view with the exclusions of a linear progress narrative. Consequently, it may encapsulate the diversity of black experiences across the diaspora in the same way that the Earth encircles the diversity of all of life.[49] One need not follow in an unbroken line from Middle Passage to live in the antiblack world it helped create.

But with so many reasons to quit the beginning, why should one need, let alone desire, to be at the origin of the world? And in particular the antiblack world? Why return, again and again, to Genesis or Equiano? To the cosmological scene of the crime? If I speak for myself, perhaps I speak for more when I say that I desire to really *be at*, and not solve or figure out, the origin of the world.

And being at, being present at, the creation of the world, it turns out, is far more a proposition of attunement than time travel. Because the world's creation is all we're ever at, is where we're still at, even when we suppose we're farther down the line. I come to Genesis and Equiano, then, desirous for not *the* beginning but a model *for* beginning. To know genesis and creation not as past event but as something we do. Can do. Have, for better and worse, done. And in the specific case of the genesis of the "world of bad spirits" that Equiano had gotten into, something we must do again, because unlike its Genesis counterpart, it was explicitly *not* good. And what strikes me in both Genesis and Equiano is a practice of beginning that consents to hover over the face of the deep.

Yet if this is why we return to the beginning, why does Equiano? Assuming he fabricated his African nativity, when granted the opportunity to choose his origin, Equiano, who could have begun elsewhere, chose Middle Passage. In doing so, Carretta argues, Equiano capitalized on a specific void in the English abolitionist movement for an authentic African voice that could bear witness to the experience of Middle Passage from the perspective of the enslaved.[50] Equiano also didn't claim to be just anybody. Rather, as an alleged African prince, he really was at least a future king. Still, the fact remains that Equiano willfully adopted a more immediate relation to Middle Passage than he possibly had. And in that choice, he may have been motivated as much by a sincerely felt historical connection as either the commitment to a just cause or what some have rather ungenerously characterized as a desire for self-gain. Whatever his motivations, the remarkable consistency of Equiano's account with what historians have subsequently come to glean about Middle Passage suggests either that he carefully sought out and attended to the accounts of survivors of Middle Passage, the way an oral historian might, or that, by the time he wrote his narrative, Middle Passage had already assumed such profound cultural significance to the African Diaspora that Equiano could faithfully reproduce even its most fleeting and gratuitous details. Details as exorbitant and nonutilitarian, for instance, as his "astonishment."

IV. astonishment

The decision to willfully assume a more immediate relation to Middle Passage than one's biography possibly necessitates on some levels confounds, insofar as we imagine that there is little about the experience of Middle Passage itself that is worth going back to fetch. Whenever we release Sankofa, how often are we hoping, like Noah and his dove, to receive confirmation of our ancestral connection to the mother*land*? To confirm that these connections endure despite the chasm we crossed. Or how often have we dreamed of returning "back to Africa" or, once upon a time in black studies, oriented ourselves toward the discovery of so-called Africanisms? Even if, in the wake of Paul Gilroy's *The Black Atlantic*, we've evolved beyond the predominance of this particular mode of black study, not even his paradigm-shifting text has inspired any like discovery of Atlanticisms. There are no calls to go back to the Atlantic. What could this even entail, if all we knew in that chasm was the terrifying hail of "a slave ship"? But our return to Equiano's narrative assures us that the very "first object which saluted [his] eyes when [he] arrived on the coast was the sea." And that when he saw it, he was astonished. That this "astonishment" was "*soon* converted to terror," in a conversion that mirrors his own conversion into cargo, suggests an interval so short as to be almost negligible, especially when considered beside the sheer scale of the antiblack world and all there is proportionally to say about such a world when held up against a moment here and already gone.[51] The agenda for black study that Equiano's record would seem to set is the study, critique, and overturning of this world. The urgent and ethical call to lay bare its "constituent elements." And I am certainly about that life. But here is where I stumble, felled perhaps too long in the passing interval of "soon." It's Equiano's "astonishment" that gets me, again and again and always. That there was, that there could be, astonishment. Then, in the time of astonishment, for a moment, but only for a moment, the Earth gathers, dancing.[52]

Equiano did not jump at this chance to see the earth before the end of his world and the beginning of ours.[53] But he did see it. And, like so many middle passing Africans encountering the ocean for the very first time, he was astonished. Just prior to being "saluted," or hailed in the classic Althusserian sense, by the slave ship—"Hey you there! Hey, cargo!"—to discovering that he really was the cargo for which the ship was waiting, and in this way being interpellated as black, Equiano was greeted by the blue face of an overwhelmingly blue planet, which, under the circumstances, he could not even be certain was *still* Earth. What if, compelled by such astonishment, we fall deep into the fleeting interval of *soon*? What would it mean to think the dawning of blackness in Middle Passage as not reducible to the "social death" hailed by the salute of the slave ship? What if, instead, we think blackness as not just responding also, but *first*, to the hailing waves of the astonishing sea? "Hey, you there! Hey, earthling." What if, as our original antiphony, blackness dawns in the ongoing response of black ecological life to the hail of a blue planet?

As it happens, such black ecological life was also held out to Bigger Thomas in the "ancient waters" we've otherwise understood to signify his social death. Richard Wright narrates that

> the feelings of [Bigger's] body reasoned that if there could be no merging with men and women about him, there should be a *merging with some other part of the natural world* in which he lived. Out of the mood of renunciation there sprang up in him again the will to kill. But this time, it was not directed outward toward people, but inward, upon himself. . . . This feeling sprang up of itself, organically, automatically; like the rotted hull of a seed forming the soil in which it should grow again.[54]

Here, the same "ancient waters" into which Bigger desired to sink in resignation to his own (social) death let out upon what may alternatively be recognized as a kind of ecological life. A merging with the more than human natural world whose ultimate horizon, like that of "the rotted hull of a seed," is not death, but life.

If Sula couldn't wait to "tell Nel," just wait'll we tell Killmonger.[55] In the film *Black Panther*, Killmonger famously invokes his ancestors who drowned during Middle Passage with his dying breath: "Bury me in the ocean with my ancestors who jumped from ships because they knew that *death* was better than bondage."[56] In the theater, this line left me breathless. I found it a cathartic elegy for those I haven't stopped thinking about since I first heard Equiano call them "*inhabitants* of the deep."[57] But how inhabitants, if humans cannot live under water? I've traveled with this phrase long enough to want to tell Killmonger the good news: that our ancestors who jumped knew not only death but also, in a way we must learn to fathom, *life*. Somebody run and tell Killmonger that the inhabitants of the deep jumped to see the Earth before the end of their worlds and the beginning of our antiblack one. Then, compelled by Equiano's astonishment, let's wade together into the deep water that there was in the beginning. Into its meaning not only for the (social) deaths we die but also, and more abundantly, for the black ecological life we live. I am about this life, too. About the life of blackness and the blackness of life. "What did we do to be so black and blue?" Louis Armstrong asked. Perhaps we lived. Took up the precarious experiment of black ecological life on a blue planet.

Introduction

THE DEEP

"Je te salue, vieil Océan!" You still preserve on your crests the silent boat of our births, your chasms are our own unconscious, furrowed with fugitive memories.
—ÉDOUARD GLISSANT, *Poetics of Relation*

I LOOKED, AND BEHOLD, a great multitude which no one could number.[1] But I tried anyway, and the jumpers and the jettisoned, across the four centuries of the transatlantic slave trade, totaled 1,818,681. I arrive at this crude and inexact number by consulting the Trans-Atlantic Slave Trade Database and subtracting the total number of Africans who ultimately disembarked in the New World from those who embarked in the Old. If you do this terrible math, you will greet the 1,818,681 who never made it across the Atlantic.[2] 1,818,681, then, who either stole (themselves) away to or were laid to un/rest in the ocean. 1,818,681 who never knew arrival. 1,818,681 who, under the circumstances, never even knew the middle that portended arrival. 1,818,681 who disembarked at sea. This number, like most related to the transatlantic slave trade, which are preserved to history in logs recorded in the spirit of inventory rather than census, yield what we might call a *statistical fabulation*.[3] It gives us data we don't really have but which we might calculate anyway to help us remember and count our immeasurable losses. Not in the spirit of exactness but in the ethical extension of a care that was not there but should have been. Black lives count. The 1,818,681 hemorrhaged into the Atlantic count and are counted here.

They are counted, too, in *The Interesting Narrative of the Life of Olaudah Equiano*. Sometimes in a traditional quantitative way: Equiano writes of "two of my wearied countrymen" who jumped over the side and the countless sick "almost daily" thrown overboard.[4] But he also uses a different manner of accounting, a curious naming of the drowned. His appellation of those who jumped or else were jettisoned to their death insists into the ocean "a kind of life":[5]

> Often did I think many of the *inhabitants* of the deep much more happy than myself. I envied them the freedom they enjoyed, and as often wished I could change my condition for theirs.[6]

It is one thing to refuse the antiblack world, to prefer death to slavery. But it is quite another thing to *inhabit* the deep. To suggest that the 1,818,681 did not (only) die but, rather, moved in. If the biblical Exodus famously begins with Moses turning aside to see the bush burning, yet not consumed, this book turns aside to see that sign and wonder that arguably founds the kindred exodus of the African Diaspora. That great, if impossible, sight that Olaudah Equiano beheld from the deck of a slave ship in the middle of the eighteenth century: the enslaved underwater, yet not dead, those he surprisingly names the "*inhabitants* of the deep." Equiano's term for those who perished over the side suggests they not only exited the antiblack world but entered a habitable elsewhere. But in a narrative explicitly committed to furnishing an unflinching witness to the horrors of the transatlantic slave trade, why does Equiano use *inhabitants*, a word typically reserved for the living, to describe those who we know drowned? And how can he claim to "env[y] them the *freedom* they enjoyed"? Yet if we suspend our initial objections to Equiano's apparent misnaming of the drowned and take seriously the lives that were *lived* underwater, awfully abbreviated as they were, then what emerges is an oceanic recalibration of human life and freedom. Perhaps the only sustainable life and freedom there is on this blue planet.

It can be easy to miss Equiano's meaning. I certainly did when I was first introduced to Equiano's narrative as a college sophomore. The knowledge that humans cannot live underwater and my sense of the ocean as a nonhuman space initially led me to mistake the "inhabitants of the deep" for fish, unwittingly perpetuating modernity's foundational confusion of blackness with the nonhuman. Not until I read Equiano's account of his "two . . . wearied countrymen" who jumped ship did I realize that the "inhabitants of the deep" were people whose unspeakable deaths were attended by unspeakable life.

In the wake of the "terror" that so quickly overwhelms Equiano's first encounter with the sea, it can also be easy to miss the surprising reply he gives to the hail of an initially astonishing ocean. *Hey, you there! Hey, earthling!* Look closely at how Equiano responds to the violence of the antiblack world: "Two of the white men offered me eatables; and, on my refusing to eat, one of them held me fast by the hands, and laid me across I think the windlass and tied my feet, while the other flogged me severely. I had never experienced anything of this kind before, and although, not being used to the water, I naturally feared that element the first time I saw it, yet nevertheless, could I have got over the nettings, *I would have jumped over the side*."[7] Is it not a little remarkable that despite his fear of this unfamiliar element, Equiano came to willfully desire the ocean, or at least the escape from slavery that it promised? On its surface, such complex willing might be interpreted as Equiano's absolute refusal of the world he "had gotten into" and what black studies has come to recognize as its "gratuitous violence."[8] Certainly, those who willfully jumped over the side, in their preference for death to a life of slavery, expressed at least this referendum on the antiblack world and its uninhabitability. And with every passing year, the evidence accumulating against this world proves these leapers prophets. Yet the life that Equiano insists into the ocean also begs the question of whether this negative refusal of the antiblack world in Equiano's desire to jump over the side can also be read as a positive apprehension of the deep as a habitable elsewhere. A place where Equiano might not only die but somehow also live.

This response to the sea's call, which can be easy to miss in Equiano's narrative, is much more conspicuous in Édouard Glissant's *Poetics of Relation* (1990). In the first chapter, "The Open Boat," which offers an extended meditation on the historical experience and cultural legacy of Middle Passage, the Martinican poet and philosopher explicitly salutes the ocean: "'Je te salue, vieil Océan!' [literally, 'I salute you, ancient ocean!'] You still preserve on your crests the silent boat of our births, your chasms are our own unconscious, furrowed with fugitive memories."[9] In Glissant's salute of the ocean, we explicitly witness at the end of the twentieth century what can already be perceived more subtly at the end of the eighteenth, in Equiano's double take at the sea that "saluted" him in the beginning. Between Equiano and Glissant, and beyond, blackness's enduring response to the hail of an astonishing ocean takes shape. *Blackness is an ongoing inhabitation of the deep; black study the perpetual discovery that if you surrender to the deep you can swim it.*

Inhabitants of the Deep: The Blueness of Blackness undertakes a black ecocritical study of the deep as the *diffuse subtext* of black literary and expressive culture. A synonym for the ocean and a potential of all waters (and lands), the *deep* is what blackness has known throughout the changing same of black life and death from the steps blinked on the face of the Atlantic to the ground we still struggle to stand upon. Extending Equiano's surprising appellation of the jumpers and the jettisoned, this book offers a vision of blackness as an ongoing inhabitation of the deep that not only originates with but persists beyond Middle Passage.[10] Yet Equiano's underwater vision of life and freedom is also our witness that we get down in the deep as much as we are cast down, wade in the water in which we have historically been weighed. Thus, *Inhabitants of the Deep* ultimately argues that the blackness which dawned in the oceanic encounter of Middle Passage set flowing an experiment of human inhabitation that is most fully apprehended not as social death hailed by the slave ship but as black ecological life hailed by a blue planet.

Focusing on the deep in this way can help attune us to the surprising turn and return to water that can be witnessed in and out of black letters. Like most, I've heard the negro speak of rivers. But I've also heard the negro speak of oceans, and bays, and creeks, and swamps, and at times water that isn't physically there. I've heard Frederick Douglass speak *to* the Chesapeake Bay and tell of Demby standing his ground in a creek. Heard Henry Bibb speak to the Ohio River after him and in a nearly identical way. Seen Otis Redding roam two thousand miles just to make his home on the dock of the San Francisco Bay. Heard M. NourbeSe Philip give

w w w   w   a   wa

w   a   w a   t

er

the first protracted word of her book-length poem *Zong!*[11] Seen Pip drown in the Pacific and live to tell about it in Herman Melville's *Moby-Dick*. Seen Avey Johnson be compelled to return to "Ibo Landing" after her great-aunt Cuney appeared to her in a dream in Paule Marshall's *Praisesong for the Widow*. Seen Aunt Ester ferry Citizen Barlow to an underwater city made of bones in August Wilson's *Gem of the Ocean*. Seen and looked away from a photograph of a boy resurrected from a Tallahatchie River grave. Stood barefoot before the grave of that same boy in ankle-deep water. Watched the *povo de santo* give Iemanjá her flowers on February 2 on a beach in Salvador da Bahia, Brazil, and been comforted by stories of how the jumpers and the jettisoned rest with Olokun. Felt the church sway to "Wade in the Water" as saints made their way to the baptismal pool. This is hardly the whole of it, but I've seen and heard and felt enough by now to appreciate something of the scope of the knowledge to which Martin Luther King Jr. alluded on the eve of his assassination, when, reflecting on the high-pressure water hoses unleashed on black backs in Birmingham, he declared that "we knew water." Indeed, with Langston Hughes, we affirm that we've known waters. That our soul has grown deep like the waters. *Deep*, of course, being the operative word.

I. take me to the water

What Equiano saw on one side of the Atlantic in *The Interesting Narrative*, Frederick Douglass saw on the other in *Narrative of the Life of Frederick Douglass* (1845). Notwithstanding the changes in coast, century, and circumstances, Douglass's account of his ritual rendezvous with the Chesapeake Bay shares several striking similarities with Equiano's encounter with the Atlantic. Although the latter's encounter with the deep comes in the context of Middle Passage and the former's in the context of New World slavery, both, for instance, are attended by profound personal transformations. Just as Equiano's encounter with the deep witnesses his transformation into mere cargo, Douglass similarly comes to stand before the Chesapeake in the immediate wake of what he famously characterizes as his transformation from a "man" into a "brute."[12]

As the narrative's organizing schema for representing the dehumanization of enslavement, this transformation is depicted throughout the narrative but is consummated by the harsh "discipline" that Douglass receives from the brutal overseer Mr. Covey during a period of Douglass's enslavement when he is made to drink "the bitterest dregs of slavery."[13] As the precipitating cause of Douglass's jaunts to the Chesapeake, this discipline represents a second point of similarity with Equiano, whose return to the ocean was similarly propelled by a severe flogging. Beyond slavery's physical violence, however, Douglass's account of the discipline to which Covey subjects him also emphasizes the existential violence whereby he "was broken in body, soul, and spirit." This comprehensive breaking inheres specifically, for Douglass, in the ubiquity of the labor he is forced to perform under Covey. Douglass is not only "*worked* in all weather" but also worked at all times, so that "work, work, work, was scarcely more the order of the day than of the night. The longest days were too short for him, and the shortest nights too long for him." Crucially, by using the passive voice, Douglass elides himself as the subject of his work. He is not a worker. Rather, he is *worked*. Evacuating the grammatical position of the subject in this way, Douglass registers the slave's fungibility as objectified labor power that, in the event of overuse, may simply be replaced. Thus, Douglass is not only reduced to but also alienated from his labor power. And because he is worked around the clock, Douglass is also alienated from time. Such is the "discipline" that compels

Douglass's famous utterance "Behold a man transformed into a brute!"[14] By it, Douglass laments a kinship with nonhuman beasts of burden who, within the logics of the plantation, were also, as it were, *on* the clock. That is, they were coerced into a relentlessly linear organization of time to maximize accumulation and profit. Also on the clock was the land, which, with the advent of monocrop agriculture, was also being worked to exhaustion. Thus, behold also time transformed into the Anthropocene, the seeds of an entire planet temporally remade in humanity's image.

Within this near-total colonization of time, however, Douglass details that "Sunday was my only leisure time," before proceeding to narrate his curious practice of using this time to repeatedly abscond to the lofty banks of the Chesapeake Bay. Here, once again, similarities between Equiano's and Douglass's respective encounters with the deep abound. In addition to sharing a basically similar mise-en-scène, Douglass's characterization of the Chesapeake can also be recognized to follow an affective trajectory parallel to Equiano's astonishment turned terror:

> Our house stood within a few rods of the Chesapeake Bay, whose broad bosom was ever white with sails from every quarter of the habitable globe. Those beautiful vessels, robed in purest white, so delightful to the eye of freemen, were to me so many shrouded ghosts, to terrify and torment me with thoughts of my wretched condition. I have often, in the deep stillness of a summer's Sabbath, stood all alone upon the lofty banks of that noble bay, and traced, with saddened heart and tearful eye, the countless number of sails moving off to the mighty ocean. The sight of these always affected me powerfully. My thoughts would compel utterance; and there, with no audience but the Almighty, I would pour out my soul's complaint, in my rude way, with an apostrophe to the moving multitude of ships.[15]

Equiano's "the sea, and a slave ship," "bad spirits," and even the whiteness of his captors are all echoed in Douglass's "Chesapeake Bay," "the moving multitude of ships," "so many shrouded ghosts," and the conspicuous whiteness of the sails. Moreover, just as "soon" as we witnessed the conversion of Equiano's astonishment into terror, what begins as a sublime description of a "beautiful" and "delightful" seascape devolves, for Douglass, into a scene of "so many shrouded ghosts, to *terrify* and torment me with thoughts of my wretched condition." What appears "to the eye of freemen" like a maritime cornucopia of commerce whose plenty is coded white is, to the eye of the enslaved Douglass, haunted.

In this characterization of the Chesapeake Bay, Douglass exhibits the same double vision as the poet Lucille Clifton in her untitled, would-be nature poem:

surely i am able to write poems
celebrating grass and how the blue
in the sky can flow green or red
and the waters lean against the
chesapeake shore like a familiar,
poems about nature and landscape
surely   but whenever i begin
"the trees wave their knotted branches
and . . ."   why
is there under that poem always
an other poem?[16]

Like Douglass, Clifton also waxes poetic about "nature and landscape" and even, as it happens, the "chesapeake." But when this nature poem turns its celebratory regard upon trees and their "*knotted* branches," it falters with a caesura that ultimately gives way to "*an other* poem." The peculiar spacing suggests not simply another, different poem that the poet is also "able to write" but a poem instead whose difference and otherness are altogether its own. A poem, in other words, that pronounces itself independently of either the poet's ability or consciousness. Involuntarily summoned, perhaps, by *knotted*, an adjective that can apply to ropes as well as branches and may, in this way, invoke, in the eyes of a black woman, the painful history of lynching. Moreover, the fact that this "other poem" surges up from "under" an otherwise one-noted celebration of nature illuminates at once a depth and a surface, a superficial celebration of the US landscape and a haunting, violent subtext.

Like Clifton's would-be nature poem, I propose that Douglass's celebration of the beauty and delight of the Chesapeake is similarly interrupted by the history of Middle Passage in a way that begins to evince the status of the deep as the diffuse subtext of the black literary tradition. Douglass stands atop the lofty banks of the Chesapeake seeing ghosts because, to the eye of a slave, these "beautiful vessels, robed in purest white," invoke what Glissant might describe as an "unconscious memory" of slave ships, if not the genuine article. It is possible that at least some of the ghosts Douglass beheld in the early nineteenth century included literal slave ships, because the Chesapeake served as an important hub for both the transatlantic and domestic slave trade. The former persisted illicitly well beyond its 1808 abolition and the latter flourished through the mid-nineteenth century. But even if they did not carry slaves, this multitude of ships almost certainly carried the fruits of slave labor:

> Coastwise shipping along the Eastern Seaboard dominated the American economy until the late 1800s. Almost all personal and business travel of more than a relatively few miles and virtually all shipping of heavy goods were conducted predominantly by water, because watercraft offered by far the fastest, cheapest, and most efficient means of transport. Coastal schooners, sloops, and brigs were the workhorses of the internal trade, in which slave-produced raw materials such as cotton and molasses were shipped northward to New England and New York factories, and northern industrial manufactured goods were shipped south. These items included finished cotton cloth, iron and steel goods, agricultural machinery, as well as third-rate salted fish used as a cheap food for enslaved populations.[17]

By shipping the produce and necessities of a slave economy, these "beautiful vessels, robed in purest white," quite literally shroud an underlying subtext of black suffering and enslavement. These ships signify Douglass's "wretched condition" as a slave in much the same way that the slave ship alerted Equiano to his status as cargo. The ships' economic implication in slavery at least partly accounts for their appearance to Douglass "as so many shrouded ghosts," haunted, as Glissant would have it, by an unconscious memory of Middle Passage.

However, neither Douglass's description of this seascape nor his rendering of his classic apostrophe to these ships explicitly alludes to Middle Passage. Instead, the explicit reason that the latter gives for why these ships affect Douglass so profoundly emphasizes the juxtaposition of their freedom of motion with Douglass's relative confinement:

> You are loosed from your moorings, and are free; I am fast in my chains, and am a slave! You move merrily before the gentle gale, and I sadly before the bloody whip! You are freedom's swift-winged angels, that fly round the world; I am confined in bands of iron! O that I were free! O, that I were on one of your gallant decks, and under your protecting wing! Alas! betwixt me and you, the turbid waters roll. Go on, go on. O that I could also go! Could I but swim! If I could fly! O, why was I born a man, of whom to make a brute![18]

Douglass not only makes no explicit mention of slave ships but, quite the opposite, he actually characterizes these vessels as "freedom's swift-winged angels."

However, I propose that these angels do not pertain to freedom so much as whiteness. Although Douglass longs to be under their "protecting wing," we've heard him previously describe these wings as robes of "purest white." His exclusion from the coverage of these wings, then, also symbolizes his social exclusion, even as a mixed-race slave, from the protections and freedoms restricted to whiteness. Furthermore, like the "knotted" branches of Clifton's "other poem," Douglass's specific wish to be on the "gallant *decks*" of these ships activates the historic subtext of the slave ship's architectural reorganization of humanity with the slave's paradigmatic exclusion from the deck and ontological reassignment to the *hold*. This Middle Passage subtext lurking beneath the freedom and protection of a deck coded white suggests a probable culprit for a disturbance that Douglass specifically characterizes, in "so many shrouded ghosts," as a haunting. That is, an insistence of the past into the present. Douglass does not specify the source of this haunting, but the symbolic coding of the history of the slave trade upon this seascape suggests an unconscious memory of Middle Passage.

As Douglass's famous apostrophe to the ships continues, his Chesapeake reverie, in a final parallel with Equiano, moves from the terror of enslavement to an ultimate resolution to run away:

> The glad ship is gone; she hides in the dim distance. I am left in the hottest hell of unending slavery. O God, save me! God, deliver me! Let me be free! Is there any God? Why am I a slave? I will run away. I will not stand it. Get caught, or get clear, I'll try it. I had as well die with ague as the fever. I have only one life to lose. I had as well be killed running as die standing. Only think of it; one hundred miles straight north, and I am free! Try it? Yes! God helping me, I will. It cannot be that I shall live and die a slave. I will take to the water. This very bay shall yet bear me into freedom.[19]

Just as Equiano's vision of the "inhabitants of the deep" ultimately insists an improbable life and freedom into the ocean he had come to fear, so the terror of Douglass's seascape belies how he ultimately comes to apprehend the Chesapeake as a crucial accomplice to his freedom. It is not the white freedom of the deck, however, because the "glad ship is gone" and "hides in the dim distance." Rather, this freedom is attributed directly to the bay itself, which, in the absence of any explicit mediating technology, "shall yet bear [Douglass] into freedom." Thus, much like Equiano, Douglass's affective relation to the Chesapeake ultimately comes to assume a defining ambivalence, not between slavery and freedom so much as between slavery and fugitivity. That is, escape unto some as of yet unrealized freedom indexed not by the fixed and docile ground of the deck—whose enabling underside is the subjugation of the hold—but by the comparatively indeterminate and *live* ground of the bay.

Much has been remarked about the significance of literacy or physical resistance to Douglass's freedom struggle. However, with respect to slavery's "bitterest dregs," and the consummation of his related transformation from a man into a brute, it is specifically Douglass's rendezvous with the Chesapeake that catalyzes his resolve to get free. In this way, it arguably represents the narrative's turning point. Immediately before, we find Douglass's famed characterization of the dehumanization of enslavement: "Behold a man transformed into a brute!" And immediately after follows perhaps the narrative's most iconic sentence, in which Douglass conversely characterizes his struggle for freedom: "You have seen how a man was made a slave; you *shall* see how a slave was made a man."[20] This is one of several instances where Douglass employs the literary device of chiasmus. And to the extent that it yields a microcosm of a narrative that generally follows a chiasmatic structure in its account of the transformations induced by slavery and subsequently inverted by freedom, the precise location of Douglass's rendezvous with the Chesapeake in the narrative renders it the very hinge upon which this inversion turns.

We also find this alternative valence of the deep as a site of freedom in two other revealing instances throughout Douglass's writings and speeches. The first can be found in Douglass's only work of fiction, *The Heroic Slave* (1852). The novella is a work of historical fiction inspired by the Creole rebellion of 1841. One of the largest and most successful slave rebellions in US history, this slave revolt took place aboard an eponymous slave brig transporting 134 enslaved persons from Virginia to New Orleans as part of the United States' still thriving domestic slave trade. Led by an enslaved cook named Madison Washington, a group of enslaved men seized control of the *Creole* and redirected its course to the free territory of the Bahamas, where the survivors ultimately gained their freedom. In *The Heroic Slave*, in the wake of the uprising and a passing storm, Madison Washington stands proudly at the helm of the *Creole* and declares, "You cannot write the bloody laws of slavery on those restless billows. The ocean, if not the land, is free."[21] Against the patriotic grain of a hallowed freedom often coded into the US landscape—the national anthem's "land of the free," for instance, or the "amber waves of grain" and "fruited plain" of "America the Beautiful"—here, it is rather the ocean that *is* free in an absolute sense, while the land and even a (slave) ship may be subject to the "bloody laws of slavery." It is further intriguing, given the strong association between literacy and freedom in Douglass's narrative, that here the ocean's absolute freedom inheres in its complete incapacitation of writing. In this way, Douglass alludes to a freedom that transcends writing or codification; that simply is, just as we often imagine the so-called inalienable rights of the individual. However, a second revealing instance of the deep in Douglass's writings troubles the grounding of such absolute freedom in the individual by applying pressure to the underlying assumption that the individual represents the most basic unit of social life. Consider the following passage from Douglass's 1859 lecture "Self-Made Men," in which the relationship between the ocean and the waves serves as an analogy for the relationship between the social and the individual:

> It must in truth be said, though it may not accord well with self-conscious individuality and self-conceit, that no possible native force of character, and no depth of wealth and originality, can lift a man into absolute independence of his fellowmen, and no generation of men can be independent of the preceding generation. The brotherhood and interdependence of mankind are guarded and defended at all points. I believe in individuality, but individuals are, to the mass, like waves to the ocean. The highest order of genius is as dependent as is the lowest. It, like the loftiest waves of the sea, derives its power and greatness from the grandeur and vastness of the ocean of which it forms a part. We differ as the waves, but are one as the sea.[22]

What Douglass characterizes as the absolute freedom of the ocean in *The Heroic Slave* here joins a second absolute—not the individual and their "inalienable rights," which we might associate with the exclusionary freedom of a deck that proceeds under the banner of sails of "purest white," but the *social*. Douglass's assertion that the social maintains an identical relation to the individual as the ocean does to individual waves inverts the traditional vision of social life enshrined by the Declaration of Independence and the US Constitution, in which the independent, or in other words *free*, individual represents the most basic unit of social life. Like the deck of a slave ship, this codified vision of social life and freedom was quite explicitly subtended by the underside of "the bloody laws of slavery." In contrast, Douglass offers a metaphor for social life that, even as it accommodates individual expression, is ultimately grounded in and irreducible beyond the social—a conception of social life that Denise Ferreira da Silva has otherwise theorized as "difference without separability."[23] These invocations of the deep elsewhere in Douglass's corpus inform how the same bay, which otherwise terrifies Douglass with thoughts of his enslavement, also and ultimately serves as the catalyst of his freedom struggle. A struggle, crucially, not for the freedom from which he is barred, the freedom of the deck, but for what he alternatively imagines, with respect to the ocean itself, as an even more absolute freedom.

We find a similar encounter with the deep in *The Life and Adventures of Henry Bibb* (1849), where in place of the sea we find the Ohio River. Notwithstanding this shift from salt to fresh water, Henry Bibb's encounter with the Ohio River may be recognized to follow a nearly identical pattern to Equiano's and Douglass's respective encounters with the ocean. Like theirs, Bibb's encounter with the deep is precipitated by both an acute awareness of his enslavement and an experience of discipline:

> As all the instrumentalities which I as a slave, could bring to bear upon the system, had utterly failed to palliate my sufferings, all hope and consolation fled. I must be a slave for life, and suffer under the lash or die. The influence which this had only tended to make me more unhappy. I resolved that I would be free if running away could make me so. I had heard that Canada was a land of liberty, somewhere in the North; and every wave of trouble that rolled across my breast, caused me to think more and more about Canada, and liberty. But more especially *after having been flogged*, I have fled to the highest hills of the forest, pressing my way to the North for refuge; but the river Ohio was my limit. To me it was an impassable gulf. I had no rod wherewith to smite the stream, and thereby divide the waters. I had no Moses to go before me and lead the way from bondage to a promised land.[24]

Much like the flogging that motivated Equiano's return to the deep, Bibb's encounter with the Ohio River is immediately preceded by a flogging. And like the ontological violence that drove Douglass to the Chesapeake, including a sense of slavery's total colonization of his time, Bibb is driven to the Ohio River by an acute sense of slavery's endurance "for life." Even the most distinguishing feature of Bibb's encounter with the deep—that it involves a river and not the ocean—is mitigated by the fact that Bibb's characterization of the Ohio River is decidedly oceanic. He not only likens it to an "impassable *gulf*," a deep inlet of the sea surrounded by land, but also alludes to the Israelites' crossing of the Red *Sea* in Exodus. Like the parallel exodus of the Israelites, Bibb's fugitivity is ultimately oriented toward the promised land of Canada, while the Ohio River, as the geographic limit to Bibb's fugitivity, colludes with his enslavement just as the Red Sea barred the escape of the Israelites. In this way, the Ohio River is haunted in a different way than Douglass's Chesapeake. Here the subtext is the Atlantic's Middle Passage tenure as an "impassable gulf" to Equiano and many other middle passing Africans who longed to return to the freedom of their homes. It may be more subtle than the Chesapeake and its ghosts, but such a haunting helps to explain the oceanic depiction of the Ohio, as well as what Bibb suggestively describes as so many *waves* of trouble *rolling* across his breast.

Yet, like Equiano and Douglass before, Bibb ultimately comes to identify the Ohio River with a kind of freedom. Consider the apostrophe that Bibb offers "on the lofty banks of the river Ohio," which uncannily echoes Douglass's apostrophe "upon the lofty banks" of the Chesapeake Bay:

> Sometimes standing on the Ohio River bluff, looking over on a free State, and as far north as my eyes could see, I have eagerly gazed upon the blue sky of the free North, which at times constrained me to cry out from the depths of my soul, Oh! Canada, sweet land of rest—Oh! when shall I get there! Oh, that I had the wings of a dove, that I might soar away to where there is no slavery; no clanking of chains, no captives, no lacerating of backs, no parting of husbands and wives; and where man ceases to be the property of his fellow man. These thoughts have revolved in my mind a thousand times. I have stood upon the lofty banks of the river Ohio, gazing upon the splendid steamboats, wafted with all their magnificence up and down the river, and I thought of the fishes of the water, the fowls of the air, the wild beasts of the forest, all appeared to be free, to go just where they pleased, and I was an unhappy slave![25]

Aside from the fact that Bibb offers his apostrophe to Canada while Douglass offers his to the Chesapeake's ships, their respective encounters with the deep are remarkably similar. Bibb cries out "from the depths of [his] soul" in the same way that Douglass pours out his "soul's complaint." Bibb also, like Douglass, juxtaposes the freedom of motion of "the splendid steamboats" with the relative constraint of his enslavement. In addition to these parallels, the two passages are so strikingly similar in language and tone that they may even be in *conscious* dialogue. Bibb's narrative was published just four years after Douglass's, and given the latter's popularity Bibb was almost certainly familiar with it. Not to mention Bibb wrote to Douglass the same year that *Narrative of the Life and Adventures of Henry Bibb* was published.[26] Finally, just as Douglass gestures toward a deep freedom beyond the purview of the deck and in excess of the deep's historical associations with slavery, so Bibb also comes to locate in the Ohio River a freedom that not only interrupts the river's collusion with slavery but whose explicit wildness also distinguishes it from the freedom indexed by the promised land of Canada. In his invocation of the freedom of the "fishes of the water," Bibb gestures toward an aqueous freedom beyond the nation-state in a manner strongly reminiscent of the absolute freedom that Douglass similarly locates in the ocean in *The Heroic Slave.*

II. the submersion narrative

The striking intertextuality between Bibb's, Douglass's, and Equiano's respective encounters with the Ohio River, Chesapeake Bay, and Atlantic Ocean suggests the early consolidation of a defining trope of the black literary tradition. In one of the inaugural genres of African American literature, how do we interpret the fact that these canonical slave narratives feature a repeated encounter with the formation that I am calling the deep? However much they may differ in their particulars, this trilogy of deep encounters set flowing by Equiano's original encounter with "the sea, and a slave ship" nevertheless share a basic aesthetic vocabulary. A bay or river may occupy the original place of the Atlantic, and a "multitude of ships" or "splendid steamboats" may occupy the original place of the slave ship, but each individual seascape nevertheless shares three basic elements: (1) a body of water, (2) watercraft(s), and (3) a fugitive slave. Here, I employ fugitivity broadly to include *any* movement away from slavery—however significant or slight, permanent or temporary, actual or imagined—such that Equiano's unrealized desire to jump over the side, Douglass's temporary rendezvous with the Chesapeake, and Bibb's limited escapes to the Ohio River all constitute enactments of fugitivity.[27] Beyond this shared aesthetic vocabulary, these repeated encounters with the deep also follow a general narrative progression that, regardless of their particulars, can likewise be delineated into three basic parts: (1) a *precipitating experience of racial subjection*, (2) a *fugitive return to the deep*, and (3) some degree of *inhabiting the deep*.

Whether a flogging in the case of Equiano and Bibb or nonphysical discipline in the case of Douglass, each of their respective encounters with the deep is precipitated by an experience of racial subjection, which inspires their acute awareness of slavery as the totality we have otherwise come to know as the antiblack world. In the immediate wake of their respective experiences of racial subjection, each also absconds to a manifestation of the deep that is haunted by an unconscious memory of Middle Passage and marked by a profound ambivalence. Hence, the deep occasions Equiano's astonishment and terror, Douglass's delight and torment, Bibb's unhappiness and hope. And for all three, the deep evokes life and death, slavery and freedom. Finally, each of their respective encounters with the deep concludes with some degree, however marginal and whether literal or figurative, of inhabiting the deep. Consider, for instance, how Equiano, Douglass, and Bibb all insist into the deep a kind of freedom. For Equiano it is the freedom of the "inhabitants of the deep," for Douglass the absolute freedom unwritten on the "restless billows" of the ocean, and for Bibb the wild freedom of the "fishes of the water." If, for Kamau Brathwaite, "the unity is submarine," so apparently is freedom.[28] And Equiano, Douglass, and Bibb inhabit the deep insofar as they, to varying degrees, adopt a sense of freedom inspired by the deep.

Of course, whatever freedom may be found in the deep seems negligible relative to the narrative supremacy of the more conventional freedom drives that define these narratives. Equiano, for example, responds to the degradation of being traded by ultimately becoming a *trader* himself. Douglass responds to his transformation into a brute by ultimately endeavoring to become a *man*.[29] And Bibb evades the "system" of slavery by ultimately making landfall in a free *country*. However, beneath the narrative primacy of these more conventional economic, gendered, and political expressions of freedom runs the steady undercurrent of a wilder freedom associated with the deep. What can seem a mere ancillary detour, or in Bibb's case an active obstruction on the way to freedom, belies what is otherwise the deep's consistent proximity to the *crucial* moment when this triumvirate of fugitive slaves resolves to *be* free. At the height of each of their respective senses of the totalizing subjugation of slavery—when Equiano sensed he "had gotten into a world," when Douglass despaired of the total colonization of his time, or when Bibb lamented his powerlessness within the "system" of enslavement—the deep looms as a consistent waterway out of no way. Moreover, its wild and absolute freedom better resonates with how the resolve to be free often precedes and exceeds the attainment of whatever existing formalizations of freedom are available to the enslaved. Consider, for example, Douglass's resolution, in the wake of his consequential fight with Mr. Covey, not to be a "slave in fact," however long he must remain "a slave in form." Could we similarly imagine the possibility of being *free in fact*, regardless of whether one has managed to become free in form? Even if Douglass explicitly identifies his fight with Covey as "the turning-point in my career as a slave" with respect to such *in-fact* freedom, we cannot discount the crucial role of his rendezvous with the Chesapeake immediately prior.[30] Within what Douglass describes as the "hell of *unending* slavery," it's specifically his encounter with the bay that leads Douglass to affirm that "there is a better *day* coming." Thus, with respect to Douglass's experience of enslavement primarily as a total subjection of his time, this encounter with the deep functions as a significant turning point in its own right.[31] What ultimately assumes the normative form of a masculinized freedom realized through violent self-defense arguably begins with the sheer possibility of freedom apprehended on the face of the deep. Apparently, you cannot write the bloody laws of slavery or freedom on these restless billows.

The shared aesthetic vocabulary and narrative progression of this repeating encounter with the deep suggests a black narrative form commensurate with "the narratives of ascent and immersion" that Robert Stepto outlines in his classic study of African American literature, *From Behind the Veil.* According to Stepto, "The classic ascent narrative launches an 'enslaved' and semi-literate figure on a ritualized journey to a symbolic North; that journey is charted through spatial expressions of social structure, invariably systems of signs that the questing figure must read in order to be both increasingly literate and increasingly free. The ascent narrative conventionally ends with the questing figure situated in the least oppressive social structure afforded by the world of the narrative, and free in the sense that he or she has gained sufficient literacy."[32] Stepto identifies both the *Narrative of the Life of Frederick Douglass* and *The Life and Adventures of Henry Bibb* as classic ascent narratives.[33] Indeed, both narratives recount northern migrations, to New Bedford and Canada respectively, that culminate with their author's freedom and literacy. Although *The Interesting Narrative of the Life of Olaudah Equiano* is not included in Stepto's analysis, Equiano's upward climb from cargo in the hold, where he "could not see how they managed the vessel," to skilled sailor and trader on the deck can also be interpreted as a type of ascent, driven by a growing literacy of the maritime and mercantile world.[34]

However, according to Stepto, a final feature of the ascent narrative—that "the least oppressive social structure afforded by the world of the narrative" is, "at best, one of solitude" and, "at worst, one of alienation"—contributes to the development of another narrative form. "Prior to *The Souls* [*of Black Folk*]," Stepto observes, "the seminal journey in Afro-American narrative literature is unquestionably the journey north." After *Souls*, however, Stepto tracks the emergence of the return journey south as a complementary vector of migration characterizing what he alternatively names the "immersion narrative."[35] Outlining this complementary narrative form, Stepto writes, "The immersion narrative is fundamentally an expression of a ritualized journey into a symbolic South, in which the protagonist seeks those aspects of tribal literacy that ameliorate, if not obliterate, the conditions imposed by solitude. The conventional immersion narrative ends almost paradoxically, with the questing figure located in or near the narrative's most oppressive social structure but free in the sense that he has regained sufficient tribal literacy."[36] If Douglass's 1845 narrative represents the "paradigmatic narrative of ascent," then Stepto reads *Souls*, which traces W. E. B. Du Bois's journey "from infancy in the Berkshires of western Massachusetts to adulthood amid the western hills of Atlanta," as the paradigmatic narrative of immersion.[37] Paule Marshall's novel *Praisesong for the Widow* can also be read as a kind of "immersion narration" that extends to the Global South, with the parallel southern journeys of the protagonist, Avey Johnson, from New York to the South Carolina Sea Islands as a child and to Carriacou as an adult.

However, the terrestrial emphasis of this Jacob's ladder of longitudinal migration processing north and south belies an equally prevalent vector of migration that has gone relatively unremarked in the study of black literature and whose strange fruition is not arrival in the existing structures of this world so much as the imagination of alternative worlds. Indeed, even longer than they've journeyed north or south, black peoples have consistently stolen (themselves) away to the deep. Especially with regard to the larger context of the African Diaspora, the journey to the deep can even be said to eclipse the journey north or south as the seminal journey of black narrative. Even if, paradoxically, it is a journey unto a placeless place where no human can hope to fully arrive.

In conversation with Stepto's delineation of the ascent and immersion narrative, I propose that this fugitive migration to the deep might alternatively be conceived, with a nod to its ultimate inhabitation of the deep, as a *submersion narrative*. In place of "a symbolic North" or "South," the submersion narrative launches an enslaved figure on a ritualized journey to the deep. Following the three-part narrative progression outlined above, it culminates not with the enslaved or questing figure situated in the least or most oppressive social structure in the world of the narrative nor with "sufficient literacy" of that world. Rather, it culminates with the realization of the possibility of a world otherwise. In the cases of Equiano, Douglass, and Bibb, this specifically manifests not just as the deep-inspired insight into freedom's very possibility but also as a rewilding of available paradigms of freedom, even if short-lived or ultimately disavowed in the pursuit of formalized freedoms.

Freedom, however, is not the only aptitude at issue in the submersion narrative. Over the course of this study, the submersion narrative will also be found to subject other significant aptitudes—constitutive of western humanism's "plan of living"—to a kind of sea change.[38] In what may be recognized as its subversive refusal of the world, the submersion narrative mirrors aspects of Stepto's "immersion narrative." Not only do they share, in the deep and in the South, similarly downward trajectories of migration, but their mutual descents enact similar refusals of the logic of ascent. According to Stepto, the immersion narrative rejects the individual, but also isolating, freedom of the North by undertaking a return journey south in a "cultural immersion ritual" that results in "tribal literacy" and "the newfound balms of group identity."[39] The submersion narrative performs a similar "cultural immersion ritual" by submersing the enslaved or questing figure in an ambivalent memory of Middle Passage.[40] Its tribal literacy and group identity, then, pertains specifically to what Saidiya Hartman has called "the tribe of Middle Passage."[41] Occasionally, as in the novel *Praisesong for the Widow*, such immersion and submersion can occur coterminously within a single text. Yet besides the latter's shift from the terrestrial to the aquatic, the submersion narrative warrants further distinction in its departure from the existing social structure of the narrative world entirely. In this way, the kind of cultural immersion it facilitates is less a balm than a window into other possible worlds.

Furthermore, unlike other narrative forms, the submersion narrative needn't exhaust the entirety of a given literary work or represent its dominant narrative. The submersion narrative is just as often—as in the case of Equiano, Douglass, and Bibb—the stuff of chapters, paragraphs, and even sentences, a subnarrative embedded within a larger text.[42] As the reference to *Praisesong* already implies, the submersion narrative also includes other genres of African American literature beyond the slave narrative or even the purview of slavery. The far more recent "(Sittin' on) The Dock of the Bay" (1968) by Otis Redding is neither a text about slavery nor, in the strictly literary sense, a text. Nevertheless, a closer inspection of Redding's hit single reveals the same aesthetic vocabulary and narrative progression witnessed in Equiano's, Douglass's, and Bibb's respective encounters with the deep.

Redding begins "The Dock of the Bay" by singing of a seascape that, no doubt by now, will appear familiar:

> Sittin' in the morning sun
> I'll be sittin' when the evening comes
> Watching the *ships* roll in
> Then I watch 'em roll away again, yeah
> I'm sittin' on the dock of the *bay*
> Watchin' the tide roll away, ooh
> I'm just sittin' on the dock of the bay
> Wastin' time[43]

In the song's opening verse and chorus, we encounter the three basic elements of the aesthetic vocabulary of the submersion narrative's repeating encounter with the deep. The first two—a body of water and watercraft(s)—are immediately apparent in the San Francisco Bay and the ships rolling in and away again, which further echo the steamboats that Bibb likewise watches wafting "up and down" the Ohio River. The final element of a fugitive slave, however, hardly seems germane to the semiautobiographical song inspired by Redding's stay on a houseboat in Sausalito, California. Nevertheless, in our consideration of "The Dock of the Bay" as a submersion narrative, we might read the figure of the fugitive slave as liberally as Stepto does the "enslaved" figure in his study of the ascent narrative. Just as Stepto interprets the protagonists of Ralph Ellison's *Invisible Man* (1952) and James Weldon Johnson's *The Autobiography of an Ex-Colored Man* (1912) as "enslaved" figures in the more general sense of a racial subjection that exceeds chattel slavery, we might read the figure of the fugitive slave in a similarly broad way. One that, regarding certain autobiographical elements of "The Dock of the Bay," resonates with the specific way in which black studies has come to define slavery more broadly as "social death."

Something approximating social death is arguably indexed by the song's concluding verse:

> Sittin' here resting my bones
> And this *loneliness* won't leave me alone
> Two thousand miles I roamed
> Just to make this dock my home[44]

In and of itself, "loneliness" is not commensurate with the radical exclusion from human society that has come to be understood in black studies under the rubric of "social death." But in the specific context of Redding's conscious search for a song that, in the racially segregated musical landscape of the United States, was "going to cross [him] over," such loneliness bears the traces of Redding's struggle against a racialized sonic isolation very much related to what is meant by the condition of social death.[45] Consider, too, the symbolic index of social death inhering in the looming signifier of *bones*, which is conspicuously tethered to *loneliness* by a conjunction. Thus, we might read Redding's journey to the dock of the bay in conversation with our previous consideration in this book's prologue of Richard Wright's Bigger Thomas, who, in response to his own loneliness, or inability "to be at home with people," resigned himself to inhabit the deep. Redding can be read as a fugitive slave, then, in the sense of a fugitive "socially dead person."[46] Furthermore, this "loneliness" can also be recognized as the *precipitating experience of racial subjection* in the basic narrative progression that defines the submersion narrative. And the subsequent lines of the verse, "Two thousand miles I *roamed* / Just to make this dock my *home*," in turn, represent both Redding's *fugitive return to* and ultimate *inhabitation of the deep*.

If all three narrative components of the submersion narrative can be found in microcosm in the final verse of "The Dock of the Bay," we can look to the rest of the song for the qualifying aspects of each part. For example, in the song's second verse we detect something like the acute awareness of slavery (or social death) as a totality that typically attends the precipitating experience of racial subjection that sets our deep-bound migrants flowing:

> I left my home in Georgia
> Headed for the 'Frisco bay
> 'Cause I've had *nothing* to live for
> And look like *nothing's* gonna come my way[47]

Here, the repeated "nothing" indexes not only a total dispossession but a dispossession that also exerts a totalizing claim upon Redding's time by consuming both his past and future. Redding's fugitive return to the deep can also be read as haunted by Middle Passage to the extent that resting his bones raises the specter of the deep's enduring significance, in the wake of the transatlantic slave trade, as an unmarked grave. This haunting is further augmented by the uncanny circumstances of Redding's tragic passing, just three days after recording "The Dock of the Bay." On December 10, 1967, the twenty-six-year-old Redding went the way of the "inhabitants of the deep" after his plane crashed in Lake Monona on the way to play a show in Madison, Wisconsin. But as much as we might therefore understand "The Dock of the Bay" to be haunted by the past, it is also haunted, in a more ambivalent sense, by the future. The iconic whistle at the end of "The Dock of the Bay" was originally intended as a placeholder for a final verse, which Redding never had the opportunity to write. To hear Redding's whistle, then, is to hear not only the future but, more precisely, future possibility or futurity. In a song whose lyrics otherwise appear to cede the future to "nothing," this is no small loophole. Finally, if in their respective submersion narratives we understand Equiano, Douglass, and Bibb to inhabit the deep with respect to their embrace of a deep-inspired freedom, Redding arguably does the same with respect to time. The song's chorus is punctuated by Redding's declaration of the one thing he is doing at the dock of the bay: "wasting time." Just as Douglass curiously spent his "leisure time" rendezvousing with the Chesapeake Bay, so we find Redding similarly wasting time before the San Francisco Bay. And he lets us know about such time-wasting in that part of a song's architecture that is always circling back on itself and that, in this way, parallels the cyclicality of the ships and the tides rolling in and away again. Thus, Redding may be recognized not merely to waste but also to free time, modeling a deep-inspired orientation to time that refuses the relentless linearity of a world that, to hear Douglass tell it, has been on the clock since at least the plantation.

III. blue nativity

Blackness's history with the deep is enough to expect a Diaspora-wide episode of aquaphobia. There is certainly enough of this in Equiano's "terror" and Douglass's "ghosts." In the unmarked grave of the 1,818,681 and the unconscious memory of what befell the felled and fallen-out of the world. There is enough too in our present: a boy laid to rest in the Tallahatchie River with a cotton-gin fan tied around his neck and the homes shipwrecked by Hurricane Katrina and the boats of African migrants left to die on the Mediterranean Sea. Yet for as long as we've feared the deep with good reason, we've also courted it. We wasted no time. No sooner did Equiano recoil from the ocean in fear than did he wish to jump over the side. And it's not just Equiano and Douglass and Bibb and Redding. It's also Harriet Jacobs, dressed like a sailor and stowing away in *Incidents in the Life of a Slave Girl* (1861). And Marcus Garvey's Black Star Line. And Langston Hughes sailing from New York out into the Atlantic in *The Big Sea* (1940). And Alexis Pauline Gumbs being discipled by whales in *Undrowned* (2020). And Rivers Solomon's vision of interspecies care and collaboration in *The Deep* (2019). Indeed, Equiano's turn and return to the sea appear to have set flowing (to borrow Farah Jasmine Griffin's language) a kind of hajj: an innumerable host, in every epoch and from every corner of the globe, making their pilgrimage to the deep. Why, then, do we come? Keep coming? Keep returning, as it were, to the scene of the crime? How could the blue-stained gate through which we passed into the hell of slavery also and for just as long (or longer, if we remember Equiano's astonishment) yield our very first "loophole of retreat"? And what might it mean that, relative to the miniscule dimensions of the hole Jacobs bored into an already impossibly circumscribed crawl space, this particular loophole constitutes the majority of Earth's surface?

One possible answer for why we come lies in history and the way we've always taken our leave of the antiblack world through the gate we came in, from the inhabitants of the deep to every deep-bound pilgrim since. In this way, the deep not only yields what Anissa Janine Wardi has theorized, following Toni Morrison, as an important "site of memory." It has also served not merely as a symbolic but as a *literal* pathway to freedom. In *Sailing to Freedom*, for example, Timothy D. Walker argues that a significant part of the Underground Railroad actually proceeded by ship and sea: "Maritime escape episodes figure prominently in the majority of published North American fugitive slave accounts written before 1865: of 103 extant pre-Emancipation slave narratives, more than 70 percent recount the use of oceangoing vessels as a means of fleeing slavery. . . . Clearly, the sea should rightly constitute a central component of the full Underground Railroad story."[48] Beside the history of the slave ship, then, we also have to acknowledge the history of what Marcus Rediker has recently surveyed as the "freedom ship." If we've previously recognized the subtext of Douglass's haunted encounter with the Chesapeake to be an unconscious memory of Middle Passage, this neglected history of what *Sailing to Freedom* reframes as the "maritime" or "saltwater Underground Railroad," may be the subtext of his ultimate conviction to "take to the water" with the belief that "this very bay shall yet bear me into freedom." Or Madison Washington's declaration in *The Heroic Slave* that "The ocean, if not the land, is free." In fact, Douglass's own "escape from Baltimore, Maryland to New York City in 1838, though conducted along an 'overland' route of less than two hundred miles, nevertheless entailed three river or estuary crossings by ferry and a steamboat passage between Wilmington, Delaware, and Philadelphia."[49] The diffusion of this alternative subtext of the deep can not only be witnessed in the slave narratives—in Bibb's ability to see a kind of freedom in the same Ohio River that otherwise restricts him—but also in Gumbs's return to the deep in *Undrowned* to learn of all things to breathe. And in Solomon's explicit return to *The Deep* in her novella about middle passing women who were thrown overboard while pregnant and gave birth to progeny who could breathe underwater. Thus, Solomon renders from whence humans are thought to have evolved into the site of humanity's further evolution, learning new ways to breathe through interspecies collaboration.

Blackness's historical relationship to the deep is therefore marked with a profound ambivalence—as a site of life and death, slavery and freedom, deep suffocation and deep breath. Another answer for why we come, then, may have to do with the generative potential, as opposed to emotional indecision or paralysis, of this ambivalence. The poetic philosophy of French philosopher Gaston Bachelard is instructive on this point. In his book *Water and Dreams*, Bachelard asserts, "I believe it is possible to establish in the realm of the imagination, a *law of the four elements* which classifies various kinds of material imagination by their connections with fire, air, water, or earth." What Bachelard calls "material imagination" names a species of imagination that learns "its particular rules and poetics" from the physical properties of matter, so that if a lyric flows, it is because a brook flowed first.[50] For Bachelard, Earth is a poet and Creation begets creation. Moreover, matter's ability to inspire imagination in this way hinges specifically on its ability to inspire ambivalence:

> *A matter to which the imagination cannot give a dual existence cannot play this psychological role of fundamental matter*. Matter that does not provide the opportunity for a psychological ambivalence cannot find a *poetic double* which allows endless transpositions. For the material element to engage the whole soul, there must be a dual participation of desire and fear, a participation of good and evil.[51]

The deep may be recognized to engage the souls of black folk in precisely this way when Douglass pours out his "*soul's* complaint" to the Chesapeake Bay or Bibb cries "out from the depths of [his] *soul*" on the Ohio River. Thus, we come to the deep as a matter to which the African Diaspora can give a dual existence because *water is our "fundamental matter."* What's *been* the matter since the rupture of Middle Passage. But what also constitutes most of the matter on this planet, and so is a fitting tutor for any who, like Celie in *The Color Purple*, would "enter the Creation."

Toward a final reason why we come, we might take our cue from Douglass's curious way of spending (or wasting, as Redding would have it) his "leisure time." Douglass, we've said, is on the clock. And that clock is totalizing. As a limited interval when the time of the enslaved was, at least in some measure, their own, Douglass's leisure time maintains the same fugitive relation to this clock that Sylvia Wynter argues that the plot maintains to the plantation. According to Wynter, the plots of land allotted to the enslaved for subsistence farming were a part of the plantation order intended to offset the costs of maintaining its labor force. However, due to its marginality, Wynter argues that the plot also served as an important "focus of resistance" to the plantation and what she saw as its fundamental reorganization of the relationship between humanity and nature:

> 1 Before the unique Western experience which began with the discovery of the New World, all societies of mankind existed in what [Léopold Sédar] Senghor describes as [a] dual oscillatory process in which Man adapts to Nature, and adapts Nature to his own needs.

2 But with the discovery of the New World and its vast exploitable lands that process which has been termed the "reduction . . . of Nature to Land" had its large scale beginning. From this moment on Western Man saw himself as "the lord and possessor of Nature." The one-way transformation of Nature began. Since man is a part of Nature, a process of dehumanization and alienation was set in train. In old societies with traditional values based on the old relation, resistance could be put up to the dominance of the new dehumanizing system. In new societies like ours, created for the market, there seemed at first to be no possibility of such a tradition.

3 But from early, the planters gave the slaves plots of land on which to grow food to feed themselves in order to maximize profits. We suggest that this plot system, was . . . the focus of resistance to the market system and market values.[52]

Because it allowed the enslaved to engage in subsistence farming at a remove from the plantation order, the plot served not only as the focus of resistance to the market system and its values but also to western humanism's consequent flattening of nature into mere "land"—a docile surface to be possessed and endlessly extracted—and the related reconstitution of the Human as the noncontingent "lords and possessors" of the land.[53] Similarly, relative to the plantation's near-total claim upon Douglass's time, his "leisure time" constitutes a kind of temporal plot. An interval when his time, at least in some measure, was his own, and in which he could resist the plantation's temporal order. Yet in the exercise of his free time, Douglass does not search out the plot but the deep, which is perhaps Earth's greatest rebuff to the reduction of nature to mere land and whose marginality to the plantation affords Douglass a similar measure of autonomy.

Against the grain of western civilization's one-way transformation of nature into a docile surface, Wynter further contends that the plot also facilitated an inverse process of indigenization whereby the displaced "multi-tribal African became the native of that area of experience that we term the New World" through the transplantation of their traditional African lifeways:[54]

4 African peasants transplanted to the plot all the structure of values that had been created by traditional societies of Africa, the land remained the Earth—and the Earth was a goddess; man used the land to feed himself; and to offer first fruits to the Earth; his funeral was the mystical reunion with the earth. Because of this traditional concept the social order remained primary. Around the growing of yam, of food for survival, he

> created on the plot a folk culture—the basis of a social order—in three hundred years.[55]

Douglass's rendezvous with the Chesapeake during the temporal plot of his "leisure time" suggests the deep as another significant coconspirator in blackness's "creation of a folk culture." As the "basis of a social order," or anything, the conspicuously instable deep may not inspire confidence. But what if this understanding of the deep offers us a way of understanding the "sea-change" that Wynter contends African culture underwent during Middle Passage: "The extra-African's cultural response to the dehumanizing alienation of the Capitalist plantation system of the New World, was to reroot himself, making use of the old cultural patterns which had undergone a true *sea-change*, in order to create the new vocabulary of the new existence." Wynter's conception of Middle Passage as inducing a sea-change troubles the logic of the horticultural metaphor of transplantation, whereby the rerooting of African culture on the plot is otherwise preceded by the implicit uprooting of "the physical and geographic disruption implied by the Middle Passage." This is arguably the prevailing characterization of Middle Passage in black studies—echoed, for instance, in Hortense Spillers's characterization of Middle Passage as a "rupture." But rather than a sea-change, which points to some active cultural influence of the ocean itself, these metaphors render the ocean a kind of void. A site of negation that may interrupt or displace but otherwise exerts no positive influence of its own. Even when we've insisted that the rupture of Middle Passage was not absolute—ultimately giving rise, for Wynter, to a cultural process of transplantation or, for Spillers, to a "radically different kind of cultural continuation"—the ocean itself remains an absolute rupture: the unmaker rather than collaborator of human culture.[56] That in spite of which African survivals or New World transplantations improbably take their shape. But what if the ocean changes us as actively as it does the humans born underwater in *The Deep*? Indeed, Glissant's metaphorization of the abyss as a "womb" holds out to us the possibility that the Africans in the middle did not wait until they arrived on New World "plots" to commence the cultural process that would transform them into "the native of . . . the New World."[57] Rather, they may have already started to live in relationship to the deep, as the first "focus of resistance" facilitating blackness's indigenization if not to a New World, which risks the erasure of Native Americans, then perhaps to a blue planet.[58] Thus, we also come because the deep is a significant precedent to the plot. Because the Africans suspended over the face of the deep also put down roots in the sea.

Gesturing toward the deep in this way can appear to disregard recent black studies scholarship that interrogates the limits of a critical overidentification of blackness with water. In *The Black Shoals*, for instance, Tiffany Lethabo King puts forward the geographic formation of the shoal, as a hybrid of land and sea, as a way of "thinking about Blackness as exceeding the metaphors and analytics of water and for thinking of indigeneity as exceeding the symbol and analytic of land." For King, the critical preponderance of "metaphors and analytics of water" in black studies works to obscure blackness's robust relationship to land and the continuities between black and indigenous struggles against conquest. The geographic formation that I am calling the deep, however, not only includes land but, even and precisely in its oceanic provenance, works to engender an interface with the planet that blackness brings to bear on both land and sea. Moreover, however much water may appear as overtrodden critical ground, Omise'eke Natasha Tinsley argues that the overabundance of aquatic metaphors and analytics in black studies nevertheless tends to overlook the materiality of water. For all our talk of water, in other words, black studies has yet, in Tinsley's estimation, to jump in. However well trodden, it appears black studies is yet to break the surface. In putting forward the deep, I attempt just that, to the surprising revelation not only of blackness's deep interface with the planet but also of a black sense of indigeneity that is careful not to erase and, I hope, holds open the possibility for solidarity with the original indigenous peoples of the Americas. As the source, then, of what we have yet to fully think as the blue nativity of blackness and as the focus of resistance to western humanism's dual reconstitution of Earth as a docile surface and the human as the "Lord and possessor" of that surface, the geographic formation that I am calling the deep yields an aquatic complement to the terrestrial formation of the plot and its insurgent afterlives.[59] Sure, insofar as humans are land creatures, blackness's ongoing inhabitation of the deep across the texts I examine, on one hand, yields a fitting symbol of the radical exclusion from human society that black studies has come to understand as social death. But on the other hand, blackness's inhabitation of the deep, precisely in its exclusion from western humanism's environmentally impoverished vision of human sociality, also uniquely positions blackness to think and enact a more genuinely social (because also ecological) life. Especially as such life would need to be imagined on a blue planet.

If the problem of being black is the problem of being an ocean *away*, this book proposes that it is also the problem of having discovered in the deep *a way*. A way out of no way, even, though persisting in the language of negation seems ill-advised when we recall that this particular no way covers the bulk of the only planet known to sustain life. If the human would enter the kingdom of Earth, the climate scientists tell us that we must be born again. Must learn to be and live differently on the Earth. This difficulty, however, is not of the order of a camel passing through the eye of a needle. The way (home) is so broad, you couldn't miss it. Yet, the vast homing of Earth indexed by the ongoing enterprise of white settler colonialism has managed to do just that. In its fetishization of terra firma, it has overlooked the ocean; forgotten, Ralph Ellison might say, the "chaos" against which every "plan of living" is conceived.

Each chapter of this study of the submersion narrative takes up a specific aptitude of western humanism's "plan of living" and explores how blackness's ongoing inhabitation of the deep has subjected it to a kind of sea change. As Elisabeth Mann Borgese observes, "The ocean is a medium different from the earth. . . . It forces us to think differently. The medium itself, where everything flows and everything is interconnected, forces us to 'unfocus,' to shed our old concepts and paradigms, to 'refocus' on a new paradigm."[60] If so, then this study of blackness's ongoing inhabitation of the deep elucidates how black life blues the human, in much the same way that John Coltrane has been known to blue a note.

Chapter 1, "Deep Humanities," undertakes a comparative analysis of Europe's and Africa's uneven encounters with the Atlantic Ocean during the eras of discovery, colonization, and the transatlantic slave trade, and interrogates how these oceanic crossings are represented in Arnold Guyot's *The Earth and Man* (1849) and Olaudah Equiano's *Interesting Narrative*, respectively. If, as Katherine McKittrick contends, "historical epochs are underwritten by differential encounters with geography," I argue that modernity is underwritten by two differential encounters with the ocean that produce whiteness as *stand-your-ground subjectivity* and blackness as *inhabitation of the deep*.[62] These respective modes of interfacing with the planet as either a docile surface or a live deep bespeak the terrible history of black foundering that, since Middle Passage, has constituted (beside native genocide and expropriation) the violent underside of white settlement. Against the grain of humanity's excessive carbon *footprint*, however, this chapter also explores how blackness's paradigmatically deep interface with the planet nevertheless yields a privileged position from which to think and imagine a more ecologically salutary relation to an Earth that is significantly more deep than terra firma.

My second chapter, "Deep Study," interrogates the mutual characterization of blackness and the ocean in Herman Melville's *Moby-Dick* (1851) as the "*dark side* of mankind" and the "*dark side* of earth," respectively.[63] It argues that this entangled binarization of humanity (white and black) and Earth (land and sea) confesses a broader sense in which blackness and blueness furnish the constitutive outside of a modern world that is fundamentally antiblack *and* terracentric.[64] Additionally, the chapter illuminates how mainstream environmentalism disavows this mutuality by perpetuating what Frank Wilderson has called the "ruse of analogy"—advocating for the environment in ways that search out analogy with, but ultimately mystify and even displace, antiblackness.[65] Yet this chapter also takes up environmentalism's turn to "blue" as perhaps the one instance where the analogy between black suffering and environmental degradation is not a ruse insofar as the ocean may also be recognized as socially dead. Finally, I illuminate how the confluence of black and blue comes to an expressive head in *Moby-Dick* in the near drowning of the "poor little negro" Pip, who is consequently consigned to the "dark side" of humanity and the earth. "Not drowned entirely," however, but "rather carried down *alive* to wondrous depths," Pip is perhaps American literature's most reliable witness that deep water and drowning are not the same thing.[66]

In chapter 3, "Deep Voice," I listen for the underwater utterance of the inhabitants of the deep—the drowned-out, would-be last words of the jumpers and the jettisoned. This historical moment of incapacitated speech mirrors what is likewise repeatedly characterized in the black literary tradition as the unspeakable "problem" of being black. But when words forsook the underwater utterance of the inhabitants of the deep, did *sound*? Instructed by the fact that water transmits sound four times more efficiently than air, this chapter queries whether, beyond its incapacitation of speech, the deep can also be apprehended as a kind of prosthesis unto some otherwise mode of expression. Furthermore, it explores the parallel way in which the black literary tradition can be recognized to speak with a *deep voice.* That is, to negotiate the ineffability of the problem of being black by recursively figuring it as a water-induced crisis of having no ground that both originates with and is subsequently haunted by Middle Passage. Through the prevalence of this trope in the black literary tradition, I observe, like M. NourbeSe Philip while writing *Zong!*, how "always what is going on seems to be about water" and as much unto the enactment of black ecological life as social death.[67]

Extending chapter 3's concern with sound and music, my fourth chapter argues that really listening to black expressive culture may be a matter of learning to detect the activity of a "Deep Imagination." The chapter reads Paule Marshall's *Praisesong for the Widow* as a prototypical submersion narrative, in which the protagonist Avey Johnson returns to a place where her great-aunt Cuney would recite a curious story about a group of Africans who disembarked a slave ship and walked on water back to Africa. I place Avey's struggle to apprehend this story in conversation with the kindred struggle of the anonymous narrator of Ralph Ellison's *Invisible Man* to "really listen" to a recording of Louis Armstrong's "(What Did I Do to Be So) Black and Blue." In their mutual concern with *really listening*, I argue that both novels model a method for the aesthetic appreciation of what Ellison calls the "blackness of blackness." However, *Praisesong* does so in a way that pushes us to consider what might constitute the material referent of "blue" in Armstrong's musical meditation on being "black." Through close readings of the Ibo landing myth at the heart of *Praisesong*, I propose that appreciating the blackness of black literature, a familiar dilemma of black literary studies, may be a matter of learning to detect the creative activity of what I call, after the poetic philosophy of Gaston Bachelard, the *material imagination of blackness*. That is, an imagination, like Old Avatara's mind in *Praisesong*, that is long "gone with the Ibos" and whose "fundamental matter," following Bachelard, is water.

Chapter 5, "Deep Life," wonders after the life of the deep by taking up another prototypical submersion narrative in August Wilson's *Gem of the Ocean*. Crucial to this wondering is an appreciation of *Gem* as the first play of Wilson's famed Century Cycle, a series of ten plays representing each decade of the twentieth century. If, according to Wilson, the cycle explicitly aims to "place the culture of black America on stage" and to demonstrate, among other things, that black people "have a ground to stand on," then this chapter interrogates why Wilson begins by locating blackness in the deep, with apparently no more ground to stand upon than blackness's nonstanding in the modern world. However, Wilson's ambivalent representation of blackness's inhabitation of the deep also invites us to question what sort of ground the deep might actually be and, more, what sort of grounds for life. Wilson writes, "Some know about the land. Some know about the water. But there is some that know about the land and the water. They got both sides of it."[68] If so, then perhaps, blackness's inhabitation of the deep harbors the knowledge of "both sides of it" and, with it, a revelation of the only ground on which any of us have to live on this deep planet.

If chapter 3 listens for the inhabitants of the deep, my final chapter, "Deep Vision," looks after them. But how can the inhabitants of the deep get a witness, if their passion unfolded below *see* level? The answer this chapter pursues is the photograph of Emmett Till, which I read as a photograph of the inhabitants of the deep. Until Emmett resurrected from his Tallahatchie grave on the third day, who had ever beheld this theretofore unseen terror? Of course, we behold Emmett only because his mother beheld him first and famously chose to "let the world see what I've seen."[69] Thus, this chapter also reads the photograph as what Mamie Till-Mobley saw—her enactment of *deep vision*. As the presiding seer of this chapter, Mamie's refusal to allow her son's broken face to be retouched is instructive for its disruption of a modern regime of visuality largely predicated upon mutual recognition. Helping to clarify the stakes of this refusal, I finally place the photograph of Emmett Till in conversation with the equally unrecognizable face of the black boy in Jason deCaires Taylor's underwater sculpture *Vicissitudes.* Notwithstanding the widely divergent circumstances of their submergence and subsequent viewing, I argue that both visualizations of the inhabitants of the deep confront their viewers with faces that, for their time spent underwater, are no longer recognizably human. In this way, they enlist viewers in an ethical exercise of attending to more-than-human life in the unrecognizability of our relation.

One of Emmett Till's murderers told on himself and all his folks when he explained that he killed Emmett "just so everybody can know how me and my folks *stand*."[70] Against the death-dealing grain of whiteness's stand-your-ground subjectivity and what we've tellingly also come to describe as humanity's "carbon *footprint*," *Inhabitants of the Deep* ultimately calls us to a recalibration of how we interface with the planet. In the face of ecological crisis, Alice Walker asks, "Where do we start? How do we reclaim a proper relationship to the world?"[71] On a blue planet such as ours, this book proposes we start with the inhabitants of the deep and their bluing of the human.

1

DEEP HUMANITIES

The land is where white people live.
—PERCIVAL EVERETT, *James*

It's terrible to have come from nothing but the sea,
which is nowhere, navigable only in its constant autodislocation.
—FRED MOTEN, *The Universal Machine*

I. blue ancestry

IT IS INDEED "terrible to have come from nothing but the sea," but perhaps we can begin to undertake what Fred Moten proceeds to describe in *The Universal Machine* as the "necessity of an investigation of that nothingness . . . which is to say the blackness, of the slave," by first recalling that technically every hue comes from blue.[1] It isn't the sort of ancestry we're hoping to discover when we pack pieces of ourselves into DNA kits promising to help us "uncover your origins," but we *all* come from "nothing but the sea," insofar as all life shares a common, if remote, ancestor in the ocean. Call it the primordial sea in so many of our creation myths (*tehom* in the Judeo-Christian tradition or Olokun in the Yoruba tradition) or the evolutionary origin of all of life.[2] But at least on this point, the theologians and the scientists agree. In the beginning was the ocean. One we land creatures still favor with the salt in our blood.

However, some of us (are made to) remember this oceanic heritage better than others. There were those for whom *Land ho*! failed to inspire the same relief as for other transatlantic migrants crossing a then unknown and dreaded ocean during the early modern era of discovery and colonization. Consider, for instance, how differently "Someone" and "we" respond to the sighting of land in Ed Roberson's poem "Comb":

> *Someone* screamed, "Land!"
> When *we* looked at the horizon everyone wept.[3]

To its intended colonizers and coerced workers, "Land!" meant very different things. The former (the poem's "Someone") celebrates the long-awaited resolution of what Moten aptly describes as the ocean's "constant autodislocation."[4] But the latter (the poem's "we") laments what will prove an *ongoing* dislocation for which "Land!" pronounces not resolution but the continuity of an oceanic experience persisting in the salt of "everyone['s]" tears. Not celebration, then, but lament. We've heard Malcolm X similarly parse our differential stakes in these first landings when he famously declared, "We *didn't land* on Plymouth Rock. The rock was landed on us."[5] X's iconoclastic refusal of this keystone of US national mythology contrasts sharply with the veneration that French political thinker and historian Alexis de Tocqueville otherwise describes in *Democracy in America* (1835): "This Rock has become an object of veneration in the United States. I have seen bits of it carefully preserved in several towns in the Union. Does this sufficiently show that all human power and greatness is in the soul of man? Here is a stone which the feet of a few outcasts pressed for an instant; and the stone becomes famous; it is treasured by a great nation; its very dust is shared as a relic."[6] The United States has built its house upon the rock—less physically than in the metaphorical sense of a kind of cohering worship, animated by the fetishization of a *certain* interface with the planet. It is not the sixty-six uncertain days that the *Mayflower* spent at sea but the mere "instant" when the Pilgrims pressed their feet upon a rock that has come to be revered as a founding part of our national mythology. The nation's worship of this totem of settlement serves to ward off the ocean's unsettling dislocation like a suppressed memory and sustain a general amnesia of the boats in our family tree such that the descendants of outcasts cast out without a hint of irony. But what to the slave is Plymouth Rock? What, to those who "didn't land," is the triumph of landing it commemorates or the triumph of landing commemorated the world over in the multinational celebration of Christopher Columbus's "discovery" of the New World? Theirs is neither the "great nation" cohered around the fetishization of Plymouth Rock nor the modern world cohered around the fetishization of perhaps the most notorious landing of all, but rather the violent underside of landing sounded out by Malcolm X.

It's from this violent underside that the fugitive slave James observes, as a kind of corollary to Moten's pronouncement about the provenance of blackness, that "the land is where white people live."[7] The inverted geographic logic of Percival Everett's *James* (2024), a retelling of Mark Twain's *Adventures of Huckleberry Finn* (1884) from the perspective of Jim, means that the eponymous James's life is paradoxically least at risk while traveling on the Mississippi River and most at risk whenever he comes ashore. Blackness, in other words, doesn't only come "*from* nothing but the sea" or whiteness, contrastingly, from "the land," but both also *continue* to inhabit these respective domains. In order to fully apprehend this racialized geography, however, I propose a shift from the arguably mystifying binary of "land" and "sea" to a distinction instead between terra firma and the *deep*, because the comparatively deep and superficial interfaces with the planet at issue in this chapter's respective conceptualizations of blackness and whiteness will be shown to manifest themselves on land and sea alike.

James, Malcolm X, and the rest of us who "didn't land," never received our invitation to the global stand-your-ground party that has evolved into what we've tellingly come to describe in terms of humanity's excessive carbon *footprint*. This party is metaphor until it isn't. Until, there, in the gruesome eye of a lynch mob of smiling bystanders, the soles of black folk gasp for ground. Of course, the racialized and violent distribution of the ground enacted during such celebrations doesn't begin or end with lynching. The history of blackness's foundering is long. It's Aunt Hester suspended from a hook "so that she stood upon the ends of her toes." It's Todd Clifton "crumpling" on the sidewalk in Ralph Ellison's *Invisible Man*.[8] It's stepping off the sidewalk in the Jim Crow South. It's Emmett Till laid to rest in the Tallahatchie River by white men preoccupied with showing "how me and my folks *stand*."[9] It's Sandra Bland discovered in a "semi-standing position" in a jail cell.[10] It's Trayvon Martin lost to a man infamously standing his ground. It's Michael Brown callously left to, on, and as the ground. But before any of these, and first, it's "the footprint on the water, filling."[11] It's the steps that middle passing Africans blinked upon the face of the Atlantic as the firstborn of those who "didn't land." It's the 1,818,681 drowned. The 1,818,681 splashes into oblivion, sounding at once the nascent pulse of white settler colonialism and the seeming geographic disinheritance that is blackness.[12] It's this ground zero of black *ab-jection*—a literal and primordial throwing away, over the side and out of the world—and the problem of meeting zero ground. It's modernity's trail of breadcrumbs. It's these black antecedents of glacier melt. *This* sea-level rise. (How much did the ocean have to rise to accommodate nearly two million new residents? It's statistically negligible, I am sure, but large masses always build momentum slowly, imperceptibly. Rise is rise.) It's Killmonger's great-great-great-great-great-great-auntie. The ancestors he passionately claims in those "who jumped from ships" but from whom, precisely because they jumped, he can't possibly be descended.[13] It's those middle passing Africans survived to us in Equiano's narrative as the "*inhabitants* of the deep," even though we know humans can't live underwater.

Those of us who are claimed by and claim this genealogy of (auto)dislocation maintain a privileged mnemonic relation to our common oceanic heritage by effectively coming from the ocean twice. Beyond the oceanic genesis in which all life shares, history has caused us to double back and begin again. How difficult it can be to forget humanity's blue ancestry when you are created by and in the dramatic reminder of Middle Passage, which Frank Wilderson has called the "dawning of blackness" and "the Black's first ontological instance."[14] Even if we would forget, history is our faithful reminder. Not just because it is full of the mnemonic spectacles of the assorted ground ceremonies of white settler colonialism indexed by lynching, but also because we take up our lives amid the regular and uneventful commemoration that is a settled world. Lynching and stepping off the sidewalk merely dramatize what are already humanity's uneven claims to the ground, before the rope goes taught. The spectacle merely lays bare the brutal interplay between white settlement and the murderous complex of dispossession and dislocation that is settlement's historical condition of possibility. They perform the terrible differences that white settler colonialism has opened up in humanity's interface with the planet—the site where our feet meet or fail to meet the ground, and the material circumstances that subtend how or if we stand.

But if "we didn't land," what did we do? To ask this question is to begin to investigate the nothingness of blackness. It is a window onto an "otherwise" interface with the planet, beyond the landing of Plymouth Rock.[15] Here, the gerund *landing* names not just the mere activity of making landfall, about which we need not think any further, but a practice, a doing, an orientation of and toward land. An interface informed not only by physics but by metaphysics. Not just the interacting materiality of what there is to land on and the entity doing the landing but the assumptions about the nature of the interactants themselves and their relationship. We gain the conviction to open this window and investigate the nothingness—which, in this case, is specifically to say the not-landing and non-standing—of blackness by first recognizing how landing itself has come under increasing suspicion both in recent critiques of US stand-your-ground law and the growing anxiety surrounding humanity's excessive carbon footprint.[16] Although these critiques have largely been elaborated independently of one another, their common indictment of how we stand interrupts the celebration of landing as an unquestionable triumph by illuminating its violent underside of antiblackness and ecological crisis. More than the racial and ecological violence of landing, however, the conviction to investigate the not-landing of blackness derives from the recognition that blackness also refuses the landing refused to it. Consider, for instance, the poet Dionne Brand's pronouncement that "I'm giving up on land to light on."[17] Or Todd Clifton's decision in Ralph Ellison's *Invisible Man* "to plunge outside of history," "instead of making a dominating stand."[18] These black refusals of the historic complex of landing, or what, following Ellison, we might label humanity's "dominating stand," suggest that exclusion from humanity's stand-your-ground party isn't the insult we think it is. Indeed, climate scientists reviewed the guest list back in 2002 and found that only 25 percent of humanity was invited.[19] So we out here. And we got company. Not commiserates either. Like Zora Neale Hurston, we "do not belong to the sobbing school of Negrohood," and we work toward the integration of this joy that we have in some other direction.[20] Let *in*? We're trying to be, practice, and turn the world *out*. Besides, the rent party, that besieged celebration of where we live beyond ownership, was always more live anyway. Not to mention that Mother Nature is about to shut that other shit down. In an irony of ironies, the eviction notice has already been served. The ninety-five theses of Martin, and Malcolm, and Baldwin, and Walker, and countless other prophets have already been posted to the door. Something about all that standing leaving too big a carbon footprint and the house getting too warm. Perhaps more than all the others, Alice Walker's thesis makes it plain: "The good news may be that Nature is phasing out the white man, but the bad news is that's who She thinks we all are."[21]

II. the atlantic opportunity

i.

Historians, too, agree that we come from nothing but the sea. Though with a purview closer to yesterday than *the* beginning, their concern is rather the more immediate oceanic origins of a modern world born largely of the advent of transatlantic migration. One way or another, we all descend from the "ships in motion across the spaces between Europe, America, Africa, and the Carribbean" because we all take up our lives in the modern world created in their wake. Paul Gilroy famously put the transatlantic traffic of these ships on the map as a defining "chronotope" of modernity in *The Black Atlantic* (1993).[22]

Before and since Gilroy's classic text, the chorus of scholars bearing witness to the significance of the Atlantic crossing in precipitating an unprecedentedly modern arrangement of time and space continues to grow. For example, Stephanie Smallwood writes in *Saltwater Slavery* (2007) that "for early modern people everywhere in the Atlantic basin, the initial encounter with the Atlantic as an arena for human activity was profoundly transformative."[23] And in *The Birth of African-American Culture* (1992), anthropologists Sidney Mintz and Richard Price write, "New World it is, for those who became its peoples remade it, and in the process, they remade themselves."[24] If this interdisciplinary consensus were not persuasive enough already, the hard sciences have also recently joined the chorus, with even more grandiose claims about these ships and their impact on not just historical but geological time. In their book *The Human Planet* (2018), climate scientists Simon Lewis and Mark Maslin propose the transatlantic traffic of the sixteenth century as the likely origin of the new geological epoch called the Anthropocene: "In the sixteenth century a new planet-wide human-driven evolutionary experiment began which will continue to play out indefinitely. What plate tectonics did over tens of millions of years is being undone by shipping in a few centuries and aviation in a few decades. We are creating a New Pangea. This fits one of the hallmarks of a new epoch, as it is a geologically significant change to life on Earth. It is an important event in the context of Earth's history."[25] New World it also is, then, insofar as the Atlantic crossings of the sixteenth century precipitated a "new planet-wide human-driven evolutionary experiment," now broadly recognized, in the Anthropocene, as the geological age of man. The historian Alfred Crosby first called attention to the massive biotic exchange between the Eastern and Western Hemispheres during this century by famously dubbing it the "Columbian Exchange."[26] But Lewis and Maslin further credit the "Columbian Exchange" with facilitating a "global reordering of life on earth," which is written indelibly into earth's fossil record as perhaps the earliest sign of humanity's emergent geological agency.[27]

So, New World, new peoples, and apparently now a new Earth. Yet I'd like to propose still another implication of this transatlantic traffic, one that takes its cue from the musings of a late contemporary of these crossings, who recognized in them a significant "opportunity." In his essay "Walking," Henry David Thoreau writes: "The Atlantic is a Lethean stream, in our passage over which we have had an *opportunity* to forget the Old World and its institutions. If we do not succeed this time, there is perhaps one more chance for the race left before it arrives on the banks of the Styx; and that is in the Lethe of the Pacific, which is three times as wide."[28] Following Thoreau, the ships in motion across the Atlantic also constituted what we might label the *Atlantic opportunity* first and explicitly "to forget the Old World and its institutions." The institution that most concerns Thoreau in "Walking" is private property and its growing encroachment upon the wilderness. Beyond the merely negative opportunity to forget, however, I want to propose that, within the context of Thoreau's broader concern in "Walking" with reimagining the human as an inhabitant, the Atlantic opportunity may also be regarded positively.

Thoreau raises the subject of human inhabitation in the opening sentence of "Walking," in which he declares, "I wish to speak a word for Nature, for absolute freedom and wildness, as contrasted with a freedom and culture merely civil—to regard man as an *inhabitant*, or a part and parcel of Nature, rather than a member of society."[29] Thus, Thoreau's reflection on the meaning of the Atlantic crossing follows in the larger context of his wish to reimagine the human as a genuine inhabitant, "part and parcel of," rather than separate from or superior to, "Nature." Thoreau viewed Europe's Atlantic crossings as a critical phase in what he generally recognized as the "westward tendency" of human history. For example, he writes, "Columbus felt the westward tendency more strongly than any before. He obeyed it, and found a New World." Thoreau also cites an extended passage from Arnold Guyot's *The Earth and Man* (1858), in which the Swedish American geographer allegorizes human history as the "adventurous career westward" of a metonymic "Old World Man" (more on this soon). Thoreau valorizes the westward tendency of human history for facilitating humanity's potentially salutary contact with the wild. He writes:

> The West of which I speak is but another name for the Wild; and what I have been preparing to say is, that in Wildness is the preservation of the World. Every tree sends its fibers forth in search of the Wild. The cities import it at any price. Men plow and sail for it. From the forest and wilderness come the tonics and barks which brace mankind. Our ancestors were savages. The story of Romulus and Remus being suckled by a wolf is not a meaningless fable. The founders of every state which has risen to eminence have drawn their nourishment and vigor from a similar wild source.[30]

This oft-cited passage from Thoreau's "Walking" has furnished the US environmentalist movement with a significant mantra: "In Wildness is the preservation of the World." With these famous words, Thoreau bespeaks a vision of environmentalism focused primarily on the conservation of the wilderness. And Thoreau suggests that by maintaining humanity's interface with the wild, the westward tendency of human history preserves humanity's prospects of becoming a genuine inhabitant "of Nature, rather than a member of society." Within this westward tendency, however, notice that Thoreau valorizes the Atlantic crossing only as a negative opportunity to forget the Old World and an institution, in private property, which he viewed as a significant barrier to genuine inhabitation. The positive opportunity to become an inhabitant is relegated to a terrestrial encounter with the wilderness. Put another way, the Atlantic crossing can only erase, while the wilderness alone yields the crayon that might *green* the human.

But what if the preservation of the world is most of all in the ocean, as Earth's wildest wild? Although no place for the walking Thoreau promotes, outside of a few rumored exceptions, the ocean not only is uniquely resistant to interpellation as private property but, with its talent for submersion, also forces the issue of becoming "part and parcel of Nature." Thus, as much as the possible origin of a new geological age marked by environmental crisis, what would it mean to also locate, in these same transatlantic crossings, the prospect of the emergence of the environmental human? What if the Atlantic opportunity inheres not merely in the negative opportunity to forget but also in the positive opportunity to discover, perhaps for the very first time, the human as the inhabitant of a blue planet?

Consider that in the voyages that proceeded throughout the transatlantic eras of discovery, colonization, and the slave trade, a critical mass of humanity was encountering the deep sea for the very first time. Although individual groups of humans had explored and even crossed the Atlantic previously, the sustained encounter with the deep sea witnessed during this era was unprecedentedly general. Moreover, because it coincided historically with the "discovery" of the Western Hemisphere, and so with the earliest possible attempts to define the species and the planet as genuine totalities (for anyone compelled to undertake such a project), this transatlantic era indexed a truly species-wide opportunity to question just what sort of planet the Earth—and by extension, what sort of creature the human—is. An opportunity, terribly, that the jettisoned debris of slave ships—as the truth of the outlandish situation of those throwaway humans coming online as black in the world—could not help but make good on.

If we are to truly survey this Atlantic opportunity, we will need to look where Thoreau did not know or think to. Not least because the Atlantic opportunity already seemed in doubt for Thoreau, so far as the European passages he primarily had in view. So much so that he had already begun to look to the second chance of the Pacific, "three times as wide." However, Europe's were not the only passages across the Atlantic. There were also the involuntary passages of those who endured the crossing from the hold rather than the deck of these ships. The remainder of this chapter, then, undertakes a comparative analysis of Europe's and Africa's uneven encounters with the Atlantic Ocean as they are respectively represented in Guyot's *The Earth and Man* and Equiano's *The Interesting Narrative of the Life of Olaudah Equiano*. Though not the only ones to make the journey, these travelers to the New World in many ways represent the Romulus and Uncle Remus of the transatlantic crossing and the ocean the wolf that suckled them. Although our Remus jumped ship and not a wall when he met his fratricidal fate.

ii.

We might think the Atlantic opportunity along a similar axis as Malcolm X's discourse on Plymouth Rock. Which is to suggest that humanity's capacity to make good on the Atlantic opportunity was significantly impacted by race. Thoreau already suggests as much, in the suspicion of whiteness he expresses elsewhere in "Walking": "A tanned skin is something more than respectable, and perhaps olive is a fitter color than white for a man,—a denizen of the woods. 'The pale white man!' I do not wonder that the African pitied him. Darwin the naturalist says, 'A white man bathing by the side of a Tahitian was like a plant bleached by the gardener's art, compared with a fine, dark green one, growing vigorously in the open fields.'"[31] Ironically, the transatlantic passages Thoreau has most in view in "Walking" are precisely those undertaken by Europeans, who went into the world proclaiming white as the ideal color of humanity. This would put them at a significant disadvantage regarding the Atlantic opportunity, because whiteness is otherwise characterized here as failed inhabitation—not "part and parcel of Nature" but uprooted "like a plant bleached" and languishing in a doomed society Thoreau proceeds to describe as an exclusive "interaction of man on man—a sort of breeding in and in, which produces . . . a civilization destined to have a speedy limit."[32] Perhaps the unspoken and unacknowledged whiteness of the specific "we," whose Atlantic crossings Thoreau has in view, has something to do with their failure to capitalize on an opportunity that the elided middle passages of the "inhabitants of the deep" were perhaps better positioned to make good on.

If, as Katherine McKittrick has observed, "historical epochs are underwritten by differential encounters with geography," then I propose that modernity is underwritten by humanity's differential encounters with the Atlantic Ocean in the wake of Columbus, an Atlantic opportunity that may be recognized as breaking along Manichean lines.[33] In fact, I suggest that more than merely being informed *by* race, humanity's uneven encounters with the Atlantic may actually be recognized to *produce* race. Precedent for such an understanding of the Atlantic crossing can be found in *Race and Nature* (2008), in which Paul Outka argues that the construction of whiteness and blackness "occurred not simply in a negotiation internal to themselves, but through reference to a third term—nature—a larger context that grounded (literally) both, while continuously enacting its own disappearance into the (literal) background."[34] According to Outka, nature grounds race by undergirding what has generally proven to be racially divergent experiences of the natural world that, in the case of whiteness, resemble traditional understandings of the *sublime* and, in the case of blackness, resemble traditional understandings of *trauma*. In his explanation of this innovative method of reading race in relationship to nature, Outka notes that both sublime and traumatic natural experiences, though following different trajectories, begin with an "eruptive moment" of encounter that entails an "experience of potent uncertainty," in which "the identities of self and world become energetically interpenetrative." "This state of uncertainty," Outka writes, "is brought about either by . . . something that suggests the infinite, such as the night sky full of stars, or the ocean—or . . . something fearful that suggests physical power much greater than we possess, such as a mountain or a storm. In both cases the mind is initially overwhelmed by the seeming incomprehensibility of the object before it."[35] It's not the experience of potent uncertainty itself, however, but how it ultimately resolves or fails to resolve that distinguishes sublimity and trauma. According to Outka, these diverging processes constitute a crucial, if neglected, aspect of the production of racialized subjectivity. On the one hand, traditional outlines of the sublime, which Outka understands to give rise to white subjectivity, culminate in resolution. In his gloss of the Kantian sublime, for example, Outka writes, "Faced with the confusion brought on by the infinite or powerful, we recover our stability and achieve sublimity through our recognition of our own essential superiority to, and difference from, the natural world that created the confusion."[36] According to Outka, the resolution of the Kantian sublime produces the "newly empowered subjectivity" of whiteness.[37] This racialization of the sublime's "essential superiority to, and difference from, the natural world" is implied by Immanuel Kant himself (albeit negatively) in his infamous declaration, in *Observations on the Feeling of the Beautiful and Sublime*, that the "Negroes of Africa have by nature no feeling that rises above the trifling."[38] The sublime and its resolution of the initial confusion of the natural encounter are therefore coded white. By contrast, Outka locates blackness in natural encounters that fail to resolve in ways consistent with conventional understandings of trauma, whose essence inheres rather in "the repeated and shattering intrusion of [the] extrasubjective world into the subject's self-construction."[39] Hence, Outka observes: "For African Americans, moments of instability between self-identity and the natural world have historically often been violently reductive, producing the traumatic inverse of white sublimity, rendering both the subject and nature abject, commodified, subaltern. Indeed, the conflation of blackness and nature served as the principal 'justification' for chattel slavery in antebellum America."[40] As the "traumatic inverse" of white sublimity's decisive resolution of the human/nature encounter, then, black trauma alternatively "collapses the distinction between the subject and nature," transforming "human subjects into natural objects, which then are available for exploitation."[41]

Outka's schema of the "sublime and the traumatic" is particularly compelling with respect to its elucidation of whiteness as the determination to be a single being. Yet our consideration of Equiano's astonishment challenges the reduction of the black experience of nature, however unconducive to individual subjectivity, to trauma. This is not to claim, or even to seek, resolution for the potent uncertainty of Equiano's fateful encounter with the ocean or the black experience of nature more broadly. Rather it is to identify this lack of resolution as basic to inhabiting a live planet. Of course, in a world ruled by subjects, to be "an object among other objects," to invoke Frantz Fanon's famous words, is certainly traumatic.[42] It is similarly traumatic for Frederick Douglass in his experience of the conflation between blackness and nonhuman nature during his valuation in *Narrative of the Life of Frederick Douglass*: "We were all ranked together at the valuation. Men and women, old and young, married and single, were ranked with horses, sheep, and swine. There were horses and men, cattle and women, pigs and children, all holding the same rank in the *scale of being*, and were all subjected to the same narrow examination."[43] Here, the collapse of the distinction between the human and nonhuman nature certainly evidences black trauma in the way that Outka argues. Yet being "ranked together" in this way, if not as a justification for exploitation, is also what it means, in Thoreau's words, to be "part and parcel of Nature." In and of itself, such being together is traumatic only insofar as we concede that being is inherently weighed on anything quite like a "scale" and sorted into naturally existing hierarchies. But hierarchies, we know well, are made, not given; and keeping company with a horse is no inherent degradation. Blackness's being together with the nonhuman world is not the *necessarily* traumatic inverse of a white sublimity predicated on the resolution of the encounter's ontological uncertainty and the restoration of the subject's a priori separation and individuation. Indeed, throughout the black literary tradition, blackness *refuses* this resolution as much as Outka demonstrates that this resolution is refused to it. In these cases, blackness is given less in the failed resolution of the encounter's uncertainty than in the consent to live an earnestly ecological life, in and with the endless eruptiveness of a *live* planet. Not only is the grouping of "horses and men," which Douglass laments as taxonomical error, not inherently degrading, but it is precisely the sort of being that our moment of ecological crisis calls for. Even if the West's philosophical musings on ontology overdetermine Douglass's experience of his nonhuman intimacy as degradation, what we've been able to discern about the irreducible entanglement of life suggests a different metaphysics: what Denise Ferreira da Silva has described as "difference without separability."[44]

To this very point, it's important to note that Outka is just as critical of white sublimity as its necessary underside of black trauma, due to what he identifies as the former's a priori separation from nature as the human's normative origin and telos:

> While traditional narrative models of sublime experience—that move first from quiescence, then to eruption, and finally to resolution—helpfully organize the chaos of the experience, they also embed the intense atemporality of the eruptive moment in a larger sequential framework of emergence from some generally unexamined and therefore normative state, and effectively make the telos of the eruption the final reflective conclusion. The sublime's eruptive moment is bracketed between an unexamined and naturalized origin it breaks out from and a resolution that exemplifies the "real" meaning of the experience. The eruption becomes an unruly middle child, a transition between realities.[45]

What if, instead of a transition between realities, we understand the potent uncertainty of the eruptive moment as constitutive of reality itself? As the exclamation of a liveness that the planet is always already expressing in more subtle and imperceptible ways? And what if the collapse of the separability between the human and nature, which Outka identifies as blackness, is not (only) trauma but ecological life? Not collapse at all but refusal of a rickety bridge to nowhere—at least nowhere sustainable. The kind of ecological life to which Outka himself gestures in his redefinition of the sublime as "the eruptive moment of radical uncertainty" itself rather than its artificial resolution within the "in-fact irreducibly open question of the relation between human identity and the nonhuman natural."[46] In Outka's schema of race and nature, blackness's experience of this indecision shows up primarily as trauma. But what if it is also a viable, even privileged, position from which to think of the human ecological life to which he gestures, in his call, for instance, for an "antiracist ecological sublime"?[47] "Terror," we know, is only part of the story and neither the first nor the half. And if Equiano's "astonishment" teaches us anything, it's that those whose living and being *is* the so-called Negro Question are uniquely positioned to shed light on the irreducibly open question of human ecological life. Especially as that question must be asked and answered on a blue planet.

Although the "nature" Outka generally has in view is limited to land and begins with the plantation, perhaps the first natural context to ground whiteness and blackness is ironically not ground at all but ocean. Even if he doesn't engage it at length, Outka explicitly cites the ocean among the natural phenomena classically associated with the sublime and its potent moment of uncertainty. Indeed, the ocean's autodislocation yields a fitting analog for what Outka suggestively characterizes as the "instability" of this eruptive moment relative to the "stability" of its eventual resolution. Similarly, the transatlantic crossing physically parallels, at least for those who managed to land, the sublime's classic trajectory from stability to instability and back again. In the ocean, in other words, the instability of the natural encounter is made literal, and resolution, likewise, is the at once physical and metaphysical effort to "recover our stability." For those who "didn't land," however, the ocean is rather the traumatic lack of this resolution. The ocean and oceanic crossings, then, yield an especially fruitful site to interrogate how natural experience produces race, and nowhen more than during humanity's first large-scale forays into a previously unknown and dreaded ocean.[48]

III. whiteness as stand-your-ground subjectivity

i.

For the Europeans coming into contact with the *deep* sea for the very first time during the age of discovery and colonization, the seemingly infinite expanse of the ocean presented a kind of gut check. Notice how Guyot's "man of the Old World," whom Thoreau cites in "Walking" as an exemplar of humanity's "westward tendency," stumbles upon reaching the Atlantic: "The man of the Old World sets out upon his way. Leaving the highlands of Asia, he descends from station to station towards Europe. Each of his steps is marked by a new civilization superior to the preceding, by a greater power of development. Arrived at the Atlantic, he *pauses* on the shore of this unknown ocean, the bounds of which he knows not, and turns upon his footprints for an instant."[49] A conspicuous "pause" worries the middle of what Guyot otherwise depicts, in the heroic metonym of the Old World Man (OWM), as the seamless westward march of European civilization. But for this pause, the OWM's "adventurous career westward" proceeds as an unbroken vector of linear progress, in which a hierarchical capacity for *civilization* is performed through the engine of *bipedalism*, such that the former linchpin of human identity is performed by the latter. Still, this proud and species-defining gait, measuring new and superior civilizations with every stride, falters conspicuously at the Atlantic. There is, in this stumble, something of the fear and anxiety that generally characterized Europe's first contact with a previously "unknown ocean." Although the Portuguese had been in the Atlantic since at least the Middle Ages and up and down the coast of West Africa by the mid-fifteenth century, the reticence of the OWM clocks what was nevertheless for most early modern Europeans a genuinely novel encounter with the Atlantic as not a coastal sea but an unbounded *deep*. Accordingly, the ambulatory powers of the OWM falter not merely at an "unknown" ocean but, more specifically, at an ocean whose "bounds" are unknown. It is specifically what Smallwood has called "the landless realm of the deep ocean" that undoes the OWM.[50] Indeed, in the imagination of the early modern humans encountering this face of the Atlantic for the very first time, the deep presented a space no less extra*terrestrial* than outer space—so alien and strange were these waters without a shore, and so precarious and uncertain these first voyages into their untested abyss.[51]

Face-to-face with this astonishingly unearthly realm, the OWM not only stops in his tracks but "turns upon his footprints" and retreats back to dry land. In this way, the deep not only interrupts but reverses the defining capacity of the OWM. This complete undoing of a human subject defined by a special talent for walking embodies the ontological instability of Outka's "eruptive moment" of "potent uncertainty" that is characteristic of sublime experience. It is a moment when the very identity of the human, here expressed as a specific interface with the planet, is radically called into question. Given the OWM's metonymic responsibility, we might recognize in his revolution the potential for a like revolution of the human species—a radical destabilization of the respective identities of the earth and humanity, in which we might begin to locate the Atlantic opportunity broadly available to the species in these transatlantic passages.

But you can't keep an OWM down. After what Guyot describes as a "long and teeming repose," the OWM returns, somehow newly empowered, to attack and subdue the ocean, at which he first stumbled: "Then recommences his adventurous career westward, as in the earliest ages. . . . Under the guidance of the genius of the age, he attacks this dreaded ocean, of which, to this time, he knows only the margin. He abandons himself to the winds and the currents, which bear him gently towards the coasts of America."[52] What changed, we might ask, to embolden the OWM to attack the ocean he first feared and subdue it into the gentle servant of his colonial desire? After being so thoroughly undone by the deep, how do we account for what Guyot specifically describes as the reanimation facilitated by his long and teeming repose? And how might this reanimation speak to a broader reanimation, in this transatlantic moment, of Europe's understanding of "Earth" and "Man," as Guyot would have it?

Even before analyzing this "long and teeming repose," perhaps one answer already lies in the fact that after he "turns upon his footprints," there is no actual mention of the OWM ever fully turning back around. In his rematch with the deep, he appears not to face the ocean so much as to back into it. If you look closely, the footprints that lead up to the threshold of the Atlantic and spawn Europe's colonization of the New World proceed heel-first. In a poor rendition of the moonwalk, the soles of white folk proceed backward, heading west but facing east. Never turning around to genuinely confront the ocean, the OWM seems to revive his confidence to resume his "adventurous career westward" by decisively reorienting himself toward the land. He gathers the strength to reenter the sea by fixating on terra firma, suppressing his dread by sustaining, even at sea, a hallucination of dry land. And we learn from Smallwood that, in this bad-faith encounter with the ocean, the OWM is very much a faithful metonym for Europe's transatlantic passages: "By the time Europeans began to colonize the New World, voyagers to the west were confident that their journey would follow a linear path, with known beginning and end points. European seamen translated the *land-based systems of time-space reckoning* of medieval Europe to the wider temporal and spatial context of life in a 'new' Atlantic world. Hourglasses and astrolabes measured time and space; and applied mathematics and geometry turned these into the Cartesian coordinates seamen used to recognize place in the seemingly formless arena of the sea."[53] In other words, Europeans made a previously "unknown ocean" knowable in terms of land. Aided by "land-based systems of time-space reckoning," whatever interruption was posed by the deep was sufficiently mitigated by the technology of the ship, which, even at sea, sustained an experience of earth as little more than a docile surface. Thus, in a letter attempting to assuage his family's fears about the transatlantic journey, a European settler could liken a ship at sea to "a cradle rocked by a careful mother's hand, which though it be moved up and down is not in danger of falling."[54] Indeed, for European settlers, the ship was, or at least aspired to be, land at sea.

An examination of the OWM's "long and teeming repose" further suggests that his unrepentant footprint embodies a decisive reorientation to not just land but, more specifically, the land practice incubated during his inland retreat, which is intriguingly said to be spent "under the influence of the soil of Europe":

> Under the influence of the soil of Europe, so richly organized, he works out slowly the numerous germs wherewith he is endowed. After this long and teeming repose, his faculties are reawakened, he is reanimated. At the close of the fifteenth century, an unaccustomed movement agitates and vexes him from one end of the continent to the other. He has tilled the impoverished soil, and yet the number of his offspring increases. He turns his looks at once towards the east and the west, and sets out in search of new countries. His horizon enlarges; his activity preys upon him; he breaks his bounds.[55]

A far cry from Thoreau's wild, the richness of Europe's soil inheres not in the soil itself, which Guyot describes as "impoverished," but in its *organization*. In other words, Guyot invokes Europe's soil not as a surface valuable in itself but as an *interface*: the site of an idealized relationship between "Earth" and "Man." The land enclosures that had begun in England by the sixteenth century help specify the nature of this idealized interface by illuminating just how "Europe's soil" was coming to be organized during this period. Lewis and Maslin tell us that "by the sixteenth century the first enclosures were occurring in England, driving commoners off communal land to give landlords the exclusive use of it for increasingly lucrative sheep farming. Every piece of land was coming to be privately owned—with one person owning exclusive rights to it—turning the whole Earth into private property, just as we think of it today."[56] To be "under the influence of the soil of Europe," then, is to be under the influence of the specific mode of relating to land as private property. Significantly, this specific human-planetary interface is also explicitly racialized in the apology Guyot offers for Europe's colonization of the New World. In a familiar rehearsal of the ideology of white settler colonialism, he reasons that "America is made for the man of the Old World" because "the human race of the New World, the Indian," had otherwise failed to "open the soil with his ploughshares, to demand the treasures it encloses" and "work out all the wealth of its inexhaustible fertility."[57] This distinction in land practice and use further maps onto the racist distinction Guyot establishes between the agricultural "white race" as "the most perfect type of humanity" and the "copper-colored . . . hunting tribes of the two Americas."[58] Of course, we know that Native Americans had robust agricultural practices, and that their reduction to mere hunters was a common justification for colonial expropriation. Nevertheless, it is significant to note how, in racial distinction to the supposedly inferior "Indian," the whiteness of the white race inheres as much in a normative way of relating to land as in skin color. The whiteness of European settlers is embodied in an exclusionary and extractive land practice that doubled as a litmus for full humanity.

If the OWM's initial encounter with the deep represents an "eruptive moment of radical uncertainty," his ultimate arrival in the New World embodies its decisive resolution. Upon reaching the "coasts of America," the OWM's impressive stride decelerates into an even greater triumph of standing. Initially, "he is enraptured as he *treads* the shore of this land of wonders." Such terrestrial rapture and wonder echoes the "eruptive moment of radical uncertainty" first instigated by the ocean and bears all the hallmarks of traditional sublimity. Especially as we might recognize the decisive resolution of this initial rapture as the OWM gradually "*establishes* himself little by little" and finally "gets a *foothold*."[59] In this way, the OWM ultimately emerges from the ontological upset of his novel encounters with the ocean and the New World with a "newly empowered subjectivity." He is not just an accomplished walker but an established stander, possessing, and no longer possessed by, the scene. Thus, at the historical moment when humanity might have otherwise discovered itself through its destabilizing encounter with the deep, to be hopelessly immersed *in* nature, the human, as reflected in the metonymic hero of the OWM, is reanimated instead as a kind of stand-your-ground subject whose defining interface with the planet is as private property.

As the culmination of the OWM's "adventurous career westward," this colonial "foothold" goes further than Thoreau is explicitly "ready to follow" in what he otherwise cites as an exemplar of the "westward tendency" that he regards as "the preservation of the World."[60] Although he does not specify the nature of his ambivalence, it is telling that Thoreau's quotation of the OWM's adventurous career westward drops off before his arrival in the Americas. Perhaps it was Guyot's explicit white supremacy, or the fact that the OWM ultimately came to a standstill. Regardless of what spooked Thoreau about the culmination of the OWM's journey, Thoreau's apparent attempt to disentangle it from exemplary beginnings is complicated by the continuity otherwise implied by the fact that the OWM, after his initial oceanic misstep, is said to recommence his journey just "as in the earliest ages." Thus, the OWM's ultimate settlement of the Americas represents not an aberration from, but the consummation of, a walking practice that was seemingly always about settlement. Perhaps if he had attended to the footprints of the OWM more closely, Thoreau would not have followed the OWM even as far as he did.

Even before his colonial "foothold," the OWM's unrepentant "footprint" already boded poorly enough for his prospects of genuine inhabitation. In it, we can recognize a set of authoritative decisions regarding the respective identities of and ideal relationship between "Earth" and "Man," which, critically, Europe made on behalf of the *entire* world before ultimately colonizing 85 percent of it.[61] The first decision was to turn away from the ocean and, with it, any experience of the earth beyond that of a docile surface. The second but related decision was that "Man" is the ruler and owner of that surface and, thus, that the life of "Man" is ideally expressed not as inhabitation or, God forbid, immersion but as possession predicated, we shall find, on a metaphysics of separation. These were the decisions which were poised to go out into the world, already exhibiting what we readily recognize today, in soil exhaustion and overpopulation, as classic signs of ecological crisis.

The OWM's turn away from and disavowal of Earth as ocean, as deep, arguably records the very first steps of what has matured into humanity's excessive carbon footprint. The disavowal of the overwhelmingly greater part of our planet which cannot be stood upon contributes to the conditions of possibility for a genre of the human that has come to stand excessively. It is no mere coincidence either that whiteness comes to be historically named against the larger backdrop of humanity's first large-scale encounter with the deep, which otherwise represented humanity's widespread opportunity to *deepen* its relationship to the planet. Because whiteness *is* the aforementioned decisions; *is* western humanism doubling down on terra firma and the stand-your-ground subject; *is* modernity's answer and resolution to the fear of a blue planet.

ii.

Beside the stand-your-ground subjectivity of whiteness, a corresponding metaphysics also landed with the OWM in the New World—a set of normative ideas about what the earth and humanity even are and the nature of their relationship. We might trace the landing of this metaphysics by interrogating the architecture of the "society," whose alienation from nature so troubles Thoreau. The process by which "man" transforms from "a part and parcel of Nature" to a "member of society" finds perhaps its most significant elaboration within "social contract" theory, a branch of political philosophy that famously considers society in juxtaposition with a much-maligned "state of nature." The famous social contract theorist Jean-Jacques Rousseau glosses this fundamental foil of western civilization in *The Social Contract* (1762): "We will suppose that men in a state of nature are arrived at that crisis, when the strength of each *individual* is insufficient to defend him from the attacks he is subject to. This primitive state can therefore subsist no longer; and the human race must perish, unless they change their manner of life."[62] In a way parallel to the uncertainty of the

OWM's initial encounter with the Atlantic, Rousseau supposes that humans in a precivilized "state of nature" are similarly faced with a debilitating "crisis." The temporality of this crisis, at which humans do not arrive but are *already* "arrived," renders the unsustainability of this speculative state absolute along with humanity's imperative to change their manner of life or perish. However, my principal interest here is not what Rousseau supposes about the "state of nature," except to emphasize that a supposition is just that. More careful attention to the actual living signified by the "state of nature" has historically turned up much more than its caricature here as mere "crisis" and "attacks." Certainly it did for Thoreau, who actually saw it the other way around, celebrating nature and rather critiquing society as the principal culprit in hastening humanity's perishing. It's also worth noting how the societies formed to protect humans from the relentless attacks they are subjected to in the state of nature historically evolved to attack, all the more efficiently, those excluded from or on the margins of society. And with respect to the contemporary threat of nuclear Armageddon, the state's protection has circled all the way back around to the attacks society originally supposed itself to be evading. But more than what Rousseau supposes about the impossibility of human life in the state of nature, I am primarily interested in what his account of the social contract arguably presupposes: namely the givenness of the "individual" as the most basic unit of social life, its organizing beginning and end.

Against the grain of what we've otherwise understood as the irreducibly open question of ecological life, the social contract, which humanity adopts to prevent its perishing, constitutes a decisive answer—a kind of fix to the global problem of life together that has arguably been operative since Plymouth Rock and every white settler colonial landing besides. It is western humanism's solving for *y*, which has been nothing but a resolving for *I*. A resolving of the open question of social life not only for the modern bastion of individual subjectivity but also, as we shall find, for that subject's property. Consider Rousseau's outline of the "problem" for which the social contract is the "solution": "Where shall we find a form of association which will defend and protect with the whole aggregate force *the person and the property of each individual*; and by which every person, while united with all, shall obey only himself, and remain as free as before the union? Such is the fundamental problem, of which the Social contract gives the solution."[63] Punctuation notwithstanding, here Rousseau doesn't ask so much as answer the open question of social life. Even before his eventual outline of the "solution" of the "social contract," there is, already hidden in his questioning, an unacknowledged answer, namely "the person and the property of each individual." This rather convoluted formulation lies at the heart not of a genuine question but rather an asking *after* something specific. It is a question already convicted of its answer, of association's ideal end. What we might alternatively recognize as the real, or at least more basic, question of social life—How do we live together?—doesn't even get a hearing in this foundational treatment of the social contract, which we might distinguish, after Ralph Ellison, as western humanism's "plan of living."[64]

At least as we find it elaborated above, the *social* contract is really quite *antisocial.* Although it unites the individual "with all," it does so in such a way that ultimately allows him to "obey only himself" and "remain as free as before the union." In other words, the social contract ultimately spares the individual the trouble of having to be in genuine relation with anyone but "himself." The problem, then, for which the social contract is the solution, is seemingly social life itself, and the imposition of the infamous Other on a vision of freedom rooted in the individual. But the seeming self-evidence of this individual notwithstanding, are we certain that relation has a "before"? That there was ever a time when the individual was free from Others in quite this way? Certainly this isn't the case in the individual's opening act, when they share another's literal flesh. Nor in the individual's closing act, when humans, as Lucille Clifton puts it in her poem "generations," become the "bottoms of trees" and start sharing their skin with the more-than-human natural world.[65] Much like the "generally unexamined and therefore normative state" from which the eruptive moment of encounter is supposed to break out in traditional accounts of sublimity, the individual standing unmolested in relation's "before" is grounded more fundamentally in metaphysics than anything we actually find in the physical world. Rather than relation's "before," the individual is arguably better perceived as the retroactive naturalization of the social contract's "after." The social contract's effect, not its motivating cause.

If we subject the social contract's "individual" to a similar scrutiny as sublimity's, it, too, may be recognized to follow the trajectory of quiescence, eruption, and resolution outlined by Outka. Leaving for the moment the individual's unexamined origin, what, if not "eruption," is the "crisis" at which the individual is arrived in the state of nature? And what but resolution is yielded by the social contract's solution? And just as sublimity transforms the individual's "potent uncertainty" into a "newly empowered subjectivity," the social contract may likewise be recognized to transform the crisis of the individual in the state of nature into a newly empowered political subjectivity. We can locate this new power in the increased "force" that the individual obtains in Rousseau's gloss of the social contract's peculiar mechanics: "In fine, each person gives himself to ALL, but not to any INDIVIDUAL, and as there is no one associate over whom the same right is not acquired which is ceded to him by others, each gains an equivalent for what he loses, and finds his *force increased* for preserving that which he possesses."[66] Thus, through the mutual alienation and aggregated force of each contractant, the individual is newly empowered, by the social contract, to do what they formerly could not, in the state of nature. Still, while the crisis of the state of nature is originally detailed as an inability to defend oneself from attacks, its resolution here is detailed as an additional matter of "preserving that which he possesses." However, we know from Rousseau's asking after a form of association that will protect both "the person and the *property* of each individual" that this curious combination of the individual and their property constitutes not only the social contract's end but also its retroactively naturalized beginning. Because rather than enabling the individual to "remain as free as before"—when such freedom is not only individual but also a matter of the individual's capacity for possession, including self-possession—the social contract actually creates the conditions of possibility for such an individual in the first place, confusing the fruits of its newfound force for original endowment.

If the individual is only retroactively projected back into relation's putative "before," then it arrives bearing some curious extra baggage. Again, it's not just the individual that the social contract is said to defend, but "the person and the property *of each individual*." As we find it here, set off by a possessive prepositional phrase, this elaboration of what was originally plainly introduced as the "individual" in a state of nature betrays something crucial about who the individual at the heart of the social contract in fact is. Less an individual than always already an *individual's*. Which is to say that the individual *is* a having, an individuated act of possession. What appears like the individual's excess baggage of person and property is, in fact, their constitutional possessions. Rousseau's elaboration of the social contract further betrays the identity of the individual by detailing how the social contract will enable him to "*obey* only himself." But even if the obedience in view here is explicitly unto one's self, why should the relationship to not only one's "person" but presumably also to one's "property" be a matter of obedience? Unless the individual were not just an individuated act of possession but also a master.

Crystallized at the heart of western humanism's "plan of living," then, is an individual whose possessive conflation of personhood and property represents not the irreducibly entangled beings we actually are but the noncontingent masters we aspire to be. Indeed, apart from private property, the individual may never even have been named as such. It is here, in this person-property hybrid at the center of the antisocial contract, that I am proposing we witness the metaphysical landing of a stand-your-ground subject whose physical landing we've already observed in the metonymic journey of the OWM and his culminating "foothold." Especially insofar as this person-property hybrid arguably finds its most significant historical expression in the conflation of the individual and that individual's land. Part of what we have to understand about the original colonial restriction of suffrage to white, male landowners is that, in practice, the authenticating property of the individuals recognized by the social contract paradigmatically consisted of their land. Cohering modern society, whose alienation from "Nature" Thoreau critiques in "Walking," is thus a social contract whose end and retroactively naturalized beginning are an individual whose operative interface with the planetary surface is that of private property and a corresponding apprehension of land as little more than a docile surface.

With this labeling of the stand-your-ground subject, I attempt to call the individual by a name more forthcoming about the social contract's transformation of personhood into an individuated act of possession—a simultaneous and consubstantial mastery over self and planet. The name also alludes to the infamous stand-your-ground laws, which entered the national spotlight after a seventeen-year-old black boy named Trayvon Martin was shot dead on a Florida sidewalk by a neighborhood watchman. Rooted in the "castle doctrine" of English common law, this complex of laws, which has come to be known in the United States under the rubric of "stand your ground," protects an individual's right to defend their "embodied castle" with lethal force by stipulating that a person under threat has no duty "to retreat from the place in which he or she is 'castled'; they can stand their ground."[67] Although the law was not formally claimed in the Trayvon Martin case—a measure which, if successful, would have avoided the necessity of a trial altogether—its logics nevertheless animated the defense and eventual acquittal of Martin's murderer, who was ultimately found "not guilty of anything but protecting his own life."[68] However, at the time that he began pursuing an unarmed teenager in the first place, suspecting he was "up to no good," the armed neighborhood watchman was not protecting his life but his gated community—what might be confused with his life only by the distinctly modern calculus whereby a person may be confused with their property and entitled to "defend" it to the violent disavowal of others. But in this case, Martin was visiting relatives who had a deed, too.

The violent exercise of individual freedom codified by US stand-your-ground law is but a local expression, however, of the racialized genre of humanity more broadly known to the world as settlement. In fact, to be castled is really to be settled by another name. It bespeaks a set of racialized expectations around being human on earth that are the specific legacy of white settler colonialism and a planetary optic that perceived the entire world as property before managing to castle 85 percent of its land by 1914.[69] The regularity with which stand-your-ground law comes to the specific defense of the extrajudicial murder of black people betrays the roots such standing claims in coloniality and a regime of standing that, since the OWM's colonial "foothold," has always been racialized. Yet something significant has needed to happen to the prevailing understanding of both humans and the ground to naturalize the expectation that humans can be anything quite like "castled" on a planet such as ours. The very idea that the ground is even ours to stand, and may at any moment be seamlessly called up into a stable enactment of human embodiment, is a possibility not only manufactured by and encoded in the antisocial contract but also, just as significantly, sustained through the metaphysical disavowal of the more than two-thirds of our planet that is ocean and, with the still precarious exception of ice caps, cannot be stood at all. The radical reorientation to land indexed by the unrepentant footprint of the OWM may be more broadly attributed to what scholars have variously critiqued as western culture's animating "terracentrism" or "terrestrial bias."[70] Indeed, the *your* in *stand your ground* presumes upon a planetary surface that, materially speaking, is not always or even mostly cooperative. This possessive and presumptuous *your* recasts what is an irreducibly ecological interaction with the earth's surface into a wholly self-contained, noncontingent, and possessive act of individuation. And this in spite of the fact that no one has ever taken a single step of or on their own. Those who can walk need just as much help as those who can't, or at least so much of the same help—namely, ground—that the added assistance of a crutch or wheelchair is too negligible to give cause for pride. Whenever we find ourselves standing, we've been helped to our feet. We're touching. *Being* touched. It's no trifling detail to the liberation of ancient Israel that God first tells Moses to take off his shoes at the burning bush. There can be no true freedom apart from this touching and being touched by the ground. If there is a future for humanity beyond the global environmental crisis, it's *this* ground ceremony, which must be found.[71]

IV. the ecologics of separability

i.

What ultimately came of Europe's Atlantic opportunity is indexed by the "newly empowered subjectivity" that the individual obtains in the parallel resolutions of the metonymic journey of the OWM and the (anti)social contract. What was humanity's opportunity, in its historical confrontation with a blue planet, to rediscover itself as an "inhabitant" culminated instead for Europe in the crystallization of the stand-your-ground subject as the animating beginning and end of social life, who, far from being "part and parcel," admits no relation to nature beyond private property. Ironically, however, what emerged in the ecological thought of Thoreau and others as an early correction to the anthropocentrism of modern society in many ways served to further naturalize and entrench the stand-your-ground subjectivity at the heart of western humanism's "plan of living." In spite of its critique of the interpellation of the ground as a mere docile surface, early US ecological thought endured several false starts, which, due to an active or passive avowal of whiteness, failed to constitute a sufficiently radical departure from the anthropocentrism of modern society.

In his history of ecological ideas, environmental historian Donald Worster identifies Thoreau as an important progenitor of US ecological thought.[72] What does it mean, then, that for his pioneering "word for nature" Thoreau draws significant inspiration from the lesser-known and remembered Guyot? Like Thoreau's "Walking," Guyot's *The Earth and Man* begins by speaking what can also be recognized as a word for nature. What culminates in a racist apology for white settler colonialism begins as an apology for the "life" of nonhuman nature, including the nature Guyot hails under the general banner of "inorganic." That is, the province of nature that we tend to dismiss as inanimate but whose "perpetual play" nevertheless, Guyot argues, constitutes a significant part of what he insists should be apprehended as "the *life* of the globe":

> But this nature, represented as dead, and contrasted in common language with living *nature*, because it has not the same life with the animal or the plant, is it then bereft of all life? If it has not life, we must acknowledge that it has at least the appearances of life. Has it not motion in the water which streams and gushes over the surface of the continents, or which tosses in the bosom of the seas?—in the winds which course with terrible rapidity and sweep the soil that we tread under our feet, covering it with ruins? Has it not its sympathies and antipathies in those mysterious elective affinities of the different molecules of matter which chemistry investigates? Has it not the powerful attractions of bodies to each other, which govern the motions of the stars scattered in the immensity of space, and keep them in an admirable harmony? Do we not see, and always with a secret astonishment, the magnetic needle agitated at the approach of a particle of iron, and leaping under the fire of the Northern light? Place any material body whatsoever by the side of another, do

they not immediately enter into relations of interchange, of molecular attraction, of electricity, of magnetism? The disturbance of equilibrium at one point induces another elsewhere, and the movement is propagated to infinity. . . .

Thus, in inorganic nature likewise, all is acting, all is changing, all is undergoing transformation. Doubtless this is not the life of the organized being, the life of the animal; but is not this assemblage of phenomena also a life? If, taking life in its most simple aspect, we define it as a mutual exchange of relations, we cannot refuse this name to those lively actions and reactions, to that perpetual play of the forces of matter, of which we are every day the witnesses.[73]

In this extended passage, Guyot speaks a word not merely for nature but for that province of the natural world that, due to its categorical exclusion from life, we most easily tend to disregard—asking us to apprehend, even in so-called dead nature, a kind of life. In this way, Guyot intervenes in a modern epistemologic, which makes a fundamental distinction between "organic" and "inorganic" matter. Since the end of the eighteenth century, "organization" has functioned as a defining characteristic of living beings and a "signal word for the animate world and its scientific analysis" (hence, the use of *organism* to describe a living being), while *inorganic* has alternatively functioned to describe inanimate or dead matter.[74] Like the late eighteenth-century musings of Rousseau about the prospects of human life in organized versus disorganized societies (i.e., the social contract versus the state of nature), science's sweeping bifurcation of the physical world into organic and inorganic matter similarly reflects a privileged relationship between organization and life. It's an intriguing parallel not because there is no such relation worth noting but because Europe went out into the world believing itself to be *the* exclusive interpreter and steward of earth's proper "order" to the disavowal of alternatives as mere "disorder."

Here, however, Guyot elaborates an apology for inorganic (i.e., unorganized) nature that recuperates its overlooked order and, by extension, its life. Today, we might recognize no such need to recuperate disorder in the first place, cognizant of how it, too, facilitates and perpetuates life. In its time, however, Guyot's intervention was significant not least for its expansion of the category of life to include any "mutual exchange of relations," and how this expansion interrupts the consolidation of a modern regard for land as private property. Although Guyot's relational apprehension of life precedes "ecology" as such, which was coined by German scientist Ernst Haeckel in 1866, it is nevertheless a deeply ecological insight. Besides his emphasis on mutuality and even equilibrium, his sense of the "life of the globe" represents an early instance of US ecological thought. To the potential disruption of stand-your-ground subjectivity, it not only teaches us to regard the surface of the planet—its waters, soils, and seas—as alive but puts pressure on the individuation of life: the idea that life is contained in discrete entities rather than inhering in the irreducible relations of those entities. It's not for nothing that the building that long housed the environmental sciences at Princeton University is named Guyot Hall.[75]

Nevertheless, we've seen how *The Earth and Man* ultimately celebrates rather than upends the stand-your-ground subject in the colonial "foothold" of the OWM. How, then, does a word for nature ultimately come to aid and abet, rather than challenge and disrupt, environmental degradation? Perhaps it has something to do with how Guyot's ecological vision of the "life of the globe" also embraces a metaphysics of separability, which undercuts the radicality of that vision. "Far from me," Guyot writes, "the idea of attempting to assimilate this *general* life of the inorganic nature of the globe to the *individual* life of the plant or the animal, as some unwise philosophers have done. I know well the wide distance which separates inorganic from organized nature. I will even go further than is ordinarily done, and I will say that there is an impassable chasm between the mineral and the plant, between the plant and the animal, an impassable chasm between the animal and the man."[76] At the same time that he insists upon life's constitutive and essential relationality, Guyot paradoxically contends that a sequence of impassable chasms neatly segregates nature into separate categories. Defined by these motes of ontology, Guyot's ecology yields what we might label, riffing on Ferreira da Silva's language, an *ecologics of separability*.[77] While there are meaningful differences between so-called organic and inorganic nature and what Guyot describes as their respective "individual" and "general life," the "impassable chasm" presumed to separate not just these but several additional taxonomical differentiations besides is traversed every day as a matter of what Guyot otherwise identifies as life's relational course. In this way, Guyot's ecologics of separability work against their own grain. Whatever democratization of life might be implied by its emphasis on nature's relationality is ultimately short-circuited by the mere replacement of one binary with another. Rather than a genuine disruption of the binary between organic and inorganic nature, a parallel binary between "individual" and "general" life bifurcates the physical world in a way that is even more, rather than less, accommodating of hierarchy. Not only does this new binary demonstrate the same metaphysical prioritization of the individual that we observed in

Rousseau's elaboration of the social contract, but its subordination of "general life" to so-called "individual life" also functionally subordinates all of nature to a humanity that represents the individual's highest and consummate expression. Thus, Guyot writes that "it is correct to say that inorganic nature is made for organized nature, and the whole globe for man."[78] This anthropocentrism at the heart of Guyot's ecological thought is logically subtended by the "impassable chasm," which supposedly sets humanity off from the rest of the life of the globe in such a way that leaves the latter utterly available to instrumentalization by the former. Moreover, just as Guyot takes the human to represent the highest expression of "individual life," we've already observed how he even more narrowly comes to identify the "white race" as the "most perfect type of humanity." The seamlessness with which Guyot's anthropocentrism bleeds into explicit white supremacy further suggests the deep entanglement of both in their mutual definition of a genre of humanity organized around the primacy of the individual and their entitlement to the surface of the earth.

ii.

The ecological false start that we find in Guyot's *The Earth and Man*, due in no small part to an anthropocentrism actively energized by white supremacy, can also be found in a US tradition of conservation, whose whiteness is, by contrast, passive—inhering less in explicit racism than in an insufficient critique of whiteness and, consequently, a reification of individual ontology inseparable from whiteness. To its significant credit, early US conservationist thought makes a significant advance beyond the anthropocentrism of the social contract and Guyot's ecologics of separability by arguing for an expanded sense of with whom humanity must learn to live. This expansion has tended to place a metonymic emphasis on humanity's relationship to land, as a microcosm of humanity's relationship to nature more broadly, and thus has predominantly assumed the form of a fundamental challenge to the modern reduction of land to mere private property. The ecological thought of Thoreau in "Walking," and subsequently of Aldo Leopold in his landmark essay "The Land Ethic," are especially emblematic of this tendency.

Between our feet and the ground lies a quiet question that, for Thoreau, still felt conspicuous in the middle of the nineteenth century. In "Walking"—from which mainstream environmentalism derives the oft-quoted conservationist mantra that "in Wildness is the preservation of the World"—it is not at all given that traversing the earth's surface should involve having to ask, Who owns this land? Today we bring variations of this question to the ground as naturally as we do shoes, feeling no great loss and registering no threat quite so significant as the downright "evil days" Thoreau feared would follow at the heels of humans grown so acclimated to the impoverished sense of land as private property:

> At present, in this vicinity, the best part of the land is not private property; the landscape is not owned, and the walker enjoys comparative freedom. But possibly the day will come when it will be partitioned off into so-called pleasure-grounds, in which a few will take a narrow and exclusive pleasure only—when fences shall be multiplied . . . and walking over the surface of God's earth shall be construed to mean trespassing on some gentleman's grounds. To enjoy a thing exclusively is commonly to exclude yourself from the true enjoyment of it. Let us improve our opportunities, then, before the evil days come.[79]

We know with the blood of Trayvon Martin that these evil days have come. We know, too, with the blood of Breonna Taylor that simply having a deed or lease is no protection against them. Murders like Martin's and Taylor's may not have been the specific evil Thoreau had in mind—and they generally evade the purview of mainstream environmentalism—but there is also a racial logic to possessing land that entitles the dispossessed and dispossesses the entitled. Indeed, there is such a thing as the complexion for possession. Even what Thoreau praises as "the best part of the land" had already become "gentleman's grounds" of a sort to the indigenous peoples who previously inhabited them and the fugitive slaves who trespassed everywhere they went. Even if he was ambivalent about it, it is important to recognize that Thoreau's walking in the wild proceeded within a *racial* claim to the land that was no less exclusive because the whites-only wilderness of the United States belonged to no one in particular.[80]

To the fugitive slave and the Native American, Thoreau's wild likely appeared "construed" and its days "evil" enough already. So long as environmentalism tends to begin with a Thoreauvian regard for the wild rather than the environmental perspectives of the former, environmentalist movements and ecological thought are fatally locked into an underestimation of their problem.[81] Redress of our ecological crisis is not only a matter of correcting the modern reduction of land to private property or the related transformation of humanity into aspiring landlords acknowledging little relation to land beyond ownership. It's these two evils that Thoreau addresses straightaway in "Walking" by expressing his "wish to speak a word for Nature" and for "man as an inhabitant, or a part and parcel of Nature, rather than a member of society."[82] To redress modern humanity's alienation from nature, "Walking" prescribes a healthy dose of walking in the wild. By bringing humans not face to face but foot to surface with land yet to go the way of private property, and so facilitating their embodiment of a relation to land beyond the narrow logic of possession, the sort of walking that Thoreau advocates may certainly engender human inhabitation.[83] But the salutary promise of such walking is mitigated by another significant transformation. Thoreau's nonwhite contemporaries knew well that those humans who had become landowners had also become *white*. And this racial transformation was in no way incidental to the new and dominating way in which they were coming to relate to the ground beneath their feet.[84] Indeed, the same white supremacy that justified the dispossession and ownership of other humans also facilitated the expropriation, private possession, and overextraction of the landscape. What bars modern humanity from genuine inhabitation, then, is not just the narrowing of human-planetary relations to a radically impoverished notion of private property but, more specifically, *whiteness* as the aestheticization of western humanism's "dominating stand": the right, superior, and most of all *Human* way of relating to land as property that was established and enforced, through the mechanism of white settler colonialism, as the global standard of genuine human being.

Even if Thoreau critiques such whiteness by one name—when, for instance, he asserts that "olive is a fitter color than white for a man"—he arguably embraces it by another, in what might be recognized as the exclusiveness and overriding individuality of his walking practice. Although he concedes to sometimes walking with a companion, Thoreau's vision of earnest walking is remarkably solitary: "If you are ready to leave father and mother, and brother and sister, and wife and child and friends, and never see them again,—if you have paid your debts, and made your will, and settled all your affairs, and are a free man, then you are ready for a walk." Setting such a high bar for earnest walking may not reflect walking's necessary isolation so much as the necessity to escape a human society erected upon its alienation from (the state of) nature. Nevertheless, the order of walkers is a remarkably exclusive one, as Thoreau explains that he has "met with but one or two persons in the course of [his] life who understood the art of Walking." This exclusiveness is opposed in "Walking" not only to the entrapments of human society but to a blithe dismissal of labor: "When sometimes I am reminded that the mechanics and shopkeepers stay in their shops not only all the forenoon, but all the afternoon too, sitting with crossed legs, so many of them,—as if the legs were made to sit upon, and not to stand or walk upon,—I think that they deserve some credit for not having all committed suicide long ago."[85] Of course, there is a critique to be made here of the exploitation of labor, but Thoreau does not make it. Nor does he quite recognize how his own privileged ability to walk for extended periods of time requires a relative leisure that is, in many ways, created by and unavailable to exploited laborers. Earnest inhabitation, however, would presumably entail labor as well as leisure, such that walking's reduction of inhabitation to mere leisure represents its own artificiality, dependent, even if antagonistically, on the backdrop of the society to which inhabitation's labor is outsourced. So far as Thoreau's passive avowal of whiteness by another name goes, the principal takeaway here is that the exclusiveness of walking is not, in and of itself, a problem for Thoreau. It is quite sufficient, if not ideal, for Thoreau to undertake his walks alone, even if alone with the world. But especially with such dubious precedents for walking as the Crusades, Columbus, and Guyot's OWM, it is difficult to distinguish such isolation from the individual ontology of whiteness.[86]

After Thoreau, perhaps the next influential US thinker to take up humanity's relationship to the ground, once the parlance of ecology has been well established, is Aldo Leopold. In his pioneering book *A Sand County Almanac* (1949), Leopold calls on humanity to develop a "land ethic": "All ethics so far evolved rest upon a single premise: that the individual is a member of a community of interdependent parts. His instincts prompt him to compete for his place in the community, but his ethics prompt him also to co-operate (perhaps in order that there may be a place to compete for). The land ethic simply enlarges the boundaries of community to include soils, waters, plants, and animals, or collectively: the land."[87] Much like Rousseau, Leopold is concerned with the general question of how individuals might live together. However, his "land ethic," in an implicit challenge to the general anthropocentrism of the social contract, expands our sense of with whom we must learn to live to a "land-community" that includes not only the human and more-than-human life with which we share the land but the land itself. Such a "land ethic," Leopold argues, would entail the mutual transformations of humanity "from conqueror of the land-community to plain member and citizen of it" and of land from mere property to fellow member of a shared biotic community.[88] And yet, because it is centered on the land and put forward as an unprecedented innovation of human ethics, Leopold's land ethic ironically also functions not only to naturalize humanity's separation from the earth but also to obscure the cooperation of racial and environmental degradation in the history of white settler colonialism whereby humanity became a conqueror of the land-community in the first place.

Leopold positions the "land ethic" as the third and final step in humanity's ethical evolution. Whereas the "first ethics dealt with the relation between individuals," and the second "dealt with the relation between the individual and society," Leopold argues: "There is as yet no ethic dealing with man's relation to land and to the animals and plants which grow upon it. . . . The extension of ethics to this third element in human environment is, if I read the evidence correctly, an evolutionary possibility and an ecological necessity. It is the third step in a sequence. The first two have already been taken."[89] I'm doubtful, though, about the prospects of any such land ethic that "simply enlarges the boundaries of [human] community to include soils, waters, plants, and animals, or collectively: the land."[90] Because once the lines of ethical community are so enlarged, they will still be found to exclude those humans who, prior to this ecological rezoning of ethics, historically were just as excluded from human community as Leopold recognized the land to be. What is brought into stark relief by interspecies lists like that which we find in *Narrative of the Life of Frederick Douglass*—"there were horses and men, cattle and women, pigs and children, all holding the same rank in the scale of being"[91]—is that the historically conquered land-community included not just "soils, waters, plants, and animals" but also other humans deemed nonhuman or less than human. This oversight further helps explain how Leopold can confidently declare, in the middle of the same century whose organizing problem W. E. B. Du Bois forecasted as the color line, that only the "third step" of extending ethics to the land remains for a humanity that has otherwise already settled the question of ethics regarding "the relation between individuals" and "the relation between the individual and society." This declaration of the finished work of intrahuman ethics is not just premature but ahistorical. It greenwashes a conquered "land-community" that historically also included red and black humans, even as it belies both the self-conscious whiteness of that conqueror and the genocidal history of his conquering. The human histories of white settler colonialism are obscured by Leopold's exclusive attention to this conqueror's status as a landowner. His equally important status as a colonizer and slave master is lost to abstraction. But in addition to the prematurity of the completed first two steps, Leopold's characterization of enviromentalism's "third step" as unprecedented also elides historical "land-communities" that *already*, prior to Columbian contact, included indigenous humans who conceived of themselves as belonging to or part of the land. Even as mainstream environmentalism orients itself toward this "third step," such land communities still exist both willfully and coercively. And in the specific case of the hold, this land community is refigured as an ocean community, whose willfulness we shall soon consider.

Notwithstanding the significance of his thought to the intellectual traditions of deep ecology and deep time, Leopold's human world is remarkably shallow.

Younger than Young Earth, the time of Leopold's world assumes the finished work of settlement as its genesis and genocidal status quo. The problem internal to both Leopold's "land ethic" and a mainstream environmentalism that tends to attribute anthropogenic climate change to the Industrial Revolution is that both think the world in *after-settlement time*. Such ahistoricity is further evidenced by Leopold's appeal to Greek mythology for an example of "human chattels" to bridge our sympathies for land reduced to mere property.[92] Sparing himself the lengthy trip to antiquity, Leopold had only to recall the nineteenth century of his own birth to retrieve relevant examples of human property. Had he considered the suffering of enslaved Africans and their descendants, he may have noted the historical interplay between owning ground and owning people and how the emergence of private property on a global scale required the mutual and simultaneous domination of both.

None of this is to claim that the "third step" of ethics isn't a step worth taking. But if we are to take it earnestly, the first step may be to realize that the ethical challenge of environmentalism is inextricably related to all that remains unfinished in the previous two ("the relation between individuals" and "the relation between the individual and society"). Moreover, these are legible as two discrete steps only because they presuppose the "individual" as the most basic unit of social and ecological life. Herein lies the second problem internal to Leopold's nonetheless important call for a land ethic: its uncritical reification of the individual (which is really the stand-your-ground subject and whiteness by another name) and, by extension, the "plan of living" that is its condition of possibility. Ironically, the greatest violence to the land, and the planetary surface more broadly, may be that it is presumed to support, a priori, anything like the individual, the naturalization of which strains against the grain of the irreducibly ecological life of the "land-community" to which Leopold would have us consent to belong. If we are to embark earnestly upon the journey of ethics, I'm not sure the individual can come along for the walk. It may even be a nonstarter. Once environmentalism unmoors itself from this reification of the individual, it will be possible to see that, as far as ethics is concerned, there is really only the one step yet unfinished. Environmental and human domination are more than related; they are a single operation. They must therefore be resolved not sequentially but together.

If not quite in Leopold's "land ethic," Thoreau's "walking," or the inspiration it derives from the "adventurous career westward" of the OWM, the remainder of this chapter searches out this one step of ethics—especially regarding the prospect of human inhabitation of a blue planet—in "the footprint on the water, filling." That is, in the more-than-human ocean communities of middle passing Africans and what we might alternatively call their *deep ethic*. I'm not sure that any genuine recalibration of the stand-your-ground subject at the heart of modernity's unsustainable "plan of living" can take place without a serious reckoning with these "inhabitants of the deep." They were there when the plans were laid, and their expulsion, as the black face of otherness, *was* the plan, along with the disavowal of the ocean. The coerced intimacy of black and blue during Middle Passage embodies the messy ecological life against which modernity's plan for life necessarily constitutes itself as a fundamentally terracentric and antiblack project. Because, in the ocean, the Earth is held out to us as ground we cannot stand and difference from which we cannot separate, in which we can only be submerged. And because blackness is this environmental submersion, which is the individual's dissolution.

V. blackness as inhabitation of the deep

i.

Europe's was not the only Atlantic opportunity. Across the four-century tenure of the transatlantic slave trade, at least twelve million captive Africans also encountered an unknown and dreaded ocean, albeit under dramatically different circumstances. In her historiography of the slave trade, Smallwood explains: "Enslaved Africans entered the Atlantic without the information and background that enabled their European captors to navigate the open sea. When confronted with the phenomenon, African captives responded to the Atlantic as Europeans had done: they made it knowable in their own terms. But the conditions of their Atlantic experience shaped that process, just as the particular conditions of maritime exploration had shaped the integration of the Atlantic into European culture and consciousness."[93] Considering that the surface of our planet is more than two-thirds ocean, the stakes of its integration into culture and consciousness are nothing short of humanity's knowledge of the Earth and, what's more, *itself* in relation to the Earth. If for Europe this process could be recognized, at least as represented in the "adventurous career westward" of the OWM, to yield a sense of Earth as little more than a docile surface and a vision of humanity as a stand-your-ground subject, what alternative visions of Earth and humanity do we imagine the black maritime experience of Middle Passage yielded? Rather than Europe's Atlantic crossing, perhaps a more promising place to begin to reimagine "man" as an "inhabitant, or part and parcel of Nature," is with the middle passages of the "inhabitants of the deep." In a way better proportioned to the material composition of our blue planet, they assume the ocean, and not the land (and still less, private property), as ground zero for social and ecological thought.

The historiography of the transatlantic slave trade teaches us that most of the captives who were gathered before the Atlantic on the coast of West Africa—poised to board slave ships as modernity's cargo—were encountering the ocean for the very first time. This blue expanse stretched now unendingly before them in a geographic harangue of landlessness, the planet's conspicuous failure to resolve back into terra firma, as water was apt to do in the rivers and lakes that served as their closest aquatic reference. Having "never before seen any water larger than a pond or rivulet," Equiano's "astonishment" at his dramatic first contact with the ocean would have been typical of those who, like him, were captured in the interior of the continent and subsequently marched to the coast.[94] There were, of course, some for whom the ocean was not a complete novelty. In *Undercurrents of Power*, Kevin Dawson chronicles the rich "aquatic culture" of coastal West African societies that had significant cultural and economic engagement with the ocean long before the rise of New World slavery.[95] However, even they were no more cosmologically prepared for the *deep* they would encounter upon the vanishing of the coast than those lacking any oceanic experience at all. As Smallwood tells us, "The landless realm of the deep ocean did not figure in pre-colonial West African societies as a domain of human (as opposed to divine) activity." Thus for middle passing Africans, "the slave ship was not just a setting for brutality and death, but also a locus of unparalleled displacement. As the sight of land grew faint, or as the land disappeared suddenly on the closing of the hatch, the disorientation that for many had begun with the process of procurement on the African coast became more marked. Out of sight of any land, enslaved Africans commenced a march through time and space that stretched their own systems of reckoning to the limits."[96] In *Barracoon*, Zora Neale Hurston registers this "unparalleled displacement" in her record of the black maritime experience of Cudjoe Lewis, the last known US survivor of Middle Passage. Consider Hurston's rendering of the visual free fall that, years later, Lewis could still recall experiencing with his shipmates when land vanished from the horizon: "We lookee and lookee and lookee and lookee and we doan see nothin' but water. Where we come from we doan know. Where we goin, we doan know."[97]

In "The Open Boat," the oft-cited first chapter of *Poetics of Relation*, Édouard Glissant approximates the terrible wonder of this black maritime experience by performing a haunting act of ventriloquy. The words may be his, but they sound out questions that, in their unmoored suspense, seem to emerge from the veritable mouths of the Africans hovering over the face of the deep: "What kind of river . . . has no middle? Is nothing there but straight ahead?"[98] With these words, Glissant sounds out what may just be the original negro question, that is, the actual questions raised by middle passing Africans in the throes of becoming black. The great irony in what is more popularly known to history as the "Negro Question" is that, like the social contract, it is really a masquerading answer. When, in *Notes on the State of Virginia*, Thomas Jefferson asks, concerning the negro, "What further is to be done with them?" he is not asking a question so much as rehearsing what we'd do better to recognize as the "Negro Answer" to the still more basic and irreducible question of social (and indeed ecological) life: *How do we live together*?[99] The Negro Answer given by modernity is racial separation, an answer that is itself inextricable from modernity's other answer to the question of life together: humanity's separation from and essential superiority to nature. In contrast to Jefferson's insincere rehearsal of the Negro Answer, Glissant's questions bespeak the negro question in earnest by voicing the sea-legged questions that captive Africans must have asked of a blue planet while huddled in the holds of slave ships. As a starting place for the thought of life together, the scope of Glissant's questions critically assume, from the very first, a horizon that extends beyond the human to the more-than-human world. Their inquiry into the nature of an ocean, whose sheer scale, according to Smallwood, "disabled many of the cognitive tools supplied by African epistemologies," registers a profound wrestling with the vicissitudes of not just social but ecological life.[100] Moreover, unlike the Negro Answer and the social contract, these questions are not masquerading answers. Rather, in a way better resembling what Outka describes as the "irreducibly open question" of ecological life, they bespeak a crisis of landlessness defined by its failure to resolve.

Brought forth in anguished naiveté, Glissant's questions impersonate the uncertainty of those who, confronted with "nothing but straight ahead," could not be certain of the land's eventual return.[101] For who was there who cared to stop and explain, in a language they could understand, *arrival*: that they were headed someplace other than this eternal now of the Atlantic? These unique circumstances meant that Middle Passage was for many of the enslaved not a crossing, which implies eventual arrival, but an extended, suspended, arrested departure. The name *Middle* Passage is both ironic and anachronistic in this respect, for it grants a knowledge of arrival where there was none, neither for those who foundered in the Atlantic along the way nor for those who did arrive on the shores of the New World but could not have known that they would. Thus, Middle Passage required African captives to perform a terrific feat of the imagination. Suddenly displaced from any and all signs of land, and not being assured of reaching some future elsewhere beyond the Atlantic, theirs was the historical labor of having to make a ground out of no ground, of having to imagine and improvise a life lived *absolutely* at sea, without even the faintest relief of a future promised land. Which is to say that for the three weeks, at least, that it took a ship to cross the Atlantic, African slaves rehearsed and practiced an unstable occupation and precarious negotiation of space that, because they could not be certain it would ever end, came to be conflated in their minds with the labor of living. With life. Thus, to speak of middle passing Africans is to speak precisely of those who were without the "middle." Belied in what we call *Middle* Passage is a lived experience whose predicament and passion are perhaps better and more faithfully apprehended as an *inhabitation of the deep*. If, in ultimate resolution of the OWM's initial stumble at the Atlantic, we witness the production of whiteness as stand-your-ground subjectivity, in the corresponding failed resolution of the crisis of groundlessness faced by middle passing Africans, we alternatively witness the production of blackness as an ongoing *inhabitation of the deep*. Yet far from being reducible to the trauma of social death, Middle Passage's failure to resolve, we will find, may alternatively be understood to produce black ecological life.

Simultaneous with the well-remarked suffering endured by enslaved Africans during the transatlantic slave trade proceeded what we have yet to fully appreciate as a collective and sustained inquiry into the nature of the ocean and the prospect of human life on a blue planet. But perhaps we are better poised to appreciate such black oceanic study now, amid the "oceanic turn" currently underway in the humanities with the emergence of what Steve Mentz has labeled the "blue humanities" and what Hester Blum has alternatively called "oceanic studies."[102] Within this general oceanic turn, Elizabeth DeLoughrey has further elucidated a still more specific shift, with growing awareness of sea-level rise, "from a long-term concern with mobility across transoceanic surfaces to theorizing oceanic submersion" in a way that renders "oceanic space into ontological place."[103] Yet the fact that there is even a need to *turn* in order to study the ocean implies that the humanities, not unlike the OWM, are otherwise somehow turned away. Dan Brayton argues precisely this in his book *Shakespeare's Ocean*, in which he questions whether our backs are to the sea and traces what he theorizes as the "terrestrial bias" of western culture.[104] That is, its defining overpreoccupation with land at the expense of a general and sustained neglect of the ocean. A 2010 documentary that identifies the ocean amid the international flow of global capital as *The Forgotten Space* further suggests this neglect.[105] To forget an ocean constituting no less than 70 percent of the earth's surface represents no small feat of amnesia. In the familiar needle/haystack analogy, we forgive and expect the loss of the needle. But by forgetting the sea, the West has somehow remarkably managed to lose the haystack. In turning to weigh the prospect of oceanic studies now and to contemplate with DeLoughrey "the submarine futures of the Anthropocene," the humanities would do well to consider that protracted oceanic study staged by the slave ship during Middle Passage. Over a period spanning five centuries, the talking commodities brimming the holds of slave ships asked bewildered questions of our blue planet. One can hardly imagine another instance when the study of the ocean more urgently or intimately coincided with what it meant to be alive.

ii.

What is at stake in stopping to attend in this way to the blue inquiry of middle passing Africans? Especially given that the "unparalleled displacement" of Middle Passage has otherwise been taken in black studies as the original, if not paradigmatic, sign of black abjection and social death. After all, if humans are land creatures, what better to signal blackness's paradigmatic exclusion from Humanity than its historical consignment to the ocean? From the very beginning, blackness, as experienced in Middle Passage, exhibits all of the symptoms of Orlando Patterson's famous definition of the slave as a "socially dead person."[106] So when Frank Wilderson invokes Middle Passage as the "dawning of blackness," he means to lay bare just how absolutely blackness not only dawns but persists in and as the "social death" of slavery, such that no meaningful distinction can be made between "Slaveness and Blackness."[107] He writes:

> The imaginary of the state and civil society is *parasitic* on the Middle Passage. Put another way, No slave, no world. And, in addition, as Patterson argues, no slave is *in* the world.
>
> If, as an ontological position . . . the Slave is not a laborer but an anti-Human, a position against which Humanity establishes, maintains, and renews its coherence, its corporeal integrity; if the slave is, to borrow from Patterson, generally dishonored, perpetually open to gratuitous violence, and void of kinship structure, that is, having no relations that need be recognized, a being outside of relationality, then our analysis cannot be approached through the rubric of gains or reversals in struggles with the state and civil society, not unless and until the interlocutor first explains how the Slave is of the world. The onus is not on one who posits the Master/Slave dichotomy but on the one who argues there is a distinction between Slaveness and Blackness. How, when, and where did such a split occur?[108]

By "the world," Wilderson explicitly means the "state and civil society"; that these bear a "parasitic" relation to Middle Passage means that the human social life housed therein is fundamentally and constitutively antiblack. And this parasitism on Middle Passage is not restricted to the past for Wilderson, as if the state sustains itself by rationing a strictly primitive accumulation of black bodies. Rather, the crisis of Middle Passage is ongoing. Bodies are still being accumulated. And the soles of black folk *still* falter, just as they did in the steps middle passing Africans blinked on the face of the Atlantic after jumping or being thrown overboard. Emmett Till jettisoned in the Tallahatchie River is Middle Passage. Trayvon Martin felled by a man standing his ground is Middle Passage. Frantz Fanon hailed by a child shouting "Look! A Negro!" and describing how his "feet no longer felt the caress of the ground" is Middle Passage.[109] For Wilderson, "the *first* ontological instance" of this "Negro," a creature with neither physical nor metaphysical ground in the world, is Middle Passage.[110] So the blackness that dawns in Middle Passage obtains not in a historical event that is past but in and as an ongoing inability to stand our ground.

Wilderson's antiblack world certainly deserves all our pessimism. But does blackness? Asked another way, does blackness need to be in the world in order for there to be any meaningful distinction between slaveness and blackness? Is the world the only place there is to be? Is it possible, even worthwhile, to be elsewhere? Wilderson's characterization of the world as "parasitic"—and parasites, on the whole, tend to be much smaller than their hosts—already begins to suggest the possibility that the world is not only not exhaustive but also, in comparison to its host, relatively small. Moreover, if no slave is in the world, then the turn of the humanities from the nation-state to an ocean characterized as forgotten further suggests that no ocean is either. And the ocean, we know, constitutes most of our planet. Then, there is the witness of ecology more generally, which critiques the exclusion of most of nonhuman life, land or sea, from our human worlds. In other words, most of life isn't in the world. The world and its Human sociality are mastery with respect not only to blackness but to the entire planet. So if black people are hosts, they are the human host to a great nonhuman company. Enough to strain a formulation like the "social death" of blackness to the point of being beside the point.

Coming to grips with the reality that no slave is in the world has been hard, but necessary, work. And the debt I owe to Wilderson's black study is considerable in this respect. But I'm also persuaded that the world is not all there is, even if it is often all that "need be recognized." That the West managed to lose the haystack of the ocean assures us that the protocols of human recognition are hardly reliable. There is a lot of elsewhere to be. By insisting on a distinction between slaveness and blackness, then, I locate blackness not in the world but rather in what the poet Ed Roberson has alternatively called "the Earth," when he writes that "the world's desires do *not* run the Earth, but the Earth *does* run the world."[111] I no more desire to be integrated into the world than I would struggle to move into a burning house. But I remain invested in disentangling blackness from its social death relative to the world in order to make visible the capaciousness of black ecological life on Earth. Black ecological life is what comes to light when knowledge of the Earth enters black study, and we adopt it, and not the world, as our critical frame.

Now in some ways, grounding a distinction between slaveness and blackness in the material recognition that the Earth is greater than the world misses Wilderson's point. The social death of blackness, for Wilderson, inheres most fundamentally in the understanding of blackness as an "ontological position." Which is to say that blackness is positioned outside the world ontologically or, more precisely, outside of the world of human ontology altogether. This grim ontological state of affairs has serious material implications, but it is not simply annulled by a mere change in one's material or existential fortunes. This is why, even after the apparent gains of emancipation and civil rights, black people for Wilderson are still slaves, in the sense that they are still socially dead. In making this argument, Wilderson reminds us of Fanon's contention that "ontology—once it is finally admitted as *leaving existence* by the wayside—does not permit us to understand the being of the black man. For not only must the black man be black; but he must be black in relation to the white man."[112] But that's just it. Ontology *has* left existence by the wayside. That is precisely the problem. It not only fails to understand the being of the black man but also fails to understand the being of the planet insofar as both are irreducibly relational, irreducibly ecological, and therefore hardly constitutive of anything like being in the traditional western sense at all. So to hell with western ontology. For that is where it is taking us, if our environmental prophets are not false. We would study and know life instead. In this time of ecological crisis, we can hardly afford to leave something as critical as existence by the wayside, even if ontology does.

The possibility that in Middle Passage blackness dawns as anything more than social death is part of what we can begin to see in Omise'eke Natasha Tinsley's consideration of the well-remarked shipmate relationship established between Africans who arrived in the New World on the same slave ship. In her article "Black Atlantic, Queer Atlantic," she writes that "the emergence of intense shipmate relationships in the water-rocked, no-person's-land of slave holds created a black Atlantic same-sex eroticism: a *feeling of, feeling for* the kidnapped that asserted the sentience of the bodies that slavers attempted to transform into brute matter." Such "feeling of, feeling for" one another in the hold of the slave ship was queer, Tinsley explains, not primarily "in the sense of a 'gay' or same-sex loving identity" but "in the sense of marking disruption to the violence of normative order" and "connecting in ways that commodified flesh was never supposed to" as a "praxis of resistance."[113] But what happens when we extend the scope of this "feeling of, feeling for" from the human to the more-than-human and the astonishing shipmate that middle passing Africans also claimed in the ocean? What comes to light in the black oceanic study of the Africans of the hold is a still more radically queer "feeling of, feeling for" the deep and, by extension, our blue planet. Which is to say that Middle Passage is humanity's Earth landing. One small step for the captives who would have taken more but could not. One giant step for humanity. Indeed, the "inhabitants of the deep" took perhaps the most earnest steps a human can take on our blue planet. Their ambulation is a significant moment in the evolution not of humanity so much as humanity's environmental humanity, and is far more significant than the flag-planting humanism that walked the moon. This ecological "feeling of, feeling for" the ocean constitutes a still greater disruption to the violence of normative order by connecting in ways that the human, imagined as separate from nature, was never supposed to. In this sense, far from a being outside of relationality or void of kinship structure, blackness dawns in and as the queer consent to the ecological conditions of life on a blue planet.

Further helping to elucidate the implications of such "feeling of, feeling for" the ocean is the aesthetic philosophy of Gaston Bachelard and the poetic import he ascribes to matter. In his book *Water and Dreams*, Bachelard argues that "it is possible to establish in the realm of the imagination, a law of the four elements which classifies various kinds of material imagination by their connections with fire, air, water, or earth." In short, these four elements, which Bachelard distinguishes as "fundamental elements," furnish the imagination with the "particular rules and poetics" expressed by their physical properties. Consider, for example, how the contemplation of the flow of water might inspire a poet or a rapper to reproduce the same phenomenon in a flowing lyric. Bachelard's term for the imagination so informed by the physiopoetic properties of one of the four fundamental elements is the "material imagination," and he speculates that ancient philosophic and aesthetic systems often made "a decisive choice along these lines."[114]

If matter indeed lends itself to imagination in the manner Bachelard describes, then beyond merely signaling black abjection or the condition of "social death," Middle Passage can be further recognized as having staged an extended meditation on the ocean, with untold poetic and imaginative potential. Thus, besides the blood-stained gate through which the enslaved serially passed into the hell of slavery, we have also to recognize the gathering and fellow*ship* of this black and blue ecclesia. These "called out" ones, gathered with and to a kindred ocean, whose fate it also was to furnish the constitutive outside of western humanism's plan of living. But beyond their mere exclusion, those who were "called out" were also calling out their own name. Calling themselves together in the cohering passion of their blue inquiry. "What kind of river has no middle? Is nothing there but straight ahead?" asked again and again and again, together, over the course of four hundred years. A kind of intergenerational mantra accompanying and announcing the birth of blackness. This blue they also passed through.

Read this way, the ocean, beyond its familiar status of rupture or unmarked grave, may also be understood to furnish the African Diaspora with the "fundamental element" of what I am calling, extending Bachelard's term, the *material imagination of blackness*. Perhaps this is the water-inspired imagination to which the poet Dionne Brand refers in *A Map to the Door of No Return* (2002), when she writes, "Water is the first thing in my imagination."[115] Or to which the poet M. NourbeSe Philip gestures in *Zong!* (2008), when she observes in the "Notanda" that "always what is going on seems to be about water."[116] Of course, to speak of some "decisive decision" on the part of the African Diaspora to adopt water as its "fundamental element" is complicated by the fact that the diaspora, at least initially, had very little choice in the matter. Blackness is devoted to the deep by history, not volition. Yet we learn from Equiano's narrative that a devotion conceived under the conditions of coercion can subsequently turn willful. After being whipped for the first time aboard the slave ship, Equiano tellingly writes, "Although, not being used to the water, I naturally feared that element the first time I saw it, yet nevertheless, could I have got over the nettings, *I would have jumped over the side*."[117] Thus, after an initially forced encounter with the ocean, Equiano subsequently comes to willfully desire the sea. And though he is prevented from jumping ship physically, we nevertheless see him jump ship in his mind, glimpsing the operation of what I am calling the material imagination of blackness, a mind or an imagination given to water. Of course, the violence that motivates Equiano's desire to jump ship complicates the willfulness of his decision as being positively for the sea as opposed to merely a negative escape from violence. Yet Equiano's curious appellation for those who did manage to jump ship physically suggests a positive vision of what it was that middle passing Africans were jumping to: "Often did I think many of the *inhabitants* of the deep much more happy than myself. I envied them the *freedom* they enjoyed, and as often wished I could change my condition for theirs."[118] Why does Equiano use *inhabitants*, a word typically reserved for the living, to describe those who jumped to their deaths? Moreover, how can he possibly claim to envy these drowned slaves their freedom? Yet if we suspend our initial objections to Equiano's apparent misnaming of the drowned, and take seriously the lives that were *lived* underwater, awfully abbreviated as they were, then what emerges is a profoundly ecological vision of human life and freedom on a blue planet. The very human ecological life after which Thoreau groped when he sounded out a word for "man as an *inhabitant*, or part and parcel of Nature." The inhabitants of the deep yield precisely such an "inhabitant," as it would need to be imagined on a planet significantly more deep than terra firma. And what the blue inquiry registered by Glissant's questions holds out to us is that *all* middle passing Africans, and not just those who jumped or were thrown overboard, were inhabitants of the deep, insofar as they all weighed the prospect of a human life lived absolutely at sea.[119]

But what are the stakes of locating, amid the incredible violence and suffering of Middle Passage, the conception and operation of the material imagination of blackness? Bachelard again is helpful here for his delineation of the problem of a materially impoverished imagination. For Bachelard, the imagination that neglects matter "deserts depth, volume, and the inner recesses of substance." Consequently, such an imagination produces images that, according to Bachelard, "cannot survive because they are merely formal play, not truly adapted to the matter they should adorn."[120] But if the imagination's failure to discover its matter is a problem for poetry, leading to insufficiently imagined images that "cannot survive," might the material impoverishment of the imagination also prove a problem for other exercises of the imagination—say, the dominant imagination of human life and freedom within a western culture that, according to Brayton, has its back turned to most of the matter on the planet? Might Bachelard condemn the superficial landing of Plymouth Rock as "merely formal play, not truly adapted to the matter" it should adorn on a blue planet? Maybe the human imaged by the "foothold" of the OWM and the stand-your-ground subject just "cannot survive."

Is this not the basic witness of ecology? That the life and freedoms of the reigning genre of the human are unsustainable? Perhaps humanity's excessive carbon footprint is all that could be reasonably expected of a western culture that has disproportionately imagined with respect to land, human life, and freedom on a planet predominantly made of water. It's in light of the terracentric and radically impoverished environmental imagination of whiteness that the stakes of the recognition of the material imagination of blackness come clear. For if life has any integrity, such that any sustainable practice of human life would need to be conceived in proportion and relation to the material realities of our blue planet, then it may just be that the inhabitants of the deep adapted the human to the matter it should adorn. That by undertaking the awful labor of conceiving and improvising human life absolutely at sea, what the Africans bereft of the middle actually managed to do was live. That within what we sometimes have occasion in black studies to appraise as "social death," we have yet and further to recognize a still more profound practice of black ecological life: the life we must all learn to live before the ocean comes home to roost, baptizing the soles of the forgetful. Faced with the prospect of our submarine futures, who knows but that, at these deepest depths, the "inhabitants of the deep" speak for us, asking their blue questions, inaugurating the ecological life of the earthling.

2

DEEP STUDY

Western Civilization has long defined the ocean as an unnatural (or prenatural) void forever evincing a hostile alterity, a void lying eternally outside—or on the margins—of human social constructs.
—DAN BRAYTON, *Shakespeare's Ocean*

Blackness is social death.
—FRANK WILDERSON, *Afropessimism*

TWICE ALONG THE EPIC VOYAGE of the *Pequod* in Herman Melville's classic novel, *Moby-Dick* (1851), the ocean is characterized as the "dark side" of the earth. The first occasion is when the novel's famous narrator, Ishmael, observes that "the sun hides not Virginia's Dismal Swamp, nor Rome's accursed Campagna, nor wide Sahara, nor all the millions of miles of deserts." Then, to consummate this survey of geographic thorns in the side of human civilization, which serve as metaphors for life's difficulties and woes, Ishmael invokes arguably the most maligned of all: "The sun hides not the ocean, which is *the dark side of this earth*, and which is two thirds of this earth."[1] Later in the novel, Captain Ahab describes the ocean in the exact same terms, brooding in one of his many asides, "So far gone am I in *the dark side of earth*, that its other side, the theoretic bright one, seems but uncertain twilight to me."[2] But why should the ocean constitute "the dark side of earth" if, as Ishmael observes, the sun rises upon it and winces not? Does the sun not shine its light on the sea as well as on terra firma? Like the equally curious case of the so-called "Dark Continent," the ocean's darkness appears immune to the sun's illumination. It is dark in and of itself, a lamp burning black. Given the anomaly of a "Dark Continent" on which the sun shines no less than on others, it's telling that the only other time we hear mention of the "dark side" in *Moby-Dick* is when the anonymous Spanish Sailor says to the "coal-black negro-savage," Daggoo, "Thy race is the undeniable *dark side of mankind*."[3]

What are we to make of the mutual characterization of blackness and the ocean as the "dark side" of humanity and the earth, respectively? Of a blackness that even the day strands as the absolute face of human otherness? Of an ocean that is likewise stranded in negative opposition to the "theoretic brightness" of land as its supposed geographic other? The theory of this "brightness" is given in the geographic orientation openly secreted in the words we've stitched together to get at the things we deem alien or strange: The fact that we call aliens extra*terrestrials*. Or that we used to call strangers out*lands* and still describe strange phenomena as out*landish*. What does this imply about the ocean—which is as far outland as you can get without a spaceship and whose deepest depths have had fewer visitors than the moon? Is the ocean the dark side of the heavens and the earth?

If, with the "discovery" of the New World and the global advent of race, modernity witnessed a revolution in our knowledge of planet and species, then what does it mean that both the ocean and blackness find themselves on the "dark side" looking in? This chapter takes up the faces of difference at which the modern world winces most. It considers how blackness and the ocean, respectively, bear the burden of representing human and nonhuman difference par excellence. If difference wears many faces, *separation* has only two; and since the dawning of the modern world, the deep and blackness have furnished the West's *constitutive* outside. There is no calling in these absolute and defining Others apart from the end of the world. But don't let that dissuade you. The end of the world is also the revelation of Earth.[4]

If in *Moby-Dick*, the confluence of blueness and blackness is apparent from their mutual characterization as the "dark side" of the modern world, this confluence comes to an expressive head in Pip, who is perhaps American literature's most famous "inhabitant of the deep." Pip's fateful jump from a whale boat and subsequent abandonment at sea is haunted by the jumpers and the jettisoned from slave ships during Middle Passage. Yet before we proceed to a reading of Pip's inhabitation of the deep, it is worth surveying the logical confluence to which black and blue have elsewhere come in the fields of black studies and the blue humanities (and environmental criticism more broadly), in their mutual, if not yet fully conversant, critiques of the color line: that is, both the classic demarcation of racial difference and the human/nature binary, which has similarly come to be conceptualized in terms of color.

I. the *color* line

The "problem" of the twenty-first century is still the problem of the color line, even if the colors that concern us today are no longer so black and white. In the years since W. E. B. Du Bois famously predicted that the organizing problem of the twentieth century would be "the relation of the darker to the lighter races of men," our understanding of the color line has evolved significantly.[5] Most basic to these evolutions is the simple insight that the color line is hardly the only line inhibiting our just relation. Not only has the conversation surrounding racial difference expanded beyond the initial dyad of black and white to include red, yellow, and brown, but other lines entirely—demarcating difference across gender, sex, sexuality, class, age, ability, and national borders—have also entered the conversation.[6] Moreover, with the rise of "intersectionality," we have also come to understand that neither these lines nor the structures of domination founded upon their exclusions—white supremacy, patriarchy, capitalism, heteronormativity, ableism, ageism, and imperialism—operate in isolation. Rather they intersect to produce irreducible confluences of oppression.[7]

This evolution in our thinking about the color line has effectively decentered it by multiplying the number of lines to which we have to attend and illuminating the abstraction of its individuated operation. The strain of black study known as "Afropessimism," however, not only preserves and intensifies the color line's centrality but also prunes the original vagueness of Du Bois's "lighter" and "darker" races to what Frank Wilderson alternatively posits as the color line's most essential differentiation: black and nonblack. Out of intersectionality's complex of oppression, Afropessimism pulls the loose and singular thread of *antiblackness* as the one form of domination, racial or otherwise, that is without analogy because it reckons its particular "Other," "the Black," *nonhuman* (in a way categorically distinct from its nonwhite, native, female, queer, disabled, or poor peers). Against the grain of the white/nonwhite variation of the color line prevalent in critical race studies, which centers white supremacy and its subjugation of various nonwhite others, Afropessimism alternatively posits black/nonblack as the color line's most essential form, arguing that it is specifically the relation of the nonblack category of the Human to the black category of the non- or anti-Human that constitutes the organizing problem of not just the twentieth century but every century since the dawning of blackness and, with it, the antiblack world.[8]

Rather than a disavowal of intersectionality, however, Afropessimism elaborates a claim about the uniqueness of antiblackness, which, even if it never operates in isolation (as in the case of black women), nevertheless singularly establishes and coheres the modern world. While it is possible to speak of many worldings, not all worldings are created equal; and the particular world at issue, here—the world founded on the paradigmatic distinction between the black and the nonblack, the Human and the non-Human—is increasingly difficult to distinguish from what geologists, albeit with more of an eye toward climate change, have begun to recognize as a profoundly human planet.[9] The parallel recognition in black studies that antiblackness coheres a Human world motivates one of the central contentions of Afropessimism: that the violence of antiblackness cannot be reconciled with the violence of colonialism, capitalism, gender oppression, or white supremacy, because "the Black" represents not a degraded Human among other Humans but rather the very "foil of Humanity." According to Wilderson, the Black's relation to violence "bears no essential analogy to the Human's relationship to violence, even when those Human subjects represent extremely abused and degraded members of the Human family." Unlike the land or profits extracted from indigenous peoples or the worker, "Blacks are not in possession of something exterior to themselves that civil society wants. . . . What civil society needs from Black people is confirmation of Human existence."[10] But even if the category of the non-Human is potentially larger and more complex than Afropessimism suggests, Wilderson's point remains that the violence that creates hierarchical relations between Humans cannot be analogized to the violence that creates the relation of domination between Humans and non-Humans.[11] The latter coheres a world in which Humans may skirmish in the first place, but "no slave is in the world."[12] As the foil of the genre of Humanity that took its first steps on the deck of the slave ship, the Black populates the constitutive outside of Human society as not merely as a forced laborer or property but what Orlando Patterson has alternatively termed a "socially dead person."[13]

More than some theoretically souped-up suffering Olympics, however, the stakes of Afropessimism's contention that antiblackness coheres the world is clarity about what liberation for the "undeniable dark side of mankind" actually entails: not a struggle for civil rights, however comprehensive, but the end of the world. So Wilderson argues that a "Black radical agenda is terrifying to most people on the Left . . . because it emanates from a condition of suffering for which there is no imaginable strategy for redress—no narrative of social, political, or national redemption."[14] In other words, I heard a prophet from Galilee say, we "must be born again." We must shed western humanism and the non-Human foil on which it depends entirely. Coincidentally, environmentalism argues something similar, but with a different nonhuman in view; in the years since Du Bois's prophetic declaration about the color line, another hue has come to represent what many alternatively regard today, in the environmental crisis, as the organizing "problem" of the modern world.

Amid the growing awareness of anthropogenic climate change, environmental thought has challenged the world not only to think but to do most everything—including buy, vote, and live—*green*. As it has specifically come to dominate environmentalist discourse, this green has nothing immediately to do with the problem of racial difference originally outlined by the color line. Instead, its purview is the hierarchical relation between humanity and nature and the line, in western humanism, generally supposed to separate the two. Like the critique of the color line in black studies, environmentalism's critique of the human/nature binary also entails a rigorous critique of the human. But if the color line indexes a racialized Human enterprise grounded in antiblackness and white supremacy, green discourse alternatively emphasizes another malady at the heart of western humanism: namely anthropocentrism, or the centering of the human and the related exclusion and subjection of the nonhuman. One of the most well-known and significant challenges to anthropocentrism comes from celebrated green thinker and environmentalist Aldo Leopold. In his environmentalist classic, *A Sand County Almanac*, Leopold laments modern humanity's regard for land as little more than property and famously calls for *Homo sapiens* to shift "from conqueror of the land-community to plain member and citizen of it."[15] To do so, he argues that human beings must develop a "land ethic" that "simply enlarges the boundaries of community to include soils, waters, plants, and animals."[16] This ethical regard and care for "land," which Leopold employs as a synecdoche for all of nonhuman nature, represents the central intervention of green thought, in its critique of the fundamental antagonism between modern humanity and a nonhuman natural world regarded as little more than property.

In the academy, green thought finds its institutional home in "environmental studies." But the more specific effort to think the *environmental* human that would be fit for citizenship in Leopold's "land-community" proceeds under the rubric of the interdisciplinary thought project known as the "environmental humanities." Among the various disciplines that have thrown in with this project, the field of literary studies represents perhaps an unlikely contributor. Its deniers notwithstanding, the climate crisis is no fiction, and literary studies is firmly in the business of stories. Is it really prudent, then, to bring a book to a climate fight? Nevertheless, it is the conviction of "ecocriticism," a subfield of literary studies that analyzes the relationship between literature and the environment, that the "stories" we tell about nature significantly inform our relationship to it. Pioneering ecocritic Lawrence Buell, for example, argues that behind the climate crisis lies a deeper "crisis of imagination": "If, as environmental philosophers contend, Western metaphysics and ethics need revision before we can address today's environmental problems, then environmental crisis involves a crisis of the imagination the amelioration of which depends on finding better ways of imaging nature and humanity's relation to it."[17] Thus, the study of literature, as an archive of the imagination and its exploits, can reveal not only how we have tended to image "nature and humanity's relation to it" but also alternative images of the same. If, as Buell contends, "how we image a thing, true or false, affects our conduct towards it," then humanity's prospects for developing a "land ethic" significantly hinge, at least in part, on the interrogation of dominant representations of humanity's relationship to nature and the discovery of more ecologically salutary representations of the same.[18]

Like environmentalism, ecocriticism has also demonstrated partiality to the color green. Indeed, according to Jeffrey Cohen, "Green has long been the favored color of ecocriticism. A green reading offers an environment minded analysis of literature and culture, and is typically concerned with how nature is represented within a text and how modes of human inhabitance unfold within an imagined natural world."[19] Although such green readings represent a significant advance upon the neglect of the natural world as mere background, recent advances in ecocriticism have begun to trouble green's representational hegemony by interrogating the logic whereby this single color has come to stand in for a many-hued nature. Buell, for example, has argued that green has perhaps "been oversold as a lumping term, thereby foreshortening one's sense of other spectrum/spectral possibilities."[20] Further specifying green's limitations, Cohen argues that "green is also too solitary, a romantic color through which individuals commune with nature and arrive at personal revelations and solipsistic calm—as if nature were an angel or messenger. To obtain such revelatory power, the wilderness must be imagined as a purified place to which one travels rather than dwells always within: separate from the human, empty, foundationally pure."[21] According to Cohen, then, the romantic greenwashing of nature can ironically function to reify the very separation between humanity and nature that green thought is otherwise meant to disrupt. By canonizing a representation of nature that is not only most appealing to humanity but also most conducive to the aspirations of the individual, green (as opposed to the hues represented in Ishmael's aforementioned catalog of undesirable geographies) fails to advance significantly beyond anthropocentrism. Nature's overrepresentation as green reduces the nonhuman natural world to a superficial, one-note association with lushness and abundance. And just as the exaggerated verdancy of the New World historically provided ideological cover for the expropriation and over-extraction of Turtle Island, so, too, the overrepresentation of nature as a green wilderness we conserve "out there" belies the ongoing environmental degradation of the "right heres" we inhabit every day.

Furthermore, for Cohen, green's overrepresentation as environmentalism's preferred metaphor for sustainability "begs the question of exactly what mode of being we are attempting to sustain, and at what environmental cost."[22] Or to recall Buell's language, what image of "nature and humanity's relation to it." Further speaking to this incisive question, in a way that similarly challenges green's hegemony, is a group of scholars relatedly concerned with nature's overrepresentation as *land*. Critiquing what he labels ecocriticism's "terrestrial bias," Dan Brayton argues in *Shakespeare's Ocean*: "Ecocritical scholarship is held inward by a centripetal force, a core commitment to all that is *green* and lives on terra firma. The fetishization of the land . . . has limited the scope of ecocritical inquiry to terrestrial topics—the American West, Wordsworthian pastoral, Milton's and Shakespeare's woods and meadows. . . . While an appeal to the land is useful shorthand . . . this terrestrial bias also situates environmental scholarship and the subject of ecocritical inquiry on shore, banishing from view the sea and its intimate connection to terrestrial phenomena."[23] Hand in hand with nature's overrepresentation as green, then, is also its overrepresentation as terra firma and a consequent neglect of the ocean. A significant case in point, for Brayton, is Leopold's "land ethic." In his classic call to expand the "boundaries of community to include soils, waters, plants, and animals, or collectively: the land," Brayton notes how the "'waters' of the Earth are encompassed by the category of 'the land.'" So, Leopold elevates "the land" to a representational height out of all proportion with our blue planet and effectively relegates "the global ocean to a kind of conceptual netherworld."[24]

According to Brayton, however, this "terrestrial bias" and consequent neglect of the ocean is hardly limited to ecocriticism. Rather, it reflects the "longstanding cultural status of the sea in Western culture as a realm of chaos and radical alterity that can scarcely be conceived, much less domesticated."[25] Western civilization has long defined the ocean as an unnatural (or prenatural) void forever evincing a hostile alterity, a void lying eternally outside—or on the margins—of human social constructs. This mythology runs through Western culture from its inception on the shores of the eastern Mediterranean to its current dispersal along every shore of this planet. As Antonis Balasopoulos has observed, water—particularly the salt water of a threateningly immense global ocean—has traditionally been perceived as "an entity whose nature paradoxically contravenes the very idea of a stability-conferring foundation." The protean sea apparently undermines the human need for a solid ground of meaning.

If civil society is antiblack, perhaps it is also antiblue. As a "radical" and "hostile alterity" situated "eternally outside . . . of human *social* constructs," the ocean is strikingly analogous to blackness as the socially dead "foil of Humanity." If blackness represents the human face of absolute difference, then, according to Brayton's survey of the "longstanding cultural status of the sea in Western culture," the ocean can be recognized to furnish the nonhuman face of absolute difference. Of all of nonhuman nature, only it is characterized in *Moby-Dick* as "the dark side of earth." Also telling are the specific qualities driving the West's aversion to the ocean, namely its inability to be "domesticated" and its disappointment of "the human need for a *solid ground*," of not just "meaning" but presumably anything. At stake in the West's fetishization of land, then, or at least such land as can be romanticized as green is the desire for a docile surface. In this way, the synecdochic power of land to stand in for all of nature reveals less about land itself and more about the idealization of land by humans as the "bright" side of the planet in opposition to the "dark side" of the sea. It's this idealization of land as the good, ideal, and most of all docile sur/face of Earth that informs humanity's historical production of enough concrete to cover the entire surface of the planet in a layer two millimeters thick. A veritable planet Terra Firma that interpellates the Earth as a mere docile surface accommodating humanity's every bipedal whim. But exceeding even the planetary, the West's affinity for "land" can also be taken to name something more on the order of what Brayton labels a "terrestrial cosmology."[26] The overrepresentation of terra *firma* evidences a metaphysical and epistemological commitment to all that is solid, stable, and sure. Yet if our backs are to the sea in the culturally sustained way that Brayton argues, then the question arises: What are the implications of disproportionately imagining, with respect to land, life on a planet predominantly made of water?

There is perhaps no site more crucial to how we image "nature and humanity's relation to it" than the everyday interface between humans and nature at the planetary surface. In the overrepresentation of "green" and "the land," this surface is held out to us as little more than a docile surface. Although a significant advance beyond western humanism's failure to regard the biophysical environment at all, the mutual overrepresentation of these prevailing categories of environmental thought smuggles a subtle but damning bit of anthropocentrism into the green revolution. The prevailing image that they offer of "nature and humanity's relation to it" is one we might otherwise recognize in the surefooted human punctuating that iconic illustration of human evolution. You know the one. A simple Google Images search for "evolution" turns up countless variations of this ubiquitous image. In it, the theory that threatened to unmoor any fixed distinction between human and nonhuman has ironically been assimilated into the popular imagination as a visual representation instead of man's (and it is always a man pictured) triumphant separation: the achievement, in bipedalism, of a new and species-defining relation to the ground. What we see in this sure-footed, perfectly upright man—hands notoriously freed up to manipulate and instrumentalize, hold and possess—is not just the fruition of humanity as evolution's crown (the image usually projects no further evolution) but also, and less conspicuously, a perfectly docile planetary surface imagined to support man faithfully and without interruption along the way. Indeed, the original image, created by Rudolph Zallinger for Time-Life Books' *Early Man* (1965), was titled "The Road to Homo Sapiens"; its many variations have subsequently come to be more widely known throughout popular culture as "The March of Progress." What does it mean, then, that in perhaps *the* most iconic image of Man, nature shows up as a "road" upon which Man can "march"? That is, not merely as a flat surface but as a man-made and utterly docile surface. And this in spite of the prevailing understanding of an evolutionary process that begins not on land but at sea. Besides the animal life subordinated to humanity's becoming, this invisible platform is the only other place that nonhuman nature shows up. This image of the stand-your-ground subject can conserve, and even love, "the land" without ever essentially transforming the dominating structure of humanity's relation to it. The significance of this prevailing image of humanity's fundamental relation to the planet may not be readily apparent. But how else do we come to walk the earth with an outsize carbon *footprint* if not by first imagining that earth is primarily a place where creatures stand? Or even understand? One look at our blue planet is enough to correct this planetary dysmorphia. It is enough to say, with Arthur C. Clarke, "How inappropriate to call this planet 'Earth' when clearly it is 'Ocean.'"[27]

Against the grain of this long-standing green, or terrestrial, bias, however, the humanities have more recently witnessed a considerable "oceanic turn," owing to a wealth of scholars who have variously started to think *blue*. The beginning of this critical turn to the ocean can arguably be traced back to the ocean-centered historicism of Marcus Rediker and the broad influence of Paul Gilroy's *The Black Atlantic*. In the specific context of the environmental humanities, however, this turn has taken shape under the rubric of what Steve Mentz has labeled the "blue humanities," which he defines as "a current of scholarly and artistic discourses that foreground human relationships with water in all its forms" and that "self-consciously distinguishes itself from familiar terrestrial (or 'green') models of the relationship with the nonhuman environment."[28] Similarly, Hester Blum has put forward the term *oceanic studies* to name a study of the ocean that takes the sea and the material conditions of the maritime world as a "point of inquiry" unto itself, with "capacious possibilities for new relational forms" beyond the overdetermining logic of land and the nation-state.[29] Thus, in their mutual turn to the ocean, Mentz and Blum alike place special emphasis on the ocean's potential to recalibrate the terrestrial modes of relation we've adopted with respect to not only one another but also the nonhuman world. And what a radically different image we get of "nature and humanity's relation to it" when the human is put out to sea, when the bottom drops out for evolutionary man and he falls back in with the life of the globe.

II. (the ruse of) analogy

Whatever its shade, environmental thought is often guilty of imagining itself the *natural* successor to the color line as the defining problem of our times. Consider, for example, how Buell invokes the color line in *The Future of Environmental Criticism* (2005): "W. E. B. Du Bois predicted that the great public issue of the twentieth century would be the problem of the color line. In the century just begun, that problem shows no sign of abating. But ultimately a still more pressing question may prove to be whether planetary life will remain viable for most of the earth's inhabitants without major changes in the way we live now. Like racism, environmental crisis is a broadly cultural issue, not the property of a single discipline. All thinking persons have a stake in it."[30] Just as Du Bois predicted about the "Negro Problem" at the turn of the twentieth century, Buell forecasts at the turn of the twenty-first a kind of passing of the torch to the "still more pressing question" of environmental crisis. Although he acknowledges that the racial antagonism of the color line remains unresolved, Buell signals a necessary pivot at least in the priority of our thinking to the human/nature antagonism presently endangering all of planetary life. In this way, the passage above performs a kind of supersessionism, wherein environmental crisis comes not just to displace race as the foundational problem of our times but also hails the attention of thinking persons of the twenty-first century in a way *analogous* to race in the twentieth. The status of race as a global crisis is rhetorically put in the service of, and at the very same time subordinated to, our ability to appreciate the environmental crisis as a problem of like, and allegedly greater, magnitude. Because racism has been borne out by the twentieth century to be precisely the order of problem that can justly concern the thought of an entire century across disciplines, or put another way, because we have already experienced race as the sort of problem that concerns all of us to the extent that it structures and coheres the world, Buell is able to argue that the environmental crisis is "like racism" and hail "all thinking persons." Threatened with climate catastrophe, now all of humanity knows how it feels to be a problem.

Buell's invocation of the color line furnishes the latest example of liberalism's ritual enactment of what Wilderson has called the "ruse of analogy," which he theorizes as a frequently accessed on-ramp to legibility for various struggles that "mystifies, rather than clarifies, Black suffering."[31] According to Wilderson, "The ruse of analogy erroneously locates Blacks in the world—a place where they have not been since the dawning of Blackness. This attempt to position the Black in the world by way of analogy is not only a mystification, and often erasure, of Blackness's grammar of suffering (accumulation and fungibility or the status of being non-Human) but simultaneously also a provision for civil society, promising an enabling modality for Human ethical dilemmas."[32] The ruse of analogy, in other words, is a favorite means for civil society to expand and reform itself to include previously excluded Humans by means of an authenticating appeal to the example of black suffering. Yet if analogy, for these Humans, is enabling, for the Black it is mystifying due to its misapprehension of the structure of black suffering. In Wilderson's terms, it "locates Blacks in the world" and so, without ever having acknowledged, let alone redressed, their fundamental exclusion from the world, pretends an inclusion that is not just premature but (for the world) impossible. The latest ethical concern of the day gains social legibility by way of extending society's formal repudiation of antiblackness to what is represented as a like or equivalent instance of oppression: ____ *is the new Black*, the grammar of the ruse goes.[33] And its repertoire is just as likely to include liberal critiques of white supremacy that whitewash antiblackness as conservative complaints about reverse racism and the White Entertainment Television station missing from our TV dials. So civil society conservatively constricts or liberally expands in a tug-of-war helmed by aggrieved Humans, who sometimes are polite enough to tip their caps to the black bellhop on their way in or out the door.

Buell's practice of analogy similarly "mystifies, rather than clarifies, black suffering." His analogization of the environmental crisis, in which all thinking persons have an indiscriminate stake, and a generalized and nondescript "racism" mystifies antiblackness. Leopold yields another, if less explicit, instance of environmentalism's perpetuation of the "ruse of analogy" in his call for a "land ethic," which rhetorically depends on an analogy between environmental degradation and slavery. Leopold begins his chapter "The Land Ethic" in *A Sand County Almanac* by recounting a deep cut of Greek mythology, in which, after returning from the wars in Troy, Odysseus hangs a "dozen slave-girls of his household whom he suspected of misbehavior during his absence." Owing to their status as "human chattel," Leopold explains that Odysseus's actions "involved no question of propriety. . . . The disposal of property was then, as now, a matter of expediency, not of right and wrong."[34] Then, after noting how humans have evolved ethically beyond the moral outrage of owning other humans, Leopold asserts, "There is as yet no ethic dealing with man's relation to land and to the animals and plants which grow upon it. Land, *like* Odysseus' slave-girls, is still property."[35] Through analogy, then, Leopold solicits our empathy for land by characterizing it as the last slave standing in an otherwise fully emancipated world, the final frontier of the unfinished work of abolition. In this case, however, Leopold's practice of analogy mystifies not only black suffering but also arguably the environment's.

In his study of the practice of slavery across human history, which extends to antiquity, Orlando Patterson demonstrates that the slave in essence is neither property nor a forced laborer but, rather, a "socially dead person." According to Afropessimism's extension of Patterson's redefinition of slavery to black people postemancipation, Leopold's celebration of the end of slavery not only mystifies black suffering but, in another way, elides it altogether. Consider, for instance, that in order to retrieve a relevant example of "human chattels," Leopold reaches all the way back to antiquity. What of the human chattel suffering just a historical stone's throw away, in the century of Leopold's own birth? This oversight helps explain how he could confidently declare—before the Civil Rights Movement and in the middle of the same century whose organizing problem Du Bois recognized as the color line—that, having settled the question of intrahuman ethics, humanity now has only to evolve a land ethic that "*simply* enlarges the boundaries of community" to include the land.[36] Were the lines of human community so extended during the writing of *A Sand County Almanac* they would still be found to exclude those human non-Humans who in 1949 were just as excluded from human community as Leopold otherwise recognized "the land" to be? Acknowledging this, however, is not to deny modern humanity's need for a "land ethic." Rather, it is to stress that this ethical challenge cannot be faced without also attending to the unfinished question of intrahuman ethics. Environmental and human domination, it turns out, are more than related; they are a single operation that must be resolved not sequentially but together. Indeed, what if environmental crisis is "like racism" after all? Not as a pretext toward racism's ultimate displacement or the "ruse of analogy" but because environmental crisis *is* racism.

In *Race and Nature from Transcendentalism to the Harlem Renaissance* (2008), Paul Outka argues precisely this when he contends that "race and nature have been profoundly entangled—and bitterly divisive—constructions since the first European colonization of the 'New' World."[37] Further illuminating the nature of this entanglement, Outka argues that "not only did nature provide a critically important origin for the production of an essential blackness and a largely invisible whiteness, the naturalization of race allowed race and racial hierarchy to piggy-back on and recursively influence a preexisting and absolute human/natural hierarchy in ways that ecocritics are only beginning to consider."[38] What if racism and slavery appear analogous to environmental degradation because they are actually consubstantial parts of a single operation of nonhuman othering? Is it possible that antiblackness, even if unparalleled by the oppression of other Humans, claims a genuine analogy in the subjugation of nonhuman nature, which, it must be acknowledged, is just as non-Human as the Black? Buell certainly implies at least this much when he contends that the environmental crisis is "like racism." Yet by pivoting from one to the other, he blunts and mutes perhaps the most significant insight of their analogization: namely the recognition that these two problems are in fact one problem. Where we've otherwise apprehended only the racial antagonism between black/nonblack, or only the human/nature binary, have we actually beheld the same line as it might be recognized, in its broadest articulation, to differentiate between the Human and the non-Human? Or, given their recent penchant for multispecies thought, have the environmental humanities no more room in the stable for the non-Humans who have also historically (been) thrown in with nonhuman nature? Or has black studies nothing to say about the animals ranked alongside Frederick Douglass in the same "scale of being" or about the other nonhuman "cargo" brimming the holds of slave ships?[39]

It is important to remember that middle passing Africans were not the only cargo occupying the slave ship's hold nor the only nonhumans playing ballast to modern Humanity. Because there were also gold, sugar, tobacco, and cotton, the slave ship's hold must be understood as an operation of both human and environmental degradation, transforming both its human and nonhuman occupants into mere holdings, and lending material heft not just to the racial separation of the Human from other (less than or non) humans but also to the equally racial separation of the human (read: white) from the rest of nonhuman nature. Both the color line and the human/nature binary are embedded in the dividing partition of the hold/deck and, in it, gain unprecedented mobility, attaining, in their treks across the Atlantic, global, and not merely local, expression and significance. The hold and its non-Human cargo are central to any holistic account of the modern world. Indeed, Europe does not come into possession of roughly 85 percent of earth's lands by 1914 without it.[40] The capacity to possess the planet on this global scale starts small; it is worked out here against not just the black body but *all* of the non-Human occupants of the hold. And it's in view of this non-Human cohort gathered in the holds of the ships in motion across the Atlantic that I also wonder if the chronology suggested by Outka's contention that racial hierarchy piggybacks on a "*preexisting* and absolute human/natural hierarchy" may be, at least in some measure, more of a simultaneous operation. Whether the *H*uman/nature (if not the *h*uman/nature) binary emerges coterminously with the color line in a necessarily co-constitutive process. Although there are various expressions of a human/natural hierarchy that predate modern racism and antiblackness, the desacralized sense of the *entire* planet as property or else an extractable resource coincides not only with the rise of the *global* standard of Human being indexed by whiteness but also the expropriation of native lands and the enslavement of black bodies, with the latter, according to Dionne Brand, serving as "the tools sent out to conquer the natural world" and "perform the tasks of exploitation of resources."[41]

Still, if it is to be more than just a ruse, the analogization of environmental degradation to racism and slavery needs to be taken as far as Afropessimism takes the latter. Buell's ecocriticism and the environmentalism spawned by Leopold's "land ethic" must adopt a kind of *ecopessimism*: not the utterly hopeless doom and gloom surrounding our apocalyptic environmental futures—which, in contrast to native genocide or transatlantic slavery, betray a historical perspective that has never had to survive the end of the world—but an understanding that what Leopold characterizes as the "slaveness" of land inheres most essentially not in its status as property but in its "social death." The recognition that "the land," like the slave, is socially dead complicates the imagined possibility of its integration into human civil society, especially in the continuous and uninterrupted sense of a "land ethic" that "*simply* enlarges the boundaries of community to include . . . the land." If, as Afropessimism contends, civil society is not elastic enough to integrate the Black or the slave, which languishes as its constitutive outside, then whence comes environmentalism's optimism that it is elastic enough to incorporate "the land"? Like Afropessimism, then, ecopessimism contends that redress of the climate crisis also demands nothing short of the end of the world, because it posits that nonhuman nature cannot be integrated into the Human civil society that requires its exclusion as its very condition of possibility.

To realize a genuine advance beyond the "ruse of analogy," perhaps the most promising shade of environmental thought is not green but blue. This "void lying eternally outside—or on the margins—of human social constructs" assumes a relation to civil society uncannily reminiscent of the Black. As "that state of barbaric vagueness and disorder out of which civilization has emerged," it laps on shores of western civilization as its constitutive outside.[42] And relative to a greenwashed "land" that unwittingly tends to reify the human/nature hierarchy as the given and docile ground of Human civil society, "the dark side of earth" embodies nature's most remote and alien face. As the outside's most "out," in a manner similar to Afropessimism's understanding of blackness's unique status among all the colors of the rainbow coalition, blue furnishes another "foil of Humanity" as the face of nonhuman otherness par excellence. It is not for nothing that Melville writes in *Moby-Dick* that "the native inhabitants of the seas have ever been regarded with emotions unspeakably *unsocial* and repelling."[43] Or that prior to Christopher Columbus's fateful voyages, a geographic imagination prevailed in Europe that partitioned the earth into a binary of habitable land and utterly uninhabitable sea. Or that, even in challenging this understanding and the related presumption of the impossibility of land in the Western Hemisphere, Columbus purportedly reasoned that "nature could not have set things on Earth so out of proportion that there should be more water than land, which was intended for *life* and the creation of souls."[44] Absolutely unsocial, uninhabitable, and antagonistically opposed to Human life, blue is not the new black. Or even like black. Rather, blue *is* black, and black is blue. Together, and not in isolation, both bear the burden of representing non-Human difference, human and nonhuman alike, par excellence. Of furnishing the constitutive outside of the modern, Human, and *antiblack/blue* world.

Given the mutual exclusion of blackness and blue from the modern world, it's fitting that in Wilderson's own resort to analogy—when he writes, "It takes an *ocean* of violence to produce a slave"—he specifically invokes this blue.[45] Sure, the ocean is unfathomably large and here specifically lends its scale to our imagination of the scale of antiblack violence. But as Tiffany Lethabo King observes, "Water, most often the ocean, has been Black studies' most faithful metaphor."[46] In her own invocation of this analogy, Hortense Spillers reminds us why, in her oft-quoted reflection on Middle Passage: "Those African persons in 'Middle Passage' were literally suspended in the 'oceanic,' if we think of the latter in its Freudian orientation as an *analogy* for undifferentiated identity."[47] Spillers's "oceanic" points us to the literal ocean behind the "ocean of violence" that, according to Wilderson, it takes to produce a slave. Her analogic appeal to the "undifferentiated identity" of Sigmund Freud's "oceanic feeling" furnishes an uneasy analogy for the lived experience of middle passing Africans insofar as their experience of the ocean was not merely metaphoric but literal: not just *like* an oceanic encounter, and evocative of that encounter's association, in psychoanalysis, with the dissolution of individual subjectivity, but a physical encounter with the ocean. For middle passing Africans, the "oceanic feeling" was subtended by material reality. Perhaps more than anything else, it's this materiality that makes the analogy of black and blue more than a ruse.

This black-and-blue reframing of the color line, of a modern world mutually organized against the "dark side of mankind" and the "dark side of earth," can be fruitfully interrogated through a black-and-blue ecocritical study of *Moby-Dick*. Buell has already helped us understand how the study of literature, as a ready-made archive of images of "nature and humanity's relation to it," is ideally suited to contend with the "crisis of imagination" behind the environmental crisis. At least part of this crisis of imagination, according to the critique of "terracentrism" elaborated in oceanic studies and the blue humanities, entails having disproportionately imagined, with respect to land, human life on an overwhelmingly blue planet. If, in its characterization of the ocean as "the dark side of earth," *Moby-Dick* seems to exemplify this disavowal of the ocean, the novel's near ubiquity throughout the blue humanities and oceanic studies otherwise attests to its significance as what Mentz has dubbed the "urtext of the human encounter with the ocean."[48] Indeed, the novel's explicit avowal of "the watery part of the world" and related critique of "landsmen" not only interrupt the West's "terrestrial bias" but also initiate a blue recalibration of the human.

III. landsmen

After William Shakespeare's ocean, ecocritics calling for a Copernican shift from an environmental study of literature that revolves around terra firma to one that proportionately attends to the ocean find perhaps their most canonical vindication in Melville's ocean.[49] With a bibliography that includes such maritime texts as *Moby-Dick*, *Billy Budd, Sailor*, and *Benito Cereno*, along with deeper cuts like *Omoo: A Narrative of Adventures in the South Seas* and *Mardi: And a Voyage Thither*, the ocean eclipses Melville's literary oeuvre as overwhelmingly as the earth's surface.[50] Given his sustained preoccupation with the ocean, the celebrated bard of the "watery part of the world" is rightly reverenced as ubiquitously as he is across oceanic studies and the blue humanities. The conspicuous oceanic emphasis of his fiction in many ways anticipates and enacts what we've already considered as the call by those fields for an oceanic recalibration of western culture's animating "terrestrial bias." Yet of all his aqueous works, nowhere does Melville's ocean roll more profoundly than in that whale of a book, *Moby-Dick*. The novel's famous opening wastes little time declaring its affinity for the sea: "Call me Ishmael. Some years ago—never mind how long precisely—having little or no money in my purse, and nothing particular to interest me on shore, I thought I would sail about a little and see the watery part of the world. . . . With a philosophical flourish Cato throws himself upon his sword; I quietly take to the ship. There is nothing surprising in this. If they but knew it, almost all men in their degree, some time or other, cherish very nearly the same feelings towards the ocean with me."[51] Although a canonical work of western literature, *Moby-Dick* opens with a profound reversal of the West's "terrestrial bias." Whereas Brayton illuminates how the West has long defined the ocean as a "void," for Ishmael, it is rather land that has "*nothing* particular to interest" him.[52] Instead, Ishmael professes his affection for the "watery part of the world" and, what's more, speculates that such affection is shared by "all men," "if they but knew it." This begs the question: Why don't they? If some degree of affinity for the ocean is indeed universal to humans, how have they otherwise come to lose it in the way that Ishmael implies and such that the West could be broadly recognized, by Brayton and others, to betray a profound "terrestrial bias"?

Although it employs different language, *Moby-Dick* displays an investment in unsettling humanity's "terrestrial bias" through repeated, and generally critical, allusions to a class of people the novel calls "landsmen." Almost totally absent from the lifeworld of a novel in which every man is basically a seaman, "landsmen" constitute an extradiegetic presence, which the narrator generally addresses or otherwise invokes in the mode of apology. For instance, after lamenting how whaling "has somehow come to be regarded among *landsmen* as a rather unpoetical and disreputable pursuit," Ishmael asserts, "I am all anxiety to convince ye, ye *landsmen*, of the injustice hereby done to us hunters of whales."[53] Elsewhere, Ishmael similarly comes to the defense of the titular whale, Moby Dick, by declaring, "So ignorant are most *landsmen* of some of the plainest and most palpable wonders of the world, that . . . they might scout at Moby Dick as a monstrous fable."[54] Perhaps the most telling invocation of "landsmen" occurs in the novel's fifty-eighth chapter, "Brit." There, we find Ishmael advocating for the ocean in an extended meditation that, even as it bespeaks an intractable antagonism between landsmen and the sea, also gestures to a kind of oceanic indigeneity that so-called landsmen have managed to forget:

> But though, to *landsmen* in general, the native inhabitants of the seas have ever been regarded with emotions unspeakably unsocial and repelling; though we know the sea to be an everlasting terra incognita, so that Columbus sailed over numberless unknown worlds to discover his one superficial western one; though, by vast odds, the most terrific of all mortal disasters have immemorially and indiscriminately befallen tens and hundreds of thousands of those who have gone upon the waters; though but a moment's consideration will teach, that however baby man may brag of his science and his skill, and however much, in a flattering future, that science and skill may augment; yet for ever and for ever, to the crack of doom, the sea will insult and murder him, and pulverize the stateliest, stiffest frigate he can make; nevertheless, by the continual repetition of these very impressions, man has lost that sense of the full awfulness of the sea which *aboriginally* belongs to it.[55]

On its surface, Ishmael's characterization of the ocean seems merely to echo, rather than to unsettle or disrupt, the way we've previously heard Brayton describe the long-standing status of the sea in western culture. For instance, where else but "eternally outside—or on the margins—of human *social* constructs" lies a marine world that Ishmael describes as "unspeakably *unsocial* and repelling"? Or what but a "hostile alterity" will "for ever and for ever, to the crack of doom . . . insult and murder"?[56] This characterization of the sea as what Ishmael goes on to describe as "such a foe to man who is an *alien* to it" seems to contradict the affection for the ocean expressed at the beginning of the novel. In its place we find an intractable antagonism that more than warrants the antipathy for the ocean that Brayton recognizes as endemic to western culture. Nor is it that humans have no reason to regard the ocean apprehensively. As air-breathing creatures, humans are unable to live at sea very long without some mediating assistance. Still, as much as the "conceptual alterity" of the ocean can be attributed to its empirical qualities as a place inhospitable to human life, that alterity, in Brayton's estimation, is also a "culturally constructed notion."[57] Although a cursory reading of the antagonistic depiction of the ocean in "Brit" may suggest otherwise, Ishmael ultimately implies something similar when he suggests that it is not the ocean itself, but rather "the continual repetition of . . . *impressions*" thereof, that has compromised humanity's "sense of the full awfulness of the sea." Presumably, what is true of the sea's awfulness is also true of the affection for the ocean that, in the opening sentences of the novel,

Ishmael speculates all humans share, "if they but knew it." In a novel that so foregrounds its affinity for the ocean, perhaps we should suspect that Ishmael represents the antagonism between humanity and the ocean not to reify it but ultimately to call it into question, by demystifying the common sense of humanity's exclusive identification with land. For how "unsocial" can the ocean really be to a humanity who shares with it a larger earth and whose life not only evolutionarily derives from but, in global processes like the hydrological cycle, is also sustained by the ocean?

With his gesture to "impressions," Ishmael, like Brayton, ultimately attributes humanity's enduring antagonism with and alienation from the ocean not to any essential or natural alterity inhering in the ocean itself but rather to the repetition of humanity's perceptions of the ocean and itself in relation to the ocean. Furthermore, it is no passing detail that this antagonistic regard for the ocean is attributed not to humanity in general but specifically "to *landsmen*." In the watery world of *Moby-Dick*, it's specifically those humans who would reckon themselves utter landsmen that are locked in an eternal antagonism with the sea. It is to them, in particular, that marine worlds are "unspeakably unsocial and repelling" and their landlocked "flattering future" that the ocean is said to frustrate. On the one hand, "landsmen" can seem the general rule of a species for which seamen are rather the exception. The designation appears to afford no more specificity than "men" might. Insofar as humans are land creatures, "landsmen" can sound almost perfectly redundant. A pleonasm akin to burning fire, in which "land" offers no *new* information about the "men" it modifies. Yet, aside from Ishmael's generally critical usage of the designation, in "Brit" "landsmen" come to be explicitly identified with Columbus, who, in Ishmael's rather unflattering account, "sailed over numberless unknown worlds to discover his one superficial western one." Rather than a perfect synonym for humans, Ishmael more specifically positions landsmen as descendants of Columbus and inheritors of the "superficial western" world spawned by his fateful voyage. And, where we've previously witnessed the uncritical celebration of Columbus's voyage in Arnold Guyot's *The Earth and Man* or even Henry David Thoreau's "Walking," Ishmael unflatteringly characterizes Columbus's voyage as a geographic oversight. Not only does Ishmael, in this way, allude to Columbus's notorious navigational blunder—the shallow knowledge of Earth whereby the celebrated navigator set out for India and accidentally arrived in a hemisphere of which Europe was yet unaware—but he recasts this geographic oversight as a literal matter of overlooking the ocean and, with it, its "numberless unknown worlds." Columbus's "superficial western *one*," in contrast and to its discredit, can be counted on a single finger. Through this critical allusion to Columbus's "discovery" of the New World, Ishmael gestures to the historical processes that have contributed to the West's oversight of the ocean and overidentification with land. These processes are namely the historical advent of white settler colonialism and coloniality's "superficial" apprehension of the planet as a mere surface, whose depths are acknowledged only insofar as they might be *surfaced* or extracted. By Ishmael's account, landsmen and their antipathy for and estrangement from the ocean are not the rule of the human species but rather the outcome of a shallow apprehension of the planet inaugurated by Columbus and elaborated through a colonial disavowal of depth and multiplicity originally worked out against the ocean.

If the empirical realities that account for the conceptual alterity of the ocean in western culture find straightforward expression in the capacity of Melville's ocean to "murder," the alterity that the ocean otherwise accrues due to cultural construction in its frustration of the colonial ambitions of landsmen can be recognized to inhere in the "insults" that the ocean adds to this injury. An ocean whose inscrutable billows roll an "everlasting terra incognita," for instance, insults a western geographic imagination that has otherwise aspired to the finished work of "the *known* world." This classic shorthand for the extent of a given period's geographic knowledge betrays a will to know the planet as cartographic fact, to speak the *one*, final word about a planet that is perhaps better apprehended as an inexhaustible mystery. Moreover, an ocean that thwarts the "flattering future" of landsmen similarly insults the West's fetishization of progress with an unrelenting past it can't get past. Later in "Brit," Ishmael makes this insult plainer, when he exclaims, "Yea, foolish mortals, Noah's flood is not yet subsided; two thirds of the fair world it yet covers."[58] So the primeval seascape of Melville's ocean remains stubbornly unintegrated into the linear march of history. Its "two thirds of the fair world" hold the planet hostage as a revolving relic.

Perhaps the ocean's greatest insult to landsmen, however, is that it precipitates their devolution into "baby man." By invalidating their progress and restoring landsmen to the historical immaturity otherwise attributed to the nonwhite humans variously demeaned by the West as native, savage, or aboriginal, Melville's ocean functions similarly to the foil that civilization claims in the "state of nature." In social contract theory, the "state of nature" refers to a hypothetical era of human existence before the advent of laws and government, which Thomas Hobbes famously characterized as "a time of war, where every man is enemy to every man," when "the life of man" was "solitary, poor, nasty, brutish, and short."[59] Hobbes's classic description of the "state of nature" as a barbaric state of "perpetual war" bears a striking resemblance to how Ishmael subsequently describes in "Brit" the "universal cannibalism of the sea; all whose creatures prey upon each other, carrying on eternal war since the world began."[60] Yet, while humans can exit the "state of nature" by forming governments, the ocean constitutes a permanent "state of nature" that, for good measure, is also conspicuously marked by the scarlet letter of cannibalism. As demonstrated by Ishmael's first contact with Queequeg, cannibalism is a familiar suspicion that the West has historically directed toward "uncivilized" and "savage" humans dwelling in a permanent (at least without western intervention) "state of nature." Perhaps it was with passages like Ishmael's description of the ocean's "eternal war" in mind that W. H. Auden wrote: "The sea, in fact, is that state of barbaric vagueness and disorder out of which civilization has emerged and into which, unless saved by the effort of gods and men, it is always liable to relapse. It is so little of a friendly symbol that the first thing which the author of the Book of Revelation notices in his vision of the new heaven and earth at the end of time is 'there was no more sea.'"[61] Something like this western apprehension toward the sea as the defining foil of human civilization can also be witnessed in the lesser-known and even less often sung second verse of the US national anthem, in which the undecided fate of a burgeoning nation is obscured by the foreboding "mists of the deep":

> On the shore dimly seen through the mists of the deep
> Where the foe's haughty host in dread silence reposes,
> *What is that* which the breeze, o'er the towering steep,
> As it fitfully blows, half conceals, half discloses?
> Now it catches the gleam of the morning's first beam,
> In full glory reflected now shines in the stream,
> *'Tis the star-spangled banner*—O long may it wave
> O'er the land of the free and the home of the brave!

The first half of the verse centers around a question—"What is that?"—whose interrogative drama transfers the historic antagonism of the British during the War of 1812 onto the Atlantic Ocean, whose "mists" obscure the US flag. The second half of the verse resolves this initial uncertainty with a triumphant answer: "'Tis the star-spangled banner." In sharp contrast to the initial question and its association with an ominous deep, the verse concludes with the triumphant image of the flag waving over "the *land* of the free." So in "The Star-Spangled Banner," the United States wrests its national being from the obscurity of the ocean in just the same way that Auden recognizes civilization to emerge out of the sea's "barbaric *vagueness* and disorder."

The antipathy for the ocean that Auden recognizes in the end, when "there was no more sea," process theologian Catherine Keller also recognizes *in the beginning*. In her book *The Face of the Deep* (2002), Keller illuminates the theological roots of the West's anxiety toward the ocean in a Christian doctrine of creation that systematically disavows the primeval sea of Genesis 1:2. In this verse, the spirit of God hovers over "the face of the deep" (*tehom* in Hebrew) and winces not. Yet according to Keller, the reigning Christian doctrine of creation ex nihilo (from nothing) has "systematically and symbolically sought to erase" the deep as disconcerting evidence of divine contingency. Because it precedes God's spoken creation ("and God said let there be"), Keller argues that the deep short-circuits the logic of divine omnipotence and sovereignty whereby God is imagined to have unilaterally created everything from nothing. Moreover, she argues that the stakes of this theological oversight exceed the realm of theology by tracing how this theo-logic gradually assumed modern, and later secular, form, in a concept and ethic of creation whereby "every kind of western originality" supposes itself to manifest "the new as if from nothing, cutting violently, ecstatically free of the abysms of the past." If, according to Keller, "it is theology that taught the West to shun the depths of creation," then Columbus proved an excellent student in what Melville represents as his oversight of the ocean.[62] What better primer than "tehomophobia"—Keller's term for the "systemic repression" of the primordial sea of Genesis—for a not incidentally Christian Europe's genocidal erasure of numberless indigenous worlds to establish its superficial western one.[63] In its expropriation of indigenous land and obliteration, in the process, of indigenous "land-communities" far older than Leopold thought to acknowledge, white settler colonialism acquits itself as a necessarily superficial enterprise, which apprehends the entire planet as a mere surface either to own or extract. What are landsmen, then, if not settlers by another name? Not the rule of a species but what Wynter might describe as a specific "genre" of humanity so thoroughly identified with the West's shallow colonial interpellation of land that it can conceive of no viable life outside of its ontological element. And this, strictly speaking, is not land, which is far from a docile surface, so much as it is the human impression of land given in and as terra firma.

IV. Planet Terra Firma

If Ishmael historicizes and therefore demystifies the apparent pleonasm of landsmen and their natural antagonism with the ocean, further along in "Brit" he also denaturalizes the land/sea binary which not only logically coheres this antagonism to begin with but arguably also warps our overall "sense of planet."[64] Just as with humanity's alienation from the ocean, a geographic common sense prevails with respect to this binary too, which takes for granted the general partitioning of our planet into the mutually exclusive domains of land and sea. Under deeper scrutiny, however, elements of the land/sea binary begin to cede their geographic facticity to social construction. Ishmael begins to disarticulate the common sense of the land/sea binary when, again in defense of the ocean, he asks: "Wherein differ the sea and the land, that a miracle upon one is not a miracle upon the other? Preternatural terrors rested upon the Hebrews, when under the feet of Korah and his company the live ground opened and swallowed them up for ever; yet not a modern sun ever sets, but in precisely the same manner the live sea swallows up ships and crews."[65] Here, Ishmael alludes to a strange episode in Judeo-Christian sacred text when land was seen to behave in a manner more readily associated with the ocean. We expect the ocean to open up. But the terror of unwanted immersion in the ocean contrasts sharply with our comparatively pedestrian experiences and expectations of land. Yet far from supplying further justification for landsmen's antipathy for an ocean that "swallows up ships and crews," Ishmael's allusion to an episode of Hebrew mythology that suspends the most basic difference between land and sea, so far as the human biped is concerned, raises the question of the absoluteness of their differentiation. Against the grain of a planet partitioned into the mutually exclusive categories of land and sea, where humanity either stands or founders, respectively, not only does Ishmael cite a moment when land was known to open up as well as ocean, but he rhetorically fashions the capacity to open up as proof of life. By opening up, ground demonstrates that it is "*live* ground" and the ocean "*live* sea." This life, made powerfully evident in an opening that discloses depth and interiority, represents what land and sea share across their supposed binary opposition, in their mutual constitution of not a docile but a *live* surface, containing land, sea, and more. That land and sea alike open up, as the former has been witnessed to do during earthquakes—when the liveness of the ground is unmistakable—leads Ishmael to question the absoluteness of a land/sea binary that, once again, can be discovered to be rooted more in repeated impressions than hard empirical fact. Taken together, land and sea constitute so singsongy a pair of antonyms that their opposition can seem beyond reproach. They settle nicely into a totalizing geographic optic as old as God's utterance in Genesis: "'Let the waters under the heavens be gathered together into one place, and let the dry *land* appear'; and it was so. And God called the dry *land* Earth, and the gathering together of the waters He called Seas. And God saw that *it was* good."[66] But if land and sea alike are good, perhaps the prevailing sense of the binary opposition to which this divine geo-logic has arguably given rise is not.

As much as the land/sea binary appears grounded in physical reality, the binary opposition of the two elements obscures what, in fact, is their profound interrelation. Whole-earth processes, like the hydrological cycle, for instance, no more countenance the division between land and sea than that between national borders. And mountain ranges like the Himalayas, which tower above sea level as perhaps terra firma's greatest flourish—consist of rocks that once rested at the bottom of the ocean and were heaved skyward by millions of years of plate tectonics.[67] Together with more basic geographic phenomena like groundwater and the ocean floor, these peculiarities of Earth unsettle the common sense of at least the absoluteness of the differentiation between land and sea that would imply utter separation. Moreover, in its function as an all-encompassing planetary optic, the land/sea binary can also be recognized to perform subtle ideological work in support of the West's terrestrial bias. First, it can imply a sense of land and sea as two halves of a whole when, in reality, the planet's geographic deck is overwhelmingly stacked in the ocean's favor. Second, this binary in many ways mystifies a complex planetary surface whose manifold forms do not always fit the neat categorization of land and sea. Tiffany King makes a similar point in her meditation on the geographic formation of the "shoal," which is both land and sea.[68] In this regard, perhaps geography's *land and sea* is critical race studies' *black and white* or gender studies' *male and female*—and in need of just as much trouble. Maybe earth is also nonbinary, and collapsing a dynamic and heterogenous planetary surface—consisting of swamp, wetland, desert, beach, shoal, and so on—into the totalizing binary of land and sea works only to impoverish and warp our overall "sense of planet."[69] The simple rebranding of *Earth* as *Ocean* by Arthur C. Clarke does not fully redress this problem because such a reversal leaves the land/sea binary intact, and in a superficial western world, landsmen *stand* just as much estranged from land as they do the sea, even if their disavowal of the sea is the primary means by which they have come to turn their backs on a live surface. This is to say that even earth isn't the earth the West wants it to be. Its historical and cultural estrangement from the ocean—and with it, depth itself—has begotten a humanism that is as alien to dry land as it is to ocean; both estrangements must be reconciled if we are to reimagine the human as a genuine inhabitant of not just our blue but, more wholistically, our deep planet.

How western humanism can, in addition to being estranged from the ocean, also be estranged from the land it has otherwise been argued to fetishize has to do with a final way in which the land/sea binary may be understood to warp our overall "sense of planet": by subscribing humanity to a vision of land and sea caricatured by their anthropocentric opposition. In the episode of sacred

Judeo-Christian text to which Ishmael alludes above, the prevailing sense of a sea that unwaveringly opens and swallows and land that unfalteringly supports obscures not only how land is also known to open up, for instance in earthquakes or quicksand, but also the 15 percent of the ocean that is covered in sea ice. And where the ocean does open, humans can be swallowed, but they can also swim, float, and dive. Bipedalism is hardly the only living way to interface with a live surface, and immersion is not always or only unto death. Thus, the land/sea binary mystifies both the land and the ocean by constituting the latter as a pure opening or void that only assails humans and the former as a pure surface that only supports humans. We have already attended to the caricatured status of the ocean in western culture as the "unspeakably unsocial" "foe to man." Yet rather than being internal to itself, that caricature is realized through a mutual and related caricature of land as terra firma.

"Terra firma" masquerades as geographic fact, but it exists nowhere on earth so much as in the minds of landsmen. As the ocean's supposed geographic other, it names not "land" but an idealized human experience of land as firm or stable and thus suitable to humans. The masquerade mostly goes unchallenged, unless we have occasion to experience those phenomena of ground that disrupt our standing and understanding. How thoroughly unsettling it can be to feel the primeval stillness of ground suddenly lurch beneath our feet. Such phenomena are so removed from our everyday expectations of the planet's surface that, for the interval, we are elsewhere, *alienated*, and might just as well be on Mars as on Earth. There is little wonder why this would be the case for a species that, in its ableist self-understanding, typically finds itself in the fullness of its powers when standing on its own two feet. That is, when assuming the biped's propulsive interface with the planet and not another, least of all the horizontal position of sleep or death. Standing, we separate ourselves from the pack, freed everywhere but at our Achilles' heel of the vulnerability of creaturely contingency. But falling, we fall back in with and are swallowed up by what Arnold Guyot once described, in a beautiful turn of phrase and early expression of US ecological thought, as the "perpetual play" of the "life of the globe."[70] What need have we as a species for Icarus's wings, when the subtler prosthesis of ground does the job well enough? We touch our feet to the ground to go forward or fly or even, as the controversial phrase goes, to stand our ground. The choreography of this reigning performance of human bipedalism enacts a verticality that is crucial to sustaining the material conditions whereby the ecologics of separation, arguably at the heart of western metaphysics, is even thinkable. As a prelude to verticality, each step enlists the planetary surface into a literalization of the human/nature or human/nonhuman binary, naturalized at the very site where it might otherwise be questioned. Much more intimacy beyond the launching pads of our feet, as when dirt begins to rub off on us, can even signal a failure of civilization.

Yet alienating as it may be, earth doesn't cease to be earth when it fails to accommodate the human aspiration to stand. Rather, it ceases to be earth to and for us, which is arguably what *terra firma* ultimately names: not only, according to the *Oxford English Dictionary*, "dry or firm land" suited to human bipedalism but also the "land as distinguished from the sea." Thus, *terra firma* caricatures land as a docile surface but in a way that depends on an opposing caricature of the ocean as its geographic other. Yet, if terra firma is a work of imagination rather than geology, it is also important to recognize, just as Barbara and Karen Fields have argued about race, how "real action creates evidence for the imagined thing."[71] Beside "racecraft," then, we have also to consider a kind of *earthcraft* by which humanity constantly works to create and solidify the world it wants. Perhaps the greatest testament to such earthcraft is the fact that humans have historically produced enough concrete to cover the entire surface of the planet in a layer two millimeters thick.[72] If *terra firma* names anything, it's this straitjacket with which Humanity has attempted to wrangle a blue planet into a veritable Planet Terra Firma. This vision of Earth as a perfectly docile surface has now dumped so much "factitious evidence for itself into the real world" that it is quite possible to forget that our planet's surface is actually much more outlandish than not.[73] With such planetary dysmorphia, perhaps landsmen, and not the ocean, are the real aliens.

Yet another example of what I've labeled Planet Terra Firma is a map representing eighteenth- and nineteenth-century shipping routes that is featured in Simon Lewis and Mark Maslin's *The Human Planet* (2018). In that book, Lewis and Maslin credit the ship-mediated "collision of Europe and the Americas" beginning in 1492 with the inauguration of a new geological epoch: what scientists have taken to calling the Anthropocene, or literally "the age of man." According to Lewis and Maslin, "What plate tectonics did over tens of millions of years is being undone by shipping in a few centuries and aviation in a few decades. We are creating a New Pangea. This fits one of the hallmarks of a new epoch, as it is a geologically significant change to life on Earth."[74] Thus, in addition to the historical, cultural, and political significance of ships, we further have to appreciate their geological import—the equal, in their capacity to reconstitute the surface of the planet, of tectonic plates. When represented on a map, the transoceanic traffic of these ships presents a vision of the planet as one uninterrupted landmass. For example, when

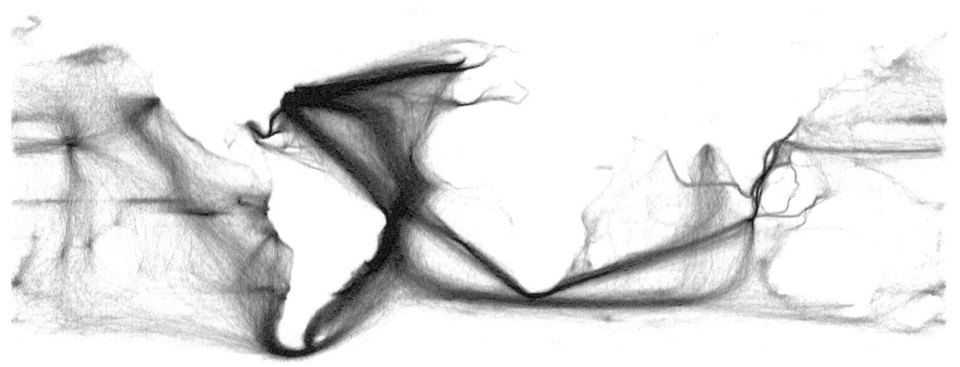

FIGURE 2.1. Digitized map of eighteenth- and nineteenth-century shipping routes. Benjamin M. Schmidt, Ghost Shipping Map, deck 701, 2018, https://creatingdata.us/ghostmaps.

viewed on a map leaving both land and sea as negative space, lines representing eighteenth- and nineteenth-century shipping routes fill the space typically occupied by the oceans to the extent of constituting a full oceanic eclipse, in contrast to which one can clearly make out the outlines of the continents (figure 2.1).[75] The legacy of this effacement of the ocean is further memorialized in the abundance of colonial world atlases appearing in the wake of the "discovery" of the Western Hemisphere, many of whose oceans are conspicuously littered with representations of ships that, particularly when scale is taken into account, rival islands and imitate their geographic permanence.[76] Like so many artificial Bering Straits eclipsing the blue void of the sea, ships do more than reinaugurate the old Pangea of our deep geological past. For even Pangea had its ocean. The geological feat of ships is more impressive still, for once they rested from their re-creation of Earth into a "New Pangea," "there was no more sea."[77]

If a sustained cultural disavowal of the ocean in the West is at least part of how we've arrived at a prevailing vision of Earth and humanity respectively as a docile surface supporting a stand-your-ground subject, then a deep and proportionate regard for the ocean, such as what oceanic studies and the blue humanities prescribe, is certainly key to reimagining the human as an inhabitant of our blue planet. But in this oceanic turn, we should be sensitive to how our regard for a "live sea" can also better attune us to the depth and life of equally "live ground." This is the deep study of Ishmael in *Moby-Dick*: not a simple inversion of the West's total identification with the land but the disarticulation of a land/sea binary that mystifies both.

Humanity's overrepresentation as landsmen in "Brit" otherwise belies the chapter's ultimate claim that "man has lost that sense of the full awfulness of the sea which *aboriginally* belongs to it." That is, "from the very beginning."[78] Significantly, everywhere else that variations of the root word *aboriginal* occur throughout *Moby-Dick*, they are explicitly in reference to either native peoples or their lands. Hence, we hear Ishmael speak of "aboriginal whalemen, the Red Men," and "natives of the Manillas," as well as "forests" and "groves." And on one other occasion, we hear Ishmael speak of the "ghostly aboriginalness of earth's primal generations."[79] One possible interpretation of the word's occurrence in "Brit" is that "awfulness" is "aboriginal" to the sea, and upstart landsmen have lost touch with that awfulness. But if, as Ishmael speculates in the beginning of *Moby-Dick*, "all men . . . cherish . . . feelings towards the ocean," then a sense of the sea's awfulness can also be said to belong to humans aboriginally in a way that gestures to a kind of oceanic indigeneity.[80] An awareness of the ocean that is not merely familiar but *indigenous* to human beings. Not merely a possession, had and then lost, but something that resides on the ontological ground floor of our species, more inalienable to whatever we are than even the rights of man, especially as those rights come to be aesthetically grounded in a complimentary vision of the ground as a docile surface. Moreover, what is true in "Brit" only of the sea's "awfulness," we can safely presume, is also true of the affection for the ocean that, according to Ishmael, all humans cherish "if they but knew it."[81] Thus, the full scope of Ishmael's musings about the ocean's "awfulness" suggests a human oceanic indigeneity that, to echo Equiano's language, is conceived as much in "astonishment" as in "terror."[82] If the superficial western world has come to know itself in and through an exclusive identification with terra firma, then it is not due to a natural alienation from the ocean nor to something that the human has utterly lost. Rather, it is due to the repression of something that the human *is*: a kind of "native inhabitant of the seas" in our own right.[83]

What greater iconoclasm for the prevailing vision of the human as an utter landsman than this oceanic indigenization of the human, by which "Brit" does not reify so much as disarticulate the common sense of modern humanity's overidentification with the land and disidentification with the ocean? In the context of a larger novel that immediately professes its oceanic allegiance and, after taking to the ship, never returns, "Brit" represents an important part of what can be recognized as the novel's broader aesthetic effort to blue the human. Just as the oceanic indigeneity of the human in "Brit" turns on the word *aboriginally*, the novel's broader bluing of the human can likewise be recognized to proceed not by way of the kin of Columbus in the novel—Ishmael, Ahab, or the mates—but by way of those alternatively and derogatorily known to western civilization as *aboriginals*, namely the Pequod's tetrad of "pagan harpooneers." Relative to the superficial western world of Columbus's kin, the native harpooneers' deep intimacy with the earth yields a significant proxy for the novel's broader effort to indigenize the human to the ocean. Yet even above the harpooneers, the reconciliation of estranged landsmen to the "dark side of earth" curiously reaches its representational apotheosis in a character that likewise hails from the "dark side of mankind." I am thinking, here, not of the indigenous African harpooneer Daggoo but of the "poor little negro" Pip. The castaway of the entire world. Our Topsy of the sea.[84]

V. Pip

All the world's the deck of the *Pequod*. Or so it appears in chapter 40 of *Moby-Dick*, where the novel assumes the form of a play and the *Pequod* becomes a literal stage. In this chapter, a crew that (aside from the narrator, captain, mates, and harpooneers) is generally silent throughout the novel steps to the mic one by one in a veritable who's who of humanity hailing from every corner of the globe. In place of conventional names, these otherwise silent sailors are identified instead by their country or place of origin. For instance, it's in this chapter that we witness the dialogic exchange between Daggoo and the Spanish Sailor who demeans the race of the former as "the undeniable dark side of mankind." The Spanish Sailor is joined by numerous other sailors, who are similarly identified: Nantucket, Dutch, French, Iceland, Maltese, Sicilian, Long-Island, Azore, China, Lascar, Tahitian, Portuguese, Danish, English, St. Jago's, and finally, Belfast Sailor. Yet if all the world's the deck of the *Pequod*, it is far from any *united* nations.[85] In fact, as can already be partially discerned from the insult of the Spanish Sailor, life together aboard the *Pequod* is beset by the color line (and more divisions besides) in every instantiation we've surveyed previously. And they all come to an illuminating head in Captain Ahab's prosthetic "bone leg," and his larger prosthetic conscription of the *Pequod* and its crew to support his stand-your-ground subjectivity.

Perhaps Captain Ahab's single most identifying feature is "the barbaric white leg upon which he partly stood." This prosthetic leg bespeaks the novel's central antagonism between humanity and nature. Fashioned "from the polished bone of the sperm whale's jaw," Ahab's prosthetic, on the one hand, alludes to the circumstances whereby he originally lost his leg, which was bitten off by the eponymous sperm whale, Moby Dick. On the other hand, as a violent appropriation of the cause of his lameness, and because he also has a "quiver of 'em," it also registers Ahab's monomaniacal desire to take revenge on Moby Dick. Supported exclusively by the jawbones of slain sperm whales, Ahab's stand is itself a vindictive expression of, and down payment on, his vengeance. Surely, it is no coincidence that in our first narrative sighting of Captain Ahab, Ishmael calls special attention to Ahab's "singular posture," which, in addition to his "bone leg," is further aided by a curious feature of the *Pequod*'s deck:[86]

> I was struck by the singular posture he maintained. Upon each side of the Pequod's quarter deck, and pretty close to the mizzen shrouds, there was an auger hole, bored about half an inch or so, into the plank. His bone leg steadied in that hole; one arm elevated, and holding by a shroud; Captain Ahab stood erect, looking straight out beyond the ship's ever-pitching prow. There was an infinity of firmest fortitude, a determinate, unsurrenderable wilfulness, in the fixed and fearless, forward dedication of that glance. Not a word he spoke; nor did his officers say aught to him; though by all their minutest gestures and expressions, they plainly showed the uneasy, if not painful, consciousness of being under a troubled master-eye. And not only that, but moody stricken Ahab stood before them with a crucifixion in his face; in all the nameless regal overbearing dignity of some mighty woe.[87]

In addition to embodying his unwavering determination to kill Moby Dick, Ahab's "singular posture" also yields a striking expression of what I have previously called stand-your-ground subjectivity. On a "bone leg" indexing the violent instrumentalization and fungibility of nonhuman nature, and in an "auger hole" indexing the interpellation of the ground as a mere docile surface, Ahab manages to stand as steadily on the "live ground" of the *Pequod*'s "ever-pitching prow" as landsmen might expect to stand on terra firma. In many ways, Ahab's singular posture can be read as a kind of metonym for the "singular posture" of the bipedal human, both in that human's imagined hierarchical relation to the nonhuman world and in our critical attempts to assess the scale of humanity's environmental impacts. Notice, first, how the rigid uprightness enabled by the combined prosthetic support of the bone leg and auger hole facilitates the performance of a kind of mastery. It grants elevated and far-seeing perspective to a "*master*-eye," in much the same way that the popular evolutionary account of our species has understood the human's "singular posture" to have freed what historically have proven to be master-hands. As a performance of mastery, Ahab's "singular posture" domineers the *Pequod* in much the same way that humanity is now critically imagined to stand atop the earth with an outsized carbon footprint. Of course, measuring only "half an inch or so," the auger hole, even on each side of the quarterdeck, hardly seems outsized and may even register just how little of our blue planet furnishes a viable foothold to the dominating stand Ahab indexes as a paragon of human uprightness. That is, at least until we consider the impact of Ahab's incessant pacing on the deck. After his initial appearance, "his steady, ivory stride was heard" throughout the *Pequod* "as to and fro he paced his old rounds, upon planks so familiar to his tread, that they were all over dented, like geological stones, with the peculiar mark of his walk."[88] So echoing the earthcraft yielding Planet Terra Firma, Ahab effectively reshapes the entire deck—dented "all over" by "the peculiar mark of his walk"—into one continuous auger hole, fit for his "singular posture." Moreover, the fact that the planks are "dented, like geological stones," yields a prescient nineteenth-century simile for the geological scale at which the "peculiar mark" of humanity's outsized carbon footprint has been recognized to have reshaped earth so profoundly that it warrants the distinction of a new geological age. The alarms we sound today concerning the Anthropocene and the global ecological crisis could already be heard more than a century ago in the foreboding knocking of Ahab's "bone leg" upon the deck of the *Pequod*. Like the ticking of the doomsday clock, this knocking sounds out a genre of western humanity defined by a superficial interface with the planet interpellated as little more than a docile surface. Just as Thoreau, in his critique of what he similarly discerned as the shallow posture of civilized man, indicts whiteness as a poor color for man, Melville's cautionary tale regarding Ahab's "singular posture" similarly, if less explicitly, comes to indict whiteness as the novel's racial litmus for who may stand and who may be stood upon.[89]

It is not just nonhuman nature that gets conscripted to perform prosthetic labor in *Moby-Dick* but also other humans. Unsurprisingly, a reliable litmus for which humans aboard the *Pequod* are available to be instrumentalized in this way is race. Consider Ishmael's characterization of the division of labor within the American whale fishery; though less than half of its sailors are American born, nearly all its officers are. In this way, observes Ishmael, "the native American liberally provides the brains," with "the rest of the world as generously supplying the muscles."[90] That in the American whale fishery "the native American"—note the erasure of the original inhabitants of America here—consistently exercises authority over "the rest of the world" as brains do muscles indexes a similar instrumentalization relative to other humans as that indexed by Ahab's prosthetic leg in relation to nonhuman nature. And although the operative distinction in Ishmael's characterization of this division of labor is nation, race is never too far behind discourses of nationalism and certainly isn't aboard the *Pequod*, whose captain and mates are not only exclusively American but also exclusively white. Further raising the specter of race regarding this differentiation between a whale crew's brains and muscles is the fact that the *Pequod*'s harpooneers are exclusively nonwhite. Unlike with the *Pequod*'s exclusively American (and white) officer class, no demographic peculiarity of the American whale fishery is offered to explain why the *Pequod*'s harpooneers are a racially caricatured set of aboriginals. Stalled out ontologically and possessing a special, even noble, intimacy with the starting line of humanity, the harpooneers are from the beginning the way most aboard the *Pequod* are from places. Still languishing in the state of nature, they are human, but only just.

More immediately than any other, it's this contingent of the *Pequod*'s crew that can be recognized to supply the "muscles" to the officers' "brains." On the one hand, there are Queequeg, Tashtego, and Daggoo—a "dark, purplish, yellow" Pacific Islander, a "red" Native American, and a "coal-black" African, assigned to the whaleboats of the first, second, and third mates, respectively. And on the other hand, there is Fedallah, a "tiger-yellow" Asian assigned to the whaleboat of Captain Ahab. Thus, each of the *Pequod*'s commanding officers is functionally paired with a racially othered counterpart. Relative to this "barbaric, heathenish, and motley set," the national distinction that Ishmael draws between the "native American" and the "rest of the world" doubles as a racial distinction between white and nonwhite.[91] Besides the fact that they derive not from civilized nations but from uncivilized lands, the added layer of racial difference distinguishing the harpooneers indexes an intensified instrumentalization relative to the officers. As the physical wielders of the harpoons, it is the harpooneers especially who, in the actual practice of whaling, furnish the muscle that executes the will of the *Pequod*'s officers, in a way that points to racial difference as a reliable, if not ultimate, index of human instrumentality aboard the *Pequod*.

Beyond the muscle they directly supply to the officers, the harpooneers perform a kind of prosthetic labor on behalf of the entire crew. Throughout *Moby-Dick*, the harpooneers, much like a body's extremities, consistently occupy the raw, unmediated, sensory edge of the *Pequod*'s interface with nature. Besides manning the harpoons and the lookouts throughout the novel as the crew's hands and eyes, they can be found falling or diving into a severed whale's head or extracting the leviathan's teeth.[92] Not even death relieves the harpooneers of their exposure. Our final sighting of Fedallah shows his lifeless body strapped to Moby Dick by the whale line, while Queequeg, Tashtego, and Daggoo are the final three to perish in the *Pequod*'s climactic wreck—three native Christs perched atop the sinking ship's three mastheads. So the harpooneers can be recognized to embody both the front lines and the rear guard of the *Pequod*'s monomaniacal pursuit of Moby Dick, securing for the rest of the crew a kind of buffer against the vicissitudes of nature, cushioning the blow for the racial kin, if not countrymen, of Columbus.

Yet for this very reason, the harpooneers, even as racial caricatures, also occupy a privileged position within the novel's broader aesthetic effort to reindigenize the human to a deep planet. With respect to Queequeg, Tashtego, and Daggoo—setting aside for the moment the somewhat different case of Fedallah—this ambivalence is made manifest in their characterization not merely as savages but as *noble* savages. Daggoo, for one, in addition to "noble savage," is also called an "imperial," "great," and even "noble negro."[93] The copious criticism surrounding the figure of the "noble savage" disabuses us of any illusion that noble savagery is any more salutary, for the actual native peoples in question, than the undiluted kind. But the trope of the noble savage does register an ambivalence about the unquestionable goodness of western civilization. Thus, while we cannot look to Queequeg, Tashtego, or Daggoo for salutary representations of racialized others, perhaps we can look to them to reveal Melville's sense of the stress points of a western civilization that he condemns as superficial. In contrast, the "nobility" of the savage harpooneers generally inheres in a celebrated embodiedness that seems to answer the superficiality of western civilization with a deep intimacy with the earth. In this sense, the harpooneers embody a kind of human loophole beyond the apparent death drive of western civilization, in a narrative about an American whaling vessel that, just as Thoreau feared in his own critique of whiteness and western civilization in "Walking," wrecks in the Pacific Ocean. And just like in "Walking," the defining stress point of western civilization in *Moby-Dick* is the human that has ceased to be an inhabitant: the shallow inhabitation indexed by Captain Ahab's stand-your-ground subjectivity and, with it, a superficial western world. In the harpooneers, Melville may be trying out and experimenting with alternative humanities in a veiled critique of whiteness that is nevertheless limited by his positionality as a white author. Indeed, to be a loophole is its own kind of prosthetic labor. But if, in their general instrumentality, the barbaric harpooneers yield the human echo of the nonhuman prosthesis indexed by "the *barbaric* white leg upon which [Captain Ahab] partly stood," this prosthesis is made even more explicit in the case of Fedallah. Beyond the fact that he lacks the nobility of the others, he is characterized as Ahab's "shadow," suggesting his derivative relation to Ahab as an entity with no personal substance of his own. And after Fedallah dies, Ahab's words to the other "tiger-yellow barbarians" in his boat during his final encounter with Moby Dick put an even finer point on it: "Ye are not other men, but my arms and my legs, and so obey me."[94]

No one, however, plays prosthesis more absolutely, more analogously to the nonhuman instrumentation figured by Ahab's "bone leg," than "Black Little Pip." In the prosthetic labor they perform, the savage harpooneers are still countenanced as men, even if not, in the suspension of their alterity, "*other* men." Ahab has to command them to serve as his arms and legs. In contrast, Pip, in the utter docility he assumes after nearly drowning and losing his mind, *asks* Ahab to "use poor me for your one lost leg; only tread upon me, sir, I ask no more, so I remain a part of ye."[95] Pip's prosthetic extension of himself may seem willful insofar as he asks to be so used by Ahab. But note that Pip asks not to become but rather to "remain" the part of Ahab that he implicitly already is. Thus, Pip's prosthetic relation to Ahab is less willful than automatic. Unlike the "tiger-yellow barbarians" in Ahab's whaleboat and without any comparable acknowledgment of his humanity, Pip doesn't need to be commanded to be Ahab's arms and legs because Pip already maintains this relation to Ahab *in potentia*. Relative to Ahab, Pip opposes no more ontological friction than the "bone leg" or "auger hole." He evinces no alterity with which Ahab must contend, even ultimately, to subordinate. Instead, Pip's subordination is simply given, the expression of the instrumentalized "being for the captor" that Hortense Spillers has illuminated as a defining predicament of black being.[96] Moreover, in coming to address Ahab as "master, master, master," Pip implies that he is not merely Ahab's instrumentalized subordinate but his slave.

Pip's request to "remain a part" of Ahab is not the first instance of his instrumentalization in *Moby-Dick*. Earlier in the novel, Pip performs a broader instrumental function in relation to the entire crew. The novel alludes to this instrumentalization in its first mention of Pip, which informs us that we "shall ere long see him, beating his tambourine."[97] If Ahab is identified by his bone leg, Pip is alternatively identified by his tambourine, which we finally see him beating as the sonic backdrop to the aforementioned drama and revelry of chapter 40:

> FRENCH SAILOR: Hist, boys! let's have a jig or two before we ride to anchor in Blanket Bay. What say ye? There comes the other watch. Stand by all legs! Pip! little Pip! hurrah with your tambourine!
>
> PIP: (*Sulky and sleepy.*) Don't know where it is.

FRENCH SAILOR: Beat thy belly, then, and wag thy ears. Jig it, men, I say; merry's the word; hurrah! Damn me, won't you dance? Form, now, Indian-file, and gallop into the double-shuffle? Throw yourselves! Legs! legs![98]

When he invites the rest of the crew to dance, the French Sailor employs a synecdoche by repeatedly referring to his fellow sailors as "legs" and telling them to "*stand* by." While certainly less imposing than Ahab's "singular posture," these "legs" nonetheless identify the sailors by their capacity to "stand," which is notably also an identifying aptitude of the human. It is telling, then, that Pip is implicitly excluded from this company of "legs." Rather than "stand by," he is instead ordered to produce the music that would facilitate his shipmates' movement. Pip also is not permitted to share the dance floor with these "legs." Later, after Azore Sailor finds Pip's tambourine, he says, "Here you are, Pip; and there's the windlass-bitts; up you mount! Now, boys!"[99] Since it is only after Pip mounts the windlass that the dancing begins, a pointedly uneven distribution of the ground grounds the revelry of chapter 40. And given the function of the windlass, in operating the anchor, mounting "up" had just as well be getting down. Pip is sonically for these "legs" what the anchor is physically in helping others maintain their place. Consider how, in the initial absence of his tambourine, Pip is ordered to "beat thy belly" and "wag thy ears." Not only is Pip excluded from the collectivity of "legs," but the body parts by which he is alternatively identified are cited as a fitting synecdoche not for bipedal humanity but for their capacity to produce sound. If in their instrumentation the harpooneers nevertheless *man* the harpoons, Pip, by contrast, *is* his tambourine. Is, in and of himself, an instrument. So much so that even with his tambourine, the China Sailor orders him to "rattle thy teeth, then, and pound away; make a pagoda of thyself."[100] Finally, after an approaching storm scatters the crew and abruptly ends the festivities, Pip, "now shrinking under the windlass," has the chapter's last word, in his only lines that are not spoken in response to his shipmates' commands:

It's worse than being in the whirled woods, the last day of the year! Who'd go climbing after chestnuts now? But there they go, all cursing, and here I don't. Fine prospects to 'em; they're on the road to heaven. Hold on hard! Jimmini, what a squall! But those chaps there are worse yet—they are your white squalls, they. White squalls? white whale, shirr! shirr! Here have I heard all their chat just now, and the white whale—shirr! shirr!—but spoken of once! and only this evening—it makes me jingle all over like my tambourine—that anaconda of an old man swore 'em in to hunt

> him! Oh, thou big white God aloft there somewhere in yon darkness, have mercy on this small black boy down here; preserve him from all men that have no bowels to feel fear![101]

Even after the party's over, Pip can still be found at the windlass, jingling all over like the tambourine he not only plays but embodies, in sharp contrast to the "legs" that otherwise people the *Pequod*. And Pip's isolation from the revelry of these legs is repeated with the approach of the storm, when Pip observes how "they go" and "I don't." Intriguingly, this differentiation between a collective "they" and a solitary "I" is further coded in Pip's concluding aside by a collectivizing whiteness, which envelops the whole crew, and an isolating blackness. In contrast to "white squalls" (by which Pip alludes to both the storm and his crewmates), the "white whale," and finally a "big white God," Pip stands alone as a "small black boy." In relation to humans, whiteness's net is cast as broadly as the synecdochical net of "legs." It signals an enclosure not of white people—since among the "chaps" that Pip identifies as "white squalls" are also those who are not white, like the harpooneers—but of an idealized humanity that all of the crew, save Pip, can more or less embody by standing. Yet as much as Pip's instrumentalization and isolation relative to the rest of the *Pequod* traffic in familiar racial stereotypes of blackness, it is important to note that Pip's isolated positionality also grants him a unique perspective of the *Pequod* and its voyage, to which the rest of his shipmates appear blind. It isn't the mastery and control characterized by Captain Ahab's "master-eye" in his unwavering pursuit of Moby Dick but an outsider's insight to know that this voyage is doomed. That even before the squall, the *Pequod*'s quest for vengeance was already endangered by a storm of whiteness, which is enough to be dubious about whatever salvation can come from a "big white God."

Pip's exclusion from the *Pequod*'s dance floor yields a microcosm for what can also be recognized as his lack of any definitive place on the broader stage of the world. In a novel that takes such care to specify where each of its characters is from, Pip is defined by a conspicuous geographic indeterminacy. We first hear passing mention of Pip as a "Poor Alabama boy" in chapter 27, in the same few sentences that tell us we shall soon see him beating his tambourine.[102] However, in chapter 93, "The Castaway," we are told that Pip is a native of Tolland County, Connecticut.[103] This discrepancy in Pip's nativity has led some scholars to speculate that Pip was originally conceived as a slave and later, over the course of Melville's composition of *Moby-Dick*, reconceived as free.[104] Whatever its explanation, this discrepancy is striking in a novel that otherwise makes a point to specify the native country or territory of nearly every member of the *Pequod*'s crew. If we know nothing else of the Spanish Sailor, we at least know that he is from Spain. And even if not from civilized nations, the harpooneers, as a tetrad of racialized native types, still come from somewhere in the world. Even the "negro-savage" Daggoo has a "native coast."[105] Meanwhile, the "blackling" Pip has no definitive seat among the *Pequod*'s united nations. And in the vacuum created by his geographic indeterminacy, his strongest geographic claim ultimately proves to be the sea.

The absolute prosthetic relation that Pip ultimately comes to assume as the "one lost leg" of his "master," Ahab, indexes an intensification of the general instrumentality we observe in chapter 40 relative to a whole crew of "legs." And intriguingly, with regard to Melville's bluing of the human and this study of the "inhabitants of the deep," the catalyst for this intensification is Pip's near drowning in "The Castaway," when Pip is abandoned at sea by his shipmates—"There they go . . . here I don't"—during a whale hunt. In this chapter, Pip is conscripted, beyond his typical duties as a cabin boy, to join Stubb's whaleboat. And while Pip's first lowering passes without incident, the second sees Pip go over the side:

> Now upon the second lowering, the boat paddled upon the whale; and as the fish received the darted iron, it gave its customary rap, which happened, in this instance, to be right under poor Pip's seat. The involuntary consternation of the moment caused him to leap, paddle in hand, out of the boat; and in such a way, that part of the slack whale line coming against his chest, he breasted it overboard with him, so as to become entangled in it, when at last plumping into the water. That instant the stricken whale started on a fierce run, the line swiftly straightened; and presto! poor Pip came all foaming up to the chocks of the boat, remorselessly dragged there by the line, which had taken several turns around his chest and neck.[106]

With whale line encircled around his neck and fastened to an entity of the nonhuman natural world, Pip leaping from the boat resembles a kind of aquatic lynching. As an antebellum novel, *Moby-Dick* predates lynching's late nineteenth-, early twentieth-century heyday as an instrument of racial terror. But whether anachronism or prophecy, *a boy was lynched yesterday*.[107] Or if not quite lynched, then entangled with nonhuman nature in the violent conflation that is essentially at issue in lynching. This confusion also inheres in the simultaneity of Pip's "leap" and the whale's "fierce run." This shared fugitive movement echoes the leaps of middle passing Africans and the contemporary fierce runs of fugitive slaves, which were also known to inconvenience the pursuit and accumulation of capital. Furthermore, the characterization of Pip's movement as "involuntary" suggests an environmental susceptibility and failure to control his body that is consistent with the racial mythologization of blackness as failed self-possession defined by excessive or unruly movement. In this respect, all that Allison Curseen teaches us in her book *Minor Moves* about Topsy's unruly movement in *Uncle Tom's Cabin* (1852) can be generatively brought to bear on Pip's in *Moby-Dick*. He is our Topsy of the sea.[108]

Ultimately, Pip is rescued after Stubb begrudgingly orders the whale line to be cut, but not without issuing Pip a pointed threat: "We can't afford to lose whales by the likes of you; a whale would sell for thirty times what you would, Pip, in *Alabama*. Bear that in mind, and don't jump any more."[109] To discourage Pip from jumping, Stubb reminds Pip of the standing reservation that the "dark side of mankind" has in the *Pequod*'s hold. That, in this way, he represents "the like" not of the other humans in the whaleboat, who under similar circumstances would be entitled to a human's ethical regard, but of the whale. And like the whale, Pip can also be bought and sold, and likely would, if the economics were different and whales not significantly more profitable. Yet the same fungibility that, under different economic conditions, could make Pip profitable also makes his life disposable in the *Pequod*'s pursuit of bigger fish. Thus, the *Pequod*'s calculus concerning Pip is economic rather than humanistic, principally a question of what these whalers can or cannot "afford." However, Stubb's not-so-veiled threat is notable for another significant reason. In the same chapter in which we learn of Pip's conflicting nativity as a freeman from Tolland County, his original geographic designation as an "Alabama boy" resurfaces like a repressed memory of Melville's possible original intentions for Pip as an enslaved character. Only, here, Alabama returns as an index not of Pip's nativity but of his "natal alienation": that is, the annulment of all claims of nativity, which Orlando Patterson identifies as a "constituent element" of the slavery's "social death."[110] No longer serving to socially situate or physically locate Pip, Alabama resurfaces instead as a place where Pip may be bought and sold to the annulment of all geographic and social claims. Despite Melville's possible reimagination of the character, Pip remains a "socially dead person": a slave in a sense that Melville could no more revise than the Emancipation Proclamation or the Thirteenth Amendment has proven capable of redressing the problem of being black.

Stubb's loaded caution notwithstanding, upon his next encounter with a whale "Pip jumped again" and this time "was left behind on the sea, *like* a hurried traveller's *trunk*."[111] Here, the likes of Pip are also literally found to include cargo. And in this way, Pip also begins to confess his likeness to the "inhabitants of the deep" who were also "left behind on the sea" like cargo during the transatlantic slave trade. This likeness comes clearer in the image of Pip's total abandonment at sea: "Bobbing up and down in that sea, Pip's ebon head showed like a head of cloves. No boat-knife was lifted when he fell so rapidly astern. Stubb's inexorable back was turned upon him; and the whale was winged. In three minutes, a whole mile of shoreless ocean was between Pip and Stubb."[112] As he is left to die by shipmates from every corner of the globe, even the most remote and uncivil, Pip's abandonment at sea stages a microcosm of Afropessimism's account of the Middle Passage dawning of blackness as the castaway of the entire world. And at the same time, Pip's near drowning *is* Middle Passage, just as those "left behind on the sea" today, whether in boats brimming with refugees fleeing emergency or on New Orleans rooftops, are Middle Passage. That is, the yet unabated intimacy that the "dark side of mankind" maintains with the "dark side of earth," in a superficial western world where the likes of Pip still have no ground to stand. Moreover, Pip's situation is hardly improved after he is ultimately rescued by the *Pequod*, though only by the "merest chance"—that is, not with the care and intention of a search and rescue but in the business as usual of whaling that happened to lead the *Pequod* into Pip's path. While preventing his physical death, Pip's rescue does nothing to abate, and perhaps even intensifies, the "social death" already implied by his exclusion from a surface shared by the *Pequod*'s "legs" and only consummated in Pip's abandonment at sea. The crushing isolation of his encounter with our blue marble caused Pip to lose his own. And "from that hour the little negro went about the deck an idiot; such, at least, they said he was. The sea had jeeringly kept his finite body up, but drowned the infinite of his soul."[113] Pip resurrects from his watery grave as a no-body. In the wake of the drowning of his soul, which has long been thought the litmus of human individuality, Pip comes to resemble mere and fungible "flesh." His inhabitation of the deep induces the same peculiarity of being that Spillers recognized in middle passing Africans, who were made flesh and coerced to perform a "being for the captor."[114] It is perhaps fitting, then, that in this slave-like state Pip addresses Captain Ahab as "master" and volunteers himself for Ahab's quiver of legs. In his utter docility and manifold likeness to the whale, Pip's proposed prosthesis is more ignoble than that of the noble savages among the harpooneers. As the equivalent of Ahab's bone leg, Pip is not from the beginning or proximate to the "state of nature." Rather, he is disappeared from the ranks of the human altogether as the fungible kin of the barrels of oil brimming the *Pequod*'s hull.

As much as Pip's inhabitation of the deep precipitates his willful docility and consummates his "social death" relative to his crewmates, it is also characterized by an ambivalence similar to what we've previously located in the Equiano phrase that lends this book its title. Like Equiano's impossible name for the drowned, Melville ultimately characterizes the drowning of Pip's soul in terms of life:

> Not drowned entirely, though. Rather carried down *alive* to wondrous depths, where strange shapes of the unwarped primal world glided to and fro before his passive eyes; and the miser-merman, Wisdom, revealed his hoarded heaps; and among the joyous, heartless, ever-juvenile eternities, Pip saw the multitudinous, God-omnipresent, coral insects, that out of the firmament of waters heaved the colossal orbs. He saw God's foot upon the treadle of the loom, and spoke it; and therefore his shipmates called him mad. So man's insanity is heaven's sense; and wandering from all mortal reason, man comes at last to that celestial thought, which, to reason, is absurd and frantic; and weal or woe, feels then uncompromised, indifferent as his God.[115]

Pip not only inhabited the deep but lived to tell about it, even if what he had to say was largely incomprehensible. But how else could the deep testimony of "God's foot upon the treadle of the loom" sound to a superficial western world? What but nonsense or insanity could a world predicated on the systematic disavowal of creation's depth discern in Pip's talk of the deep origins of creation? Against the grain of the theological suppression of the primordial sea, and what Keller reads as its secular and modern mutation into a generalized shunning of depth of all kinds, Pip speaks *tehom's* unspeakable and silenced name. Puts in a word for everything that, in relation to the terrestrial order of landsmen, gets maligned as disorder, chaos, or nothingness. Within a terrestrial cosmology, such talk of *tehom* is spoken out of cosmological turn, as if the mute jawbone propping up Ahab's "singular posture" suddenly learned speech. Indeed, Pip voices the elided abyssal beginnings of creation before the creation is otherwise recorded to have become articulate, when, per the Christian doctrine of creation ex nihilo, God spoke creation into existence out of nothing. By speaking "God's foot upon the treadle" of a loom situated in the deep, Pip resurfaces the much-maligned beginning of the beginning, in a way that not only echoes but deepens the creative footing that God otherwise appears content to adopt in the oft-elided creational drama of God's spirit "hovering over the face of the waters."[116]

In ways far exceeding the violence of racial subjection, Pip's blackness as a representative of the "dark side of mankind" also resonates with, and finds aesthetic vindication in, the "darkness" that also looms "on the face of the deep" in Genesis 1:2. In its resonance with this primordial darkness, blackness, rather than being wholly contained within the antiblack logics of white supremacy, escapes into what Nathaniel Mackey might call an "insistent previousness," anterior to both the Human and its constitutional others.[117] Such blackness, cosmologically dislodged from the binary logics of Manicheism, yields to Melville an aesthetic loophole of retreat. Just as Melville's turn to "the dark side of earth" affords him the aesthetic opportunity to imagine the earth beyond the "superficial western" world, so the "dark side of mankind" similarly affords him the aesthetic opportunity to think the human beyond whiteness's colonial reinscription of humanity as utter landsmen. In contrast, the twitchy, leap-happy Pip, though expressly commanded not to, can't help but jump ship. His unruly movement is as involuntary as the prosthetic labor he extends to Captain Ahab is voluntary. Just as much as he plays prosthesis, Pip also can't keep still, frustrating every ambition of those who would run a "tight ship." In his excessive movement, he represents the human analog of a planet that Captain Ahab bemoans as slippery when he divulges to the carpenter that would fashion him a new leg, "I like a good grip; I like to feel something in this slippery world that can hold."[118]

In his utter docility, stereotypical musicality, and unruly movement, Pip is not very far from the empty Sambo paper doll in Ralph Ellison's *Invisible Man*. Yet, like Melville's insurgent representation of the "dark side of earth," I suspect that Melville is up to something more complex, if limited, in his representation of this geographically unmoored representative of the "dark side of mankind": that here, too, Melville's intent is not to reify but rather to destabilize the racial order of the human that has yielded a dark and light side. Ishmael tells us that "Pip, though over tender-hearted, was at bottom very bright, with that pleasant, genial, jolly brightness peculiar to his tribe; a tribe, which ever enjoy all holidays and festivities with finer, freer relish than any other race. For blacks, the year's calendar should show naught but three hundred and sixty-five Fourth of Julys and New Year's Days. Nor smile so, while I write that this little black was brilliant, for even blackness has its brilliancy; behold yon lustrous ebony, panelled in king's cabinets."[119] I do not put Pip forward as an ideal or unproblematic representation of blackness. Like Harriet Beecher Stowe's description of Topsy, Melville's excessive characterization of Pip, however sympathetic, is deeply racist. Yet at the same time that he rehearses these familiar racial stereotypes of blackness, he also upsets the binary upon which they are founded when he writes that even "blackness has its brilliancy." Moreover, it is telling that, in his effort to carve out a space of human affiliation with the ocean, the nearest Melville can come, before language fails him, is an image of blackness's inhabitation of the deep:

> Out from the centre of the sea, poor Pip turned his crisp, curling, black head to the sun, another lonely castaway, though the loftiest and the brightest.
>
> Now, in calm weather, to swim in the open ocean is as easy to the practised swimmer as to ride in a spring-carriage ashore. But the awful lonesomeness is intolerable. The intense concentration of self in the middle of such a heartless immensity, my God! who can tell it?[120]

In the next chapter, we will consider how black writers negotiate the telling of a story that cannot be told. Yet in our search for more careful and salutary images of blackness's ongoing inhabitation of the deep, we should not fail to remember Pip, who not only inhabited the deep but lived to tell about it. In *Moby-Dick*, it is to him most of all that a sense of the ocean can be said to be aboriginal. This representative of both the "dark side of mankind" and "the dark side of earth" is the only human to be carried down alive to the depths of the sea and so our most reliable witness that if you surrender to the deep you can swim it.

3

DEEP VOICE

always what is going on seems to be about water
—M. NOURBESE PHILIP, *Zong!*

I. sound

NO EAR HAS HEARD the underwater utterance of the inhabitants of the deep. There were things spoken underwater that can never be repeated. Things unspeakable in the most literal sense—not simply because there are no words but because even what words there were had no more ground on which to stand than those who tried to speak them. How many *Mama*s and *I can't breathe*s unraveled in the ocean, with nothing so stable to support them as the implicit line upholding this and every sentence? Lasting last *words* were not a dignity extended to the 1,818,681. The closest we might come to representing their submarine speech textually is _____. But even this wordless line is straighter than it would need to be.

When words forsook the underwater utterance of the inhabitants of the deep, was there not water in their stead? We may be more wont to consider and lament water's incapacitation of speech. I certainly was when I first began to wonder about so many last words muted by the ocean. But while pursuing my scuba diving certification, I learned that water, however problematic for human *speech*, actually transmits *sound* far more efficiently than air. According to the PADI (Professional Association of Diving Instructors) *Open Water Diver Manual*, "sound travels about four times faster in water than in air. This makes it difficult to determine its source—underwater, it usually seems like sound is coming from all around, or directly overhead." In addition, "underwater sound travels over longer distances. For example, a boat that you can't hear at the surface may sound relatively close underwater."[1] What my diving instructor dismissed as mere "theory" I later experienced in practice during my first open-water dive, when a light rain at the surface paradoxically seemed to grow louder and nearer when I descended. Even at a depth of sixty feet the rain sounded as if it were smacking my own skin. If something like sharing a skin with the earth is what Sigmund Freud called the "oceanic feeling," such was my oceanic *hearing*. And with every sound seeming to come from directly overhead, sound also sounds remarkably immersive underwater, giving new resonance to the gospel standard "Up Above My Head (I Hear Music in the Air)" and renewed conviction that "there must be a God somewhere."

Thus, if the deep can be perceived as the enemy of human speech, it is also a remarkable friend of sound. This is true not only physically but also etymologically. The word *sound* has long kept company with the deep as a name for a narrow body of water, for what we do when we measure depth (especially of water), and for what whales do when they dive into the deep. The multiple registers of *sound* come to an awful confluence in the underwater utterance of the inhabitants of the deep. But they also grant greater complexity to a singular moment in the multivalent history of black sound. This complexity interrupts our sense of the deep's incapacitation of would-be last words by gesturing instead to the deep's sonic enablement. A remarkable photograph of a parallel moment in the history of black sound helps to illuminate this sonic enablement. It's a photograph of Dizzy Gillespie standing knee-deep in the ocean while playing his famous bent horn. But it's not just his choice of stage that is remarkable, it's also that Dizzy is hunched over and sounding his horn underwater (figure 3.1). Who can know what possessed the famed wielder of the bent horn to bend his trumpet toward the deep? Maybe a man who became a puffer fish every time he picked up his horn was bound to find his way to the ocean. Or maybe Dizzy was persuaded, like Saint Francis of Assisi and his congregation of fish, that the good news of bebop should be shared with more than just humans. Or maybe the sonic innovator was simply curious about what it might sound like to exchange his conventional mute for the sea. You have heard it played con sordino, but I play unto you con oceano. If mutes are known to alter

FIGURE 3.1. Dizzy Gillespie playing the trumpet underwater. Photo: Jean-Marie Périer, *Dizzy Gillespie dans l'eau, Juan les Pins*, 1958.

the timbre and volume of sound, then what kind of mute is the deep, which conducts sound faster and farther than air?

What if we imagine the greater distance sound can travel in water in relation not only to space but to time? The way, for instance, August Wilson seems to imagine with these lines from Aunt Ester in *Gem of the Ocean* (2003): "The people got a burning tongue, Mr. Citizen. Their mouths are on fire with song. That water can't put it out. That song is powerful. It rise up and come across the water. Ten thousand tongues and ten thousand chariots coming across the water. They on their way, Mr. Citizen. They coming across the water."[2] In his own meditation on the underwater utterance of the inhabitants of the deep, Wilson alludes to the famous biblical episode of Pentecost, when "tongues, as of fire," rested on the disciples and enabled them to speak in other languages. So the gospel was not content to hold itself up in its original language but addressed bewildered passersby in their mother tongues. That the inhabitants of the deep "got a burning tongue," then, distinguishes their underwater utterance as a like miracle of mediation, where space and time, rather than language barriers, are being crossed. Not only could water not put out the powerful song of the 1,818,681, but it also enabled that song to travel farther than it otherwise might have in air. Perhaps when Dizzy rested his fire-hued trumpet on the face of the deep, some antiphonal exchange between these parallel moments in the history of black sound took place: the distress call of the inhabitants of the deep and, centuries later, conscious or not, the response of a luminary descendant, resounding in their own deep voice.

So, too, might we imagine the poet M. NourbeSe Philip to respond when she gives *water* the first protracted word of her book-length poem *Zong!*:[3]

w w w   w   a   wa
                  w   a   w a   t
er

The thing about *water*, as we find it here, is that the verbal sign is unraveling in the element it signifies. Breaking up, spreading out, and diffusing as things are wont to do in water. Philip, in other words, sings her *Zong!* in a deep voice. We may not know what possessed Dizzy to sound his horn underwater, but Philip tells us plainly that *Zong!* was "told to the author by Setaey Adamu Boateng," an imagined victim of the historic *Zong* massacre, and so an inhabitant of the deep. In November 1781, some 150 Africans were thrown overboard the British slave ship *Zong* because the captain reckoned that the policy insuring the enslaved would be more lucrative than their eventual sale. *Cargo among other cargo.*

"There is," according to Philip, "no telling this story," and yet, she insists, "it must be told." Philip's approach to the expressive dilemma she faces in *Zong!*, then, is paradoxically "to *not tell* the story that must be told."[4] To tell it, that is, precisely by not telling it—not in a refusal of expression, but rather in the struggle to sound out an expressive way out of no way. And Philip's first recourse in her not telling of the *Zong* massacre is to water. Are there things, then, that only the water can say?

II. water's voice

While writing *Zong!*, Philip kept a journal in which she observed: "Always what is going on seems to be about water."[5] Of course, given *Zong!*'s subject matter and the final resting place of Philip's informant, it is reasonable to expect that water would figure prominently in a poem not merely about but technically by an inhabitant of the deep. Yet these details alone do not fully explain the elevated status Philip grants to water, or the nature of the element's ubiquitous relation to her writing practice. Indeed, what does it mean for water to be "going on" in writing, and for it to be going on "always"? This characterization of water goes far beyond what literary critics know to analyze as an important motif, theme, or symbol. The seeming omnipresence of water's "going on" suggests less the incident of any particular literary device and more an atmospheric observation about the writing in general. "Always what is going on," whatever is being written, in whatever way, "seems to be about water." Taking my cue from this passing remark in Philip's writing journal, I want to investigate the possibility that a *reading* journal might similarly conclude that water is the animating element of not only *Zong!* but all black writing. That "always what is going" in the black literary tradition also "seems to be about water."

Consider, for instance, the black folk in Ralph Ellison's *Invisible Man* (1952), who "shoot up from the South" with a gait "like that of deep sea divers suffering from the bends."[6] Or the Invisible Man himself, whose legs become "watery beneath me."[7] Or Bigger Thomas in Richard Wright's *Native Son* (1940), whose "fear rendered his legs like water."[8] Or "the people" in August Wilson's *Gem of the Ocean*, "who got the law tied to their toe" so that "every time they try to swim, the law pull them under."[9] Individually, these repeated appeals to the symbolic power of water represent isolated instances of simile or metaphor. But taken in their aggregate, across multiple texts, they suggest a more general strategy of analogy that I submit has long facilitated the witness of a literary tradition, which harbors the terrible testimony of how it feels to be a problem. More than figuring in isolated figures of speech, water flows across these texts, even in their twentieth-century and predominantly urban settings where, in contrast to a text like *Zong!*, we might not expect water to show up. And what's more, water surfaces in these texts in a strikingly similar way. In each of the examples cited above, water troubles the otherwise pedestrian activities of standing or walking. At issue in each analogical appeal to water is specifically its precarity as ground, or at least the sort of ground on which humans can hope to stand. I propose that this recurring image of blackness's sea legs evinces a generalized way in which black writers repeatedly figure the "problem" of being black as a water-induced crisis of having no ground that both originates with and is subsequently haunted by the waters of Middle Passage.

This insight is born of the years I've spent eavesdropping in classrooms, coffee shops, and the library—anywhere two or more books are gathered—on how black literature struggles to wrestle into words how it feels to be a problem. In many ways, W. E. B. Du Bois's struggle to reply to this familiar question in *The Souls of Black Folk* (1903) embodies the expressive bind of black literature more broadly.

> Between me and the other world there is ever an unasked question: unasked by some through feelings of delicacy; by others through the difficulty of rightly framing it. All, nevertheless, flutter round it. They approach me in a half-hesitant sort of way, eye me curiously or compassionately, and then, instead of saying directly, How does it feel to be a problem? they say, I know an excellent colored man in my town; or, I fought at Mechanicsville; or, Do not these Southern outrages make your blood boil? At these I smile, or am interested, or reduce the boiling to a simmer, as the occasion may require. To the real question, How does it feel to be a problem? I answer seldom a word.[10]

Du Bois's answering "seldom a word" speaks to the expressive bind of a black literary tradition often charged with speaking the unspeakable. And yet, like Philip's "not telling" of the *Zong* massacre, we might similarly understand Du Bois's wordless reply as a kind (and not the absence) of an answer—one that necessarily appeals to extraverbal forms of expression. Although we should be careful not to reduce the black literary tradition to an exclusive meditation on the "problem" of being black, it is also true that, from its origins in the slave narrative, black literature has long engaged in a practice of testimony and witness that brings it, again and again, to the brink of the expressive power of words. Of course, what I've put forward as the analogy of blackness's sea legs is a verbal phenomenon, but it nevertheless depends significantly for its effect on material and embodied experience. If all words are abstractions of whatever they signify, analogy walks meaning on something of a shorter leash by directly alluding to experiences of the physical world that are nonverbal. Analogy's more conspicuous appeal to this material excess beyond verbal signification represents one of the strategies available to black literature to "not tell" its unspeakable story.

Black writers' diffuse appeal to the analogical power of water can be thought in relation to the well-remarked way in which black literature similarly appeals to music. Two famous incidents of this appeal to music are found in the expressive power that Frederick Douglass and Du Bois attribute to negro spirituals in *Narrative of the Life of Frederick Douglass* (1845) and *The Souls of Black Folk*. In *Narrative*, for instance, Douglass remarks that the "deep meaning of those rude and apparently incoherent songs" could do "more to impress some minds with the horrible character of slavery than the reading of whole volumes of philosophy on the subject could do." Somehow despite their rudeness and incoherence (qualities we do not typically associate with eloquence), Douglass explains that these songs

> told a tale of woe which was then altogether beyond my feeble comprehension; they were tones loud, long, and deep; they breathed the prayer and complaint of souls boiling over with the bitterest anguish. Every tone was a testimony against slavery, and a prayer to God for deliverance from chains. The hearing of those wild notes always depressed my spirit, and filled me with ineffable sadness. I have frequently found myself in tears while hearing them. The mere recurrence to those songs, even now, afflicts me; and while I am writing these lines, an *expression of feeling has already found its way down my cheek*. To those songs I trace my first glimmering conception of the dehumanizing character of slavery. I can never get rid of that conception. Those songs still follow me, to deepen my hatred of slavery, and quicken my sympathies for my brethren in bonds. If any one wishes to be impressed with the soul-killing effects of slavery, let him go to Colonel Lloyd's plantation, and, on allowance-day, place himself in the deep pine woods, and there let him, in silence, analyze the sounds that shall pass through the chambers of his soul—and if he is not thus impressed, it will only be because "there is no flesh in his obdurate heart."[11]

So Douglass describes the expressive power of spirituals, and sound more generally, to render the otherwise "ineffable" effects of slavery. But it is also worth noting, given this project's immediate concern with water, the other expressive medium that supplements words in the passage above: "the *expression* of feeling," or tear, that Douglass informs his reader is concurrent with the writing of these words. Perhaps he, too, might have remarked with Philip that "always what is going on seems to be about water." In the context of the passage above, sound in fact shares the burden of extraverbal expression with the materiality of water.

Spirituals fulfill this same function in *Souls*, and in a way that similarly suggests some semiotic collaboration with water. In "The Sorrow Songs," a chapter devoted entirely to negro spirituals, Du Bois describes the "heart-touching witness of these songs": "I know that these songs are the articulate message of the slave to the world. . . . They are the music of an unhappy people, of the children of disappointment; they tell of death and suffering and unvoiced longing toward a truer world, of misty wanderings and hidden ways."[12] Yet Du Bois's appeal to sound is not limited to this chapter alone but operates as a primary means of expressing the problem of being black throughout the text. Each chapter of *Souls* begins with the same general epigraphic pattern: a poem from the Euro-American literary canon followed by a lyricless fragment of sheet music from a number of prominent negro spirituals. Explaining this aesthetic decision, Du Bois writes: "Before each thought that I have written in this book I have set a phrase, a haunting echo of these weird old songs in which the soul of the black slave spoke to men. Ever since I was a child these songs have stirred me strangely. They came out of the South unknown to me, one by one, and yet at once I knew them as of me and of mine."[13] That "these weird old songs" come before the words "written in this book" once again privileges sound as a medium suited to the expression of a problem that exceeds what words alone can say. It also bears mentioning that, while unknown on the level of understanding in a way echoed by Douglass in *Narrative*, these songs are instead known to Du Bois on the level of expressing a cultural and aesthetic relation, of expressing a unity between "me and mine," which we are otherwise in the habit of calling blackness. But I want to call specific attention to the epigraph that begins the first chapter of *Souls*, "Of Our Spiritual Strivings," and immediately precedes Du Bois's account of the ineffable "problem" of being black. I submit that, in addition to gesturing, once again, toward the expressive power of sound, this epigraph also, in a manner similar to Douglass's, solicits the expressive power of water in a way that further develops and informs the analogous relation between water and the "problem" of being black that I am attempting to elucidate.

The poem-song combination that furnishes the epigraph of "Of Our Spiritual Strivings" begins with an untitled poem by British poet Arthur Symons, in which one can immediately recognize the prominence of water:

> O water, voice of my heart, crying in the sand,
> All night long crying with a mournful cry,
> As I lie and listen, and cannot understand
> The voice of my heart in my side or the voice of the sea,
> O water, crying for rest, is it I, is it I?
> All night long the water is crying to me.
>
> Unresting water, there shall never be rest
> Till the last moon droop and the last tide fail,
> And the fire of the end begin to burn in the west;
> And the heart shall be weary and wonder and cry like the sea,
> All life long crying without avail,
> As the water all night long is crying to me.[14]

Suggestively, this poem, which opens the first chapter of *Souls*, is addressed to water. And given our specific interrogation of water's relation to the ineffable problem of being black, it is further suggestive that water appears in the poem as "the voice of the sea." A voice, moreover, that is "crying" and which the poem's first-person and presumably white speaker "cannot understand." Then there is the fact that the poem is followed by an untitled and wordless fragment of sheet music belonging, we only belatedly learn in "The Sorrow Songs," to the well-known spiritual "No Body Knows the Trouble I've Seen." Arriving at this musical phrase in the wake of the poem, readers confront a problem for reading. In the absence of a title or lyrics, the only instrument a reader might avail themselves of to read this musical phrase is their voice and, what's more, their speechless voice. This assumes, of course, that Du Bois's readers can even read music. If not, these musical notes cry out to readers who, much like the poem's speaker, "cannot understand."

Taken together, as their presence in a single epigraph seems to encourage, this white poem and black song establish a dynamic of communication that fails across the color line. The very construction of the epigraph, poem followed by song, not only structurally renders the song as a response to the poem, which is written in the mode of address, but suggests that this black and illegible song actually sustains the incomprehensibility first attributed to the ocean in the poem. Just as the poem is addressed to "the voice of the sea," which the speaker cannot understand, the song sounds out a trouble that nobody, speaker presumably included, knows. This failed communication across the color line in the epigraph is redoubled in Du Bois's account of the ever-unasked question, to which he also illegibly answers "seldom a word." Taken together, they establish a layered parallel between the "voice of the sea," which the poem's speaker cannot understand, the musical "trouble," which nobody knows and which readers fail to read, and the "problem" of being black, which cannot be spoken. This layered parallel invites our speculation that water, and particularly the sea, *is* the trouble and problem that no body knows and that can't be spoken. But perhaps it can be voiced if, as the phrase "voice of the sea" suggests, water can be recognized to furnish a kind of voice.

Du Bois's account of the specific circumstances that precipitated the creation of "No Body Knows the Trouble I've Seen" further suggests this relationship between the problem of being black and water. Du Bois writes: "When, struck with a sudden poverty, the United States *refused to fulfill its promises of land to the freedmen*, a brigadier-general went down to the Sea Islands to carry the news. An old woman on the outskirts of the throng began singing this song; all the mass joined her, swaying. And the soldier wept."[15] This specific sorrow song, then, is rooted in the trouble of having no land, a "swaying" relation to the ground that echoes the self-same trouble visited upon the slaves of the *Zong*, who in steps too brief on the face of the Atlantic were also refused the promises of land. It echoes, too, the water-frustrated posture of Bigger Thomas and the sea-legged black folk in *Invisible Man*.

The white general may further be read as a kind of foil to the first-person speaker of the poem. Like the speaker, who is close enough to the sea to hear its voice, the general goes down to the Sea Islands and hears a song. In a way, both participate, in different locations, in the type of listening session prescribed by Douglass when he suggests that to be impressed by the soul-killing effects of slavery, one has only to visit the deep pine woods of Colonel Lloyd's plantation and "analyze the sounds that shall pass through the chambers of his soul." On the one hand, if we accept Douglass as a suitable judge of the listening experiment he prescribes, we might conclude that "there is no flesh in [the] obdurate heart" of the speaker who "cannot understand / . . . the voice of the sea" crying out to him. On the other hand, the weeping soldier gets got by the sound in much the same way as the tearful Douglass. If not on account of the soldier's own heart of flesh, then on account of "the heart-touching witness of these songs."

III. the soles of black folk

The recurring image of blackness's sea legs is no mere fiction. It's literal as well as literary. Its claim to analogy in the strictly figurative sense is not pure. Rather, the growing literary catalog of the water-beset soles of black folk is attended by a material history of foundering that stretches all the way back to what the historian Stephanie Smallwood has described as the "unparalleled displacement" of Middle Passage due to the novel encounter of middle passing Africans with the "landless realm of the deep sea."[16] In *Poetics of Relation* (1990), Édouard Glissant remembers the literal crisis of groundlessness that history visited upon those inhabitants of the deep, who, like the 150 captives aboard the *Zong*, were thrown overboard during the Middle Passage: "Whenever a fleet of ships gave chase to slave ships, it was easiest just to lighten the boat by throwing cargo overboard, weighing it down with balls and chains. These underwater signposts mark the course between the Gold Coast and the Leeward Islands. Navigating the green splendor of the sea . . . still brings to mind, coming to light like seaweed, these lowest depths, these deeps, with their punctuation of scarcely corroded balls and chains."[17] Glissant's meditation on the inhabitants of the deep calls our attention to the historical moment when the inability to stand on water was not merely like, but quite literally *was*, how it felt to be a problem. The 1,818,681 crises of literal groundlessness endured by the jumpers and the jettisoned throughout the transatlantic slave trade threaten the purely literary status of the analogy of blackness's sea legs even more than analogy can already be said to appeal to material experience for its meaning. Could this painful and protracted history be the extraverbal source of water's voice? Its power to express the problem of being black when words alone fail? If, according to Gaston Bachelard, "images discovered by men evolve slowly, painfully," and if, according to Jacques Bousquet, "a new image costs humanity as much labor as a new characteristic costs a plant," then how many painful centuries and how much labor did it cost the inhabitants of the deep to discover the image of the water-beset soles of black folk?[18] To, in effect, *blue* the human (much like Dizzy was known to blue a note) by learning to blink with their feet as well as their eyes?

Perhaps Ed Roberson had these failed steps in mind when he wrote these lines in *Voices Cast Out to Talk Us In* (1995):

> The footprint on the water, filling.
>
> Often you don't even notice the steps,
> that is that each
> is *bridged* by the falling body to the next,
>
> discontinuous through the ground.[19]

Here, Roberson zeroes in on and decelerates the infinitesimal instant that a foot contacts the water and challenges us, however counterintuitively, to apprehend in this fleeting moment an actual footprint. Even if it is one that, in comparison to the cleanly delineated molds we delight to leave in sand or snow, takes on water like a sinking ship. Perhaps we "don't even notice the steps" swallowed by the Atlantic because they disappoint our basic expectation of what a viable step is: namely, if I may hazard a definition, a *pedestrian* engagement with ground that continuously propels a body forward. *Pedestrian*'s connotation as uneventful or commonplace bespeaks just how given we expect a pedestrian's engagement with ground to be. It implies a remarkably impoverished notion of ground as little more than a docile surface. It's in contrast to how we typically imagine a step, and the arguably reduced notion of ground implicit therein, that Roberson's "footprint on the water, filling," appears illegible. Rather than an interstitial unit of *continuous* motion, it flounders "*discontinuous* through the ground." Far from given, here, the ground gives too much.

Nevertheless, Roberson insists that we apprehend in this failed footprint an actual step. And this noticing, for Roberson, is a matter of attending not just to isolated steps that we might otherwise overlook but also to the connections between these steps: the fact "that each / is bridged by the falling body to the next." These lines from Roberson articulate an ethic of noticing, of bearing witness to not only the steps that faltered on the face of the Atlantic but also the bridge connecting each awful step to the next in what might be recognized as a genealogy of the faltering soles of black folk. Moreover, I propose that the purview of this bridge of the falling black body is not only limited to the water, in the way glimpsed by Glissant's underwater columns of the drowned, but also extends to wherever and whenever it is that black bodies *still* fall. In other words, there is a history of falling to which I am arguing we must attend that, even if precipitated by the waters of Middle Passage, persists beyond them as a *fundamental* expression of the "problem" of being black. The problem of an ongoing precarious relation to ground that did not end when the inhabitants of the deep made landfall.

Indeed, the history of blackness's foundering is long. It's Frederick Douglass's Aunt Hester suspended from a hook "so that she stood upon the ends of her toes."[20] It's Frantz Fanon, for whom, at the interpellating cry of "Look, a Negro!," the ground began "to rock with laughter" until his "feet no longer felt the caress of the ground."[21] It's Emmett Till laid to rest in the Tallahatchie River by a white man trying to show "how me and my folks stand."[22] It's Trayvon Martin also lost to a man standing his ground. But before any of these, and first, it is "the footprint on the water, filling," the steps middle passing Africans blinked on the face of the Atlantic during the centuries-long tenure of the transatlantic slave trade.[23] This genealogy of the soles of black folk foundering outside of the black literary tradition (until, in Aunt Hester's case, it finds its way inside) constitutes the cacophonous wreckage that ever accumulates, though never quite piles *up*, at the feet of the Angel of Black History. In contrast to Walter Benjamin's famed Angel of History in his meditation on the "Angelus Novus," the domain of this angel's flight pertains not to the land but to the sea. It may be spotted in an early passage in *The Interesting Narrative of the Life of Olaudah Equiano*, when a slave ship looks as though it were about to move away from something Equiano is staring at: "Soon after this the blacks who brought me on board went off, and left me abandoned to despair. I now saw myself deprived of all chance of returning to my native country, or even the least glimpse of hope of gaining the shore."[24] What I am calling the Angel of Black History must look just like this slave ship, ever receding from land as the winds of modernity propel its winged sails into the deep. Frederick Douglass establishes sufficient precedent for reading the ship in this way when he writes of the "swift winged *angels*" in motion across the Chesapeake Bay.[25] But further precedent still may be found in Derek Walcott's insistence that "the sea is History."[26] Where we might see, in the aforementioned catalog of the faltering soles of black folk, a chain of discrete events, our angel sees only the "one single catastrophe" of Middle Passage and its racially uneven distribution of ground. Moreover, the strange pile created by this black maritime disaster is inverted, growing ocean-deep rather than sky-high. The "rubble on top of rubble" that it heaps at the feet of our angel consists rather harrowingly of slave on top of sinking slave.[27] I am putting forward a possible vision of the history of black peoples, then, in which the chains binding the underwater columns of drowned Africans extend unbroken unto figures as diverse as Aunt Hester, Frantz Fanon, Emmett Till, and Trayvon Martin. I am putting forward, too, a vision of black literary history where we might recognize in the wobbly gait of Ellison's "deep sea divers" or in the water-frustrated posture of Bigger something of the crisis originally visited upon the "inhabitants of the deep." In other words, I propose that, like Equiano, who saw himself deprived of all "hope of gaining the shore," the black literary tradition also sees itself as profoundly divested of the ground, thinks this divestment as the problem of being black, and figures this problem through a recursive appeal to water.

IV. "Sturm und Drang"

A parallel tradition of black study imagines the "problem" of being black as not just a physical but also an ontological crisis of groundlessness precipitated by the transatlantic slave trade. For example, in her famous essay "Mama's Baby, Papa's Maybe" (1987), Hortense Spillers outlines a "grammar" of black being that begins with the "rupture" of Middle Passage:

> The symbolic order that I wish to trace in this writing, calling it an "American grammar," begins at the "*beginning*," which is really a rupture and a radically different kind of cultural continuation. The massive demographic shifts, the violent formation of a modern African consciousness, that take place on the subsaharan Continent during the initiative strikes which open the Atlantic Slave Trade in the fifteenth century of our Christ, interrupted hundreds of years of black African culture. We write and think, then, about an outcome of aspects of African-American life in the United States under the pressure of those events.[28]

This oft-cited passage from Spillers exemplifies a significant tradition of black study, which understands the ordeal of being black to have first emerged during the forced abduction and transatlantic migration of millions of captives from the African continent to the New World. Among the "we" who so "write and think" not just about "African-American life in the United States" but black diasporic life more broadly, we can also include Glissant, who, in the opening chapter of *Poetics of Relation*, identifies the hold of the slave ship as a "womb" and further contends that "the entire ocean, the entire sea . . . make one vast beginning."[29] More recently, Frank Wilderson described Middle Passage as the "dawning of blackness" and the "Black's first ontological instance."[30] Christina Sharpe has likewise theorized black being as existing in the "wake" of transatlantic slavery and its manifold afterlives.[31] And finally, Fred Moten has written regarding blackness that "it's terrible to have come from nothing but the sea, which is *nowhere*, navigable only in its constant autodislocation."[32] Whatever differences may obtain in their ultimate understandings of the "problem" of being black, the scholars included in this brief genealogy of black study all trace this "problem" back to Middle Passage.

Glissant especially helps us better apprehend Middle Passage, which we've already heard Spillers call a "rupture," by taking inventory of all that was lost in the rending. Enumerating the magnitude of this loss, Glissant imagines middle passing Africans "feeling a language vanish, the word of the gods vanish, and the sealed image of even the most everyday object, of even the most familiar animal, vanish. The evanescent taste of what you ate. The hounded scent of ochre earth and savannas."[33] Yet as much as any physical rupture obtaining in the "unparalleled displacement" of Middle Passage, this genealogy of black study also emphasizes a corresponding *ontological* rupture, for which the mere prospect of re-placement, in the New World or anywhere, offers no resolution. On this point, it's worth revisiting Spillers's extended account of how, for middle passing Africans suspended in the "oceanic," the bottom dropped out of not just the world but, perhaps even more devastatingly, being:

> Those African persons in "Middle Passage" were literally suspended in the "oceanic," if we think of the latter in its Freudian orientation as an analogy for undifferentiated identity: removed from the indigenous land and culture, and not-yet "American" either, these captive persons, without names that their captors would recognize, were in movement across the Atlantic, but they were also *nowhere* at all. Inasmuch as, on any given day, we might imagine, the captive personality did not know where s/he was, we could say that they were the culturally "unmade," thrown in the midst of a figurative darkness that "exposed" their destinies to an unknown course. Often enough for the captains of these galleys, navigational science of the day was not sufficient to guarantee the intended destination. We might say that the slave ship, its crew, and its human-as-cargo stand for a wild and unclaimed richness of possibility that is not interrupted, not "counted"/"accounted," or differentiated, until its movement gains the land thousands of miles away from the point of departure.

Under these conditions, one is neither female, nor male, as both subjects are taken into "account" as quantities. The female in "Middle Passage," as the apparently smaller physical mass, occupies "less room" in a directly translatable money economy. But she is, nevertheless, quantifiable by the same rules of accounting as her male counterpart.[34]

Following Spillers, the Africans in the middle were *nowhere*, not only in the physical sense of being suspended between Africa and the Americas but also in a related ontological sense of being "not-yet 'American'" nor fully African. But more than this basic complication of identity, whose cultural unmaking might be sutured effectively enough with time and a hyphen, the Africans in the middle also suffer an ontological transformation from persons into mere quantities of "flesh," for which human social categories such as gender are no more applicable than they are for meat in a grocery store. This abolition of personhood has led Wilderson and others to argue that blackness, in an extension of Orlando Patterson's famous definition of slavery, is "social death."[35] That is, an ontological position "against which Humanity establishes, maintains, and renews its coherence, its corporeal integrity."[36] In other words, the Africans in the middle not only fell out of a world bottomed by terra firma; they also fell out of human being in a way that surviving the transatlantic crossing could not resolve.

Black studies' characterization of this fall out of humanity is haunted, whether consciously or not, by the terrible physics of what originally befell the inhabitants of the deep. Moten, for example, speaks of blackness's lack of a "standpoint."[37] And Wilderson asserts that "no slave," and by extension, no Black, "is in the world."[38] An earlier example of this characterization of blackness's fall out of the world can also be found in the archetypal scene of racial interpellation narrated by Fanon in *Black Skin, White Masks* (1952) in the oft-cited chapter "The Lived Experience of the Black Man." Although he was on a train, Fanon might just as well have been on a slave ship when he was hailed by a child shouting "Look! A Negro!" Note his description of how "the ground, up till now a bridled steed, begins to rock with laughter."[39] Later in the chapter, we witness the ground give way entirely: "Truthfully, I'm telling you, I sensed my shoulders slipping from this world, and my feet no longer felt the caress of the ground."[40] At the sound of "Look! A Negro!", in other words, Fanon *sounds*. The recurring index of his racial interpellation in "The Lived Experience of the Black Man" is an instable relationship to the ground. His experience of the world grows as uncertain and instable as that of his middle passing ancestors. Like them, he "was unable to discover the feverish coordinates of the world."[41]

And in the "nausea" to which he repeatedly succumbs, there is also something of the "vertigo" that Glissant associates with the Africans suspended in the middle.[42] Moreover, just as Equiano gave himself up as cargo after being carried on board the slave ship, Fanon writes: "I . . . gave myself up as an object. . . . Yet this reconsideration of myself, this thematization, was not my idea. I wanted quite simply to be a man among men."[43] Elsewhere in *Black Skin, White Masks*, Fanon describes this falling out of humanity as a descent into a "veritable hell": "There is a zone of nonbeing, an extraordinarily sterile and arid region, an incline stripped bare of every essential from which a genuine new departure can emerge. In most cases, the black man cannot take advantage of this descent into a veritable hell."[44] In many ways, this ontological "descent into a veritable hell" mirrors the physical descent of the 1,818,681. Fanon's "zone of nonbeing" may even be ontology's *deep*. Given in and as his falling out of the world and humanity, Fanon's archetypal scene of racial interpellation is haunted by the original foundering of the inhabitants of the deep.

We might understand Du Bois's curious characterization of the problem of being black at the end of the first chapter of *Souls* to be similarly haunted. At the turn of the twentieth century, Du Bois still recognized enough in the vicissitudes of black life to warrant its representation as an embattled boat at sea. Just when it appeared we had historically disembarked for good, at the close of the last century to know the prowling of the slave ship, Du Bois curiously announces the dawning of "the time of *Sturm und Drang*," in which "storm and stress today rocks our little boat on the mad waters of the world-sea."[45] So it would appear that the consistent witness of black study is that we have yet to disembark the boats of our births. Blackness is an ongoing inhabitation of the deep.

But as humanity *stands* on the brink of climate catastrophe with its outsize carbon *footprint*, a damning of a different sort calls the damning of blackness as social death radically into question. An ecocritical interrogation of Fanon's characterization of his dislocation from the ground, for instance, might ask how humanity has come to expect the ground to behave as a "bridled steed" in the first place. On some levels, this represents a rather strange metaphor for a planetary surface that consists overwhelmingly of water and that, even with respect to land, constitutes far more than a docile surface. We'd do well to question the apprehension of the ground as a "bridled steed" with the same incredulity as the Invisible Man, when he declares: "My world has become one of infinite possibilities. What a phrase—still it's a good phrase and a good view of life, and a man shouldn't accept any other; that much I've learned underground. Until some gang succeeds in putting the world in a strait jacket, its definition is possibility."[46] Indeed, some gang has at least tried to straitjacket the planet. What, but a kind of straitjacket, do we apprehend in the advent of the Anthropocene or the fact that humanity has historically produced enough concrete to cover the planet in a layer two millimeters thick?[47] Yet given what this bridling of the planet has meant for the flourishing of all life on Earth, it seems that the Invisible Man's alternative view of the planet as one of infinite possibility is, indeed, a "good view of life," to which the faltering soles of black folk, precisely in their comparative inability to stand their ground, maintain a privileged relation. A relation that puts pressure on the idea of black social death, by gesturing toward what we might alternatively apprehend as black ecological life. For even if Fanon and his middle passing ancestors have fallen out of a bridled *world*, do we imagine that they have also fallen out of the *Earth*, which, to hear Ed Roberson tell it, "there is no step out of"?[48] And if humanity's efforts to bridle the world have been found to be a problem, then how should we understand the "problem" of being black given in and as exclusion from this world?

V. "giving up on land to light on"

At every turn, the tradition of black study that I survey above, which imagines the "problem" of being black as a crisis of groundlessness precipitated by Middle Passage, is characterized by a profound ambivalence. What Spillers, on the one hand, describes as the "rupture" of Middle Passage she also terms "a radically different kind of cultural continuation." And what she describes as the cultural unmaking of the Africans "suspended in the oceanic" she also apprehends as "a wild and unclaimed richness of possibility." So, too, is Fanon's "hell" or "zone of nonbeing" also a place in which some "advantage" can be claimed and "from which a genuine new departure can emerge." If the disadvantage of falling out of the world is what has generally come to be known in black study under the rubric of "social death," then what is the nature of its "advantage," its "wild and unclaimed richness of possibility"?

The pursuit of such a question requires a different orientation to black study's "problem." This orientation would not be overdetermined by *problem*'s dominant sense as "a matter or situation regarded as unwelcome, harmful, or wrong and needing to be overcome." Instead, it would remain open to that older and more open sense of *problem* as "a *question* proposed for academic discussion."[49] In contrast to the former sense, you'll notice that in the latter connotation of the word, the problem of being black is an open question, leaving open the possibility for an understanding of and orientation toward blackness as something other than a problematic condition needing to be overcome. This possibility is already apparent in the usage of Du Bois, from whom black studies inherits the critical language of the "problem" of being black. Immediately after offering a comprehensive delineation of the "Negro Problem" in "Of Our Spiritual Strivings," Du Bois writes at the conclusion of *Souls'* opening chapter, "And now what I have briefly sketched in large outline let me on coming pages *tell again* in many ways, with *loving* emphasis and *deeper* detail, that men may listen to the striving in the souls of black folk."[50] No sooner does Du Bois tell it than he resolves to tell it again, to retell it. And this retelling, it is important to point out, is an act of *love* expressed in the measure of its *depth*, its exhaustion. This stuttering announcement of our problem is nothing but black studies' faithful stammer, its telling again and again, in depth and love, of the problem in which we *get down* as much as we are cast down. We hear something like this stammering in Jared Sexton's improvisational rehearsal of Du Bois's original question in "The Social Life of Social Death":

> What is the nature of a form of being that presents a problem for the thought of being itself? More precisely, what is the nature of a human being whose human being is put into question radically and by definition, a human being whose being human raises the question of being human at all? Or, rather, whose being is the generative force, historic occasion, and essential byproduct of the question of human being in general? How might it be thought that there exists a being about which the question of its particular being is the condition of possibility and the condition of impossibility for any thought about being whatsoever? What can be said about such a being, and how, if at stake in the question is the very possibility of human being and perhaps even possibility as such? What is the being of a problem?
>
> The formulation of a sustained response to such an inquiry is the province of the field of investigation called black studies, or African American studies, or, more recently, African diaspora studies.[51]

What was true for Du Bois, after his systematic delineation of the "problem" of being black in "Of Our Spiritual Strivings," is also, following Sexton, true of black studies more broadly. Indeed, after all these years, we're still asking and answering how it feels to be a problem. We still aren't through with our question. And there is, in our serial and ceremonial revisiting and recasting of Du Bois's original question, a commitment that very much resembles love. We are in no ways tired, and we persist, not just because we have yet to overcome the "problem" of being black but because we *wouldn't*. Our questionable humanity, it turns out, has also proven to be what is increasingly coming to be recognized globally as the necessary occasion to question the Human and to think a genuinely new departure from the ecological dead end of western humanism and its dominating stand.

We can locate something like this departure in the alternative orientation to the crisis of having no ground, which the poet Dionne Brand adopts in her collection *Land to Light On* (1997):

> You come to this, here's the marrow of it, not
> moving, not standing, it's too much to hold up, what I
> really want to say is, I don't want no fucking country, here
> or there and all the way back, I don't like it, none of it,
> easy as that. I'm giving up on land to light on—[52]

Here, Brand elaborates a refusal of the bridled ground refused to her, as a black woman living in the unsettled wake of Middle Passage. But she also notably refuses, as "too much to hold up," the subjectivity that the bridling of the ground is meant to hold up: namely the stand-your-ground subjectivity made possible by the exclusionary formation of the nation-state. If humanity's outsize carbon footprint is any indication, then this subject is indeed too much to hold up. And it's not only the ground but the underground and submarine inhabitants of the deep that are doing the holding. Following Brand, then, what would it mean to think inhabitation of the deep not as blackness's problem to be overcome but as the ethical refusal of the stand-your-ground subject's "land to light on," of the Human's dominating stand? What if, relative to a reductive notion of standing your ground as territory or private property, inhabitation of the deep elaborates an ethical posture of being in the world that, in "giving up on land to light on," as Brand so beautifully puts it, consents to the precarious and ecological conditions of life on a deep planet?

To help illuminate this possibility, let us return to Du Bois's pronouncement of the dawning of "the time of *Sturm und Drang*" at the conclusion of "Of Our Spiritual Strivings." You'll recall that we have previously referred to this declaration as an index of the traumatic afterlife of Middle Passage. However, a more extended look at Du Bois's characterization of this time yields one final example of black ambivalence:

> So dawned the time of *Sturm und Drang*: storm and stress today rocks our little boat on the mad waters of the world-sea; there is within and without the sound of conflict, the burning of body and rending of soul; inspiration strives with doubt, and faith with vain questionings. The bright ideals of the past,—physical freedom, political power, the training

> of brains and the training of hands,—all these in turn have waxed and waned, until even the last grows dim and overcast. Are they all wrong,—all false? No, not that, but each alone was over-simple and incomplete. . . . Work, culture, liberty,—all these we need, not singly but together, not successively but together, each growing and aiding each, and all striving toward that vaster ideal that *swims* before the Negro people, the ideal of human brotherhood.[53]

Notice that in the very same waters that assail "our little boat," there curiously also "swims" what Du Bois describes as "the ideal of human brotherhood." Insofar as humans are understood as land creatures, and their life together exclusively a venture undertaken on land, we might reasonably expect to find the *ideal* of human fraternity (preserving for the moment Du Bois's masculinist language) on terra firma. However, Du Bois curiously locates this ideal at sea where, owing to its ongoing inhabitation of the deep, blackness presumably is in a privileged position to pursue it. Moreover, Du Bois reimagines Earth as a "world-sea" that better reflects the proportions of our blue planet.

If the outsize carbon footprint of the stand-your-ground subject has been weighed and found to be too much, perhaps such swimming as Du Bois imagines yields a more ecologically salutary way of envisioning not merely human brotherhood but more-than-human ecological life. To further elucidate what such swimming might entail for humans, consider this passage from *Being and Nothingness* (1943), in which Jean-Paul Sartre narrates his understanding of the ontological drama set in motion with the "appearance of the Other in the world": "Thus suddenly an object has appeared which has stolen the world from me. Everything is in place; everything still exists for me; but everything is traversed by an invisible flight and fixed in the direction of a new object. The appearance of the Other in the world corresponds therefore to a fixed sliding of the whole universe, to a decentralization of the world which undermines the centralization which I am simultaneously effecting."[54] I am interested in Sartre's interpretation of the Other as that which not only puts the world to flight—interesting in itself insofar as this fugitive world resists its own territorialization in the form of private property—but also that which sets the world flowing. For now that the other sees me, Sartre writes, "it appears that the world has a kind of drain hole in the middle of its being and that it is perpetually flowing off through this hole."[55] What if the drama that Sartre describes is not a crisis, but rather the gracious teaching of *all* difference, both human and more-than-human? What would it mean to be open to the terra firma flowing beneath our feet as the given ground of ecological life, and not that which we might seek to bridle or possess? What if, when we meet each other, we consent to walk on water? To be found upon the given relations that give us, and so, in this way, to join the ranks of the "inhabitants of the deep"? The Ibos, to whom we turn now in Paule Marshall's *Praisesong for the Widow*, learned to walk in just this way. When they went walking on the water, they too sang out with a deep voice; and their singing spawned a deep imagination.

4

DEEP IMAGINATION

What did I do to be so black and blue?
—LOUIS ARMSTRONG, "Black and Blue"

I. "black and blue"

THAT'S SALT WATER COMING OUT of Louis's spit valve, our faithful witness to the liquid residue of the music and the way it sounds. We forget this crude matter when we attend to the poetry black and blues people make out of being invisible. Lose the sense of its relation to the music, of the saliva all bound up in the way it sounds. We could go to the excessive lengths of the anonymous narrator in Ralph Ellison's *Invisible Man* to really hear Armstrong's "Black and Blue":

> Now I have one radio-phonograph; I plan to have five. There is a certain acoustical deadness in my hole, and when I have music I want to *feel* its vibration, not only with my ear but with my whole body. I'd like to hear five recordings of Louis Armstrong playing and singing "What Did I Do to Be so Black and Blue"—all at the same time. . . . Perhaps I like Louis Armstrong because he's made poetry out of being invisible. I think it must be because he's unaware that he *is* invisible. And my own grasp of invisibility aids me to understand his music.[1]

All five phonographs can be playing. But have we *really* heard unless we've somehow managed to hear the spit too?

Claiming "few really listen to this music," the Invisible Man proposes and performs in the novel's famous prologue what he calls "a new analytical way of listening to music."[2] The newness of his method can be located in its augmented sense of what's available to be heard. It listens to not only sound's time but also its space; not only sound's sound but also its silence. This excessive hearing calls for *five* phonographs instead of the usual one. A detail, which, along with the Invisible Man's aspiration to also *feel* the music with his whole body, suggests a desire to employ all *five* senses in a single but expanded act of listening. This chapter is in many ways kin to this effort of conceiving an augmented listening practice, one as suited to hearing the poetry as the music. Our concern here, then, is not only how we listen but how we read.

With Louis's spit valve as my witness, I propose that the expressive traditions of the African Diaspora are wet. By which I mean to say, profoundly given to what Gaston Bachelard has called a "primitive material reverie" about water.[3] This, I argue, is what we must ultimately come to understand and appreciate about the *mind* that is "gone with the Ibos," those middle passing Africans we find songfully hovering over the face of the deep in Paule Marshall's *Praisesong for the Widow* (1983).[4] But prior to any discussion of this mind or its relationship to the expressive traditions of the African Diaspora, we have first to understand just where the Ibos have gone and wrestle a while with the improbable testimony about what they did there. And in that Benjaminian sort of way, flinching not to wrestle with the angels of history even when we find them underwater.

In concerning itself with where the Ibos have gone, this chapter's black study by way of *Praisesong* and other texts invites us to go with them. In this way, our critical journey will mirror that to which a reluctant Avatara (Avey) Johnson, the novel's protagonist, consents after her deceased great-aunt Cuney implores her in a dream to resume their ceremonial walks to a place called "Ibo Landing":

> Three nights ago, in the dream, there the old woman had been after all those years, drawn up waiting for her on the road. . . . Standing there unmarked by the grave . . . beckoning to her with a hand that should have been fleshless bone by now. . . .
>
> . . . She was pleading with her now to join her, silently exhorting her, transformed into a preacher in a Holiness church imploring the sinners and backsliders to come forward to the mercy seat. "*Come / O will you come . . . ?*"[5]

As a child, Avey traveled every August from Harlem to visit her great-aunt Cuney in Tatem, a fictional South Carolina Sea Island. The novel details Avey's annual trips to the South as a child in multiple flashbacks, while a significantly older and recently widowed Avey undertakes a journey to the Caribbean island of Grenada and, later, Carriacou. Thus, *Praisesong* yields a type of what Robert Stepto has called the "immersion narrative"—an African American narrative form characterized by a "ritualized journey into a symbolic South" and, in this case, the Global South.[6] In addition to demonstrating the classic properties of the "immersion narrative," however, *Praisesong* also typifies the black narrative form, which this book has called the "submersion narrative" and which is alternatively characterized by a ritualized journey to a symbolic deep. During Avey's annual visits to the South, Aunt Cuney ritually took Avey to a place known locally in Tatem as "the Landing," where a group of enslaved Ibos once purportedly landed from a slave ship and, not liking what they saw, walked on water back to Africa. It's to the Landing, in the dream above, that the now deceased Aunt Cuney exhorts a much older and recently widowed Avey to "*Come*." And the spiritual disturbance created by this oneiric invitation causes Avey to embark on a parallel journey to another symbolic deep, which she encounters on a boat ride from the mainland of Grenada to Carriacou and whose circumstances strongly evoke the Middle Passage.

Because "people in Tatem said she had made the Landing her religion," Aunt Cuney's transformation into a preacher in Avey's dream is fitting.[7] If the text of the preacher hooping in Ellison's "underworld of sound" is the "Blackness of Blackness," Aunt Cuney's text is the story of the Ibo Landing. She's been coming from this same scripture ever since Avey turned seven and Aunt Cuney "ordered [Avey's] father to bring and deposit her every August in Tatem . . . and there year after year had filled her head with some far-fetched story of people walking on water which she in her childish faith had believed till the age of ten."[8] Seated, as it were, in Aunt Cuney's waterfront church between Sister Avey and Brother Invisible, in the pages to follow we will consider how black study in general, and black literary study in particular, always begins with a reading of the "Blackness of Blackness." Always begins, that is, by concluding something about what blackness is. It is certainly no mistake that the "Blackness of Blackness" resounds from the *ground* floor of Brother Invisible's "underworld of sound," his concentrated listening to Louis's horn. Nevertheless, we are gathered in Aunt Cuney's church and not that of Ellison's preacher because of how the ambivalent valuations of blackness overheard by the Invisible Man are profoundly echoed with respect to water in the story of the Ibos.

So profoundly, in fact, that even before we turn to Aunt Cuney's sermon in full, we might summarize it in this undoubtedly familiar way:

> "Brothers and sisters, my text this morning is 'the Landing of the water-walking Ibos.'"
>
> And a congregation of voices answered: "That water is most blue, sister, most blue . . ."
>
> "In the beginning . . ."
>
> "At the very start," they cried.
>
> ". . . There was water . . ."
>
> "Preach it . . ."
>
> "Now water is . . ." Aunt Cuney shouted.
>
> "Bloody . . ."
>
> "I said water is . . ."
>
> "Preach it, sister . . ."
>
> ". . . an' water ain't . . ."
>
> "Amen, sister . . ."
>
> "Water will git you . . ."
>
> "Yes, it will . . ."
>
> "Yes, it will . . ."
>
> ". . . An' water won't . . ."
>
> Naw, it won't!"
>
> "It do . . ."
>
> "It do, Lawd . . ."
>
> ". . . an' it don't."
>
> "Halleluiah . . ."
>
> ". . . It'll put you, glory, glory, Oh my Lawd, in the WHALE'S BELLY."
>
> "Preach it, dear sister . . ."
>
> ". . . an' make you tempt . . ."
>
> "Good God a-mighty!"
>
> "Old Aunt Cuney!"
>
> "Water will make you . . ."
>
> "Water . . ."
>
> ". . . or water will un-make you."[9]

Recalling that the "Blackness of Blackness" resounds somewhere deep down in the depths of Armstrong's "Black and Blue," the text of the Ibo Landing takes up this blue. Thinks the blue(s) of black by way of blackness's primordial relation to the water that there was in the beginning. Teaches us to hear the spit.

II. food! for (black) thought

i.

Each time they reached Ibo Landing, after miles of walking, Aunt Cuney started into telling the story:

> It was here that they brought 'em. They taken 'em out of the boats right here where we's standing. Nobody remembers how many of 'em it was, but they was a good few 'cording to my gran' who was a little girl no bigger than you when it happened. The small boats was dragged up here and the ship they had just come from was out in the deep water. Great big ol' ship with sails. And the minute those Ibos was brought on shore they just stopped, my gran' said, and taken a look around. A good long look. Not saying a word. Just studying the place real good. Just taking their time and studying on it.[10]

Later we will have occasion to consider the Ibos' studying as an enactment of black study. For now, however, we give our attention to the moment in Aunt Cuney's story where the suggested parallel with Ellison's preacher appears to break down. For if, in the traditional antiphonal mode of black preaching, he solicits the free participation of his congregation, Aunt Cuney, for all of her obvious calling, seems relatively uninterested in Avey's response. As Aunt Cuney starts to tell how the Ibos turned to the water, a point in the story where she routinely asks Avey a question, she strangely ignores the girl's answer:

> "Do you know what the Ibos did? Do you? . . ."
>
> "I do." (It wasn't meant for her to answer but she always did anyway.) "Want me to finish telling about 'em? I know the story good as you." (Which was true. Back home after only her first summer in Tatem she had recounted the whole thing almost word for word to her three brothers, complete with the old woman's inflections and gestures.)
>
> ". . . They just turned, my gran' said, all of 'em—" she would have ignored the *interruption* as usual, *wouldn't even have heard it over the voice that possessed her*—"and walked on back down to the edge of the river here. Every las' man, woman, and chile. . . . And they didn't bother getting back into the small boats drawed up here—boats take too much time. They just kept walking right on out over the river. Now you wouldna thought they'd of got very far seeing as it was water they was walking on. Besides they had all that iron on 'em . . . and chains hooking up the iron. But

> chains didn't stop those Ibos none. Neither iron. The way my gran' tol' it (other folks in Tatem said it wasn't so and that she was crazy but she never paid 'em no mind) 'cording to her they just kept on walking like the water was solid ground.[11]

Yet if Aunt Cuney ignores Avey, it is not because she prefers to be alone in the telling. In fact, because of "the voice that possessed her," she isn't alone at all. Rather she is accompanied by her gran', Avatara, who first passed the story on to her. Far from demonstrating an aversion to antiphony, then, Aunt Cuney's story may actually be read as her response to a call first sounded by her gran'. Nevertheless, I argue that the story should also be read as Aunt Cuney's call to Avey. The mere fact that she now tells Avey a story she received from her own gran', and that she does so regularly, suggests a desire that Avey one day be able to tell it too. Telling the story may even be the mission the old woman was entrusting to her: "in instilling the story of the Ibos in her child's mind, the old woman had entrusted her with a mission she couldn't even name yet had felt duty-bound to fulfill. It had taken [Avey] years to rid herself of the notion."[12] When Avey finally succeeds in ridding herself of this vague notion, Aunt Cuney appears to her in a dream as a "preacher" imploring her to return to the place "she had made her . . . religion." Despite the evidence to the contrary, then, Aunt Cuney not only desires Avey's participation as a future teller of the story, but she also wishes to make Avey her disciple.[13]

If in this way we can be sure that Aunt Cuney wants Avey's participation, how then do we explain the refusal to allow her to "finish telling about 'em," especially since Avey insists (and Marshall even confirms), "I know the story"? If we understand Aunt Cuney to also *hear* the story she tells (from the voice possessing her), then the fact that she doesn't even hear what's significantly called Avey's "interruption" suggests that the story Avey believes she knows somehow differs from Aunt Cuney's. It is true that Avey can perfectly render the story's content ("word for word") and form ("the old woman's inflections and gestures"). But perhaps that is not all there is to tell. In this sense, Aunt Cuney ignoring Avey may be read as an attempt to guard the story's integrity or at the very least as a fidelity to the voice possessing her. It implies that something about Avey's knowledge is not quite up to the telling. What more of the story would Avey have to know, then, if content and form alone are insufficient, in order to "finish telling about 'em"?

Because Aunt Cuney hears the story she tells, perhaps Avey's incomplete knowledge of the story can be attributed to a failure of her listening. In other words, Avey can't really tell it because she hasn't really heard it. Yet Aunt Cuney does not simply hear the story. Her hearing takes the specific form of being possessed by Avatara. It's certainly telling, then, that Avey, who I have already suggested is hard of hearing, also expresses an aversion to being possessed by Avatara. During the dream sequence in which Aunt Cuney implores Avey to return to "the Landing," Marshall voices Avey's resistance to being Avatara's "little girl" and resentment for having been "saddled with her name":

> Couldn't [Aunt Cuney] see she was no longer the child . . . scrambling along at her side over the wrecked fields? No longer the Avey (or Avatara as she insisted on calling her) she had laid claim to for a month each summer from the time she was seven. Before she was seven! Before she had been born even! There was the story of how she had sent word months before her birth that it would be a girl and she was to be called after her grandmother who had come to her in a dream with the news: "It's my gran' done sent her. She's her little girl."
>
> Great-aunt Cuney had saddled her with the name of some-one people had sworn was crazy.[14]

I propose that Avey's inability to "finish telling about 'em" is ultimately rooted in her aversion to being possessed by her namesake in the way we have understood Aunt Cuney to be when she tells the story. But what exactly would it mean for Avey to consent to be possessed in this way? Perhaps Aunt Cuney's insistence on *calling* Avey "Avatara" offers some insight, given what it arguably reveals about how she expects Avey to *respond*. In this respect, I propose that the original question—"Do you know what the Ibos did?"—should be understood as a call intended for Avey only insofar as she might learn to respond in the spirit of her name. Then Avey would have recognized that Aunt Cuney's hail was really addressed to her, that it was really Avatara who was meant by the hailing (and not someone else). Here, I employ the rhetoric of Louis Althusser's drama of interpellation intentionally, but not without some amendment of its original spirit in order to better suit our purposes.[15] In Avey's specific case, we are discussing not the interpellation of the subject but rather that very subject's unmaking. Like the Ibos, who, to hear Aunt Cuney tell it, also "turned," the "one-hundred-and-eighty-degree physical *conversion*" solicited from the "backslider" Avey is precisely a turn unto the water. This water that, like blackness, *will make you and unmake you*. Since Avey's aversion to her name manifests in her dream precisely as a stubborn reluctance to return with Aunt Cuney to "the Landing," we can already suspect that Avey's ability to "finish telling about 'em" in the novel would require an oneiric turn to the water.

ii.

Perhaps at this point, as an illuminating foil to Aunt Cuney's inspired hearing (and Avey's lack thereof), it will prove useful to remember the symptoms of Brother Invisible's "new analytical way of listening to music" as well as the fact that it is induced by a drug trip:

> I know now that few really listen to this music. I sat on the chair's edge in a soaking sweat. . . . It was exhausting—as though I had held my breath continuously for an hour under the terrifying serenity that comes from days of intense hunger. And yet, it was a strangely satisfying experience for an invisible man to hear the silence of sound. I had discovered unrecognized compulsions of my being—even though I could not answer "yes" to their promptings. I haven't smoked a reefer since, however; not because they're illegal, but because to *see* around corners is enough (that is not unusual when you are invisible). But to hear around them is too much; it inhibits action. And . . . I believe in nothing if not action.[16]

Brother Invisible may not be concerned with the fact that reefer is illegal, but we can charge him with possession anyway. Don't mistake me. I certainly don't mean to conflate the spiritual phenomenon of possession with drug use. But I do want to call attention to how they similarly inhibit our faculties of self-possession. Both have a way of making us vulnerable to getting got. And while Brother Invisible decided never to smoke reefer again, it is important to point out that not all forms of getting got inhibit action. Spiritual possession, in particular—that is, being in the spirit—even has a record of prompting it. Nevertheless, it's unclear whether the Invisible Man's decision not to smoke expresses a belief that action is exclusively the work of the self-possessed. He concludes that it is enough just to be invisible in order to sense in the augmented way he desires. If Brother Invisible thinks there is actually something to if not invisibility, then blackness—something more than the mere nightmarish consequence of white fantasy—then to be invisible because one has consented to be got by blackness (and not the other way around) may instance a kind of possession in its own right. Blackness, in this sense, is a call to which one may or may not respond. A vocation to which one may or may not consent. It "*will git you.*" And "*it won't.*"

The symptoms of Brother Invisible's drug trip are more interesting still for how they resemble and even illuminate elements of Aunt Cuney's inspired hearing that are absent from Avey's prior to her oneiric turn. If the Invisible Man wanted not only to hear the music with his ears but to *feel* it with his whole body, then the "soaking sweat" in which he emerges from his descent into the depths of sound suggests that the music may just feel wet. But wet in such a way that calls to mind the black maritime experiences of those who also held their breath continuously. For where else do we hold our breath but underwater? In other words, when Brother Invisible gives an expanded ear to Armstrong's sounding of the travails of being black and blue, he "feels" a drowning.

It is important to note how the Ibos of the historical Ibo Landing, per the testimony of the slave trader William Mein, preserved to us in a letter dated May 24, 1803, are also numbered among the drowned slaves who shared in this experience of the water. Especially because, to Mein's eye, these Ibos didn't walk on water at all. They drowned:

> We have had a great many Ibo and Angolas—all of which have readily sold about L.E.100 round of his prime. Spaulding and Couper bought a whole bay of Ibos and have suffered much by mismanagement of Mr. Couper's overseer Paterson who poor fellow lost his life. The Negroes rose by being confined in a small vessel. Patterson was frightened and in swimming ashore he with two sailors were drowned. The Negroes took to the Marsh and they have lost at least ten or twelve in recovering them besides being subject to an expense [of] ten dollars a head for salvage.[17]

If for Aunt Cuney and her gran' "*water is*," and *is* ground, in Mein's estimation "*water ain't*." His letter has helped researchers determine the historical events that likely inspired what has been preserved in the oral and folk traditions of the Georgia and South Carolina Sea Islands alternately as the myth of the Flying Africans and the Ibo Landing story. From this archival record, Timothy Powell has offered the following summary of what we know for sure:

> What we do know for sure is that in May 1803, a group of Ibo . . . slaves arrived at Skidaway Island, just south of Savannah, Georgia, after enduring the nightmare of the Middle Passage. The slave dealer William Mein sold the Ibo to Thomas Spalding and James Couper. . . . On the short voyage from Skidaway to St. Simon Island, the Ibo rose in rebellion, leading to the death of the white overseer and two sailors aboard the *York*. According to archival evidence, the Ibo did not fly, but instead committed collective suicide by drowning themselves in Dunbar Creek, at a place now called Ebos Landing.

Powell has insightfully argued that "the distinction between suicide and flight may very well depend on whether the analysis takes into consideration the spiritual dimension of the story, the realm of the ancestors."[18] While for Mein the story clearly ends with the Ibos' death, Powell explains that "the oral histories of the black community . . . focus most intently on what happens immediately after Mein's conclusion, when the Ibo are transformed into powerful ancestral spirits."[19] It is this afterward, according to Powell, that is dramatized in the Ibos' "flying" or "walking" home to Africa.

By privileging the more cyclical (as opposed to linear) sense of time that Powell reasons the Ibos likely possessed, Powell submits Mein's letter to "a more expansive reading" that should call to mind Brother Invisible's expanded hearing. His reading unpacks the more complex spiritual elements inhering in the events reductively detailed by Mein as "the Negroes rose" and "the Negroes took to the Marsh," and it illuminates two additional events elided by the letter's sparing attention to the Ibos and their cyclical sense of time. In addition to the Ibos' uprising and mass suicide, Powell draws our attention, on the one hand, to their initial capture in Africa and, on the other, to their subsequent return home to Africa as ancestral spirits. While I generally affirm and agree with Powell's reading, I want to call special attention to his assessment of this very first event, which, precisely because it is first, overdetermines what it is possible to see in the subsequent events he so nimbly illuminates in Mein's letter. "The first event . . . can be construed as the capture of 'ten or twelve' souls who were transformed from freemen to slaves and thrown into a state of spiritual crisis. This crisis constitutes a dam of time . . . wherein the Ibo undergo a transformation of energy that Orlando Patterson calls the 'social death' of slavery."[20] I am particularly interested in how this assessment of the initial capture of the Ibos overdetermines what can be seen in the Ibos' collective suicide. By regarding slavery as social death, Powell divests the Ibos' suicide of any meaning in itself, at least insofar as it might bear significance for life. It is meaningful, even to the survivors who would later tell the story, only insofar as it allows the Ibos to escape the living death of slavery and return home to Africa as ancestral spirits. The claim that the Ibos walked on water, then, lapses into a metaphor for the afterlife. The Ibos still drown, and only drown. But their spirits walk. The problem with this reading, however, is that it obscures the tremendous implications for *life*, and not just the afterlife, of the literal walking insisted on by those left behind to tell the story. If, as Powell has explained, "the African American community that was left behind after the Ibo flew away is ultimately responsible for the creation and preservation of the many different versions of the story that have been passed down to the present day," then the rendering of the Ibos' walking as mere metaphor obscures the foundational aesthetic decision guiding and inspiring the "creation and preservation" of these stories.[21]

Namely the decision to regard water as a kind of ground. The widespread implications of such a decision, particularly with respect to what we might discern about the Gullah Geechee imagination, are especially apparent in light of the story's ubiquity throughout the Sea Islands. While Mein's letter locates the original events of the Ibo Landing on Saint Simons Island in Georgia, Marshall stages her rendering of the Ibo Landing myth on the fictional Tatem Island in South Carolina. And in her film *Daughters of the Dust*, director Julie Dash, who incorporates an extensive retelling of Marshall's version of the myth into the film's script, stages her own representation of the Ibo Landing myth on Dataw Island, South Carolina.[22] Helping to explain this geographic proliferation of Ibo Landings, Sara Clarke Kaplan details Dash's observation that "nearly every island off the Carolina/Georgia coast has an 'Ibo Landing,' a place renowned as the site where a group of newly-disembarked captive Africans returned to the waters of the Atlantic rather than become slaves."[23]

What drops out of view in Powell's reading of the Ibo Landing story is a sense of the character of the collective imagination of those left behind to create it. What can be discerned about the Gullah Geechee imagination given the widespread aesthetic decision to regard water as ground? What species of imagination does such a decision found? To what manner of creation does it give rise? How might we characterize the poetic orientation of the imagination whose ground floor is the water? Can we now begin to think about Aunt Cuney's possession as a matter of having been got by the water? Indeed, if this aesthetic decision or judgment about water is taken to decide one's participation in the imagination that is able to "finish telling about 'em," then we might begin to detect the lack of such imagination in the question Avey asks about the improbable feat of the water-walking Ibos.

iii.

The germ of the aversion to possession Avey demonstrates in her dream as an adult may already be discerned in the question she asks Aunt Cuney as a child. After four straight summers of hearing the improbable story of the water-walking Ibos, Avey finally thinks to ask:

> "But how come they didn't drown, Aunt Cuney?"
>
> She had been ten—that old!—and had been hearing the story for four summers straight before she had thought to ask.
>
> Slowly, standing on the consecrated ground . . . her great-aunt had turned and regarded her in silence for the longest time. It was to take Avey years to forget the look on the face under the field hat, the disappointment

> and sadness there. If she could have reached up that day and snatched her question like a fly out of the air and swallowed it whole, she would have done so.[24]

Just as it would take Avey years to rid herself of the vague notion of a call inhering in her name, it would take her years to forget the look bounding into her from beneath the brim of Aunt Cuney's hat. And even once she finally manages to forget, the look stubbornly resurfaces when she dreams of Aunt Cuney imploring her to return to "the Landing" with eyes that "were filled . . . with the same disappointment and sadness that had greeted the thoughtless question she had asked as the ten-year-old long ago. In them was reflected also the mute plea: '*Come/Won't you come.*'"[25] This later instance of Aunt Cuney's look informs our understanding of the nature of her "disappointment" so many years before. It reveals that Aunt Cuney was disappointed with Avey's "thoughtless question" only insofar as it revealed that she had yet to *come*. And to come is precisely to come to the water and learn to regard it as ground. This is the aesthetic decision animating the story of the water-walking Ibos. All who would *really* tell the story must make it. I want to insist, however, that Avey's question is not utterly thoughtless. It simply lacks the sort of thought with which the story's foundational conceit must be apprehended: faith and imagination. Still, though the query is reprimanded, it seems to me at least that Avey's question *should* be asked; that we cannot fully appreciate Aunt Cuney's claim about what the Ibos did unless we feel the terrible need to ask it. In fact, Avey can't even begin to *come* without asking. Because it's precisely here, in her recognition of the questionable, that she even approaches the opportunity to exercise the kind of "thought" Aunt Cuney accuses her question of lacking.

Aunt Cuney's answer to Avey's question offers some insight into the sort of thought by which the story should be apprehended:

> "Did it say Jesus drowned when he went walking on the water in that Sunday School book your momma always sends with you?"
>
> "No, ma'am."
>
> "I din' think so. You got any more questions?"[26]

In response to Avey's question, Aunt Cuney claims the precedence and authority of two signature ground miracles of the Judeo-Christian religious tradition. The Ibo slaves take off their boats in that Moses way: "And when they got to where the ship was they didn't so much as give it a look. Just walked on past it. Didn't want nothing to do with that ol' ship. They feets was gonna take 'em wherever they was going that day."[27] The ground of Ibo Landing is not just "consecrated." It's *holy*. By which I mean to suggest a relation between this ground and that which is disclosed to Moses at the burning bush. But this ground, as in the second of our ground miracles, includes the water. The Ibos walk on it as ably as Jesus is purported to have walked on water in the New Testament. If "the Landing" is Aunt Cuney's religion, then its name derives from its founding miracle. The Landing. The improvisation of land, the revelation of holy ground. *Ground*, Aunt Cuney insists, and yet the daughter of the Ibos has no place to rest her feet. No place but the no-place of the water.

By invoking the precedent of Jesus walking on water, Aunt Cuney at once signals that this story calls for *faith* even as she critiques the racially coded processes by which what is dignified as faith in one context is arbitrarily denigrated as superstition in another. Or put another way, she critiques the restriction of faith as viable, if at all, only in relation to the miracles recorded in the canonical scriptures of the Christian Bible. That said, I think that belief in Jesus is precisely what Aunt Cuney *wants*, at least insofar as he walked on water. Only she understands his feat, and the kindred miracle performed by the Ibos, not primarily as a demonstration of transcendent power but rather as a teaching about how we too might walk. Blessed are those who walk on water, for they will inherit the earth before the end of the world. This earth, whose surface is more than 70 percent water, such that no truer steps have ever been taken than those taken at sea. To say that Aunt Cuney wants faith in Jesus, then, is to say she believes in the way he and the Ibos walked, and she would have others *come* and believe, too. The tone is less "If you believe Jesus did, then why not the Ibos?" and more "If not the Ibos, then you could hardly really believe Jesus did either." By not drowning when he went walking on the water, as Aunt Cuney reminds Avey, Jesus takes hold of boatless human engagement with the water in a way that imagines something other and more than just our drowning. There are actual steps here. However brief. What remains to us now is the work of coming to believe in them. To believe in these steps, however, also requires a feat of imagination, that faculty able to produce images that, by many accounts, aren't there.

Besides its lack of faith, then, Avey's question is also "thoughtless" with respect to its lack of imagination. Aunt Cuney's invocation of Jesus in relation to the Ibos is also telling in this regard. The stories concerning the two feature tremendous suffering as well as incredible beauty. And because the presence of the former obscures our recognition of the latter, these stories pose a severe challenge to our imaginations if we hope to faithfully bear witness to both. Consider James Cone's comments on the imagination it takes to apprehend the mysteries of black life in *The Cross and the Lynching Tree* (2011): "It takes a powerful imagination, grounded in historical experience, to uncover the great *mysteries* of black life. . . . The beauty in black existence is as real as the brutality, and the beauty prevents the brutality from having the final word. Black suffering needs radical and creative voices, prophetic advocates who can tell brutal and beautiful stories of how oppressed black people survived with a measure of dignity when they were not meant to."[28] The thing about a mystery—about the moment we apprehend not knowing something and find it so exhilarating that we need a word for it that we set about naming it with the precision of a poet, because we'd like to somehow formalize for posterity a way to know not-knowing—is that it's nothing if not aesthetic. If it weren't, there wouldn't be such delight when you find yourself on the inside of one—marveling at its finishes, all the ways it kept itself from being known, until you even find yourself wishing you could not know again. The Ibo Landing story, as a portrait of black life or the lived experience of blackness, is beautiful in this way. Not because it is a fantasy of flight from the historical realities inspiring it but precisely because it isn't. The story, I argue, is terribly aware of the brutal history of the drowned, yet it still insists on the co-presence of the beautiful. And the beautiful keeps the brutal from having the final word, because its sheer being there is a mystery that is itself beautiful. In this way, beauty can't help but finish brutality's sentences. This, by the way, is why it would be a mistake to think that Armstrong is able to make poetry out of being invisible because he's somehow unaware. Quite the opposite is true, in fact. Because even if invisibility can't sing, since as the phantom of some white nightmare it could hardly be said even to exist, blackness can. Which is to say there is more to blackness than being invisible. But detecting awareness of this is not so straightforward as poring over the song's content and form or turning up the volume. I'm not refuting that a grasp of invisibility (or blackness) helps Brother Invisible understand the music, but I am refuting the assumption that a similar awareness of being black (if not invisible) can't likewise aid Louis's playing.

It's a matter, then, of learning to hear *in the music* the operation of the "powerful imagination" that it takes to uncover the great mysteries of being black and blue. The playing *is* already this uncovering. When we really hear it, we uncover it, too. But it's the musician and the poet, long before the critic, who first lend their "radical and creative voices" to the revelation. Louis is the prophet sounding out the brutal-beautiful story on his trumpet. Indeed, it takes "a powerful imagination, grounded in historical experience," to make poetry out of blackness. Especially when that historical experience is precisely the experience of having no ground. This, the operation of this imagination, *is* the mystery we only belatedly uncover with the hole of Louis's spit valve.

With respect to the mysterious paradoxes and contradictions of black life uncovered in the Ibo Landing story, the faith and imagination missing from Avey's question are, according to Cone, poignantly exercised by black Christians with respect to the kindred example of the cross of Jesus:

> That God could "make a way out of no way" in Jesus' cross was truly absurd to the intellect, yet profoundly real in the souls of black folk. Enslaved blacks who first heard the gospel message seized on the power of the cross. Christ crucified manifested God's loving and liberating presence *in* the contradictions of black life—that transcendent presence in the lives of black Christians that empowered them to believe that *ultimately*, in God's eschatological future, they would not be defeated by the "troubles of this world," no matter how great and painful their suffering. Believing this paradox, this absurd claim of faith, was only possible through God's "amazing grace" and the gift of faith, grounded in humility and repentance. There was no place for the proud and mighty, for people who think that God called them to rule over others. The cross was God's critique of power—white power—with powerless love, snatching victory out of defeat.[29]

If the cross of Jesus, as a "way out of no way," is real to the souls of black folk, I wonder if that other miracle of his invoked by Aunt Cuney isn't all the more real to their *soles*. When Jesus "went walking on water," he made a ground out of no ground. Just as the water-walking Ibos were purported to have done. And just as Brother Invisible arguably does if, beside the more brutal symptoms accompanying the discovery of his invisibility, we also take note of his sea legs: "It occurred to me that the man had not seen me, actually; that he, as far as he knew, was in the midst of a walking nightmare! . . . I stared at him hard as the lights of a car stabbed through the darkness. He lay there, moaning on the asphalt; a man almost killed by a phantom. It unnerved me. I was both disgusted and ashamed. I was like a drunken man myself, wavering about on weakened legs."[30] Brother Invisible's experience of invisibility here is not unlike Bigger Thomas's experience, in Richard Wright's *Native Son*, of a "fear" that "rendered his legs like water."[31] Both moments speak to what blackness serially confronts in a myriad of historically shifting ways as the situation of having no ground. But the sorrow songs demonstrate that "wavering about on weakened legs," this symptom marking Brother Invisible's experience of invisibility, can nonetheless provide sufficient ground for poetry or song. Recall from "Deep Voice" Du Bois's narration of the peculiar circumstances that precipitated the creation of the well-known spiritual "No Body Knows the Trouble I've Seen":

"When, struck with sudden poverty, the United States *refused to fulfill its promises of land* to the freedmen, a brigadier-general went down to the Sea Islands to carry the news. An old woman on the outskirts of the throng began singing this song; all the mass joined with her, swaying."[32] The old woman might just be Aunt Cuney. Not only because the song, like her story, arises in the context of the Sea Islands but also because both the song and the story demonstrate the creative potential of "swaying," of "wavering about on weakened legs." In this way, the sorrow songs (and "No Body Knows" especially) bear witness to how poetry can be made from the *awareness* of having no ground. And since we find strains of this song in the epigraph of the first chapter of *The Souls of Black Folk*, which also includes a poem in which the speaker is straining to hear water's voice, *really hearing* this song might just require an ear for water as the enduring sign of the condition of having no ground. But an ear for water in the sense of detecting the operation of the imagination that has found its sea legs and learned to make this situation sing—learned, however paradoxically, to regard no ground as grounds for singing. So it's not like Armstrong makes his poetry out of absolutely nothing. The potter, as it were, is not quite grasping at a phantom on the wheel. There's water there. Sure, it's a trickier substance than clay, but it's something all the same.

Ultimately, Aunt Cuney's allusion to the precedent of Jesus for the miraculous feat of the water-walking Ibos suggests that, instead of suspending the conditions of thought's possibility, paradox can actually sustain and propel it. Though a stumbling block to what Cone calls "the intellect," it is food for faith and imagination. We might finally name the joint operation of their thought in this way: if the story of the Ibo Landing is to be apprehended, it must be *fathomed*. That is, it must be appreciated as a mystery by a mind unafraid of getting wet.

iv.

Yet even if the question must be asked in order even to have the opportunity to fathom in the way we have described, there is a way in which we ask questions that betrays that we really want nothing to do with them. We much prefer answers. Often this preference is so strong that one wonders whether we have any genuine investment in the question at all. We can further consider the fault Aunt Cuney finds with Avey's question in precisely this way. Consider that in response to the old woman's reprimanding look, Avey's remorse manifests as a desire to reach out and swallow her question. If this response tells us anything about the nature of the reprimand itself, perhaps it's not Avey's question that disappoints Aunt Cuney so much as Avey's little regard for her question, or Aunt Cuney's before it, as something she might actually eat. The distinct orientations Avey and Aunt Cuney maintain toward their respective questions further illuminates this point. Recall that to hear the Ibo Landing story is, in fact, to hear Aunt Cuney's answer to her own question ("Do you know what the Ibos did?"). The answer, the subsequent story about "*what the Ibos did*," is *in* her question. And the story itself is questionable. Even in her answer, Aunt Cuney preserves something of the character of the question to which she responds. In this sense, Aunt Cuney turns to her question in the same way the Ibos turn to the water, preparing to wade, to fathom. So committed is she to the mysterious object of her inquiry that, far from seeking its resolution in some armored answer, she is content to tell a wounded story, untroubled by its vulnerability to being questioned.

If, in this way, Aunt Cuney's question demonstrates a genuine investment in what the Ibos did, then Avey's ("How come they didn't drown . . . ?") by contrast disinvests from their improbable feat to weigh, instead, the conditions making it unlikely. Again, not that Avey's question shouldn't be asked. Only that it should be asked *with* this first question, and its persevering interest in the mystery of what the Ibos did, and not *without* it. Asked alone, it is hardly a question at all. Jettisoning a genuine inquiry into what the Ibos did, Avey's "question" becomes only the veiled desire for an answer to what is rendered as the mere "problem" of having no ground. But what would it mean, if rather than a problem to be done away with, Avey regarded her question, and not just its possible answer, as something she might actually eat? Fred Moten might have advised Avey to "beware, in yourself, the effects of the kind of thinking that produces certain traditional ideas of unlikeliness," and he would not have been very far off from the heart of Aunt Cuney's disappointment.[33] The kind of thinking behind Avey's question, which struggles to maintain its interest in the questionable object of its inquiry, may still be able to relay the story's content and form, but of the mystery of the Ibos walking on water it can speak seldom a word.

That Moten's caution to black studies scholars in his essay "Notes on Passage" so nearly approximates Aunt Cuney's is also telling. For like Avey, we, too, have a question, the "Negro Question" so famously articulated by Du Bois in *Souls*: "How does it feel to be a problem?"[34] Following Jared Sexton, "The formulation of a sustained response to such an inquiry is the province of the field of black studies."[35] Yet if we accept this characterization of the field, it remains for us to examine the orientation we assume toward our question, one perhaps belied in the interchangeability that the "Negro Question" has historically enjoyed with the "Negro Problem." Precisely how do we regard the being of the problem into which we are inquiring? Do we find therein a proposition no less baffling than the Ibos who didn't drown? Surely a problem, which is a problem precisely because of its exclusion from being, cannot *be* any more than slaves can walk on water. In what ways, then, has a question to which we might respond, and in such a way that genuinely invests in the questionable object of our inquiry, become only a problem to be answered and done away with? Is it very long after we ask "How come they didn't drown?" that we find ourselves asking, "How do we get out of the water?"

Perhaps, like Avey, we, too, must learn to eat our question, take and eat in remembrance of the Ibos, imagining that if we reach out and swallow it, we just might be filled. The "Negro Problem" alone just doesn't tell it. It may be perfectly adept to tell the (hi)story of how we drowned or elaborate the sociological implications of our drowning. But this will not fully tell this story that M. NourbeSe Philip insists "must be told."[36] Something remains after the question is cast in the anemic terms of a problem. If we are to "finish telling about 'em," we must tell that, too. A whole meal lies in the break between the question and the problem, one we miss if we do not maintain our interest in the questionable gait of the Ibos or the being of the problem. It may even be our Eucharist.

III. long gone

i.

If we are not prepared to fathom the feat of the water-walking Ibos, then we are almost certainly assured of neglecting the creativity of the mind that has elected to go with them. This, by far, is the larger oversight. For even greater works than walking on water has the mind that has "gone with the Ibos" performed. This mind, whose first and ongoing work is to tell the story. We only begin to suspect the costliness of this oversight once we finally allow Aunt Cuney to "finish telling about 'em," and we learn that the Ibos not only walked on water but "started in to singing":

> And when they got to where the ship was they didn't so much as give it a look. Just walked on past it. Didn't want nothing to do with that ol' ship. They feets was gonna take 'em wherever they was going that day. And they were singing by then, so my gran' said. When they realized there wasn't nothing between them and home but some water and that wasn't giving 'em no trouble they got so tickled they started in to singing. You could hear 'em clear across Tatem 'cording to her. They sounded like they was having such a good time my gran' declared she just picked herself up and

> took off after 'em in her mind. Her body she always usta say might be in Tatem but her mind, her mind was long gone with the Ibos.[37]

It's not just that the Ibos went walking on the water. Contending with this claim alone does not exhaust our wrestling. There's also the fact that they "started in to singing." We wrestle as much with a song as we do with the underwater angels of history. If the feet of the water-walking Ibos prompted us to ask what kind of ground is no ground, their singing lures us one wavering step further into asking: What kind of grounds for singing is no ground? Is the water? This second question, you'll notice, has a made-up mind when it comes to the water, because it recognizes that, whatever our valuations of its viability as ground, it is ground *enough* for singing. The joy of this discovery so gripped Old Avatara that "she just picked herself up and took off after 'em in her mind." We'd do well, then, to attend to it.

Significantly, this discovery by Old Avatara (who personally witnessed the Ibo Landing and recounted it to Aunt Cuney) means that the Ibo Landing story is the product of a mind that is "gone with the Ibos." Avey's ability to really hear the story then becomes a matter of learning to appreciate the secreted activity of this mind, this imagination. Likewise, her ability to really tell it becomes a matter of coming to have this mind in her that was also in the Ibos. In other words, I am suggesting that what Old Avatara discovered in the singing at Ibo Landing was, if not literal steps, a sea-legged posture of mind, an imagination swaying on the deep, poised for creation. To be gone with the Ibos, then, is more elaborately to consent to participate in their poetic posture and mode of creating. It's for us to decide if this is reason enough to linger with the terrible steps blinked upon the face of the Atlantic. To be patient with the faltering soles of black folk. To learn to think of ground in the broadest sense possible so as to include whatever it is we find beneath our feet, however precarious its give.

The discovery of this imagination has tremendous implications for any discussion of "black aesthetics." It suggests more is available to being heard or read as black than the content or form of a thing. If, as recent scholarship has argued, aesthetic inquiries into the "blackness of blackness" typically run aground in attempts to rigidly delineate essentially black "form" or "content," it is certainly compelling that in Avey's case knowledge of the story's "content" and "form" alone prove insufficient to "finish telling about 'em."[38] And that she is able to do so only after her oneiric decision to "*Come*"—a decision she significantly makes in her mind—to a place Old Avatara's mind had already long gone. A brief overview of the novel's narrative structure in relation to Avey's dream helps illuminate this point.

Praisesong begins with Avey's sudden decision to leave a luxurious cruise prematurely and embark on an impromptu journey of cultural and spiritual rediscovery. Only belatedly do we learn that her perplexing decision is inspired by the dream, in which she reluctantly consents to go with her Aunt Cuney to "the Landing." Poet Ed Roberson may have unwittingly summarized the novel when, regarding dreams, he mused: "The dream itself, a vision, is created by creating its completion, its accomplishment, creating its waking. Otherwise, it's just sleep. But that's only an introduction to the real question: of waking. . . . The question is how to wake into the continuum of creating, into life, rather than a dried-up eternal sleep. It's about the life of creation, trying to live a life of creativity—and about the works themselves."[39] All of *Praisesong* can be reduced to Avey's attempt to "wake" in precisely the way Roberson describes. Its pages narrate Avey's endeavor to consummate *in life* her oneiric decision to join Aunt Cuney on the road to Ibo Landing, to create her waking by venturing fully into the ongoing creative life of a mind gone with the Ibos. Thus, the novel fittingly concludes with Avey having finally learned, after so many years, to "finish telling about 'em":

> At least twice a week in the late afternoon, when the juniper trees around Tatem began sending out their cool and stately shadows, [Avey] would lead them, grandchildren and visitors alike, in a troop over to the Landing.
>
> "It was here that they brought them," she would begin—as had been ordained. "They took them out of the boats right here where we're standing."[40]

That Avey's oneiric consent to go to the water ultimately enables her to tell the story, and not her knowledge of its content or form, challenges and renews our understandings of black aesthetics. It suggests the possibility that, in detecting the blackness of a text, we have to consider not only its form or content but also its *matter*. Bachelard has established a precedent for thinking of literature in this way by arguing that "it is possible to establish in the realm of the imagination, a *law of the four elements* which classifies various kinds of material imagination by their connections with fire, air, water, or earth."[41] Further elucidating the operation of what he calls the "material imagination," Bachelard writes:

> If a reverie is to be pursued with the constancy of a written work, it must discover its matter. A material element must provide its own substance, its particular rules and poetics. It is not simply coincidental that primitive philosophies often made a decisive choice along these lines. They associated with their formal principles one of the four fundamental

> elements, which thus became signs of philosophic disposition. In these philosophic systems, learned thought is linked to a primitive material reverie, serene and lasting wisdom is rooted in a substantial invariability. If we still find these simple and powerful philosophies convincing, it is because by studying them we may discover completely natural imaginative powers.[42]

Psychoanalyst that he was, Bachelard might have interpreted the significance of Avey's dream as having enabled her "to finish telling about 'em" by facilitating her discovery of the story's matter: water. In James Baldwin's short story "Sonny's Blues," Creole and his bass fiddle help Sonny and his piano do the same: "[Creole] wanted Sonny to leave the shoreline and strike out for the deep water. He was Sonny's witness that deep water and drowning were not the same thing—he had been there, and he knew. And he wanted Sonny to know. He was waiting for Sonny to do the things on the keys which would let Creole know that Sonny was in the water."[43] And Creole finally succeeded when he

> began to tell us what the blues were all about. They were not about anything very new. He and his boys up there were keeping it new, at the risk of ruin, destruction, madness, and death, in order to find new ways to make us listen. For, while the tale of how we suffer, and how we are delighted, and how we may triumph is never new, it always must be heard. There isn't any other tale to tell; it's the only light we've got in all this darkness.
>
> And this tale, according to that face, that body, those strong hands on those strings, has another aspect in every country, and a new depth in every generation. Listen, Creole seemed to be saying, listen. Now these are Sonny's blues. . . . Creole wasn't trying any longer to get Sonny in the water. He was wishing him Godspeed. Then he stepped back, very slowly, filling the air with the immense suggestion that Sonny speak for himself.
>
> Then they all gathered around Sonny and Sonny played. Every now and again one of them seemed to say, amen. Sonny's fingers filled the air with life, his life. But that life contained so many others. And Sonny went all the way back, he really began with the spare, flat statement of the opening phrase of the song. Then he began to make it his. . . . He had made it his: that long line, of which we knew only Mama and Daddy.[44]

Just as Aunt Cuney helped Avey discover her matter, Creole helped Sonny discover his. And suggestively, in both cases the matter animating their creativity in the way Bachelard theorizes is water. Perhaps, somewhere along the long line of trouble "of which [Sonny] knew only Mama and Daddy," stood the Ibos, songfully hovering over the face of the deep, much like Sonny's brother, the story's narrator, imagines Sonny to do while playing his piano: "All I know about music is that not many people ever *really hear* it. And even then, on the rare occasions when something opens within, and the music enters, what we mainly hear, or hear corroborated, are personal, private, vanishing evocations. But the man who creates the music is hearing something else, is dealing with *the roar rising from the void and imposing order on it as it hits the air*."[45] In other words, Sonny's body may have been seated in front of his piano, but his mind was gone with the Ibos, learning with them the difference between deep water and drowning, making the water sing.

The fact that Armstrong's horn, the Ibos' song, and Sonny's blues each present not-so-straightforward exercises in *really hearing*, and that each discovers its matter in the water, at once stages a familiar quandary to students of the expressive traditions of the African Diaspora—namely, how do we name the "blackness of blackness" that's supposed to cohere these traditions—and suggests a possible, if unlikely, way forward. Evie Shockley's recent theorization of "black aesthetics" argues that "blackness" should be read as inhering not in any specifically black form or content but rather, and more flexibly, in "aesthetic decisions" motivated by, to borrow a common Fanonian phrase, "the lived experience of blackness."[46] I elaborate upon this important innovation in our conception of black aesthetics by calling attention to the ways in which this experience is repeatedly cast throughout African Diasporic literature as an experience of water. Bachelard's literary regard for matter, then, can perhaps yield a fitting and refreshing waterway out of no way for really hearing and reading blackness. If Shockley aids us in thinking the relationship between the water giving way beneath the Ibos' feet and their song, then Bachelard gives us a way to understand the creative potential of the mind that goes with them. Perhaps Old Avatara's long gone mind is the index of what we might label, after Bachelard, the "material imagination" of blackness. An imagination, that is, whose "fundamental element" is water.

It's the creative activity of the material imagination of blackness and its operation behind the variable content and form of the expressive traditions of the African Diaspora that we risk overlooking when we fail to fathom the ground miracle of the Ibo Landing. How, then, might we begin to sketch the contours of the creative history of the mind that is gone with the Ibos—and *long* gone, that is, gone for quite some time? Perhaps we might start with a slave narrative penned by another Ibo, Equiano's *Interesting Narrative*. The fictional Old

Avatara was hardly the only one with a made-up mind about water during the transatlantic slave trade. If Old Avatara witnessed "the Landing" in 1803 (assuming Marshall was true in this way to the historical events inspiring it), then Equiano's *Interesting Narrative* yields a contemporary nonfictional account of a landing from elsewhere in the diaspora. His narrative bears witness to a mind gone in ways kindred to Old Avatara's, and in such a way as to provoke the consideration of this mind's relation not just to the Ibo Landing story but the expressive traditions of the African Diaspora more broadly. Together they will offer us some insight into just how long this mind has been gone.

ii.

The Ibos did not hover over the face of the deep idly. Rather they *started*. Specifically, they "started in to singing," but here, I want to call special attention to their starting. Under the circumstances of being forcefully transported to a New World, one can imagine how the power to start or start over, begin or begin again, possessed special appeal for enslaved Africans. In this sense, starting is not limited to singing alone. It extends to the capacity to start into any number of things. Or, with respect to the antiblack world, to even start into the remaking of the whole damn thing. You'll remember that the Ibos took to the water only after a protracted study of this world. Let us finally consider more carefully Aunt Cuney's report about what they saw:

> They seen things that day you and me don't have the power to see. 'Cause those pure born Africans was peoples my gran' said could see in more ways than one. The kind can tell you 'bout things to come long after they's dead. Well, they seen everything that was to happen 'round here that day. The slavery time and the war my gran' always talked about, the 'mancipation and everything after that right on up to the hard times today. Those Ibos didn't miss anything. Even seen you and me standing here talking about 'em. And when they got through sizing up the place real good and seen what was to come, they *turned*, my gran' said, and looked at the white folks what brought 'em here. Took their time again and gived them the same long hard look. Tell you the truth, I don't know how those white folks stood it. I know I wouldn't have wanted 'em looking at me that way. And when they got to studying 'em, when they knew just from looking at 'em how those folks was gonna do, do you know what the Ibos did?[47]

By now we know they turned. But at issue here is the turn before the turn to go walking out on the water. After "studying the place real good," the Ibos turn to look at "the white folks what brought 'em here." And if Aunt Cuney wouldn't want them looking at her that way, it is because this look is a look of judgment. As if to ask with no small bite of condemnation, "Just what sort of world are you creating here?" Such a look recalls the nonfictional study of white folk performed by another Ibo, though much more subtly, given the tight space in which he writes. Early in his slave narrative, Equiano offers this description of his encounter with "the white folks what [*bought*]" him. Though referenced several times in this study already, it bears quoting again here:

> The first object which saluted my eyes when I arrived on the coast was the sea, and a slave ship, which was then riding at anchor, and waiting for its cargo. These filled me with astonishment, which was soon converted into terror when I was carried on board. I was immediately handled and tossed up to see if I were sound by some of the crew; and I was now persuaded that I had gotten into a world of *bad spirits*, and that they were *going to kill me*. Their complexions, too, differing so much from ours, their long hair, and the language they spoke (which was very different from any I had ever heard), united to confirm me in this belief. Indeed such was the horror of my views and fears at the moment, that, if 10,000 worlds had been my own, I would have freely parted with them all to have exchanged my condition with that of the meanest slave in my own country.[48]

In the beginning, Equiano neared the end. The earth, quite suddenly, was "without form, and void," and "bad spirits" were moving on the face of the deep in slave ships. Versed in the Bible as he was, one wonders whether Equiano didn't have Genesis in mind while relating this moment in his narrative. Is there not a deep irony and critique in the recognition that those who arrived on the African continent with knowledge of the beginning are here judged by Equiano to be beginning badly? Is there any implied relationship between their knowledge of the beginning and the manner in which they begin? If we understand Equiano to be alluding to the biblical account of creation, then the particular verse to which he alludes is significant. It reads: "And the earth was without form, and void; and darkness was upon the face of the deep. And the spirit of God moved upon the face of the waters."[49] Theologian Catherine Keller has argued in *The Face of the Deep* (2003) that this verse has been systematically elided from the western theological imaginary.[50] A similar elision would be much more difficult for the likes of Equiano and his shipmates. Indeed, Africans in the New World can hardly speak of their beginnings without also speaking of the water. What, then, would it mean if the spirit of creation ceased to hover over the face of the deep? Or worse, grabbed a boat? And not just any boat, but this boat that, similarly to his countrymen in *Praisesong*, Equiano wants no part of. This boat that transforms his astonishment into terror precisely at the moment he realizes the ship "waiting for its cargo" was waiting for *him*. The moment he realizes he had been bought. Might such a disavowal of the water constitute the stuff of a "bad spirit"?

Of course, when Equiano takes the phrase "bad spirit" into his mouth, we should recognize that he wears the mask.[51] He has taken on nothing less than the denigration of African religions as demonic, irrational superstition. By which I mean to suggest how an African speaking of "bad spirits" in the eighteenth century goes down easy. Nonetheless, the spoonful of sugar should not distract us from the medicine it helps go down. And what has just gone down is a black man calling a bunch of white folk "bad," if not outright demonic. From within a negative valuation of black religion he tastefully condemns the bad spirit prowling over the face of the deep in slave ships. That is, he condemns the bad spirit of whiteness animating the creation of the New World of slavery. A spirit condemned by its fear of getting wet, its overinfatuation with land, its idolatrous worship of Plymouth Rock. Although we've encountered it already in "Deep Humanities," it bears revisiting Alexis de Tocqueville's gloss of this worship in *Democracy in America* (1835): "This Rock has become an object of veneration in the United States. I have seen bits of it carefully preserved in several towns in the Union. Does this sufficiently show that all human power and greatness is in the soul of man? Here is a stone which the feet of a few outcasts pressed for an instant; and the stone becomes famous; it is treasured by a great nation; its very dust is shared as a relic."[52] Perhaps more than anything it might say about the soul of man, the veneration of Plymouth Rock reveals a great deal about the overinfatuation of white soles with the land. The time the *Mayflower* spent on the water dwarfs the mere "instant" the stone was pressed, and yet it is the stone that is remembered. Such a landing as was happy to forget the water was always going to be a problem. Equiano and his fellow Ibos in *Praisesong* anticipate the New World to which the bad spirit of whiteness and its aversion to water would inevitably give rise. They discerned from the very start that Plymouth Rock was going to land on them, that this world was going to kill them. Hence the need to start over. Begin again.

But if the look of the Ibos is a look of judgment, we must be precise about the fact that it is a judgment not of white folk so much as whiteness. Their struggle was not against flesh and blood but against bad spirits. Which is what we have to understand about the echo in the Ibos' turning to look at these white folk in the moment when Aunt Cuney "turned and regarded [Avey] in silence for the longest time" after she asked her thoughtless question. This, too, is a look of judgment. "What sort of world will you create?" she might have asked. Yet we also know that it is also an invitation to *Come*. If we allow this look to inform that of the Ibos, then perhaps theirs was an invitation too. Maybe they would have had those white folks go with them. Then, perhaps, they could have done their water-walking on land, together.

Like Avey, Equiano has a similar opportunity to *Come*, in such a way that recalls what we have spoken of in terms of an amended sense of Althusser's notion of interpellation. If Avey is hailed by the vague calling expressed in her birthname (Avatara), Equiano undergoes a similar process of hailing that is perhaps obscured by the more obvious instances of hailing (now in the traditional sense of Althusser's use of the word) to which he is subjected. Recall that the very "first object which *saluted* [his] eyes when [he] arrived on the coast was the sea." This salute filled him with an astonishment that was converted into terror only after he "was carried on board" the second object to salute him, the slave ship. There are two hails to be distinguished here. On the one hand, there is the hail of the slave ship, which, true to Althusser's original use of the word in his drama of interpellation, subjects Equiano as a slave. This is the hail epitomized by the new names to which Equiano and his countless shipmates were made to answer. But there is also, and *before*, the hail of the astonishing sea. Its "salute," its *wave*, is nothing but the aquatic announcement of a kind of hail: "Hey, you there! *Come* and see the Earth before the beginning of the New World."[53] With regard to this very first hail, Equiano's turn is delayed until some moments after his initial confrontation with the ocean, once he is subjected to the violence of slavery: "Soon, to my grief, two of the white men offered me eatables; and, on my refusing to eat, one of them held me fast by the hands, and laid me across I think the windlass, and tied my feet, while the other flogged me severely. I had never experienced anything of this kind before; and although, not being used to the water, I naturally feared that element the first time I saw it, yet nevertheless, could I have got over the nettings, *I would have jumped over the side*."[54] Equiano's body might be on the ship, but this Ibo's mind was gone with the "inhabitants of the deep," whom he often thought "much more happy than myself" and whose "freedom" he envied.[55] Like Old Avatara, then, it's a celebration that causes Equiano, after an initial fear of the water, to pick himself up and take off after 'em in his mind. And while Equiano does not claim that the "*inhabitants* of the deep" walked on water, he does imply that they managed to *live* there. But, once again, if we suspend what may be our initial objections to Equiano's apparent misnaming of the drowned, and take seriously the lives that were *lived* underwater, awfully abbreviated as they were, then what emerges is a deep recalibration of human life and freedom on a blue planet. The blueness of blackness, in other words, is not only a question of blackness's interpellation as slaveness. It's also, and *first*, a matter of consenting to inhabit the deep. We are hailed as much by the astonishment of the ocean as by the terror of the slave ship. From the very first, there is this fork in the road of black study yielding paths to optimism and pessimism.[56] And while I don't propose we do away with the fork, I do propose we recognize that there is one. Perhaps then we might find ourselves better equipped to eat our question.

Helping us to a final appreciation of the significance of the "home" Equiano locates in the water is Bachelard: "The region we call home is less expanse than matter; it is granite or soil, wind or dryness, water or light. It is in it that we materialize our reveries, through it that our dream seizes upon its true substance. From it we solicit our fundamental color. Dreaming by the river, I dedicated my imagination to the water."[57] So, too, has the African Diaspora dedicated its imagination, dreaming by the Atlantic its primitive material reverie about water. For what I am calling the material imagination of blackness is a development historically rooted in the bewildering encounter of middle passing Africans with the deep. While Africans undoubtedly possessed their own conceptions of water prior to slavery, if, as historian Stephanie Smallwood has argued, "the landless realm of the deep ocean did not figure in precolonial West African societies," as it didn't for Equiano, then what we must understand about Middle Passage is that it required African captives to perform a terrific feat of the imagination.[58] Theirs was the historical labor of having to make a ground out of no ground, of having to imagine and improvise a life lived absolutely at sea without even the faintest relief of a future promised land. We read "black aesthetics," then, in the wake of this imaginative feat as the expression of a mind long gone with the Ibos.

5

DEEP LIFE

He could have come out of the water.
—BLACK MARY IN AUGUST WILSON, *Gem of the Ocean*

So live.
—ELI IN AUGUST WILSON, *Gem of the Ocean*

IN THE MIDST OF SO MUCH DEATH—physical, social, premature, and otherwise—I want to put in a word for life. Or, I want to put in a word for *black* life. I want to do both these things. Not because I'm indecisive or can't make up my mind. But because in *this* world, I'm not sure that there is any other kind. Because, finally, I am persuaded that these two things—life and black life—are, in fact, one thing. I got *a* word. Just one.

Turn to your neighbor and tell them, "Life is black."

I'm straining for a way to hear in *black life* not fundamentally a word concerning the lives of black people, our miraculous still-beating hearts and breath-filled lungs in a world that both Equiano and the water-walking Ibos knew was going to kill them. Black life certainly includes these phenomena, but I wish to speak a more extreme word, one where *black* relinquishes its nominal powers and, for a moment, plays the adjective straight. One where the only noun we hear is *life*. Black *life*. Such a word, if I could ever manage to sound it out, would prove even more extreme than that which Henry David Thoreau offers at the outset of his essay "Walking": "I wish to speak a word for Nature, for absolute freedom and wildness, as contrasted with a freedom and culture merely civil—to regard man as an inhabitant, or a part and parcel of Nature, rather than a member of society. I wish to make an extreme statement, if so I may make an emphatic one, for there are enough champions of civilization: the minister and the school committee and every one of you will take care of that."[1] Recoiling from western humanism's imagined separation from nature, Thoreau hazarded to speak what he characterized in the middle of the nineteenth century as an *extreme* "word for Nature." The extremity of his nature word lay in the fact that it also and at once purported to be a human word. Thoreau had just one word, too: "Nature," of which he understood the human species to be irrevocably "part and parcel," and this against the grain of a western humanism that had begun to imagine the human as not only separated from but indeed superior and free of any ethical obligation to the category of nonhuman nature. Moreover, Thoreau offered his word at a historical moment when inclusion in this emerging performance of the Human was being adjudicated globally by racial ideology. Thus, those humans who were really or paradigmatically Human knew their Humanity specifically by their whiteness, which not only distinguished them as the most evolved of the human species in realizing civilization's defining break from nature and the state thereof but also consequently entitled them to the possession of the lands of their nonwhite human peers and, moreover, to the bodies, breath, and blood of those interpellated by the modern world as black. To his credit, in "Walking" Thoreau makes plain his suspicions regarding the specific performance of the human inhering in and as whiteness. He writes: "That is mere sentimentality that lies abed by day and thinks itself white, far from the tan and callus of experience." Or again, "A tanned skin is something more than respectable, and perhaps olive is a fitter color than white for a man—a denizen of the woods."[2]

Yet if we have learned anything from the racial blind spots of mainstream environmentalism, which has located in Thoreau's "word for Nature" the famed conservationist mantra that "in Wildness is the preservation of the world," it is that there are quite enough champions of an unspoiled, romantic, or nonhuman nature and not enough *inhabitants*. And there are still fewer "inhabitants of the deep," who, as the submerged of Earth, come by their status as "part and parcel" of this blue planet honestly, albeit also precariously. Being part and parcel of nature, it turns out, is no walk in the park, not even Walden. To speak a word for nature that is at once also a word for the human *in*habitant of nature may require an even more radical break from whiteness than tan or olive. I wish, then, to go all the way to the other side of the color line and that portion of the rainbow coalition that has historically signaled not just less human but *non*human. I want to speak a word of black life. A word for the life of blackness that is really a word for the blackness of life. A word as extreme as that living word spoken of the dead in *The Interesting Narrative of the Life of Olaudah Equiano* where Equiano refers to those drowned in Middle Passage as the "*inhabitants* of the deep."[3] I want to speak an extreme word of black life. If so, I will not have been the first. Indeed, I will have managed only to echo a word I heard years ago during a 2014 production of August Wilson's *Gem of the Ocean* (2003), a play set in 1904 in Pittsburgh's predominantly black Hill District. Perhaps you've heard and wondered at this word too. You'd remember if you had. It comes at the very end.

I. so

Were the last word of the play simply *live*, the dramatic conclusion of Wilson's *Gem of the Ocean* would be perplexing enough given the circumstances. Just moments before the play offers its final word, we hear words of a far different sort ring out from the stage: "Caesar shot Solly."[4]

This is how we learn that Solly, a former slave and veteran conductor on the Underground Railroad, has been shot by Caesar, the Hill District's black constable with an itching trigger finger and dogmatic devotion to the law. "The law is everything," we've heard him say. Then, with hardly any time to brace ourselves, we are enlisted as witnesses to the emergency that the words "Caesar shot Solly" herald. We watch Solly's broken body being helped onstage. Watch him stumble to the ground. Watch him being laid across a kitchen table that has anchored too much of the life of this play to suit this new purpose. The entire play has taken place here in the parlor of 1839 Wylie Avenue, and it has come abruptly to this. A stage direction we can't hear right now, but one we still feel, calls it an "old, old, unwelcome visitation."[5]

Just last scene we saw Solly exiting the stage on his own two feet, resolved to head down to Alabama to help his sister escape the post-Reconstruction reactionary terror of the Jim Crow South. He was also leaving, we learned, as a fugitive, on the run from Caesar after he discovered that Solly was the one responsible for burning down the local steel mill at the end of the first act because it was holding its black workers in a form of debt slavery. At the time, all this felt like a fitting resolution for a character who had carried "sixty-two people . . . to Freedom" and who was "looking to make it sixty-three when

Abraham Lincoln come along and changed all that."[6] On his way to Alabama, however, we learn that Solly decided to double back and burn down the Hill District's jail, for good measure. One of the characters tells us, "He didn't feel right being free and the rest of the people in bondage."[7] But before he could reach the jail, "Caesar shot Solly." That we see Solly now, crumpled and overflowing with his own life, is a tearing open of the resolution of his character arc that mirrors the tearing open of his flesh. It is a plot revelation of brutal suddenness, and with it, the play seems to accelerate toward its finale, entering more thickly and conspicuously into the time measured and experienced in the *emergency* of the blood flowing out of Solly's chest and the communal effort to stop it. This time—felt in the way the world always seems to stop with the announcement of news like Solly's, but paradoxically also to quicken in the steadily building momentum of a deathly happening that keeps happening—is all too familiar to those who stand ever within earshot of the bad news of being black in the world. The particulars are always revolving, but the grammar remains remarkably consistent. They shot Tamir Rice. They shot Michael Brown. They shot Breonna Taylor. They shot Ahmaud Arbery. They shot. They shot. They shot. Subject, harming verb, harmed black object. It may be a play, but there is nothing fictional about "Caesar shot Solly" when we hear it. We've heard it before. Said variations of the words ourselves. Sent the texts, shared the articles, watched the videos. Our extradiegetic share in the play's time is the first sign that we are no longer safe. We feel our skin enter the game and struggle to play the audience straight.

Now we are watching all of the residents and friends of 1839 Wylie Avenue play the wound dresser. Everyone onstage has set their hands to the labor and care of keeping blood and breath in Solly's body. But by the time Eli, Solly's dear friend and a fellow conductor on the Underground Railroad, speaks the play's final word, too much of Solly's blood has flowed out of the hole opened up in his chest by Caesar's bullet for "live" not to sound misplaced. Solly has just died. His body lies broken and bled out on a kitchen table where we've otherwise watched the characters of the play break bread. His body lies transubstantiated before us as the still-accumulating debris of a long genealogy of black not here no more, of black gone and gone on:

> *I opened up the curtain and he was gone. My grandson was gone.*[8]

In the midst of so much black death, now hardly seems the time to put in a word for life. Still less to pour a drink of whiskey and raise it in a toast.[9] But Eli's is an extreme word. Greedy even. While it bears the special responsibility of closing the play down, it sounds rather more intent on ripping the play open. Not content with its two acts, the play wants into our world. It's in the way Eli breaks from the clearly delineated lifeworld of the play and turns conspicuously in our direction. The way he raises his glass toward us and speaks the word *live* with such clear ambitions on us, who are gathered just outside the dramatic world of Pittsburgh's Hill District in 1904. With this simple gesture, we, who had been mere spectators, are surprised to learn of our status as witnesses. We are attending, not watching, this wake. We are its congregation, not merely its audience. Eli, suddenly imbued with all of the ceremony of a priest presiding over some black Eucharist, is exhorting *us* to "live."

And because Eli is doing all of this in plain view of Solly's dead body, "live" resounds with the same dissonance as Equiano's living word concerning the "*inhabitants* of the deep." It's their faltering steps on the face of the Atlantic that offer us a sense of just how old visitations like Solly's felled body are. There's something of their "footprint[s] on the water, filling," in Solly collapsing on the floor.[10] The very same 1839 Wylie Avenue floor that we saw go to water some scenes ago, when we watched Aunt Ester take the play's protagonist, a troubled young man named Citizen Barlow, on a ceremonial journey to the "City of Bones": the underwater kingdom made from the bones of the "people that didn't make it across the water." The City of Bones is where Aunt Ester, the 285-year-old matriarch of 1839 Wylie Avenue, is known to take the Hill District's poor in spirit who, for various reasons, need to get their souls washed. How the lighting, blue and rippling, softened the stage into water. Not unlike every stage playing ground to Alvin Ailey's *Revelations*. The dancers leaping and landing on flowing blue sheets, wading in the water beneath their feet with embodied faith and a special irreverence for all of Isaac Newton's laws (figure 5.1). Or the stage similarly become ocean in Bill T. Jones's *Deep Blue Sea*, with W. E. B. Du Bois's familiar question—How does it feel to be a problem?—superimposed on the automated waves. How Citizen stumbled about with significantly less grace than Ailey's or Jones's dancers, trying to balance himself on the way to the City of Bones. "I feel it moving! The land . . . it's moving away," we heard him say.[11] How the stage enfleshed what it is that we, inhabitants of the deep, have to stand on. The terrible continuity, so far as the soles of black folk are concerned, between the land and the sea. Or not so terrible, if, like Ailey's or Jones's dancers, we surrendered to the deep and learned to swim it.

Yet *Gem*'s final exhortation is not "Live" but "*So* live." Under the circumstances, "Live" is already exhortation extreme enough. But "So live" is more extreme still. Live anyway or anyhow, we might have anticipated. Something more along the lines of Claude McKay's "If we must die." But "*So* live"? As in,

FIGURE 5.1. Jacqueline Green in Alvin Ailey's *Revelations*. Photo: Paul Kolnik.

live *like* this. Live "in the way or manner described, indicated or suggested."[12] But how, when *so*'s referent is Solly, and Solly is dead? What way or manner to live can death, the ultimate no-way, offer life? What do the deaths we die here in the deep possibly have to teach us about how we might or must live? Another register of *so* is no less baffling: *Therefore* live. Live for this reason or on this account. Consequently or accordingly.[13] But when did the eternal foes of life and death strike their agreement? Or how can we live because or on the account of our death? The scandal of *Gem*'s final exhortation is not a misplaced word of life so much as this *so*. The conjunction stages what Christina Sharpe has described as "the fact of Black life as proximate to death" and yet performs that proximity in a way that suggests something other than the anticipated opposition of McKay's "dying, *but* fighting back."[14] In place of this opposition, we find instead a confounding continuity. Live like we die. Or live as enabled by our death. Can you hear how outrageous this *so* is? It implies that there is something in the deaths we die as inhabitants of the deep that is useful, and perhaps even necessary, to life. To living. Something we, in the spirit of another kind of Sankofa, may actually need to go back and fetch. Something Aunt Ester keeps ferrying black folks back to the City of Bones to retrieve in a ceremonial reenactment of Middle Passage that, charged with the musical accompaniment of negro spirituals and hymns, bears the familiar textures of an ecstatic black church service. Back to Middle Passage to retrieve something that presents not an obstacle in spite of which black life flourishes but the actual source of its flourishing. Back to what black studies scholar Frank Wilderson has called the "dawning of blackness" and "the Black's first ontological instance," but not to locate the origins of what he theorizes and defines as black "social death" but rather to identify what the play instead positions as the source of what we might alternatively call black ecological life.[15]

This *so* is a problem. It's a problem for the common sense of life and death as total opposites and it's a problem for the thought of how it feels to be a "problem." Especially insofar as our thinking around the problem of being black and blackness has come to be expressed explicitly in terms of death, be it blackness's structural vulnerability and proximity to "premature death" or, perhaps most notoriously of all, "social death." This is because the confounding continuity of life and death in *so* unsettles what thought about (black) life and (black) death can otherwise uncritically tend to accept as their total opposition, the sense of life and death as equal and opposite foes of an absolute binary. Unmoored by *so* from the poles of their absolute opposition, and thus no longer fully accessible to knowledge as *totally* different, the nature of life and death and their relation are thrown radically into question. Barred from the logical shorthand of knowing life as totally different from death, *so* compels us to revisit just what life and death are, if not reducible to mere opposition. It compels us to ask all over again some very basic questions: What is life? What is death? And what, by extension, is the nature of the relation between black life and black death?

The first and most basic sense in which *so* compels us to reconsider life inheres in the simple fact that living is something we have to be told to *do*. Why should the living need to be told to live? Do our hearts and lungs not settle the matter quite automatically? Would Eli's words not be better spent on Solly than on us? Just what is life if, even in death, Solly seems to maintain a more privileged relationship to it than we do, who still haunt the land of the living? At the very least, needing to be exhorted to live calls into question the assumption of the automatic relation of our living to life. It raises the possibility that humanity's modern "plan of living," to again invoke Ralph Ellison's phrase, has somehow alienated modern humanity from life, in much the same way that Thoreau feared that "civilization," with its "freedom and culture merely civil," had alienated modern humanity from the "absolute freedom and wildness" of nature.[16] *So* is about, because it solicits, our consent to live life on its own terms and according to its own integrity, which includes vulnerability to death. So that death, even black death, may not be the opposition to life we think it is.

There is also the specific way that Solly's death, framed by *so* and held out to us as a model for living, compels us to revisit our settled thinking around black death. How might our conceptions of black death change if even death, while in no way to be confused with life, nevertheless maintains a relation to life that is not reducible to opposition? If by insisting on the life of the "inhabitants of the deep," the black literary tradition invites us to recognize *black life in death* or "Black life insisted from death," as Christina Sharpe has put it, then by inviting us to consider a continuity between Solly's death and our living, *so* even more bafflingly asks us also to recognize *black death in life*.[17] An Earth of difference inheres in this simple reversal. At stake in it is our sense of what the Aunt Esters and Aunt Cuneys in my life have often called the everlasting arms. Their prayerful assurances about the life that ultimately bottoms the world and is always there to catch us when we fall. Even we, inhabitants of the deep, who fall in the world as the paradigmatically *fallen*. At stake, too, is our awareness of our positionality in the "Earth," which, to hear Ed Roberson tell it, there is "no step out of."[18] To locate black death *in life*, then, is ultimately to apprehend life, and not death, as the ground. It is, in the words of Howard Thurman, to apprehend death as "an event in Life." As "something that occurs in life rather than something that occurs to life."[19] Implicit in *so* is a deeper claim about the fundamental status of life on this planet and our unassailable position in the Earth, which should not be conflated with the life of civil society or the world, outside of which blackness finds itself. *So* guides us unto an awareness of a planetary surface given ultimately and fundamentally to the grounding of life. A planetary surface whose one word and mantra, spoken as much to body as to seed, is "Live!" That receives everything the world throws at it (even death) and turns it back to life. Armed with the trump card of death, Father Time may indeed be undefeated. But my money is on life every time. For who has beheld the end of life? Not his or her or their life, but life. Not even in the stubbornly verdant cemetery is life defeated. It's life through and through, including through death. But we'll have to weigh the extent to which life such as this, unmoored from the human and the individual, matters, and matters to our thinking about blackness and black death. We'll have to weigh whether such life might be valuable precisely because, as Wilderson points out, it is "not analogous" to the life of a civil society in ecological peril, or a civilization, as Thoreau laments, triumphantly separated from nature.[20] Indeed, if Thurman is right, and life, not death, ultimately bottoms existence, then how might this insight inform conceptions of blackness that otherwise recognize (and with good reason) black death to be the ground? That is, to be both foundational and necessary to the world? If, under the pressure of people dying in the streets, to borrow Stuart Hall's famous words, it has been necessary to think about blackness fundamentally in terms of its relationship to a death and violence not only physical but structural, what would it mean for black study to alternatively center blackness's relation to the life it can't fall out of? Especially if, in the light of *so*, we are able to constellate the deaths we've died as inhabitants of the deep in relation to life.

And because *so* also denotes similarity, and is capable of mimicking the literary function of *like* or *as*, *so* is also about the fundamental simile of a black literary tradition that over and over again represents the problem of being black in aqueous terms.[21] Sounded at the end of a play whose title invokes the ocean, and that both begins in the wake of a black man's willful drowning and features a ceremonial reenactment of Middle Passage, *so* is finally about what this study conceives as blackness's original and ongoing inhabitation of the deep. About how we attend to black being in the deep and recognize in this physical and ontological position of blackness not only or even primarily death but ultimately the stuff of life. I want to think through, with, and about this *so*. About the light it sheds on the deep life of blackness and the black life of the deep. And about how it might lead us to treasure and not despise blackness's inhabitation of the deep as our gem of the ocean.

II. what kind of beginning is the water?

Just as resonant as *Gem*'s end is its beginning, which, like the former, is more than itself. In fact, it's hard to imagine two bookends any more porous or delinquent in the task of starting and stopping a thing than the beginning and end of *Gem*. For just as the end of the play imbricates its drama in the ongoing drama of our living, its beginning is charged with the energy of beginnings (and ends) that likewise exceed the immediate lifeworld of the play. This is because *Gem* is the first installment of a series of ten plays dubbed the Century Cycle, which together undertake the ambitious feat of dramatizing the black American experience over the course of each decade of the twentieth century.[22] But despite being chronologically first, *Gem* was the second to last of Wilson's famed cycle plays to be written:

With the completion of my latest play, *King Hedley II*, I have only the "bookends," the first and last decades of the 20th century, remaining. As I approach the cycle's end, I find myself a different person than when I started. The experience of writing the plays has altered me in ways I cannot yet fully articulate.

As with any journey, the only real question is: "Is the port worthy of the cruise?" The answer is a resounding "Yes." I often remark that I am a struggling playwright. I'm struggling to get the next play on the page. Eight down and counting. The struggle continues.[23]

At the end, Wilson chose to begin at the beginning. He started drafting the "bookend" devoted to the first decade of the twentieth century in 2000. The play that ultimately developed from the first lines he managed to get down on a napkin in Eddie's restaurant, one of Wilson's favorite Hill District haunts, eventually opened at Chicago's Goodman Theatre in 2003, just two years before Wilson died from liver cancer.[24] So at the end—of the century, of the cycle, of his life's work, of his life—Wilson confronted the question of how to begin. Written in the light of most of the whole, *Gem* represents a self-conscious and layered "struggle" to get the beginning on the page. And as the first play in the cycle, *Gem*'s beginning doubles as the beginning of the entire cycle.

It's not a little significant, then, that *Gem*, charged with beginning more than itself, opens in the wake of a drowning. It's not long into the play's first scene that we hear the bad news about a local mill worker named Garret Brown who drowned after jumping into a river to avoid being arrested and jailed for a crime he didn't commit:

ELI: They had a man named Garret Brown who jumped into the river. Caesar chased him and he jumped in and wouldn't come out. They say he stole a bucket of nails. He said he didn't do it. They having his funeral today.[25]

Thus, *Gem* and the Century Cycle begin in the turbulent wake of Garret Brown's drowning. The play's primary narrative arc is centered around the spiritual turmoil of Citizen Barlow, who has come to Aunt Ester to get his "soul washed" because, as the one who actually stole the bucket of nails, he is indirectly responsible for Brown's death. This arc unfolds against the backdrop of an offstage climate of deep social unrest, as we hear of mill workers striking and "rioting" in protest of Brown's death and the mill's exploitative labor practices. Opening post rem, in this way, after a drowning that has already happened, but which nevertheless gives shape to the ensuing drama of the play, *Gem*'s beginning might be described as transparent. That is, we are invited to look through Eli's bad news as we otherwise would a window to a still earlier beginning that precedes and exceeds the play itself. In this way, *Gem* and the Century Cycle begin by referring us to a past external to both, with a trail of breadcrumbs that leads conspicuously, for a book concerned with the blueness of blackness, to the water.

What I am proposing might be read as *Gem*'s transparent beginning corresponds with Wilson's own sense of the temporality of the "black experience in America" that he explicitly hoped to chronicle in his Century Cycle—what he termed the "black American odyssey" spanning "from the first black in 1619 until now."[26] Wilson spoke more elaborately of this "first black" when he expressed his desire to place himself and his work "in that long continuum that goes all the way back to the first African who set foot on the continent. The African who arrived chained and malnourished in the hold of a 350-ton Portuguese vessel—he has not vanished from the face of the earth; he is here, in whatever manifestation, alive in the thirty million black people who are in this country now."[27] And presumably alive, too, in Garret Brown, who—as an uncast character we never quite see, but whose death nonetheless gives shape to the events of the play—haunts *Gem* as a type of this "first black" to arrive in 1619 "chained and malnourished in the hold." Not least because as a mistaken thief who "jumped into the river," Brown founders in ecclesial conversation with those middle passing Africans who also jumped into the Atlantic as mistaken thieves in their own right, insofar as by stealing away they were also supposed to have stolen themselves. Indeed, Brown's drowning is charged with the living memory of the "inhabitants of the deep" who never made it across the water but whom Wilson nevertheless imagines washing ashore in the cycle's second entry, *Joe Turner's Come and Gone* (1986), and whose bones in *Gem* constitute an underwater city.[28]

Also suggestive of the way *Gem*'s transparent beginning extends back through the drowning of Garret Brown to the genesis Wilson ultimately locates in 1619 and the famed "20 and odd" is the impossibly old Aunt Ester, whom Wilson dubbed "the most significant persona of the cycle." Before *Gem*, Aunt Ester first surfaced in the cycle as an offstage presence in two other cycle plays. She had yet to appear in the flesh, because Wilson, who famously talked to his characters as part of his creative process, had only heard talk about her secondhand from other characters. Over the course of his work on the cycle, however, he had come to consider Aunt Ester a "repository of the entire black experience and wisdom" and an embodiment of "our history all the way back to 1619."[29] Who better, then, to consult in the hard work of beginning than the woman who was there when it happened?

> In *Two Trains Running*, there's an offstage character named Aunt Ester. She's 349 years old during this play. In *King Hedley II*, she's also an offstage character but by now she's 366 years old when she dies in this play. Aunt Ester obviously represents our history all the way back to 1619 and that's the connection that if we don't value it, you lose it. So, to make the new connection, I will bring Aunt Ester back, but on stage this time in 1904. As usual, I started listening to my music . . . then wrote her name down: Aunt Ester. I said "Okay," and then I have her say: "there's a lot of things I don't talk about . . . I don't talk about the water . . ." and then she begins to talk about the water. . . . After getting these first lines down, I knew I was on my way.[30]

When the time for beginning came, Wilson reckoned it was about time for him to have a word with Aunt Ester directly. *Gem* and the cycle begin in earnest, then, with a conversation between Wilson and Aunt Ester and these "first lines" entrusted to a napkin in Eddie's about the water that there was in the beginning. Aunt Ester does not talk about this water in the same way that M. NourbeSe Philip does "not tell the story that must be told" in her poem *Zong!*[31] If the problem of black art is established in the slave narratives as the problem of offering expression to the ineffable and inexpressible, if this problem would only be compounded in an expressive venture proposing to attend to an entire century of black struggle, and if this represents at least part of Wilson's struggle to begin, then in the transparent beginning of *Gem* we once again find water, as I have argued elsewhere in this book, poured into the expressive gap. Lending a well-suited prosthesis, a deep voice to all of our *not telling* about the problem of being black.

Through the transparent beginning of *Gem* and the Century Cycle, then, we are invited, like Bigger Thomas, to look "upon the dark face of the ancient waters upon which some spirit had breathed and created him."[32] To look upon the face of the deep that astonished Equiano and embraced his shipmates. Inflected by these unspeakable "ancient waters," Garret Brown's drowning, which precipitates the drama not only of *Gem* but of the entire cycle, serves as a powerful symbol of what the black literary tradition often imagines as the blue beginnings of blackness. It also yields still another representation of the problem of being black as an enduring, no less in 1904 than in 1619, inhabitation of the deep. And in this sense of the beginning, Wilson and the black literary tradition are not alone. They are also joined by a significant thread of black study. Take Hortense Spillers, for example, who in her watermark essay "Mama's Baby, Papa's Maybe" "begins at the 'beginning'":

> The symbolic order that I wish to trace in this writing, calling it an "American grammar," begins at the "beginning," which is really a rupture and a radically different kind of cultural continuation. The massive demographic shifts, the violent formation of a modern African consciousness, that take place on the subsaharan Continent during the initiative strikes which open the Atlantic Slave Trade in the fifteenth century of our Christ, interrupted hundreds of years of black African culture. We write and think, then, about an outcome of aspects of African-American life in the United States under the pressure of those events.[33]

So Spillers positions the writing and thinking called black study in the wake of the unorthodox genesis of the transatlantic slave trade, which, as "really a rupture and a radically different kind of cultural continuation," is transparent in its own right insofar as it, too, can send us deeper into the past to recover still earlier and perhaps more desirable beginnings. While some black study, tending more toward the "continuation" than the "rupture" outlined by Spillers, performs this work by endeavoring to hunt down the survival of so-called Africanisms, more recently the field has seemed largely to consent to Saidiya Hartman's imperative to "lose your mother," recognizing in Middle Passage a more opaque and decisive beginning, which looms historically as a "door of no return" not only for blackness but for the entire modern world.[34] Writing from a Caribbean context, Édouard Glissant, for example, theorizes Middle Passage as "one *vast* beginning, but a beginning whose time is marked by these balls and chains gone green."[35] Likewise, in addition to "the dawning of blackness" and "the Black's first ontological instance," Wilderson also recognizes in Middle Passage the dawning of the modern world.[36] And Fred Moten has similarly argued that "it's terrible to have come from nothing but the sea, which is nowhere, navigable only in its constant autodislocation. The absence of solidity seems to demand some other ceremony of hailing that will have been carried out on some more exalted frequency."[37] If, per this genealogy of black study, our beginnings are indeed blue, and if, at the beginning of the twentieth century and per the witness of Garret Brown, we are *still* in the water and have progressed no further, then what *sort* of beginning is the water? What's so terrible about having "come from nothing but the sea" and apparently progressed no further? And what should our orientation toward such a beginning be? Is it one we should aspire to distance ourselves from as a runner hopes to create distance between themselves and the starting line? Or can the water be foundational? Though it lacks the solidity of both the rock and the sand in Jesus's well-known parable, are we fools to attempt to build a kind of life on it?

And what of the fact that when Garret Brown finally surfaces in the play, in a dramatic encounter with Citizen during his journey to the City of Bones, he is impersonated by Solly, our confoundingly dead model for living? What if, like Solly's death, Garret Brown's refusal to come out of the water has something important to tell us about life and how we might live it? Beyond serving as the perhaps paradigmatic expression of black death, how might blackness's inhabitation of the deep be understood to animate not a dying but a living?

III. "the people drowning"

If Garret Brown is literally in the water, "the people" of the Hill District are in the water metaphorically. Solly, for example, declares that "the people drowning in sorrow and grief. That's a mighty big ocean. They got the law tied to their toe. Every time they try and swim the law pull them under."[38] These lines foreshadow how Solly will eventually be pulled under by the law when Caesar shoots him. But while it can at least be said that Solly actively transgressed the law by burning down the mill, we see, in the example of Citizen Barlow and his initial run-in with Caesar, how the people are always already weighed down by the law as transgressions enough in and of themselves:

> CAESAR: Are you a troublemaker, Citizen Barlow? You ever been in jail?
>
> CITIZEN: I ain't never been in jail.
>
> CAESAR: That's where you heading. You got to have visible means of support around here. If I see you standing around looking to steal something and you ain't got two dollars in your pocket you going to jail. You understand. Get you a job and stay out of trouble. Stay off the streets.[39]

In a not so subtle critique of the unfinished freedom granted to black Americans by mere emancipation and the extension of citizenship, notice how the conspicuously named Citizen is already, in the eyes of Caesar and the law, headed to prison, is already saddled with a kind of passive guilt, even before actively committing any infraction. In fact, this passive guilt can be offset only through the demonstration of "*visible* means of support" or "two dollars." In other words, Citizen must actively demonstrate external signs of economic proficiency; without the aid of these signs, he is hampered by a semiotic regime of race in which he is visually positioned, in and of himself, as already on the way to jail, on the basis of no other transgression than that which inheres in the color of his skin. And in the same way that the drowning of the people, in Solly's estimation, manifests as a compromised relation to the ground and a hampered capacity to move (the people "got the law tied to their toe," he says), Citizen's passive guilt is expressed as a compromised relation to the ground and an incapacity to stand. He is prohibited from "standing around" and instructed by Caesar to "stay off the streets." Besides this passive guilt and the threat of incarceration, the people's precarious and interrupted relationship to the ground also shows up in the play in the form of evictions. We learn that, in addition to the constable, Caesar is a prominent landlord in the Hill District and has been overcharging people for rent and evicting them when they fail to make even a single payment.

Thus, whether through eviction or incarceration, the people of the Hill District can no more stand their ground than can the "inhabitants of the deep." What they have to stand on may not give way as suddenly and spectacularly as water, but their relationship to the ground is no less unsteady or impermanent. Nor is it the guarantee of private landownership that, in the play, is explicitly associated with the entitlements of whiteness. After Caesar manages to buy his first property, he tellingly complains, "Niggers got mad at me. Said I must have thought I was a white man 'cause I got hold to a little something."[40] Here, getting "*hold* to a little something" is coded white, and expressive, I would add, of a general mode of relating to the ground exclusively as private property that is historically coincident with the global advent of whiteness and white settler colonialism. And to the extent that, à la Aldo Leopold's "land ethic," ground can be taken as a proxy for all of nonhuman nature, we can arguably generalize from this reductive land relation a broader orientation toward the environment. In this way, getting "hold to a little something" bespeaks the reigning and racialized performance of the Human indexed by whiteness, and which we might trace back to the "hold" historically practiced and worked out against the non-Human occupants of the slave ship's hold. That is, its human and nonhuman cargo. If Caesar's feat of getting "hold to a little something" is inflected by whiteness's hold on *all* of the non-Human world, including black people, then "the people" in *Gem of the Ocean* struggling to stand their ground are, in contrast, *held* and held down by the law in a way that is symbolically haunted by the waters of Middle Passage.

If, through the physical drowning of Garret Brown and the metaphorical drowning of the people, Wilson positions blackness in the water and portrays blackness as an ongoing inhabitation of the deep, how do we reconcile this aesthetic decision with what Wilson otherwise describes as his desire, in writing the Century Cycle plays, to "place the culture of black America on stage" and demonstrate that black people "have a ground to stand on . . . that has been developed by [their] ancestors"?[41] If Wilson desired to illuminate blackness's grounds, why does he open the cycle with a play that positions blackness so conspicuously and thoroughly in the water? What kind of ground is water? Is no-ground? Or at least no-ground fit to stand or, even less, to hold and possess? In pursuit of these questions—which are nothing but variations of the negro question, which is to say the question of black being—I want to consider how *Gem* stages our black study.

IV. staging black study

Beyond the kindred way in which Wilson's Century Cycle and black study both "begin at the beginning," Wilson's dramatic interest in the twentieth century parallels that of another luminary of black studies, who famously pronounced that "the problem of the twentieth century is the problem of the color line."[42] In *The Souls of Black Folk* (1903), W. E. B. Du Bois forecasted at the outset of the twentieth century what Wilson—whose work on the cycle spanned from his first draft of *Jitney* in 1979 to the 2005 opening of *Radio Golf* at the Yale Repertory Theatre—reflected on at its end. I place these bookending bards of the twentieth century in conversation in hopes of situating Wilson as a significant practitioner of the black study we more readily attribute to Du Bois. Not only does the Century Cycle "place the culture of black America on stage" and, so, dramatically represent Wilson's individual black study, but as plays intended to be seen and heard, the cycle also stages the black study of its audiences. What the cycle ultimately asks people to attend to is the problem of being black across the very same century that Du Bois predicted would be defined by that problem. And as the inaugural play of the cycle, *Gem* stages this problem specifically as the problem of inhabiting the deep. In this way, we who see the play are not unlike the "five hundred people" who, according to Caesar, watched Brown drown:

> CAESAR: Five hundred people standing around watching the man drown. I tried to break it up. Get them to go home. But they wanna stand around and watch a damn fool drown himself in the river. . . . People wanna blame me but I got to keep order. Just like them niggers wanna riot over a bucket of nails. Talking about they ain't going to work. Talking about closing the mill down.[43]

To this already substantial cloud of witnesses we can add the numerous audiences *Gem* has assembled since it opened at the Goodman Theatre in Chicago on April 28, 2003. This simple "watching the man drown" and the audience's parallel witness to blackness's broader inhabitation of the deep in this play represent an enactment of what might be termed lay black study. That is, the bare act of bearing witness to the problem of being black through which all further and more sustained study must come. Such lay black study has yet to make any specific conclusions or consequent plans of action, but it is the first line of defense against oblivion. Its bare attention is already disruptive to Caesar and Caesar's order simply by seeing it and telling it. Or trying and failing anyway. Remember the eulogy that the Invisible Man gives to honor his fallen brother Todd Clifton?

> Here are the facts. He was standing and he fell. He fell and he kneeled. He kneeled and he bled. He bled and he died. He fell in a heap like any man and his blood spilled out like any blood; *red* as any blood, wet as any blood and reflecting the sky and the buildings and the birds and the trees, or your face if you'd look into its dulling mirror—and it dried in the sun as blood dries. That's all. They spilled his blood and he bled. They cut him down and he died; the blood flowed on the walk in a pool, gleamed a while, and, after a while, became dull then dusty, then dried. That's the story and that's how it ended. It's an old story and there's been too much blood to excite you.[44]

Lay black study is the attention we pay to the "old story" of our falling, which Wilson invokes in *Gem* with the "old, old unwelcome visitation" of Solly's felling by a policeman's bullet. But before the death that ends the play, we are witnesses first, beside the five hundred, to the drowning of Garret Brown and thus the oldest chapter in the story of our falling. When we peer through *Gem*'s transparent beginning and see Garret Brown, we bear witness to the problem of being black as an ongoing inhabitation of the deep.

This attention to the problem of being black that *Gem* and the Century Cycle elicit as plays, and which I am calling lay black study, disrupts what Wilson otherwise perceives and critiques as "the glancing manner" in which black and white Americans can attend to black life. "Blacks in America," Wilson writes, "have so little to make life with compared to whites, yet they do so with a certain energy that is fascinating because they make life out of nothing—yet it is charged and luminous and has all the qualities of any one else's life. I think a lot of this is hidden by the *glancing* manner in which white America looks at blacks, and the way blacks look at themselves."[45] What glancing risks, for which the Century Cycle attempts aesthetic reparation, is an underappreciation of black life due to the comparatively "little" or "nothing" from which black life, relative to the seeming abundance of white life, is made. What but an enactment of glancing, for example, do we witness in Caesar's declaration, "I got to play the hand that was dealt to me. You look around and see you black. . . . I'm starting out with *nothing* so I got to get a little something."[46] When Caesar looks around and sees he's black, in other words, he merely glances and sees what he esteems as "nothing." The problem with such glancing for black people in particular, Wilson writes elsewhere, is that "we don't know who we are, and we're not willing to recognize the *value* in claiming that."[47] And who we are, per the witness of a play that proceeds in the wake of a drowning, are inhabitants of the deep. In contrast to Caesar's dismissal of Garret Brown, then, what would it mean to "value" blackness's being in the deep? To apprehend in the deep not the "little" or "nothing" a glance might apprehend but someplace worth inhabiting the way Aunt Ester ritually invites seekers to inhabit the City of Bones?

By staging our double take at the deep, the journey to the City of Bones in *Gem* not only discourages glancing, but works to fulfill Wilson's explicit motivation for creating the Century Cycle:

> The suffering is only a part of black history. What I want to do is place the culture of black America on stage, to demonstrate that it has the ability to offer sustenance, so that when you leave your parents' house, you are not in the world alone. You have something that is yours, you have a *ground* to stand on, and you have a *viewpoint*, and you have a *way of proceeding* in the world that has been developed by your ancestors. It was James Baldwin who called for a "profound articulation of the black tradition," which he defined as that field of manners and rituals that sustains a man once he has left his father's house. And I said, Ah-hah! I am going to answer that call. I am going to show that this culture exists and that it is capable of offering sustenance. Now, if in the process of doing that, you have to explore the sufferings of black America, then that is also part of who we are. And I don't think you can ignore that because our culture was fired in the kiln of slavery and survival.[48]

Beyond the "little," "nothing," or mere suffering suggested by a superficial glance at black history, Wilson's Century Cycle pursues a "profound articulation" of what he perceives as blackness's "ground," "viewpoint," and "way of proceeding in the world." Like Aunt Cuney in Paule Marshall's *Praisesong for the Widow*, then, it seems that Wilson would also have us eat the Negro Question. Not as Caesar hopes to go from nothing to something but with the conviction that the question of black being itself—here, given in and as blackness's ongoing inhabitation of the deep—"is capable of offering sustenance." Of sustaining, that is, not only black (social) death but also life. If so, the question Wilson would have us chew may just be the one Aunt Ester puts to Citizen when he comes to her to get his soul washed: "You got to find out why it was important for Garret Brown to die rather than to take his thirty days. Do you know why he didn't come out the water, Mr. Citizen? Do you know why he chose to die rather than to be branded a thief?"[49] We, too, have to find out why Garret Brown refused to come out of the water and thus extend more than a glance to his and blackness's inhabitation of the deep. At a glance, Brown's drowning illuminates no "ground" on which blackness has to stand, no "viewpoint" beyond that of one whom Caesar dismisses as a damned fool, and no "way of proceeding" so much as an untimely end. But with Aunt Ester's questions, Wilson discourages such glancing by soliciting our curious and patient interest in the drowning of Garret Brown as possibly enunciative of more than just black suffering and death. Note how Aunt Ester's questions emphasize the willfulness of Brown's decision as not just a negative refusal but a positive choice. In this way, Aunt Ester elicits the same patience with blackness's inhabitation of the deep that Christians have come to relate to Jesus's death on the cross. She explicitly invites this comparison when she tells Citizen that Brown "was like Jesus."[50] Perhaps like Jesus's (or Solly's, for that matter), Brown's death can also be discovered to bear some significant relationship to not just death but life.

By eliciting the lay black study of its audiences in this way, *Gem* powerfully intervenes in the thought of how it feels to be a problem and how such thought can otherwise tend, and not without good reason, to define blackness primarily in relationship to death, including especially the status of "social death." Garret Brown's inhabitation of the deep, however, speaks a different word. On the one hand, an Afropessimist reading of Brown's refusal to come out of the water would rightly apprehend a radical embrace of something very much like blackness's "social death." In this sense, Brown's inhabitation of the deep indexes blackness's ontological exclusion from the world—not only in the ocean's historical association with the Middle Passage "dawning of blackness" but also in the sense that the ocean has long figured in the western cultural imagination as "a void, lying eternally outside or on the margins of human social constructs."[51] Bearing witness to Brown's, the people's, and ultimately Solly's inhabitation of a deep situated as the constitutive outside of the western world may seem to warrant a Eucharist closer to what Wilderson describes in *Afropessimism* than Eli's perplexing "So Live" at the end of *Gem*: "There is no world without Blacks, yet there are no Blacks who are in the world. You had to be young or you had to be old for this Eucharist to touch your lips."[52] Yet if an Afropessimist reading of Garret Brown interprets his refusal to come out of the water as a radical embrace of his exclusion from a fundamentally antiblack world, then, according to Wilderson, this embrace is not fatalistic so much as the first and necessary step toward social death's destruction: "like class and gender, which are also constructs, not divine designations, social death can be destroyed. But the first step toward the destruction is to assume one's position (*assume, not celebrate or disavow*), and then burn the ship or the plantation, in its past and present incarnations, from the inside out."[53] By refusing to come out of the water Brown indeed assumes and does not disavow his position as an inhabitant of the deep. And although he does not live to engage personally in the subsequent pyrotechnics that Wilderson prescribes as an important follow-up to so getting in formation, his death does galvanize Solly to burn down the mill and at least attempt to burn down the jail. It's precisely because Wilson means not to disavow the truth of the black position that he begins *Gem* and the Century Cycle with the deep. Like a good Afropessimist, he saw "no avenues open for [black Americans] to participate in society," and there is even something of Afropessimism's conflation of blackness and slaveness in Wilson's insistence that the "first black," a slave, "has not vanished from the face of the earth" and is still "alive in the thirty million black people who are in this country right now."[54]

But after the last smoldering ember gives up the ghost, what will there be? Even if the world is flammable, is the Earth? Doesn't whatever survives the end of the world do so precisely because it also precedes and exceeds the world? And what is the relationship between the black position and it? Not only after the final flame dies out but right now? I raise these questions as one who has drunk from the cup of the Eucharist that touches our lips at the end of *Gem*. And judging from that cup's spiritous contents, a celebration may very well be in order. I raise these questions as one who has been hailed by Eli's exhortation to live like a man who recognized far more in his position than merely being excluded from the world. When Caesar places Solly under arrest, just as he did Brown, Solly replies with an emphatic spatial pronouncement that further complicates just where we imagine Brown to have been when he drowned under arrest:

> CAESAR: Solly, you didn't know somebody seen you when you set fire to the mill. You didn't know that. You thought you was gonna get away with it. But you can't get away with nothing like that. You under arrest.
>
> SOLLY: I'm under God's sky, motherfucker! That's what I'm under![55]

What if our position is not reducible to, or even primarily a question of, being under arrest as the constitutive outside of the modern world? What if, like Solly, we are also under God's sky? What if, as I've argued elsewhere, blackness is not only outside of the antiblack world but in the Earth?[56] And what if, when the final flame dies out, we will *still* be black with a blackness that was never reducible to social death, slaveness, or being excluded from the world? What if what survives the fire is black *life*? The good news of *Gem* is not that we are or can be in the world. That ship has literally sailed. Rather it is the revelation that the world is not total, nor the only meaningful frame for black study. There is a lot of elsewhere to be. And what is to be celebrated, even now, about the black position is illuminated in the light of this elsewhere, which not only reaches up to "God's sky" but down to the deep we inhabit. Here is where Wilson's black study and Wilderson's begin to diverge. For although Brown assumes blackness's paradigmatic position in the deep, Wilson's sense of that position is far less defined by black social death than what we might alternatively apprehend as black ecological life. Wilson's description of the basic difference between the "worldview," or *viewpoint*, of whiteness and blackness helps to illuminate this point: "The basic difference in worldview between blacks and whites can be expressed as follows: Western culture sees man as being *apart from* the world, and African culture just sees man as *a part of* the world. . . . For the white man, nature exists to be conquered. Whereas, for Africans, they see themselves as part of everything, the trees, all of life on the planet."[57] In his perception of western culture and the white worldview, Wilson has company in Thoreau, who similarly expresses in "Walking" his sense of whiteness as the human's aspirational separation from nature.[58] Yet, all available evidence suggests that Earth will not indefinitely tolerate the environmental devastation of this "genre of Man."[59] Does it quite make sense, then, to allow death to have the defining word about a mode of human life whose inhabitation of the deep may just be modern humanity's "loophole of retreat" to a viable environmental future as *a part of* our blue planet? Less due to an essential or original African essence but, rather, as a function of blackness's profound encounter with the deep during and in the wake of Middle Passage.

In pursuit of this question, it's worth exploring one final resonance between the black study of Wilson and Du Bois. In chapter 3, "Deep Voice," we considered how Du Bois represents emancipation in *Souls* as the dawning of a "time of *Sturm und Drang*," in which "storm and stress to-day rocks our little boat on the mad waters of the world-sea" just as fiercely as they troubled slave ships during the transatlantic slave trade.[60] Similarly, in *Gem*, which is set in the same decade as the publication of *Souls*, Wilson also represents blackness as *still* at sea, whether in the drowning of Garret Brown, "the people drowning," or finally, in the journey to the City of Bones. In our consideration of Du Bois's appropriation of nautical imagery in "Deep Voice," we noted how "the ideal of human brotherhood" "swims before the Negro people," such that they are uniquely positioned to pursue that ideal in their "little boat."[61] So, too, might we apprehend, swimming before Citizen's boat on his journey to the City of Bones in *Gem*, not only a *social* "ideal of human brotherhood" but the even more radical *ecological* ideal of a more-than-human creaturehood.

v. "the center of the world"

The social implications of Citizen's journey to the City of Bones are made explicit in the stage direction that immediately follows its conclusion. Citizen has just reached the Gatekeeper of the City of Bones, played by a masked Solly, who won't let Citizen pass and who Citizen dramatically discovers is Garret Brown. Aunt Ester instructs Citizen that if he does not confess that he stole the bucket of nails that cost Brown his life, Citizen will "never be right with [himself]. Peter denied Christ three times. You might not get lucky like Peter to have three chances." Citizen confesses, the masked Solly/Brown lets him pass, the city gates open, and we read the following stage direction: "Overwhelmed by the sheer beauty of the city . . . , Citizen Barlow, now reborn as a *man of the people*, sits down and begins to cry. Solly removes his mask. The journey is over."[62]

Aunt Ester's analogization of Citizen and Brown to Peter and Jesus suggests that the fault denying Citizen entry to the City of Bones is not his theft so much as his denial. Not the economic exploitation that drove him to steal the bucket of nails but Citizen's disavowal of and failure to express solidarity with Brown. This disavowal finds expression early in the play when Citizen reasons, in response to Brown's senseless death, that "he could have come out the river."[63] Indeed, should have come out the river and taken his thirty days rather than lose his life. Jesus, too, was scornfully commanded to come down from the cross if he was indeed the Son of God, and it was largely Jesus's willful embrace of the cross that spurred Peter's denial. In a parallel way, we can understand the declaration that "he could have come out the river" as Citizen's disavowal of Brown's inhabitation of the deep as unnecessary and purposeless. Also, Citizen notably does not join the rioters protesting Brown's death. His response to Brown's death is individual; he seeks only to alleviate *his* guilt and get *his* soul washed. In this way, Citizen's worldview recalls Wilson's gloss of a white worldview where humans stand "apart from" not only nature but also, given the primacy of the individual in western culture, one another. This viewpoint finds additional expression in an exchange between Citizen and Black Mary when Citizen makes a pass at her:

BLACK MARY: Okay, Mr. Citizen. I'll come to your room tonight. But the morning got to come, Mr. Citizen. What you got then? You tell me tomorrow. You wake up and look at your hands and see what you got.

CITIZEN: I got me. That's all there is.

BLACK MARY: That ain't never gonna be enough.[64]

Citizen's declaration not only rehearses the logic of the self-possessed individual ("I got me"), which is the beating heart of western sociality, but also makes an existential claim. All there is, all that ultimately exists, is the individual and whatever that individual can *get hold to*, to recall Caesar's language. Existence, in other words, is a holding, not least of our very selves.

With such a worldview, Citizen bears no obligation, responsibility, or relation to Brown or anyone. His disavowal of Brown and, more, Brown's inhabitation of the deep is rooted in a disavowal of sociality itself and a subscription instead to a metaphysics of separability and individuation. It is little wonder, then, that during his journey to the City of Bones, Aunt Ester makes such a point of asking Citizen about "the people":

AUNT ESTER: What about the people? Where are the people?

CITIZEN: I don't see no people.

AUNT ESTER: Look close. Do you see any people? Look real close now.

CITIZEN: I see the people. They chained to the boat.

AUNT ESTER: Them people you seen got some powerful gods, Mr. Citizen. But they ain't on the boat with them. They don't know to call him on their own. God don't answer to no one man. God answer to the all. All the people. They need all the people. Them people you see is without God.[65]

This crucial moment in Citizen's journey to the City of Bones grants him nothing short of a different worldview, perhaps the very "viewpoint" Wilson hoped to put on stage with the Century cycle and its "profound articulation of the black tradition." Against the grain of the primacy of the individual, this worldview prioritizes not "one man," but "the all." And, crucially, this viewpoint is situated in the black tradition not as a so-called "Africanism" but specifically as an inheritance of Middle Passage. Namely, the socialization whereby the individual strangers in the hold, possessing individual gods and cosmologies, became a "people" assembled under the banner of blackness, and further indexed in the historiography of the slave trade by the shipmate relation established between Africans, who arrived in the New World on the same slave ship.[66] Citizen's exposure to this "viewpoint"—which, besides blackness, also dawned in Middle Passage—enables him to see not just himself but also other people, including, finally, Garret Brown. If Afropessimism's concern is the disavowal of blackness's "social death" relative to an antiblack world, Wilson's concern in *Gem* is Citizen's disavowal of the black social life given in and as blackness's inhabitation of the deep. It's only through his avowal and participation in the black social life of Middle Passage that Citizen gains entry into the City of Bones and is "reborn as a man of the people."

But I have said that the journey to the City of Bones has not only social but *ecological* import; and it is in this way, especially, that the journey to the City of Bones can be said to illuminate blackness's "ground," "viewpoint," and "way of proceeding in the world." Consider, for example, the following stage direction, which signals the start of Citizen's journey to the City of Bones: "Citizen gets up and makes a sudden move to balance himself." Citizen has not moved from his position in Aunt Ester's parlor, but we nevertheless hear him exclaim: "I feel it moving! The land . . . it's moving away."[67] This, too, middle passing Africans observed of their world. The land moving away, the bottom falling out of the world, the spectacular vanishing of terra firma. As the beginning of Citizen's journey to the City of Bones, these lines and the embodied performance of the unsteady gait that accompany them register blackness's "ground." What this book otherwise thinks in terms of blackness's ongoing "inhabitation of the deep," its paradigmatic exclusion from, if not land per se, then the settled and stable experience of land as terra firma. And yet, this unsteady experience of the ground is here desired, willfully sought out, and intentionally reproduced in sacred ceremony. It is holy ground. Even if it fails to meet the settled expectations we typically bring to ground. And if this revelation of blackness's ground appears impractical, consider that land is hardly the static and docile surface we imagine it to be. Is not land always moving, if not in the spectacle of earthquakes then in the imperceptible shifting of tectonic plates beneath our feet? And would not the human inhabitant of a planet such as ours, whose surface is just as dynamic, need to consent to live with such dynamism? Would not the human inhabitant of a planet such as ours need to feel the land moving, need to know their engagement with earth's dynamic surface as the dialogue that it is?

Even if such ground is not ground enough for us, it was ground enough, Aunt Ester assures Citizen, for the inhabitants of the deep:

Take a look at this Map, Mr. Citizen. See that right there . . . that's a city. It's only a half mile by a half mile but that's a city. It's made of bones. Pearly white bones. All the buildings and everything is made of bones. I seen it. I been there, Mr. Citizen. My mother live there. I got an aunt and three uncles live down there in that city made of bones. You want to go there, Mr. Citizen? I can take you there if you want to go. That's the center of the world. In time it will all come to light. The people made a kingdom out of nothing. They were the people that didn't make it across the water. They sat down right there. They say, "Let's make a kingdom. Let's make a city of bones."[68]

I read in these lines not only an illumination of blackness's "ground" but what we might further recognize as its "way of proceeding in the world." A consent, that is, to be with and inhabit Earth as it really is. According to Aunt Ester, the inhabitants of the deep "sat down right there," wading in the water in which they had also been weighed, swimming, if not standing, their ground. On the one hand, it would be easy to dismiss Aunt Ester's words as a kind of euphemism, a nicer, more poetic way to say that they drowned. But, like Equiano, Aunt Ester insists that her ancestors "*live* down there" in a way that challenges us to imagine what meaning their inhabitation of the deep may have for life. Two things in particular come to light in Aunt Ester's reflection on "the people who didn't make it across the water." Two things, I propose, that elucidate the ecological viability of the "ground" and "way of proceeding in the world" conjured during the journey to the City of Bones and its ritual reenactment of Middle Passage. First, Aunt Ester ascribes to the inhabitants of the deep an expanded and deepened sense of the planet: "Some know about the land. Some know about the water. But there is some that know about the land and the water, they got both sides of it."[69] If the binary partitioning of Earth into the mutually exclusive domains of land and sea actually obscures both—that is, obscures land as a docile surface on the one hand and ocean as an utterly uninhabitable, antihuman, and chaotic void on the other—then the black culture that takes shape in the wake of Middle Passage and its profound oceanic encounter alternatively harbors a sense of the planet as an ecological unity. It is a kind of *Earthrise*, one of the earliest photographs of Earth from outer space and dubbed by nature photographer Galen Rowell "the most influential environmental photograph ever taken." Second, Aunt Ester attributes to the inhabitants of the deep a hidden geographic insight. Incredibly, Aunt Ester claims that the City of Bones is "the center of the world" and that "in time it will all come to light." Perhaps, with the advent of sea-level rise, this time has already come. Regardless, Aunt Ester's claim that the City of the Bones is "the center of the world" anticipates the critique in the blue humanities of the animating "terracentrism" or "terrestrial bias" of western culture.[70] Through the geographic knowledge of the inhabitants of the deep, Aunt Ester forwards an alternative vision of Earth as Ocean. And insofar as the ocean constitutes more than 70 percent of the surface of the planet, water may be the ideal ground for any humanism that hopes to have an environmental future.

In this way, although Citizen is explicitly "reborn as a man of the people," he is even more radically born again as a man of the more than people.[71] Consider that even before "the people" the first thing that Aunt Ester asks Citizen to look for on his journey to the City of Bones is the sky:

> AUNT ESTER: Do you see the sky?
>
> CITIZEN: I see the sky.
>
> AUNT ESTER: What color is it?
>
> CITIZEN: It's blue color up close but farther along it's gray.[72]

Why, at the very outset of his journey to the City of Bones, does Aunt Ester prompt Citizen, who can see only himself, to look at the sky? At stake in this look, I propose, is the ecological, and not merely the social, "viewpoint" conjured by this ritual reenactment of Middle Passage. Consider, for instance, Aunt Ester's account of her personal experience of Middle Passage:

> I came across that ocean, Mr. Citizen. I cried. I had lost everything. Everything I had ever known in this life I lost that. I cried a ocean of tears. Did you ever lose anything like that, Mr. Citizen? Where you so lost the only thing that can guide you is the stars. That's all I had left. Everything I had ever known was gone to me. The only thing I had was the stars. I say well I got something. I wanted to hold on to them so I started naming them. I named them after my children. I say there go Cephus and that's Jasper and that's Cecilia, and that big one over there that's Junebug. You ever look at the stars, Mr. Citizen? I bet you seen my Junebug and didn't even know it. You come by here sometime when the stars are out and I'll show you my Junebug.[73]

Just as Caesar saw that he was black and thus starting out with "nothing," Aunt Ester apprehends in the Middle Passage dawning of blackness a similarly total dispossession. She "lost everything." Everything, that is, but the stars. But unlike Caesar's black study in nothingness, which sets him down the antiblack path of getting hold to "a little something," Aunt Ester's study of the seeming nothingness of blackness lets out upon the cosmos. And with it an altogether different kind of having and holding predicated not on private property but on kinship and relation. Having lost the world, she gained not just the Earth but the universe, such that having nothing bleeds into having not merely "something" but effectively everything. Perhaps by instructing Citizen to look at the sky, Aunt Ester was inviting a man who had only himself to have the stars—not as a possession but as a mother, father, sister, brother, or even child. That is, as a matter of ecological belonging. We know that during his journey to the City of Bones Citizen must have seen the stars because we hear him ask, after being symbolically forced into the slave ship's hold: "The stars. Where are the stars?"[74] If by seeing "the people," Citizen was born again as a "man of the people," what rebirth do we imagine was catalyzed by his vision of the stars, if not Aunt Ester's more-than-human cosmological creaturehood? None of this is to claim that inhabitation, on a blue planet such as ours, is any walk in the park. But it just might be a dive.

PLATE 1. J. M.W. Turner's *The Slave Ship*, 1840. Oil on canvas, 35¾ × 48¼ in. Henry Lillie Pierce Fund, Museum of Fine Arts, Boston.

PLATE 2. Underwater still from the 1997 movie *Amistad* of an enslaved woman thrown overboard from a slave ship during Middle Passage. Source: Paramount Studios.

PLATE 3. Jason deCaires Taylor's *Vicissitudes*, an underwater sculpture in the Molinere Bay Underwater Sculpture Park in Grenada, 2007. Twenty-six life-size sculptures cast in reduced-pH cement. Photo: © Jason deCaires Taylor.

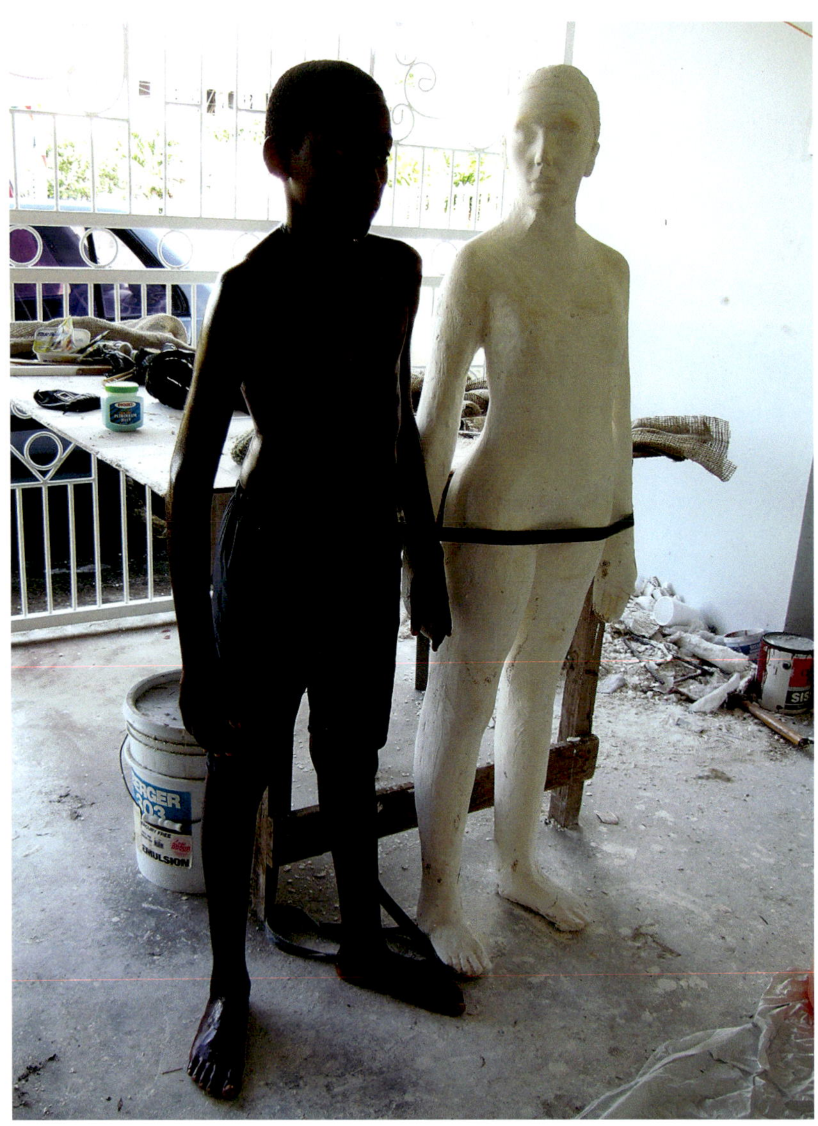

PLATE 4. A black Grenadian boy, one of two child models for *Vicissitudes*, poses beside his sculpture. Photo: © Jason deCaires Taylor.

PLATE 5. Close-up image of *Vicissitudes* showing the sculpture's dramatic transformation over time. Photo: © Jason deCaires Taylor.

PLATE 6. The author visiting Jason deCaires Taylor's *Vicissitudes* during a dive, August 2023.

PLATE 7. The author standing in ankle-deep water before the submerged grave of Emmett Till. Burr Oak Cemetery, Alsip, Illinois, April 2022.

PLATE 8. The grave of Emmett Till underwater after a heavy rain. Burr Oak Cemetery, Alsip, Illinois, April 2022.

6

DEEP VISION

The Tallahatchie River was "the big bang" of the civil rights movement.
—REV. JESSE L. JACKSON SR.

Let the people see what I've seen.
—MAMIE TILL-MOBLEY

I. unrecognizable

NO EYE HAS SEEN the underwater perishing of the inhabitants of the deep. The passion of their submarine inhabitation is a vision utterly vanished to history. It's not just that underwater archaeology is by definition belated, or that the technologies we use to record light had largely yet to be invented, or even that the sun's powers of illumination begin to fail below 660 feet of seawater, rendering the deep a literal blind spot. Rather, and more straightforward, it's that this submerged life wants historically for eyewitnesses, elapsing as it did below see level.

> *Witness: One who is or was present and is able to testify from personal observation; one present as a spectator or auditor.*[1]

Not even Equiano, who supposedly was there, gets us there. His narrative vision halts at the ocular event horizon of the ocean's surface. What seeing we do manage of the oblivion underwater we owe mostly to the prosthesis of visual art and media. Perhaps most famous is J. M. W. Turner's 1840 painting *The Slave Ship*, inspired by the infamous *Zong* massacre of 1781 (plate 1). The painting's original title, *Slavers Throwing Overboard the Dead and Dying, Typhon Coming On*, explicitly invokes the some 150 captive Africans who were thrown overboard the British slave ship *Zong* because the insurance money for these supposed commodities was reckoned more valuable than their lives. Still, I imagine the earliest onlookers had to tarry awhile to make good on the terrible promise of that lengthier, more expository title. At first glance, the painting seems to depict only a ship (and not yet a slave ship) pitching sublimely in the distance of a churning sea at sunset. There's little that immediately suggests the painful history awash in the fire-hued haze of this indistinct and seemingly innocent seascape. Until we can just begin to make out, foundering in the foreground, unapparent until conspicuous—what? A hand? Another? Too many outstretched hands that would be gasping for air if they were mouths. And there in the right corner, projecting crudely out of the sea, is that a leg? Are those manacles hanging from this horrible litany of limbs? And surrounding them, are those fish? And why where the fish swim most does the sea soak reddest? Hortense Spillers might describe *The Slave Ship* as a painting of the "flesh," pictured precisely where she first theorized the flesh in its "seared, divided, ripped-apartness, riveted to the ship's hole, fallen, or 'escaped' overboard."[2] Indeed, the painting depicts not bodies (not even broken bodies) but pained, fragmented, and, crucially, *faceless* "flesh," in whose subjugation the ocean, its weather (the coming typhoon), and its ecologies (the feasting fish) are all complicit. We may see only its surface, but it's enough to know that Turner's is an uninhabitable deep.

A similar illumination of the deep can be found in Steven Spielberg's 1997 film *Amistad* and what might be recognized as its parallel representation of the inhabitants of the deep. Based on the eponymous Spanish slave ship *La Amistad*, which was apprehended off the coast of Long Island, New York, in 1839 after a successful slave revolt, the film primarily treats the ensuing, international legal battle that ultimately decided the free status of the so-called *Amistad* Africans. Fittingly interrupting the *middle* of the film's dramatic arc, however, is a dramatized flashback to Middle Passage, rendered as the legal testimony of Joseph Cinquez, the historic leader of the *Amistad* rebellion and the film's protagonist. Like Turner's painting, Spielberg's dramatization of Middle Passage contains a representation of "slavers throwing overboard the dead and dying." But instead of stopping at the ocean's surface, *Amistad* lifts the veil of the Atlantic and affords its viewers a terrible glimpse of the oblivion below. After showing a series of nude bodies splash one by one into the sea, chained together and preceded by a net full of weights, the film makes an impossible cut, granting visual access where history otherwise does not. As if cued by the screams of the final woman to be pulled into the sea—our Aunt Hester of the Atlantic—the perspective of the lens suddenly jump-cuts over the side (plate 2). Now that we've passed through the blue gate previously barring all human witness to this horror, a column of drowning Africans thrashes before us, surrounded by bubbling exhalations. The focus of the lens eschews faces for flailing limbs, which is notable in a film that otherwise opens with an intense close-up of Cinquez working to free himself moments before the uprising. In this shot, however, there are no close-ups. In fact, the face-preoccupied shot is almost entirely absent from the film's treatment of Middle Passage, outside of the moments when the lens lights on Cinquez's face. In contrast, those listed in the credits either as "Amistad African," "Additional Amistad African," or "Amistad African Extra" appear so indistinguishably on-screen that they may just as well have been cast as "flesh." And once all flesh has sunk out of our underwater view, and all that remains in the shot is ocean and traces of breath half-taken, we hear, once again, the piercing sound of a woman's scream. Like, but higher pitched than, the one that originally sent us over the side and resounding with an uncanny clarity belying the seawater suffocating the screen at the time of its emission. Then, finally and mercifully, a cut to a perfectly calm and quiet sea, "all implicated, all / unconcerned."[3] Yet if the human voice sounds different underwater, from where does this second, perfectly unmuffled scream emerge? With no flesh on-screen to claim it, perhaps this impossible scream escapes extradiegetically into the film's score. Maybe, in this way, it sounds out the film's "total climate" of antiblackness, which Christina Sharpe has theorized in terms of "weather."[4] The "typhon coming on" in Turner's painting. Or, further extradiegetically still, perhaps this impossible scream is our own.

Despite whatever prosthetic access they grant to a horror no human eye has seen, Saidiya Hartman's contention that the spectacular paradoxically obscures more than it illuminates puts pressure on these parallel representations of the inhabitants of the deep. As spectacles of black suffering, they can unwittingly work to mystify the violence of a racial subjugation that operates most insidiously at the level of the quotidian.[5] The problem in the case of either image is that it's quite enough to look away. Enough, in order to resolve whatever ethical disturbance they provoke, merely to blink, look around, and see that there are no more slaves staining our seascapes. Never mind the images of black folk stranded on rooftops after Hurricane Katrina—"HELP! The Water is Rising Pleas"—or of ships brimming with African migrants on the Mediterranean Sea, left to die like Pip but without his resurrection (figure 6.1).[6] Except for these exceptional anachronisms, the inhabitants of the deep belong safely, if regrettably, to a distant past. By the time Turner's painting was exhibited in 1840, spectators could look to the fait accompli of the abolition of the transatlantic slave trade, and by the time *Amistad* was released in 1997, they could look to both the abolition of slavery and the passing of landmark civil rights legislation. But what of the less conspicuous violence already saturating the everyday of black life before flesh hits water, which the abolition of neither the slave trade nor slavery nor Jim Crow has fully managed to redress? The violence of racial subjugation that Frantz Fanon famously characterizes as a quieter matter of visuality. All that "Look, a Negro!" business in his archetypal scene of racial subjugation, whose visual tyranny led him to conclude that "the black man has no ontological resistance in the eyes of the white man."[7] Or, reaching even further back into the origins of this ordeal, Equiano's related observation that "we were all put under deck *so that we could not see* how they managed the vessel."[8] Taken together, Fanon and Equiano gesture to a broader visual dilemma basic to the problem of black being: the incapacity either to see or be seen. The specific implications of this visual situation keep getting worked out in the "changing same" of every century since Europe's fateful encounter with the so-called *Dark* Continent. What visualization, then, might facilitate the exposure of its violence? Its abolition? And, if not quite in *The Slave Ship* or *Amistad*, where can the inhabitants of the deep get a witness?

In asking specifically after a witness, I'm searching for a practice of regard informed by what Hartman has denoted as "the thin line between witness and spectator."[9] Relative to the latter, "a person who sees," the former, a "spectator *or auditor*," practices an elevated mode of perception that exceeds not only sight but, for one who also "gives evidence" and "testifies," the moment of perception itself. If the looking of the spectator exhausts itself in the moment and exerts no further or enduring claim, the witness, by contrast, is caught in the wake of their perception and bears it interminably into the future as potential energy for expression.[10] We would be witnesses to, and not mere spectators of, the inhabitants of the deep. Yet even this we do not attempt without reservation, as if it were an unquestionable good. Indeed, why peer beneath the surface of the Atlantic and disturb the dead at all? Do the inhabitants of the deep *need* our witness, or is it rather that we somehow need theirs? Maybe if they couldn't be free, they can and should, as Farah Jasmine Griffin has taught us, be a mystery.[11] This question of whether or how to look is a matter of frequent debate in black studies. What do ethics, care, and thoughtfulness all require, when, in our teaching and writing and living, we are faced with painful material? Do I watch this video? Do I show these photographs? Who should or shouldn't reproduce

FIGURE 6.1. Residents wait to be rescued from a rooftop in New Orleans after Hurricane Katrina, September 1, 2005. Photo: David J. Phillip/Pool/Reuters/Corbis.

these images? And how? Wherever one lands in the tension between the critique of the overexposure of black suffering or an unflinching commitment to bear it all, I agree with Elleza Kelley's vulnerable observation that "we still do not have a failsafe method for handling painful material." So, following Kelley, what this chapter labors to do instead, with deep thought and care, is try: "We are just trying. . . . Trying to write proper epitaphs. Trying to read, trying to breathe."[12] I recognize no inherent good in the elucidation of the inhabitants of the deep, or ill in their opacity.[13] In fact, the most significant risk I run in trying to bear witness to the inhabitants of the deep is their overexposure. Still there must be some way to regard a mystery *as a mystery*, especially when that mystery is all bound up in the mystery of being alive.[14]

I do not risk trying to bear witness to the inhabitants of the deep primarily to "never forget," as it were, although many need to remember and many are hard at work legislating our amnesia. The impulse to "never forget" alone, however, often paradoxically has more to do with securing the status quo of the present than faithfully remembering the past. The progress beyond past injustice it seeks to secure is often foreshortened by a too-narrow horizon of grievance, envisioning redress for individual entities rather than the solidarities a more thorough reckoning with our intersecting colonial, enslaved, and imperial pasts might yield. Nor, in peering beneath the veil of the Atlantic, do I mean to place a disproportionate emphasis on sight relative to the other senses and so reify the West's well-noted ocular centrism. Indeed, I'm persuaded that any meaningful witness to the inhabitants of the deep must be *born*. That is, carried or even birthed. It's not for nothing that we speak of bearing witness, but isolating the verb *bear* makes clear the more that witnessing entails beyond what can be performed by eyes alone.

No, I risk trying to bear witness to the inhabitants of the deep because I've discovered it to be a matter of both ethical and existential necessity. It's not only our care for the dead in the violence of their invisibilization. We also need to see them if we are to earnestly see ourselves—but, to be clear, not at all the way Narcissus saw himself. In Greek mythology, the hunter's superficial engagement with the water fatally stops at its surface, where he beholds himself to death. If Equiano and Fanon glimpse the visual dilemma of blackness, we may alternatively take Narcissus to embody the visual dilemma of whiteness, since western civilization has long seen fit to locate its roots in ancient Greece. Relative to the supposed visual incapacity of the progeny of the Dark Continent, it is perhaps strange to claim that the offspring of Europe, who went into the earth as the self-proclaimed "light of the world," are beset by their own visual dilemma. Yet, as the most beloved (at least nominally) prophet of the West has said, "If the light within you is darkness, how great is that darkness."[15] The darkness of light, in this case, inheres in what this same prophet might call out as the plank in the eye of modern visuality, in its fetishization of the individual subject as the most basic unit of social life. If throughout this book I have spoken, after Ralph Ellison, of modernity's "plan of living," here I am more precisely concerned with modernity's plan for *looking*. That is, the visual protocols and conventions—and behind these, the epistemology—that order and organize not only how we see ourselves and each other, whenever we meet, here, there, or anywhere, but also how we see the earth. The mirrors we are wont to make of each other as we hurry past the seeming interruptions of our encounters with human and nonhuman difference on to ontology's varied, individuated resolutions. First, the intrahuman plan for looking by which, in (visual) relation with others, we manage—like Narcissus and not unlike what we have understood of the (a)social contract—merely to see ourselves back to ourselves, in a rehearsal of encounter that only feels like interruption because we've fetishized the individual it seems to interrupt. Not to mention, the restrictions on whom we even owe the courtesy of this rolling stop masquerading as ethics. And second, the extrahuman plan for looking first exercised against the earliest images of Earth as a totality in the 2D maps of colonization, which return a reflection less of ourselves than of the conditions of possibility for the individual selves we believe ourselves to be.

In contrast to the superficiality of the visuality exemplified by Narcissus, the sort of vision with which this chapter is primarily concerned—what I call *deep vision*—is irreducibly social (read: ecological) and concerned with depth. In trying to bear witness to the inhabitants of the deep, I am interested in thinking toward some other practice of encounter with human and more-than-human difference. One that interrogates the thoroughly naturalized grammar of the preexisting singular beings always imagined to arrive on the scene, even if, quiet as it's kept, they are the aspiration and not the source of our looking. Against the grain of western humanism's "plan for looking" and what Fanon exposes as its fundamental antiblackness, the inhabitants of the deep confront us with a more radically immersed and involved vision of human life on Earth. As the modern world's original castaways, the inhabitants of the deep reflect back to us not only the violence and deathliness of our world in its present ecocidal arrangements—all its throwaways, both human and more-than-human—but also, could we learn to regard it, a profound bluing of the human. Like a blue note in jazz, their inhabitation of the deep performs the human against the standard grain of an exclusive identification with land and, in this way, glimpses the sort of human ecological life demanded by a planet that is significantly more blue than terra firma.

But if not in *The Slave Ship* or *Amistad*, which endeavor to represent them explicitly, this chapter explores whether the inhabitants of the deep can get a witness in two images that, at least on their surface, bear no explicit relation to Middle Passage: the photograph of Emmett Till and photographs of the black boy in Jason deCaires Taylor's underwater sculpture *Vicissitudes* (2007). In the painful photograph of Emmett Till's mutilated face, we bear witness to a body that was thrown into the Tallahatchie River during the era of Jim Crow. And in *Vicissitudes*, although it is often mistaken for a memorial to Middle Passage, we bear witness to a work of eco-art explicitly intended by Taylor, who is white, to promote ocean conservation by developing over time, with numerous other sculptures forming an entire underwater sculpture park, into an artificial coral reef. Whether pertaining to a later era of antiblackness or what is commonly understood by mainstream environmentalism as a different crisis altogether, the prospect of bearing witness to the inhabitants of the deep in these respective visualizations is further complicated by their exacerbation of what, by a certain logic, is already debilitating about *The Slave Ship* and *Amistad*. That is, neither offers prospective witnesses a recognizable face to light on. Within modernity's plan for looking, the face arguably represents the privileged seat of "recognition," in the absence of which ethics is almost unthinkable. The ethical philosophy of Emmanuel Levinas, for example, famously centers entirely on what he describes as our encounter with "the face of the Other."[16] Indeed, the (ethical) subject of modern visuality declares itself in the dictum *I recognize, therefore I am ethical.* And above all, what this subject recognizes is the face. However, the effacement we already observe in *The Slave Ship* and *Amistad* intensifies into an active *defacement* in the photographs of Till and the black boy of *Vicissitudes.* Till's face was notoriously beaten beyond human recognition, and the coral-covered face of the black boy of *Vicissitudes* grows increasingly unrecognizable over the course of what Christina Sharpe might call his "residence time."[17] It's not that these images eschew the face. They are even close-ups of a kind. Rather, it's that in their pan over the face, they offer nothing to see. Or at least nothing human, which might facilitate the "recognition" necessary to ethics' face-to-face. But as troubling as the circumstances that produce this effacement are, at least in the case of Till, it is also important to recognize that most of life lacks the sort of face that might ground our ethical regard and that our inability to apprehend not just more-than-human but more-than-individual life beyond the horizon of the face is a defining crisis of our times. Indeed, what is the Anthropocene but the height of *human* recognition? Has this recognition precisely of ourselves been the win for ethics that recognition promises? It just won't do to go on expanding whom we recognize as Human and eligible for the respect of their inalienable rights if, as the climate crisis makes clear, the modern category and performance of the Human, along with its enabling flattening of nonhuman life, is precisely the problem. But what if we just agree, with Fred Moten, that "our existence is unrecognizable, if we could only imagine it"?[18] In what follows, I want to try to imagine the unrecognizable life we live together on this blue planet, and I want to try this by trying to bear witness to the inhabitants of the deep in the unrecognizable faces of two black boys.

II. negative exposure

My first look at the photograph of Emmett Till came in the seventh grade, during a screening of the opening episode of the acclaimed civil rights documentary *Eyes on the Prize.*[19] Moments before the b(e)aring of Till's face, my teacher paused the video to warn us about the something it costs to look. About the weight there would be for pupils to carry. This weight, which was also a wounding. He repeated this warning, only this time making it mine, the only black student in the class, by extending to me a special invitation to be excused from the classroom. I accepted not because I sincerely wanted to but because of some vague sense that I could not be black and look at this.[20] Still I wondered why my white classmates could better afford to look than I. True, they could better afford most things, but this had nothing to do with money. Curious, I found myself, in a horrible inverse of Harriet Jacobs's "loophole of retreat," peeping through the door's windowpane, which was "scarcely large enough to give me a glimpse" of the faceless face that flashed upon the screen.[21] And I remember looking away, in that frantic prayer eyes pray for somewhere rid of what should not be. Prayers to a God whose son I'd heard had also been beaten beyond human recognition. Was this—and not the notorious blond-haired, blue-eyed portraits—how his face looked as he hung there, lynched?[22]

> *his visage was so marred more than any man,*
> *and his form more than the sons of men*[23]

What does it mean to bear witness to the marred visage in the photograph of Emmett Till? To a face that overflows the frames of family photos and human recognition, that suspends the Hegelian logics of recognition altogether?[24] What even can be seen in the photograph if not quite the face and form of a "man"? And what would a witness beyond recognition even entail?

The photograph that flashed on the television screen in my seventh-grade classroom appeared for the very first time in print in the September 15, 1955, issue of the weekly black periodical *Jet*, in a short photo-essay headlined NATION HORRIFIED BY MURDER OF KIDNAPED CHICAGO YOUTH.[25] The text of the essay relays a brutal set of facts. While visiting family in Mississippi, Emmett Till, a fourteen-year-old black boy from Chicago, was brutally lynched for allegedly whistling at a white woman. Three days later, his horribly disfigured body was discovered by a local fisherman in the Tallahatchie River with a seventy-five-pound cotton-gin fan wrapped around his neck. Spanning just four pages of a magazine designed to fit easily in a pocket or purse, the length of "Nation Horrified" belies the historical significance of the events it recounts.[26] Its actual *text* is shorter still, appearing on only three pages and sharing its limited paginal real estate with numerous photographs. But what is there to say about a story that, in M. NourbeSe Philip's words, "cannot be told"? That can be only "not told"?[27] What "Nation Horrified" cannot tell, however, it *shows*. The article, distinguished for baring the broken face of Emmett Till to the world, goes about the "not telling" of its story through a persistent and ultimately absolute appeal to the visual. No sooner do we begin reading the account of Emmett's murder than we encounter the extraverbal aid of a photograph of

Emmett and his mother, Mamie Till-Mobley. It is a typical family portrait. Mamie's arm encircles her son's shoulders in an embrace, and both smile toward the camera. Our convention of reading left-to-right prioritizes the photograph. Appearing in the upper left-hand corner and sharing a paginal latitude with the opening lines of text, it "speaks" the photo essay's first word. And, fittingly for the genre, a photograph also speaks the essay's last. The fourth and final page of "Nation Horrified" succumbs entirely to the visual.[28] Accompanied by no text besides its caption, the full-page image, which I identify as *the* photograph of Emmett Till, has the essay's final harrowing word.[29] It is described this way in its caption: "*Close up* of lynch victim bares mute evidence of horrible slaying. Chicago undertaker A. A. Raynor said youth had not been castrated as was rumored. Mutilated face of victim was left un-retouched by mortician at mother's request. She said she wanted 'all the world' to witness this atrocity."[30] Thus, "Nation Horrified" culminates its "not telling" of the murder of Emmett Till with the "mute evidence" of this historic photograph and the terrible difference between it and the essay's first photographic word. What, we ask involuntarily, would need to happen to the bright and boyish visage we behold at the beginning of "Nation Horrified" to cause it to assume the outlandish form we confront at the end? Emmett Till's broken face is moving in the most literal sense. It demands of one's body physical movement—wherever, however, or however much. Indeed, the Civil Rights *Movement*, commonly attributed to the galvanizing force of Emmett Till's murder, was conceived for many in look-aways, winces, and shudders at this photograph, which, in "Nation Horrified," immediately follows two other photographs, found side by side at the bottom of the essay's penultimate page, that also feature the ruin of Emmett's face. In the first, that ruin looms in the bottom right-hand corner of a photograph less of Emmett than of what is identified in the caption as Mamie's "first look" at her son in the casket. As the horrible inverse of the earlier mother-son family portrait, it instead pictures this family's undoing. The second photograph, as if offering Mamie's vantage point, is a head-on shot of Emmett's upper torso and face, in which the ruin of Emmett's face only begins to take center stage. As the final image in this sequence, *the* photograph of Emmett Till is indeed a "close-up," twice zoomed in from Mamie's "first look." Yet, what sort of close-up is the photograph of Emmett Till if the quintessential object of the close-up is the face? And if, in its approximation to the face, the close-up is generally supposed to afford a closer, more illuminating look at the individual subject, what are we approximating when we draw near to the heap of flesh that used to be Emmett's face? If it is a close-up at all, perhaps the photograph of Emmett Till is a failed close-up, approximating not the face but a terrible defacement. One to which Emmett's mother nevertheless demonstrates a curious commitment with her refusal to have the body retouched.

There is no seeing the photograph of Emmett Till; it must be seen. Following Philip's characterization of the bind of the ineffable and extending it to the visual, my study of the photograph of Emmett Till will not rely on its visual reproduction here. However, what I'd risk by doing so—namely, Emmett's overexposure and the perpetuation of a pornography of black pain—I likely still risk by writing and thinking about the photograph as attentively as I do. Still, I do so for no reason much more complex than that I feel that I must. I am beholden to it, be*held* by it—have been since the seventh grade. I just want to be a faithful witness. But since there is no seeing the photograph of Emmett Till, at least according to the protocols of recognition we typically bring to close-ups, it must be *not-seen*, or not only seen, or not-(only-)seen, which is finally just to say *witnessed*. On the occasion of this writing, not-(only-)seeing or bearing witness to the photograph of Emmett Till will mean beholding not straight on, but obliquely and aslant, in the way, for instance, modeled by Fred Moten when he undertakes to *listen* to the photograph.[31] Similarly, my study of the photograph is no straightforward or straightforwardly visual exercise. Bearing witness, as I hope to demonstrate, never is. Looking aslant at the photograph of Emmett Till—and, in this first instance, eschewing the conspicuous for the inconspicuous—I take note of something I had not previously. It's the photograph's negative exposure and, as a result and in distinction to other images of Emmett, its utterly black background. Suspended in the very blackness of blackness, the photograph of Emmett Till is its own afterimage. What we'd still see if we closed our eyes. Scrubbed of the contextualizing mise-en-scène of its specific physical setting, the ruin of Emmett's face could be any-, every-, and nowhere. It appears to us not in any specific place but rather in pure space. It is a photograph of Fanon's "zone of nonbeing" or what Frank Wilderson has otherwise described in terms of blackness's "ontological position."[32] A theoretical space that is essentially placeless until it *takes place*, until it happens in the world.

To interpret the photograph of Emmett Till as a photograph of blackness's "zone" or "position" is, on the one hand, to recognize in the photograph the "example" that his murderers, J. W. Milam and his half brother Roy Bryant, set out to make of Emmett. An example, namely, of blackness's "place." Consider these words from Milam in the murder confession that he and Bryant sold to *Look* magazine mere months after their acquittal:

> Well, what else could we do? He was hopeless. I'm no bully; I never hurt a nigger in my life. I like niggers—in their place—I know how to work 'em. But I just decided it was time a few people got put on notice. As long as I live and can do anything about it, niggers are gonna stay in their place. Niggers ain't gonna vote where I live. If they did, they'd control the government. They ain't gonna go to school with my kids. And when a nigger gets close to mentioning sex with a white woman, he's tired o' livin'. I'm likely to kill him. Me and my folks fought for this country, and we got some rights. I stood there in that shed and listened to that nigger throw that poison at me, and I just made up my mind. "Chicago boy," I said, "I'm tired of 'em sending your kind down here to stir up trouble. Goddamn you, *I'm going to make an example of you*—just so everybody can know how me and my folks stand.[33]

As a visual record of the terrible "example" Emmett was made into, the photograph of Emmett Till is what blackness's "place" looks like. Yet what we also need to understand about Milam's preoccupation with demonstrating "how me and my folks *stand*" is that an entire racial geography is at stake in Emmett's murder. A complementary set of ideas and assumptions about the "place" not only of blackness but also, through its so-called stand and the spatial practice implicit therein, whiteness. What, then, do the circumstances of Emmett's murder ultimately disclose about the nature of blackness's "place," as Emmett was ultimately made to occupy it at the bottom of the Tallahatchie River? And what is the relationship between this "place" and however it is that whiteness can be recognized to "stand"?

Prior to outlining the racial geography indexed by blackness's "place" and whiteness's "stand," it is crucial, first, to understand that it need never take the gruesome form it assumes in the photograph. In fact, as rhetorically expressed by Milam, this racial geography is essentially nonviolent. He claims, for instance, that he is "no bully," has "never hurt a nigger in [his] life," and even "like[s] niggers," albeit in their place. Moreover, as far as human postures go, a "stand" is relatively innocuous. It represents the human body not in any considerable posture of aggression but at arguably its most basic and least elaborated. Milam's insistence upon his "rights" is likewise basic, asking no more than a functional democracy should already guarantee. How, then, do we reconcile one of the most spectacular displays of racial violence in US history with what is otherwise jarringly figured, at least rhetorically, as nonviolent and unexceptional? Rather than dismiss Milam offhand, I propose we take him at his word and take seriously the specious nonviolence and unremarkability of Emmett's murder. How else would we know so clearly that our fight is not against incidents of racial violence but the ground? That, as Christina Sharpe has argued, the "ongoing state-sanctioned legal and extralegal murders of Black people are *normative* and, for this so-called democracy, necessary; it is the *ground* we walk on."[34] Emmett's was not a hit job performed in racial malice but the routine maintenance of a geographic status quo that may even look idyllic, if it isn't the death of you.

We can begin to discern the nature of blackness's "place" in the racial geography of the Jim Crow South by attending to the notable imprecision of Milam's response to the specific trespass of Emmett's whistle. Notice how indiscriminately the imagined suggestion of "sex with a white woman" also triggers anxieties about the integrity of voting polls and schools in a confession to the murder of a "Chicago boy" of no immediate threat to either. On the one hand, Milam's apparent overestimation of the spatial trespass of Emmett's whistle can be attributed to the fact that Emmett had managed to trespass the racial geography of the Jim Crow South at the site of its most anxiously guarded bastion. Or the historical context that Emmett's whistle was sounded out in the immediate wake of the 1954 *Brown v. Board of Education* decision and its generalized threat at least to the legality of racial segregation altogether. Even so, Milam's sense of the seemingly ubiquitous spatial incursion of Emmett's whistle suggests that Milam was less concerned with the integrity of any specific *place* so much as the integrity of social *space*. So distinguishing physical place from social space, I take the latter to mean something like the "placeless spaces" that concern Michel Foucault in his essay "Of Other Spaces." There, he argues that "we do not live in a kind of void, inside of which we could place individuals and things." Rather, "we live inside of a set of relations that delineates sites."[35] By social space, I mean precisely this "set of relations" that mediates our relationship to the physical world. Meanwhile, I take *place* to alternatively name the space, or "set of relations," that has *taken place*, that has happened in the world and taken root in physical space. In this sense, what initially may appear imprecise about Milam's estimation of Emmett's whistle can actually be recognized as thorough. For more than any single place, even a place as charged as a white woman's bedroom, Emmett was out of space. That is, outside of the "set of relations" that had come to define the Jim Crow South and so, it only follows, made to look like something that, his mother later remarked, "came from outer space."[36]

If what Milam calls blackness's "place" is ultimately a reference to social space, so, too, is what he alternatively characterizes as whiteness's "stand." We can discern this aspect of whiteness's "stand" in the frequent conceptualization of white space in the era of legal segregation in terms of a racially segregated "plane." Consider, for instance, the denunciation of the *Brown* decision by contemporary Mississippi Senator James Eastland as "an attempt to put the races together, physically, upon a *plane* of social equality."[37] Or, even more pertinent to the case of Emmett Till, the Swedish sociologist Gunnar Myrdal's similar observation that "it is assumed that Negro men have a strong desire for intermarriage, and that white women would be open to proposals from negro men, if they were not guarded from even meeting them on an equal *plane*."[38] One way in which Milam and his folks can be recognized to stand, in other words, is precisely on this so-called plane, which the *Oxford English Dictionary* otherwise defines as "an *imaginary* flat surface" that delineates a shared field of relation.[39] Being, in the first place, imaginary, the "plane" on which whiteness stands again refers not to any specific physical place but to social space. However, the geometrical construct of a plane is also what makes the material world thinkable and orderable, by reckoning its density and depth as a flat and fungible surface.

Even as relative positions within social space, however, the racial geography of the Jim Crow South had nevertheless to take place. And in a post-*Brown* United States facing the theoretical end of white and black space altogether, a heightened pressure fell upon the "racial etiquette" which maintained the segregated "plane" of whiteness as a physical, and not merely imagined, reality. According to Jerrold Packard, "Racial etiquette had come to control practically every public or semipublic facet of the lives of African-Americans in the South. No less dangerous than breaches of statute, lapses in race etiquette resulted in many of the criminal assaults that beset black American life: the so-called back talk or sassing that whites were taught from earliest childhood not to tolerate from blacks, the 'crime' of blacks *getting above themselves* ... or—deadliest of all for the transgressor—an inadvertent or casual or misplaced indication of a black man's interest in a white female."[40] By allegedly whistling at a white woman, Emmett transgressed the racial etiquette of the Jim Crow South in the especially deadly way that Packard describes above. Prior to his whistle, however, nothing, topographically speaking, guarded Carolyn Bryant from encountering Emmett "on an equal plane," as Myrdal wrote. Still, their physically coplanar existence became evident and *problematic* only in a lapse of racial etiquette. Emmett got "above" himself not by climbing a ladder but by upsurging onto whiteness's plane by hailing Carolyn with his whistle. What guarded Carolyn from meeting Emmett on an equal plane, then, was not a physical reality but rather the spectacle of racial etiquette and its remarkable capacity to maintain the illusion of physical separation even in the absence of physical distance. How the racial geography of the Jim Crow South takes place through the spectacle of racial etiquette is further evidenced in the question William Faulkner put to his fellow white Southerners in the wake of Emmett's murder: "Why do we have so low an opinion of our blood and traditions as to fear that, as soon as the Negro enters our house by the front door, he will propose marriage to our daughter and she will immediately accept him?"[41] Again, according to Faulkner, the South did not fear encounters between white women and black men in and of themselves. These were tolerated in places as intimate as the home. Rather, what white Southerners feared was how such meetings would go down without the mitigation of the racial etiquette of entering through the back door. Echoing the Door of No Return centuries prior, passage through the back door was no mere indignity but a spectacle effecting blackness's eviction from whiteness's plane.

Because you could "hold your head *up* in Chicago," Mamie anticipated that not getting above himself would be a significant adjustment for Emmett.[42] So before putting him on a train to Mississippi, she offered him a lesson in racial etiquette that generally cautioned him to "get down":

> I told him when he was coming down here that he would have to adapt himself to a new way of life. And I told him to be very careful about how he spoke and to whom he spoke, and to always remember to say "Yes, Sir" and "No, Ma'am" at all times. And I told him that if ever an incident should arise where there would be any trouble of any kind with white people, then if it got to a point where he even had to *get down* on his knees before them, well, I told him not to hesitate to do so. Like, if he bumped into somebody on the street, well, and then they might get belligerent or something, well, I told him to go ahead and humble himself so as not to get into any trouble of any kind.[43]

The general rhetoric of declension that characterizes Mamie's lesson in racial etiquette—the multiple ways in which she counsels Emmett to "get *down*"—grants significant insight into the nature of the "place" he had vacated by otherwise getting "above" himself in his failure to observe racial etiquette. By getting down in the manner Mamie prescribes and in accordance with racial etiquette, blackness manifested its supposed racial inferiority, while simultaneously grounding whiteness's own experience of its relative racial superiority. In this way, blackness's "place" and whiteness's "stand" can be recognized to take place together as two sides of a single geographical coin. Not only are they best apprehended as social spaces, but, here, we also discover that these spaces are relative and mutually constitutive.

Nowhere in the various rituals of racial etiquette did whiteness's "stand" or blackness's "place" take place more conspicuously or literally than on the occasions when black people were expected to "get down" off the sidewalk, at the approach of their white peers. This particular expression of racial etiquette epitomizes how Milam and his folks can be recognized to stand both in hierarchical relation to blackness and on a "plane" of their own. In blackness's step down from the sidewalk, we glimpse the necessary underside relative to which the stand of whiteness realizes the conditions of its own possibility. In it, the "zone of non-being" can be recognized to take place in the world precisely as the "utterly naked *declivity*" that Fanon imagined. The marginal descent from the sidewalk may hardly seem to warrant what Fanon characterizes as a "descent into a real hell."[44] And yet, geometrically speaking, even the slightest longitudinal difference is enough to signal a different plane. However, it is important to notice that in the examples we've surveyed, "plane" only ever appears in the singular and pertains exclusively to whiteness. Blackness has no like, or even inferior, plane to speak of. There is only the one "*plane* of social equality." Thus, when black people step down from the sidewalk, they land not on a lower plane but in the putative nowhere this book has otherwise interrogated under the rubric of the deep. Indeed, they do not *land* at all so much as founder. When the plane of whiteness is the only plane countenanced by the world, any descent, however marginal, is a "descent into a real hell."

It is also this drama of the sidewalk, and its illumination of whiteness's plane, that perhaps most justifies Mamie's sense that racial etiquette entailed nothing short of a "way of life." If, as J. Kameron Carter has argued, "whiteness is the enactment of a cosmology," or a set of ideas and beliefs about the nature of the universe and the material world, then we might otherwise recognize whiteness's "stand"—as the embodiment of this "way of life"—to enact this cosmology. As it is given in blackness's step down from the sidewalk and arguably further bottomed by the interpellation of the ground as a mere docile surface, whiteness's "stand" can be recognized to express an orientation to matter "in which the earth itself, its material stuff-ness or its very thingliness, is believed to be ownable or in which an extractive logic of property governs one's orientation toward the earth."[45] Recalling our previous encounters with whiteness's "plane," consider how white women show up on it as a mere opening. Myrdal explains that it is assumed that they "would be open" to the sexual advances of black men almost automatically if not guarded from meeting them "on an equal plane." And Faulkner likewise writes of Southerners' fear that they would accept the proposals of black men "immediately." But if the racial exclusiveness of whiteness's plane, and no agency of white women themselves, is the only thing imagined to guard them from the sexual advances of black men, then what does this say about white women's sexual availability to white men, who do share their plane? Would it not also be immediate and automatic? And does whiteness's plane, in this way, also prove itself to be male? Or does it mean nothing in our interrogation of Milam's "rights" that the right to vote throughout all of Europe's colonies in the Americas was originally restricted not just to whites but also to men and landowners?

The automatic and immediate availability of women on what is not only whiteness's but also maleness's plane suggests how "an extractive logic of property" may animate both this plane at large and the far from innocuous way in which Milam and his folks can be recognized to "stand" up on it. Beyond its racial subjugation, in other words, the seeming innocuousness of Milam's "stand" further belies a sexual and environmental subjugation. If the former is indexed in the characterization of women as being "immediately" "open," we might apprehend the latter in the abstraction of the planetary surface as a "plane," in the first place. In this way, the varied topography of the earth is flattened into a frictionless, fungible, and docile surface that is also "open" to extraction and "immediately" given as the automatic prosthesis of stand-your-ground subjectivity. Thus, Milam and his folks "stand" on a plane not of social equality but of the democratization of mastery. Carter again is helpful here, in his critique of "Man's freedom":

> This Subject . . . can subject other things to itself. It can rule. It can own things, beginning with itself, though this properly self-possessed and self-determining Subject cannot be subjected to another. In rationally owning itself as the basis of owning things, including the capacity to lay claim to the earth itself, it declares itself to be the veritable embodiment of "freedom." And yet, it is also the case that within this cosmology, within this imagination of "the world," Man's freedom expresses a capacity of self-rule for the sake of ruling over other things. Within the world, or more precisely within such a cosmology, this is what freedom means. Freedom is a function of sovereignty and sovereignty is a function, an expression, of freedom.[46]

So we might also understand Milam to express his "rights," within a cosmology defined by a hierarchical reckoning of and orientation toward the material world and requiring an enabling "set of relations" of domination. The domination inherent in these relations makes clear that the "*life*, liberty and pursuit of happiness" constituting Milam's "rights," and embodied by his "stand," are neither neutral nor basic, and far from innocuous, but rather an aspirational mastery with a necessary underside.

The social performances constituting the racial etiquette of the Jim Crow South—entry through the back door or the step down from the sidewalk—were all spectacles that needed to be seen. And whose being seen created the illusion and ruse by which white women were guarded from meeting black men "on an equal plane." This ruse reigned over interracial encounters in the Jim Crow South with a bluff so potent that, even in the absence of topographical assurances, blackness could be perceived as excluded from whiteness's "plane." However, when Emmett Till blew the whistle on racial etiquette's enchantment of the interracial encounter, such topographical assurance became urgently necessary. So necessary in fact, that Till's murderers "drove close to 75 miles" searching for the bluff that might affirm Jim Crow's bluff:

> Their intention was to "just whip him . . . and scare some sense into him." And for this chore, Big Milam knew "the scariest place in the Delta." He had come upon it last year hunting wild geese. Over close to Rosedale, the Big River bends around under a bluff. "Brother, she's a 100-foot sheer drop, and she's a 100 feet deep after you hit."
>
> Big Milam's idea was to stand him up there on that bluff, "whip" him with the .45, and then shine the light on down there toward that water and make him think you're gonna knock him in.
>
> "Brother, if that won't scare the Chicago——, hell won't."
>
> Searching for this bluff, they drove close to 75 miles.[47]

Suggestively, in his effort to put Emmett in his place, Milam sought out a bluff not only that was a "100-foot sheer drop" and "100 feet deep after you hit" but which he also femininizes and previously subjected to a level of environmental mastery by "hunting wild geese." Thus, Milam sought out a place where, for each of these reasons, the racial geography of the Jim Crow South might ideally take place. A place whose two-hundred-foot topographical variability would physically accommodate not only the inferiority of blackness's place "down there toward that water" but also the relative superiority of whiteness's "stand" upon a feminized "plane" where it was open season for a lot more than wild geese.

But in addition to the preoccupation with height and depth betrayed by the seventy-five miles, what we must understand about the flashlight is that Emmett's murderers were equally concerned with lighting. Lighting not merely to see in the dark but also, and more critically, because they needed to *see* Emmett to his place, if not by some illusion of racial etiquette, then by the threat of the one hundred feet. Lighting, because they themselves were numbered in the "everybody" who needed to know how they stood and were, in fact, the only bodies, besides Emmett's body, who would attend this viewing. And finally, lighting, because by "shin[ing] the light on down there toward that *water*," they also needed Emmett to see, and accept, not only his place but space. What, in the light of Milam's flashlight, becomes visible is not only the Tallahatchie River but the *deep*—ground zero of blackness's crisis of having zero ground. With the flashlight, they undertook to show Emmett that he really was an "inhabitant of the deep" whose lease on terra firma could be revoked at any moment.

After seventy-five miles of driving, however, Milam never did find his bluff. And Emmett never gave his murderers the satisfaction of his compliance. So in the end, they decided to coerce in death the descent Emmett refused in life. For this they secured a cotton-gin fan and settled for a less exalted place possessing the same basic elements of the bluff:

> About 1.5 miles southeast of the Boyce home is a lonely spot where Big Milam has hunted squirrels. The river bank is steep. The truck stopped 30 yards from the water.
>
> Big Milam ordered Bobo to pick up the fan.
>
> He staggered under its weight . . . carried it to the river bank. They stood silently . . . just hating one another.
>
> Milam: "Take off your clothes."
>
> Slowly, Bobo pulled off his shoes, his socks. He stood up, unbuttoned his shirt, dropped his pants, his shorts.
>
> He stood there naked.
>
> It was Sunday morning, a little before 7.
>
> Milam: "You still as good as I am?"
>
> Bobo: "Yeah."
>
> Milam: "You still 'had' white women?"
>
> Bobo: "Yeah."
>
> That big .45 jumped in Big Milam's hand. The youth turned to catch that big, expanding bullet at his right ear. He dropped.
>
> They barb-wired the gin fan to his neck, rolled him into 20 feet of water.[48]

If in this way Milam and Bryant made Emmett into an example of blackness's "place" and whiteness's "stand," then their use of the cotton-gin fan assures that this example was intended to inhere not in what is preserved to us in the photograph but rather in the illuminated spectacle of Emmett's physical eviction from whiteness's plane. Like blackness's step down from the sidewalk into nowhere, it was the spectacle of Emmett's absence, of his complete disappearance, that was meant to provide the "notice" about blackness's place and help everybody "know" how Milam and his folks stand. But earth is significantly more than sidewalk, and our designated nowheres are "where" enough, far more than we often know to give them credit for. And in Milam and Bryant's rehearsal of the racial geography of the Jim Crow South, the nowhere of the Tallahatchie is precisely where their visual autonomy over their intended example slips and something unintended takes place. Where the Tallahatchie comes to manifest Fanon's "zone of nonbeing" indeed, by also proving to be a site "where an authentic upheaval can be born."[49] The upheaval I have in mind begins with what Mamie characterizes as the mis/use of the cotton-gin fan: "Emmett's murderers had tied a gin fan around his neck to weigh him down, figuring he never would be found. But they figured wrong. They had failed to weigh his feet down."[50] Consequently, when Emmett's body resurfaced three days later due to its natural buoyancy, it was "Emmett's *foot* rising above the surface of the river" that was spotted by a local fisherman, in an uncanny echo of the crude leg jutting out of the Atlantic in Turner's *The Slave Ship*.[51]

This echo constitutes more than a haunting coincidence. Rather, I propose that Emmett's leg-first resurfacing indexes a veritable *haunting*. Not in the sense of Casper, or even the sense in which the past is never past and so can always be said to haunt the present, particularly in the case of black life. But in the sense that Avery Gordon has otherwise described in *Ghostly Matters* (2008) as

> an animated state in which a repressed or unresolved social violence is making itself known, sometimes very directly, sometimes more obliquely. I [use] the term *haunting* to describe those singular yet repetitive instances when home becomes unfamiliar, when your bearings on the world lose direction, when the over-and-done-with comes alive, when what's been in your blind spot comes into view. Haunting raises specters, and it alters the experience of being in time, the way we separate the past, the present, and the future. These specters or ghosts appear when the trouble they represent and symptomize is no longer being contained or repressed or blocked from view. The ghost, as I understand it, is not the invisible or some ineffable excess. The whole essence, if you can use that word, of a ghost is that it has a real presence and demands its due, your attention. Haunting and the appearance of specters or ghosts is one way . . . we are notified that what's been concealed is very much alive and present, interfering precisely with those always incomplete forms of containment and repression ceaselessly directed toward us.[52]

In what I am proposing can be read as Emmett's haunted resurfacing, the repressed and unresolved social violence making itself known, in excess of what

Milam otherwise meant for "everybody [to] know," is *Slavers Throwing Overboard the Dead and Dying*. That is, the throwing overboard of middle passing Africans during the transatlantic slave trade. Nor does this haunting inhere only in Emmett's resurfacing. It also registers in the actions of his murderers, who, by jettisoning Emmett's body into the Tallahatchie River, offered their best impersonation of Turner's "slavers." Not to mention the conspicuous signifier of US slavery that Milam and Bryant used to weigh Emmett's body down. The profound haunting effected by each of these elements makes known the foundational repression of the antiblack world: the 1,818,681 bodies disappeared into the sea without a trace. And it makes it known not as a perceived over-and-done-with catastrophe in the past but as the ongoing racially uneven distribution of the ground still founding our present. The mise-en-scène may not always be as uncanny, but all black life, as an ongoing inhabitation of the deep, is arguably haunted in this way.

Yet if haunting "raises specters," then Emmett's haunted resurfacing, as it was ultimately captured in the photograph of Emmett Till, also resurfaces the inhabitants of the deep. Mamie Till-Mobley likely did not know or intend it. But when she instigated the photograph of her son, so many cameras flashed underwater. Years before *Amistad* lifted the veil of the Atlantic, the inhabitants of the deep had arguably already resurfaced in our visual consciousness on the pages of *Jet* magazine and subsequently in newspapers and periodicals throughout the United States and the world. In other words, I am proposing that the photograph of Emmett Till *is* a photograph of the inhabitants of the deep. That in it, the inhabitants of the deep are really presenced, and the world unwittingly comes face-to-face with the image of a drowned slave. When else had the entire world had the occasion to see what an inhabitant of the deep looks like? Indeed, prior to the revelation of Emmett's broken and bloated face, who had ever beheld this buried evidence of the antiblack world's original sin?[53]

Emmett's murderers figured wrong indeed. Their mis/use of the cotton-gin fan assured the eventual discovery not just of Emmett's body but also, through a profound haunting, of the inhabitants of the deep. And unlike trauma, haunting, Gordon tells us, "is distinctive for producing a *something-to-be-done*. Indeed . . . haunting [is] precisely the domain of turmoil and trouble, that moment (of however long duration) when things are not in their assigned places . . . when the people who are meant to be invisible show up without any sign of leaving, when disturbed feelings cannot be put away, when something else, something different from before, seems like it must be done."[54] Haunted by the disappeared host of the 1,818,681 who perished during Middle Passage, a body never intended to be seen again ultimately resurfaced in newspapers and television sets across the globe, "set[ting] in motion this nation's profoundest political insurrection and resurrection, the resurrection of reconstruction, a second reconstruction like a second coming of the Lord."[55] A photograph of an unmade face, recklessly eyeballing not only a nation but a world with its "something-to-be-done."

Take up your fan and follow me.

III. "*Let* the world see"

When the "Nation Horrified" article cedes its final devastating word to the photograph of Emmett Till, it emblematizes its distinctly visual times. Its decisive shift from the verbal to the visual yields a microcosm of what Jacqueline Goldsby illuminates as the broader visual turn of 1950s media with the popularization of photojournalism and the advent of television. The revolutionary proliferation of representational technologies in media was marked, according to Goldsby, by a corresponding transformation of the US public from a primarily "wordminded" to an "eyeminded people," for whom seeing, above all else, was believing.[56] Thus, it was with newfound eyes to see that a horrified nation beheld not only the photograph of Emmett Till but also what Goldsby frames as the broader "discursive event" of Emmett's murder, open-casket memorial, and subsequent murder and kidnapping trials from August to November 1955. Situating this "discursive event" in the historical context of the 1950s visual turn, Goldsby argues that Emmett Till, and the enduring force with which he "haunts our political conscience," is a specific "construction of 1950s mass visual culture."[57] Due to the amplifying power of this visual culture, the viewing, which might have ended in Chicago as a four-day open-casket memorial attended by an estimated 100,000 people, evolved into an even more protracted viewing staged not only in newspapers and magazines but on living room television sets. The latter technology was especially significant to the coverage of the trial. In addition to being covered by sixty to seventy reporters, all three major television networks flew film footage of the trial to New York for nightly broadcasts.[58] Hailing so many eyes, the discursive event of Emmett Till approached a level of protovirality that was not only national but international in scope, receiving media coverage in at least six foreign countries and likely more.[59] Nor has this viewing ever really concluded. Rather, as evidenced in several recent flash points in just the past ten years, it is ongoing: in Dana Schutz's *Open Casket* and the controversy surrounding the inclusion of the white artist's painting of Emmett's disfigured face in the 2017 Whitney Biennial in New York; in the 2022 film *Till*; in the now bulletproof sign (after the vandalization of two others) commemorating Emmett Till at Graball Landing, where Emmett's body is believed to have been pulled from the Tallahatchie River and which was recently declared a national monument with the signing of the Emmett Till Antilynching Act in 2022; and in whoever may be filing past the exhibition of Emmett's casket in the National Museum of African American History and Culture as you read this sentence.

What Goldsby terms "1950s mass visual culture" offers important context to what has long been acknowledged as Emmett Till's historical significance as a major catalyst for the US Civil Rights Movement. If, as David Halberstam has contended, "the murder of Emmett Till and the trial of the two men accused of murdering him became the first great media event of the civil rights movement," then it was precisely owing to a novel mass visual culture that, according to Goldsby, was characterized not just by the prevalence of photography and television but also the shared belief in a "visual realism" that dictated that "what was 'true' or 'real' was that which could be seen."[60] In this visual climate, the protracted viewing of Emmett Till wielded the epistemological authority to reveal the truth about the United States' oft-debated race problem, however wildly interpretations of that truth might vary in the eye of the beholder. For instance, in Mississippi, though the state would ultimately close rank around and exonerate Emmett's murderers, a local newspaper editor initially denounced Emmett's murder as "way, way, beyond the bounds of human decency." Likewise, Mississippi Governor Hugh White declared that "Mississippi does not condone such conduct."[61] However, fearing its negative implications for Mississippi and the South more broadly, Governor White also refuted the characterization of Emmett's murder in the national media as a racially motivated lynching, claiming instead that it was a "straight out murder."[62] If the South, in this way, initially viewed Emmett's murder as the barbaric actions of a few bad apples, the national press in contrast came to indict the whole of not only Mississippi but the Jim Crow South. In their eyes, Emmett Till revealed "a rare glimpse beneath the Deep South's genteel surface at how the white power structure kept blacks in line—using the rawest violence, if necessary."[63] Others, in the international press especially, wondered whether the murder of Emmett Till revealed a broader truth about the United States as a whole. In addition to the discrepancy between Emmett's face in life and death, they were appalled by what that discrepancy revealed about the incongruity between the United States' democratic ideals and its treatment of its black citizens. As the headline of one article in Belgium read: "Killing a black person isn't a crime in the home of the Yankees: The white killers of young Emmett Till are acquitted!"[64] But whatever the protracted viewing of Emmett Till revealed, all believed that it revealed the truth.

The looking we've done and continue to do at the photograph of Emmett Till is perhaps a fitting synecdoche for all this viewing. Not only does the photograph persist as the most frequently reproduced and accessed rallying point for the witness to Emmett Till that endures today, but more than any other constitutive part of the broader "discursive event," the photograph and its original circulation among *Jet* magazine's national readership of 425,000 best qualifies as the "*first* great media event of the civil rights movement." It specifically precipitated the spread of Emmett's story from a local to a national audience. Thus, Charles Diggs Jr., Michigan's first black congressman and the only congressman to attend the murder trial, distinguishes the photograph as "probably the greatest media product in the last 40 or 50 years because that picture stimulated a lot of interest and anger on the part of blacks all over the country."[65] Yet even as Diggs justifies our estimation of the photograph of Emmett Till as a fitting synecdoche for the protracted viewing of a broader discursive event, his specific emphasis on the "interest and anger on the part of blacks" also suggests a distinctly black witness to Emmett. The distinction I am attempting to make here between the initially black and subsequently more general witness of a horrified nation breaks not on the racially essential lines of black and white people but, rather, on this book's broader understanding of the difference between blackness and whiteness, and the respective performance of the (non)Human implicit therein. Nor, in calling attention to a distinctly black witness to the photograph of Emmett Till, do I mean to disavow the historical significance of the more general witness of a horrified nation. The Civil Rights Movement that Emmett's murder helped galvanize was significantly a multiracial coalition, in which both white and black protesters placed their bodies on the line. Nevertheless, the distinctly black witness I want to distinguish, while overlapping with the Civil Rights Movement, also exceeds, and in some ways even contradicts, the dominant characterization of that movement by also partaking in the "black radical tradition" and, more, constituting a luminary visual moment within that tradition.[66]

It is especially with respect to the black witness to the photograph of Emmett Till that I want to probe the meaning of Rev. Jesse Jackson's compelling declaration that "Emmett Till was the 'big bang,' the Tallahatchie River was the 'big bang' of the civil rights movement."[67] My own emphasis on the photograph suggests that we might locate this bang even more precisely in the fateful flash of a camera in A. A. Rayner Funeral Home. In any case, it is striking that in Reverend Jackson's compelling formulation, Emmett Till and the Tallahatchie River *both*, and not one more than the other, are analogized to the

Big Bang. How, then, can a river help catalyze a movement? And where exactly is the Tallahatchie in the photograph I've otherwise put forward as the "first great media event of the civil rights movement"? I want to propose that not only are the waters of the Tallahatchie not incidental to the beginnings of the Civil Rights Movement but that they constitute a significant aspect of the revelatory witness of the photograph of Emmett Till.

One way to think of the Tallahatchie's specific function as a catalyst for the Civil Rights Movement is the resonance the river arguably gains, in its analogization with the Big Bang and in the mouth of a black Baptist preacher, with the primordial deep in the creation narrative of the Bible. Like Richard Wright's invocation of the Atlantic as a type of *tehom* in the creation of Bigger Thomas in *Native Son*, as rhetorically invoked by Jackson, the Tallahatchie similarly evinces a type of *tehom* that catalyzes the re-creation of a nation.[68] What Christina Sharpe might describe as the "track left on the surface of the [Tallahatchie] by [Emmett]" is rhetorically imbued with the same creative power of God's movement over the face of the deep in Genesis 1:2. In this way, the Civil Rights Movement may be located not only figuratively but physically in Emmett's "wake."[69] Perhaps, as the very trouble God promised, like and not like the old spiritual goes, to children, weighed in the water.

In the photograph itself, the troubled waters of the Tallahatchie might be located in the image's negative exposure and a background black as the "darkness [that] was upon the face of the deep." Or, more straightforwardly, in the awful bloat that had settled into Emmett's face as the visual trace of his three-day underwater inhabitation. But if we behold the photograph obliquely, another related sense in which the photograph is troubled by water comes to light: the sense in which we have already understood the photograph of Emmett Till to be a photograph of the "inhabitants of the deep." Picturing in this way the outermost out, the photograph haunts our "political conscience," to recall Goldsby's phrasing, by revealing the terrible and foundational violence of every *in*.

But when understood primarily as a struggle for political *recognition*, the Civil Rights Movement represents a strange fruition of the roots it claims in the photograph of Emmett Till, which otherwise comes to us precisely in Mamie's refusal of recognition. She, who loved every detail of her son's precious face, nevertheless refused to have it retouched. Whatever marginal recovery, whatever rescue from unrecognizability retouching a faceless face like Emmett's might have yielded, she who beheld his face first and loved it most refused. Mamie recounts this refusal in her memoir:

> I told Mr. Rayner I wanted an open-casket funeral. He looked at Emmett, that horribly distorted face, then he looked back at me. He asked me if I was sure. I was never more certain of anything. He asked me if I wanted him to retouch Emmett. If I wanted him to work on my son. If I wanted to make him more presentable.
>
> I shook my head. "No," I said. That was the way I wanted him presented. "*Let the world see what I've seen.*"[70]

If Emmett and the Tallahatchie are the Big Bang of the Civil Rights Movement, then, with her now famous declaration, Mamie may have spoken the movement's "Let there be light." Like this and other well-known *let*s throughout the Bible—*Let the redeemed of the Lord say so, Let everything that has breath praise the Lord, Let the little children come to me*, and so on[71]—Mamie's *let* performs a creative utterance, conjuring conditions that do not currently exist but, for the flourishing of life, should and would, if we would only learn to get out of life's way. And that which Mamie specifically speaks into existence here is a kind of global vision. *Let the world see*, if not also *let us see the world*. And what the world has the opportunity to see, in the photograph of Emmett Till, is not just the horror of racism but also what Moten might call our unrecognizable existence. The willful unrecognizability of the photograph of Emmett Till creates a tension between a sense of civil rights as a struggle for recognition, on the one hand, and recognition's refusal, on the other. These two registers of freedom struggle can be usefully mapped onto what we've already glossed as Fanon's characterization of blackness's visual dilemma. If "the black man has no ontological resistance in the eyes of the white man," then one possible register of freedom struggle is the black man's struggle precisely to obtain or assert a recognizable ontology. Recall, for example, the ontological emphasis of the iconic "I *am* a Man" protest signs, which can be read as civil rights' emphatic answer to abolition's earlier and equally iconic protest image of a kneeling and supplicating slave asking, "AM I NOT A MAN AND A BROTHER?" As powerful appeals for recognition, these canonical protest images respectively interrogate and interrupt the violent erasure of black humanity. However, scholars have also come to question the limitations of their respective visions of freedom as either uncritically masculinist or defined in the normative terms of whiteness.[72] Turns out a man gaining recognition as a man does not get us *all* free. In many cases, it actually enlists more masters. Moreover, whatever freedom can be gained through supplication is limited by the imagination of the giver, who excluded the unfree in the first place. Driven by these significant limitations, we may therefore imagine another register of freedom struggle, not as the ontological appeal for recognition but as a profound interrogation of the "eyes of the white man" that established the terms of recognition to begin with. This latter mode of freedom struggle crucially locates blackness's visual dilemma not in any black visual incapacity, either to see or be seen, but instead in what J. Kameron Carter might describe as the "cosmological" vision of whiteness. That is, its peculiar way of seeing the world. The problem of black (non)being, then, lies first and foremost "in the eyes of the white man": those eyes that surveyed the world and everything therein and apprehended only a docile surface to be possessed and extracted, including but not limited to the surface they beheld in black skin.

This is not to disavow the connection Reverend Jackson suggests between the photograph of Emmett Till and the US Civil Rights Movement. Rather, I understand the implications of Mamie Till-Mobley's decision to "let the world see what I've seen" to be precisely as *cosmic* as Reverend Jackson suggests. Thus, if Emmett and the Tallahatchie are the Big Bang, they are the Big Bang, I propose, not of a struggle for (political) recognition, which would merely integrate rather than re-create the world, but of a radical refusal of the world's constitutive visual logics and, in the clearing of that refusal, what Sharon Sliwinski might call the "virtual community" that was and continues to be hailed not just by the photograph of Emmett Till but, in it, Mamie's refusal of recognition. Finally, then, in my oblique look at the photograph of Emmett Till, and against the visuality of "the eyes of the white man," I propose an understanding of the photograph as the look of a black woman. It matters that the photograph of Emmett Till in *Jet* follows in the wake of Mamie Till-Mobley's "first look." The implications of this sequencing are hidden in every recitation of Mamie's famous words, "Let the world see *what I've seen*." What we ultimately see in the photograph of Emmett Till, then, is a look. Is Mamie Till-Mobley's black looking. Mamie Till-Mobley staged one of the most significant visual moments of the twentieth century. It's her wake, as much as Emmett's, that we're caught up in.

IV. "what I've *seen*"

When the most recognized prophet of the US Civil Rights Movement ascended the mountaintop, he may well have seen Mamie Till-Mobley on her way back down. Echoing the visual denouement of "Nation Horrified," Martin Luther King Jr. closed what would prove to be the final sermon of his life by narrating a look:

> Well, I don't know what will happen now. We've got some difficult days ahead. But it really doesn't matter with me now. Because I've been to the mountaintop. And I don't mind. Like anybody, I would like to live a long life. Longevity has its place. But I'm not concerned about that now. I just want to do God's will. And He's allowed me to go up to the mountain. And I've looked over. And I've *seen* the promised land. I may not get there with you. But I want you to know tonight, that we, as a people, will get to the promised land. So I'm happy, tonight. I'm not worried about anything. I'm not fearing any man. Mine *eyes* have seen the glory of the coming of the Lord.[73]

Like the crowd gathered in Mason Temple (the Church of God in Christ headquarters in Memphis, Tennessee) on April 3, 1968, you really need to hear this look.[74] The way King specifically emphasizes "seen" and "eyes," sonically extending two words having to do with vision for a full second. In their stretched-out pronunciation, we can actually hear King "look[ing] *over*." Spoken in his characteristic "vibrato"—which Maurice Wallace has helped us better hear[75]—these vacillating words, like stairs, also bear us up to the mountaintop so that we, too, might see what King has seen: the "promised land" and the "coming of the Lord." These biblical allusions represent a utopian space and time, respectively—and, in King's usage, express a vision of human life unmoored from the individual.[76] Individual longevity has no more or less than "its place" and, beyond that, there are other meaningful ways for black life to "matter with" and to those who would see its flourishing. Yet King inspires little confidence in his mountaintop vision of the promised land when he confesses that he "may not get there," which is also to say that he has never been there, and regrettably we know that he never arrived. Nor, for that matter, have we. If, in this way, King forfeits the most basic qualification of a witness as "one who is or was *present*," then how did he see what he claims to have seen? Moreover, how can we possibly "know *tonight* that we, as a people, will get to the promised land," while the "coming of the Lord" still tarries?

King's dubious mountaintop vision, like Equiano's underwater vision of life and freedom, raises an important question about epistemology. On what grounds can we reliably claim to know something? And is it possible to know that which we cannot know for certain? That is, as a perfect and indisputable fact? In an epistemological milieu in which seeing has long enjoyed a conflation with believing, King's grounds for seeing and knowing what he purports to see and know, as one who was *not* present, are as dubious as what the inhabitants of the deep had to stand on. Yet just as we have come to understand about the latter's *physical* position, the precarity of King's *epistemological* position is not owing to any natural intellectual inferiority rooted in racial difference. Rather, it is the artificial outcome of a racially uneven distribution of ground, which, as the animating logic of modernity, obtains as much metaphysically as physically. At issue in King's dubious mountaintop vision, then, is the modern world's historic foreclosure to blackness of the capacity not just to see, as already glimpsed in our outline of blackness's visual dilemma, but consequently also to know, given modernity's epistemological conflation of vision and knowledge. *I'll believe it when I see it* or *I see*, we say when we otherwise mean we understand. Still, I propose that the uncertainty of blackness's epistemological position in the modern world represents the opposite not of knowledge but of absolute certainty, which we might in turn recognize as the equally artificial epistemological standpoint of whiteness. Certainty is epistemology's equivalent of terra firma, fetishized by whiteness as knowledge's consummate, if not only, form in much the same way that whiteness apprehends the earth merely as a docile surface. What we can know, however, is hardly limited to facts. Moreover, black uncertainty, even if artificial in its constructed hyperprecarity and negation relative to white certainty, can also be apprehended, when beheld beyond this opposition, as real insofar as knowledge is discovered, as it inevitably is for those who earnestly seek it, to be a growing awareness precisely of what we do not and cannot ever know for certain. Ignorance, too, or at least the awareness thereof, is power.

So barred from vision and knowledge, King's stretched-out pronunciation of "see" and "eyes" also represents the audible trace of a similar and necessary stretching of the faculty of vision itself from a strictly ocular to also an aural phenomenon. Beyond what eyes alone can perform, such vision as *feels its help*, as black preachers are wont to say when the preaching is preaching, represents the necessary recourse of those who, owing to no blindness of their own, cannot (or else are not authorized to) see what they need to see. Caught, as they often are in the antiblack world, between what Nicholas Mirzoeff has insightfully parsed as "a real that did exist but should not have, and one that should exist but was as yet becoming."[77] Gathered in Mason Temple, King and the "people" he wanted "to know tonight" were so caught between their *un*reality of racial and economic injustice and the "promised land" and "coming of the Lord," in which they believed as an ultimate, if deferred, reality. One they needed to stretch to see, even as they walked through the unillumined shadow of the Jim Crow South.

King's mountaintop vision in many ways captures the visionary spirit of a movement that, not for nothing, is chronicled in the documentary series *Eyes on the Prize*. Its opening theme pictures people marching single-file, like the Israelites, through a wilderness of unfreedom to, we can safely assume, the "promised land" of full integration into US society, because, as the camera pans out, the single files are revealed to be the "stripes" of the US flag. Yet as iconic as King's mountaintop vision is, it claims a significant and illuminating precedent in what Mamie Till-Mobley saw. If King's vision proceeds from the transcendent vantage point of the mountaintop, Mamie's vision, by contrast, proceeds from and in the deep. Hers is not the mountaintop vision enabling King to glimpse a "promised land" to come but what we might alternatively label *deep vision*, the subversive genre of black looking that this chapter has been building toward. Because, far from any promised *land*, what deep vision perceives in the watermarked ruin of Emmett's face is blackness's ongoing inhabitation of the deep. This it sees not only as a vision of black death or abjection, which is evident enough in the photograph of Emmett Till. Rather, as with Equiano's underwater vision of the "inhabitants of the deep" and their improbable "freedom," the focus of deep vision is life and freedom—not only to come in the "not yet" but "already" perceptible here, in the absence of land's promise. Furthermore, Mamie's vision is also deep in the sense that the photograph of Emmett Till yields no recognizable face to light on, and so suspends the visual equivalent of land in western philosophy's traditional configuration of the encounter between "I and the Other." In its willful refusal of recognition, I argue that Mamie's deep vision stages an iconoclastic revision of the traditional encounter and its fetishization of recognition. Instead, it exhausts itself in an interminable relay with difference which, even in this painful instance, we must learn to apprehend as the always unfinished work of social and ecological life.

In distinguishing King's mountaintop from Mamie's deep vision in this way, I do not mean to valorize one over the other. Each has its place in the black freedom struggle. But if the significance of the former is generally well-remarked, particularly for a movement that has already been popularly imagined as a matter of keeping our "eyes on the prize," the latter's significance both to the Civil Rights Movement and to the black freedom struggle more broadly is relatively less so. I want to propose that what Mamie saw is as historically significant as we already recognize King's "mountaintop" vision and "dream" to be. But if on his ascent to the mountaintop King encountered Mamie on her way down, then her descent was not from, but *to*, vision. Even more than King's, her deep vision is the greater assurance that black looking can and does take place, even in what Equiano glimpses as the intended blind spot of the "hold" and its historical analogs.

Mamie Till-Mobley is nothing if not a seer. Consider the preponderance and multiple registers of visual language in her explanation of the decision to bare her son to the world:

> It would be important for people to *look* at what had happened on a late Mississippi night when nobody was *looking*, to consider what might happen again if we didn't *look* out. . . . I knew that I could talk for the rest of my life about what had happened to my baby, I could explain it in great detail, I could describe what I *saw* laid out there on that slab at A. A. Rayner's, one piece, one inch, one body part at a time. I could do all of that and people still would not get the full impact. They would not be able to *visualize* what had happened, unless they were allowed to *see* the results of what had happened. They had to *see* what I had *seen*. The whole nation had to *bear witness* to this. So I wanted to make it as real and as *visible* to people as I could possibly make it.[78]

With a profound understanding of her visual moment, and a deep conviction in the power of the visual, Mamie struggled to make Emmett visible, and with her efforts she staged one of the most significant media events not just of the Civil Rights Movement but also, for reasons to be explored, of a black radical tradition that has never found sufficient recourse in narrow discourses either of the human or of human rights. I want, then, to take a closer look at this look. Not only as we find it in the photograph of Emmett Till, but also as it was first performed in the viewing room of A. A. Rayner Funeral Home and repeatedly narrated thereafter during her speaking tour with the NAACP and, later, in multiple documentaries. Like King's, then, Mamie's is a look to which we will ultimately need to listen and which likewise will be demonstrated to stretch the faculty of vision beyond its typical scope.

What Mamie saw, she saw, first, as an act of resistance against significant opposition. It's not just that the photograph of Emmett Till comes to us against the intentions of those who weighed his body in a watery grave. But it's also all that state and local officials did subsequently, to assure that Emmett would remain buried visually, if not physically. After Emmett's great-uncle Moses Wright positively identified the body at Graball Landing, Tallahatchie County Sheriff Strider reportedly ordered him to, "Get that body in the ground immediately."[79] A grave had already been dug before word arrived from Mamie insisting that her son was to be buried in Chicago, which introduced an additional financial and legal barrier to what Mamie saw. First, it cost $3,300, or most of Mamie's $4,000 annual salary, to have the body shipped back to

Chicago. And second, to get the body out of Mississippi, the black undertakers in both Chicago and Mississippi and Mamie's Mississippi relatives all had to sign paperwork assuring the casket would remain closed. When the body reached Chicago on the *City of New Orleans*, it was "locked up with the seal of the State of Mississippi" and technically illegal to open.[80] What Mamie saw, then, represented an act of visual insurgency. Echoing the absurdity whereby over-the-side or runaway slaves could be reckoned thieves, by insisting on taking one last look at her son before placing him in the ground, Mamie effectively stole the visual property of the state of Mississippi.

Moreover, before voicing her deep vision during her NAACP speaking tour, Mamie's testimony concerning what she saw encountered further legal opposition during the murder trial whose infamous not-guilty verdict ultimately hinged on the sustained invalidation of her and other instances of black looking: the repeated contention, over and over again, that black witnesses simply could not have seen what they purported to have seen. Moses Wright could not have seen the men who kidnapped Emmett that night and, even more significantly for the defense's case, Mamie could not have recognized her son. On the one hand, the defense's closing argument to an all-male, all-white jury—"Every last Anglo-Saxon one of you has the courage to free these men"—tells us everything we need to know about a trial that was ultimately judging, regardless of its particulars, between white and black, and whose decision in this respect was never in doubt.[81] Thus, it can seem gratuitous to interrogate the proceedings of a trial that was little more than a formality, and whose jury deliberated as long as they did only because they were instructed to "make it look good." On the other hand, it is precisely this effort to "make it *look* good" that interests me because, if nothing else, it betrays a prevailing understanding about what could be viewed as not only plausible but also aesthetic. Even in their explicit pretense, then, the proceedings of the murder trial betray a broader epistemological and aesthetic regime defined by a general schema of visuality predicated, on the one hand, on a black incapacity to see and, on the other, on whiteness's exclusive claim to what Mirzoeff has called the "right to look."[82]

One of the murder trial's most dramatic moments came on its third day, when Moses Wright identified J. W. Milam and Roy Bryant as Emmett's murderers in open court. An article in the *New York Post*, "He Went All the Way," offered this account of the moment: "Moses Wright, making a formation no white man in this county really believed he would dare to make, stood on his tiptoes to the full limit of his 64 years and his 5 feet 3 inches yesterday, pointed his black, work-worn finger straight at the huge and stormy head of J. W. Milam and swore that this was the man who dragged 14-year-old Emmett Louis Till out of his cotton-field cabin the night the boy was murdered. 'There he is,' said Moses Wright. . . . 'And there's Mr. Bryant.'"[83] Mamie later declared Ernest Withers's iconic photograph of this dramatic moment "the single most significant photograph of the entire trial."[84] But just like this historic photograph, because the judge explicitly declared photography impermissible during the trial, Moses's black looking would ultimately be declared impermissible during cross-examination, with a line of questioning that established it was too dark for Moses to see that night:

Q *Was the moon shining?*
A It was not.
Q *There was no light there at all?*
A No light.
Q *And you didn't turn on the lights in your house?*
A That's right.[85]

Despite this lack of light, however, Moses insisted that he "knowed" both Milam and Bryant that night, if not exclusively through the visual means of facial recognition—Moses did testify that he was able to make out Milam's face—then also by noting Milam's stature and Bryant's voice.[86] As in the multisensory visions of King and Mamie, Moses's use of the verb *knowed*, rather than *saw*, also registers a more-than-visual perception that more fully accounts for the complex ways in which we actually recognize one another. Nevertheless, this lack of light enabled the court to ignore the looking that Moses managed in the dark in a way that looked good.

If Moses had "no light" by which to credibly see, the defense also embarked upon a line of questioning that otherwise established "light" as the exclusive possession of whiteness. Note the distribution of light, and thus vision, established by the defense's inquiry into Milam's flashlight:

Q *And he had the flashlight in his left hand, is that right?*
A Yes, Sir.
Q *And where was the flashlight pointed?*
A It was out like this (indicating with his hand).
Q *Do you mean it was out in front of his body, in front of the other hand in which you say he had the pistol?*
A That's right.
Q *Was there any light in your house that night?*
A No light.[87]

As in his murder of Emmett Till, Milam's flashlight proves no less an injurious weapon than his pistol. The emphasis on the positioning of the flashlight, "in front of his body," facilitates not only Milam's ability to see his victims but also his inability to be seen in return. Oriented in this way, the lighting from the flashlight creates a visual scene in which blackness is overexposed while whiteness is hidden in a blind spot. It ultimately didn't matter that, by the light of the flashlight, Moses claimed to have been able to make out Milam's face as he moved through the house. It mattered only that the light was in Milam's exclusive possession and that, with it, he intended only to see and not be seen. Under these visual conditions, whiteness exclusively reserves "the right to look" while simultaneously wielding the visual authority to declare that, behind the flashlight, there is "nothing to see."

I borrow the language above from Mirzoeff's pioneering study of modern visuality, *The Right to Look* (2011), which opens with a meditation on the similarly unequal visual dynamic activated whenever we hear a police officer declare, "Move on, there's nothing to see here."[88] According to Mirzoeff, the alignment between sovereignty and vision expressed in this familiar declaration characterizes modern visuality, more generally, as the "exclusive claim to be able to look," which can be traced back to the figure of the plantation overseer. According to Mirzoeff, "Visuality's first domains were the slave plantation, monitored by the surveillance of the overseer, operating as the surrogate of the sovereign. This sovereign surveillance was reinforced by violent punishment but sustained a modern division of labor."[89] Reflecting its origins on the slave plantation, Mirzoeff's general term for such "sovereign surveillance" as it has expressed itself through time is "oversight." That the flashlight-wielding Milam, described in the *Look* confession as "slavery's plantation overseer," is elsewhere already suggests how Mirzoeff's theory of oversight may be usefully brought to bear upon the dynamics of visuality at play in the murder trial, if not also in our first encounter with Milam's flashlight during Emmett Till's murder. But if Mirzoeff's genealogy of "oversight" proceeds from the plantation ultimately to an analysis of the military-industrial complex, in which antiblack racism factors minimally, I propose that the twentieth-century examples of Moses Wright and (as we shall find) Mamie Till-Mobley, along with the familiar prohibition against "reckless eyeballing" in the Jim Crow South, suggest that antiblackness is *constitutive* and enduring, and not merely incidental or original, to modern visuality. Some consideration of an overlooked ancestor that oversight arguably claims in slave ship "watches" further substantiates this point.

Cycles of maritime labor and the sailors that worked them were organized into starboard and larboard "watches." So named, the complex of skills performed by sailors could reasonably be distilled down to a look. In fact, according to Marcus Rediker, looking was particularly crucial for vessels engaged in the transatlantic slave trade, where, once captive Africans were brought aboard, "the primary purposes of the sailor's work were now to keep a vigilant watch."[90] Echoing Mirzoeff's language of oversight, Rediker offers the following description of the vigilance peculiar to the slave ship: "As the ship filled up, sailors *oversaw* the routines of the captives on both the lower and main decks. Below deck the sailor would assist in 'stowing' the slaves—that is, the assignment of a particular space where each person was to lie or sit whenever below deck, while on the coast and during the Middle Passage. The chief mate and the boatswain . . . supervised stowing the men; the second mate and gunner, the women. The sailors helped to pack the enslaved together tightly, 'adjusting their arms and legs, and prescribing a fixed place for each.'" The activity of "stowing" is as functionally ocular as it is manual. Sailors needed not only to see the descent of African captives belowdecks, just as Milam needed to see Emmett drop the one hundred feet, but also to supervise them within this assigned place. Moreover, stowing did not constitute merely passive spectatorship but also actively produced space through the *fixing* of blackness in place. Such production occurs in the silent elapse of time between stowing and supervision. That is, between the initial seeing of African captives to their place, as Milam might say, belowdecks, and the subsequent still seeing them there, either through their presence below or absence above deck. It's this *still seeing* them there that accomplishes the fixing of blackness in place and consequentially works both to produce and to naturalize blackness's space or social location in the modern world. That is, the "hold," but only as a physical expression, if not ur-type, of what can be more broadly recognized as the constitutive underside of the Human and that Human's faculties, including vision. Thus, the ocular stowing of African captives in the hold, as one face of Édouard Glissant's "abyss," may be understood to actively produce the spatial formation that this book otherwise explores as the deep.[91]

Slave ship watches not only actively produced the deep but, recalling once again Equiano's testimony that "we were all put under deck, so that we could not see," also reserved "the right to look" as a sovereign and exclusive one, just as Mirzoeff argues of oversight. At stake in excavating the deeper roots of oversight in Middle Passage, however, is not the vain distinction of being first but, rather, the recognition of what consequently amounts to modern visuality's *foundational* pattern of antiblackness. If, on both the slave ship and the plantation, modern visuality comes online as a specifically antiblack enterprise, in which whiteness reserves "the right to look" exclusively, and white vision is further enabled by the visual underside of black blindness, then antiblackness should be understood as foundational and constitutive rather than incidental to modern visuality. In that case, we would expect the antiblackness of modern visuality to persist, as an organizing factor, beyond slavery's abolition.

This is precisely what we witness in Emmett Till's murder trial with respect, first, to the invalidation of Moses Wright's positive identification of Roy Bryant and J. W. Milam and, second, to the defense's contention that Mamie could not have seen what she purported to have seen. Instead, as one juror later recalled the defense's core argument: "The body fished out of the Tallahatchie River was not that of Emmett Till—who was, they claimed, still very much alive and hiding out in Chicago or Detroit or somewhere else up North—but someone else's, a corpse planted there by the N.A.A.C.P. for the express purpose of stirring up a racial tornado that would tear through Sumner, and through all of Mississippi, and through the rest of the South, for that matter." For all of this argument's patent absurdity, the process by which it was made to "look good" in court is nevertheless instructive. Consider the implications for what Mamie saw of the testimony of two of the defense's key witnesses: a doctor and the aforementioned Sheriff Strider, each of whom, though for different reasons, was ruled by the court to be "an expert witness in his field."[92]

If, according to Mirzoeff, the encapsulating formulation of modern visuality is the police officer's "Move on, there is nothing to see here," the testimony of the doctor may be recognized to forward a slight revision of this statement:

> Q *Doctor, explain to the jury—and you may use medical or scientific terms, if you so desire—but will you please explain to the jury and describe the condition of that body to the jury as you saw it at that time?*
>
> A This body was badly swollen, badly bloated. . . . The skin and the flesh was beginning to slip on it. The head was badly mutilated. The right eye was protruding. And the tongue was protruding from the mouth. . . .
>
> Q *Doctor, I want to ask this question: from the condition that you saw that body in, in your opinion, could anybody have identified any particular person as being that body? . . .*
>
> A I don't think you could. I don't think you could have identified that body.
>
> Q *Now suppose if the man had been another person's brother, could he have identified it, in your opinion?*
>
> A I doubt it.
>
> Q *Or if it had been a person's son, could a mother have identified that body, in your opinion?*
>
> A I doubt it.[93]

In so many words, the doctor's testimony declares, "Move on, there is *no one* to see here." The doctor exercises his right to look, then, to the exclusion and negation of Mamie Till-Mobley's black looking, by which she was able to behold a body protruding beyond the frames of family photos and the normatively identifiable and nevertheless recognize her son. By refining the question from "Could anybody?" to "Could a mother have identified that body?" the defense isolates the more a mother could know that would enable her to identify a body like Emmett's. Against the validity of this deeply personal and subjective knowledge, the doctor opposes the authority of objective, empirical knowledge. As do the lawyers who invite the doctor to speak in "medical or scientific terms." In this way, the defense solicits the doctor's performance of what Michel Foucault has theorized in terms of a "clinical gaze," which claims "sovereignty in a world of language":

> Over all these endeavors on the part of clinical thought to define its methods and scientific norms hovers the great myth of a pure Gaze that would be pure Language: a speaking eye. It would scan the entire hospital field, taking in and gathering together each of the singular events that occurred within it; and as it saw, as it saw ever more and more clearly, it would be turned into speech that states and teaches; the truth, which events, in their repetitions and convergence, would outline under its gaze, would, by this same gaze and in the same order, be reserved, in the form of teaching, to those who do not know and have not yet seen. This speaking eye would be the servant of things and the master of truth.[94]

Thus, the doctor speaks his eye, translating his pure—which is to say objective and disinterested—examination of Emmett's body "into speech that states and teaches" the court the truth reserved to the doctor by his specialized medical language. Namely that there is no one to see in the photograph of Emmett Till. If the recourse to speech is, for both Martin and Mamie, a means of negotiating modern visuality's interdiction against black looking, here it is rather the means by which whiteness lays sovereign and exclusive claim to the "right to look." In this case, the doctor's "medical or scientific terms" illuminate Emmett's body as "no one in particular." That is, a nobody or, worse, flesh. With his clinical gaze, he sees the very impossibility of seeing.

The doctor's testimony follows a line of questioning that results in the court ruling that he is qualified as "an expert witness in his field." Since this was never said of Mamie, the specific grounds of the doctor's qualifications, beyond what we've already seen as his scientific and medical expertise, are telling. In contrast and opposition to Mamie's maternal knowledge of her son, what specifically qualifies the doctor is instead his extensive experience with corpses:

Q *Doctor, during that experience, in your hospital training, and in your regular practice, and also your service in the Army, did you ever have occasion to examine any dead bodies?*
A Yes, Sir, I did.
Q *And Doctor, have you ever had occasion to examine dead bodies that have been in the air and also those that have been in water?*
A I have.
Q *Would you please tell the jury or give the jury some kind of estimate as to the number of those dead bodies you have seen?*
A Oh, that would be hard for me to just say offhand, as to just how many of those bodies I have seen.
Q *Well, would it be a few or a large number?*
A What?
Q *Have you seen a few or a large number of those bodies?*
A I would say a large number.
MR. BRELAND: We submit, Your Honor, that he is an expert witness in his field.
THE COURT: I think the gentleman qualifies.[95]

A similar logic likewise qualifies Sheriff Strider, who, though lacking the doctor's scientific and medical expertise, because of his experience with numerous bodies, proved an equally qualified witness, no less capable of invalidating what Mamie saw:

Q *What then, Mr. Strider, is your opinion based on your past experience in taking bodies from the river, as to how long this particular body that was removed from the water on August 31st had been in the river?*
MR. SMITH: We object to that, if Your Honor please. He is not a doctor, and he is not qualified to testify about that.
THE COURT: He is not qualified as a doctor, but he stated that he has had experience with other bodies taken from the river from time to time. And I think he is qualified.
Q *You may state your opinion on that, Mr. Strider.*
A I would say at least ten days, if not fifteen . . .
Q *Was that body recognizable to be that of any particular person's?"*
A Well, if one of my own boys had been missing, I couldn't really say if it was my own son or not, or anybody else's. I couldn't tell that. All I could tell, it was a *human being.*[96]

Both the doctor and sheriff, then, illuminate Emmett as a nobody. Even without the doctor's "clinical gaze," the sheriff is nevertheless endorsed by the court as a qualified witness because of the wealth of his experience pulling dead bodies from the river. Endowed with the authority of this endorsement, the sheriff is no less qualified than the doctor to invalidate what Mamie saw.

Yet it is not simply a given that this illumination of Emmett as a nobody, belonging to "no one in particular," could "look good." In fact, it did *not* to Mamie, who beyond insisting that she was able to identify her son also later objected that the defense "didn't try to explain *whose body it was*. It seems that bodies are pretty plentiful down there. And the only point that they were trying to prove is that the body, that I had, did not belong to me."[97] That this body, scrubbed of personhood, as an empty signifier of humanity, did *not* "look good" to Mamie suggests that there has first to exist a palate, if not an appetite, for such bodies. That they are an acquired look.

Where, in the elaborate discourse of western humanism, might the court have acquired the eyes to see this body as a depersonalized and empty signifier of the human? That in a legal setting the knowledge of numerous *other* bodies sanctions and qualifies the doctor's and sheriff's authoritative looking at *this* particular body, and negates a mother's personal and intimate knowledge of a specific body, perhaps exemplifies the underside of Ian Baucom's argument that "the humanity to which the Euromodern witness . . . has attached itself over the course of the past 250 years is . . . a humanity apprehensible as a speculative idea and a speculative (and regulatory) ideal, a humanity grounded in natural law and natural right, an abstract humanity called into existence by the discourses of the right of man and of human rights."[98] If, on the one hand, the speculative idea and ideal of the human as an individual subject "with certain inalienable rights" (to recall the language of the Constitution) is what makes "human rights" thinkable, and therefore protectable, then what sense do we make of its weaponization, on the other hand, against what Mamie saw by a court that ultimately sanctioned and sustained the violation of Emmett's human rights? This paradox is proof of concept that, as Frank Wilderson argues, the Black "is an anti-Human, a position against which Humanity establishes, maintains, and renews its coherence, its corporeal integrity."[99] Wilderson names what from the jump—and the jump over the side—has always furnished the constitutional underside of discourses of the Human. Baucom's emphasis on the abstracted nature of these discourses, however, also guides us toward another way of thinking about blackness's exclusion from the Human. On the one hand, the elevation of the doctor's and sheriff's knowledge of a quantity of bodies over Mamie's particular knowledge of her son is certainly suggestive of the natal alienation characteristic of "social death" and of Mamie's and Emmett's exclusion from the protections otherwise guaranteed to individual human subjects. But it also evidences the court's subscription to an "Enlightenment philosophical discourse" whose speculative investment in the concept of humanity "abstracts the concept of humanity from the observed turn of human events, contracts itself and its audience to agree disinterestedly to recognize a transcendent category relieved from its entanglement in all brute particulars, and binds itself to honor that agreement (regardless of the singularity of any given case)."[100] The court's aesthetic preference for a nobody over Mamie's particular and personal knowledge of her son, then, is not just about Emmett's exclusion from the protections and entitlements of the individual but also about a concept of humanity whose thorough abstraction, to its own impoverishment, from the particulars and contingencies of the social relations that situate human existence is what renders the individual thinkable to begin with. All this is to say, it's not that Mamie can't see this body that the court adopts as an empty signifier of "a transcendent category relieved from its entanglement in all brute particulars"—but rather that she won't. What, then, did she see?

V. "*what* I've seen"

What Mamie saw was also irreducibly social. You cannot look long at Mamie's look before noticing how, at each stage and scale of its expression—from her private look at her son to the four-day open-casket memorial to the elaboration of her look during her NAACP speaking tour and, finally, to the "virtual community" hailed by the photograph—Mamie "consents not to be a single" seer.[101] How consistently she looks, not alone but with others. *With* may even mystify what I mean here. We go to the movies with others and still head to our individual and often, these days, assigned seat. But the radically social vision I'm trying to get at is not this collection of nonetheless individual visions. Rather, it is social all the way down to the retina—as troubling to individual enactments of vision as when, again at the movies, we find a stranger in our seat. The irreducible sociality of Mamie's vision is apparent from the moment she arrives at Twelfth Street Station to receive the crate carrying her son. As is the immediate contrast it provides to the hypothetical and aspirational performance of "oversight" by "slavery's overseer," Milam, in his *Look* magazine confession. If atop the hundred-foot bluff Milam wanted to show how "me and my folks *stand*," Mamie's deep vision forgoes standing almost entirely:[102] "I had to be brought up in a wheelchair. I was too weak and just couldn't stand up at the moment the train pulled in. But I was quite alert. I was aware of everything, everything that was going on. Even with that large crowd of people milling about, if a tiny mouse had peeked his head up, I would have noticed that, too. My father was there with me, and Gene Mobley, Rayfield Mooty, a few cousins. Bishop Henry Ford and Bishop Isaiah Roberts were also there. And, of course, Uncle Crosby."[103] If the "stand" of whiteness is otherwise the stand of the individual liberal subject who has "some rights," it is telling that in her performance of deep vision, Mamie, by contrast, "couldn't stand up." In the absence of this autonomous stand, Mamie's vision feels its help from a range of sources, both human and nonhuman. Not only is she accompanied in this look by her family, partner, and several leaders of the Church of God in Christ, but she is also "brought up in a wheelchair." Yet here in particular, Mamie feels her help not just as the temporary disability of a woman crucified by grief but rather as an expression of the often-disavowed help underlying all ability, even, unbeknownst to him, the bluff that would have supported Milam's hypothetical "stand." Moreover, Mamie's more-than-human help is also mirrored by her more-than-human attention. Like the God of whom she had heard it said that "his eye is on the sparrow," so too the awareness that she would eventually bring to bear upon her son was so careful and capacious that she "would have noticed" even a "tiny mouse."

Mamie's help continued when, approaching the pine box, her stand again faltered:

> I reached out, as if to embrace the box moving toward us. I stood and I nearly fainted. Gene was right there, standing over me, helping me. So many other people rushed to my aid. People were trying to comfort me and keep the large crowd back to give me air. I wanted to pray.
>
> The ministers helped me to my knees. "Lord, take my soul," I began, "show me what you want me to do, and make me able to do it."[104]

If Mamie's initial inability to stand reads as a temporary disability precipitated by grief, here not standing constitutes her willful refusal. Mamie "*wanted* to pray" and thus eschewed her own two feet for the spiritual vision that she could realize only on her knees. Once again, she descends unto vision. However, this vision feels its help too, both in the form of the attending ministers who "helped" Mamie to her knees and in the God she was asking both to "show" her what to do and to empower her to do it. In this way, what Mamie saw at Central Station, as we will discover in her subsequent enactments of deep vision, proved both a this- and an otherworldly proposition. Indeed, we consider her a seer for good reason. It also is no coincidence that Mamie's prayer for vision, to be shown something from another world, immediately follows her initial sighting of the box containing her son. "At that moment," she writes, "there was nothing in the world but that giant crate. Death to me was so much larger than life."[105] Presuming she really was shown what to do, our clearest window into what Mamie saw on her knees is what she did. Which was not just to see but to "let the world see what I've seen."

What I am describing as the irreducible sociality of what Mamie, whose awareness of the more-than-human also introduces a significant ecological dimension, saw is even present at its most private and intimate: what the "Nation Horrified" photo-essay termed Mamie's "first look" at her son in A. A. Rayner's Funeral Home. In the *Jet* photograph of this moment, Mamie is being held up by her partner, and as she later recounts in her memoir, "Gennie held one of my arms and my father held the other." In this photograph, the sociality of Mamie's "first look" is initially unmistakable but seems to drop out once, to hear Mamie tell it, they "reached the table" and she "told Gennie and Daddy to release me. I needed to stand alone. . . . I had a *job* to do."[106] One way to think about this "job" is as an expression of what Sharpe has called "wake work," a "keeping *watch* with the dead" that Mamie performs here through the care and careful attention she pays to her son in death.[107] Yet it would be a mistake to read Mamie's need "to stand alone" as a momentary departure from what otherwise consistently and increasingly shows up as the irreducible sociality of what she saw. It's not just the social conditions that sustained and enabled her to reach the table in the first place. It's also, for what it's worth—and I confess that I'm unsure how much it is worth, though I'm certain that it's not enough—the fleeting eruption of sociality that we find in Mamie's account of her "first look." How, in the middle of her careful examination of her son's body, she

> stopped at his private area. Just long enough, really, to see that everything was still there. That had been one of the terrible rumors that had spread—that Emmett had been castrated. I was relieved for a moment before I caught myself. Oh, my God. Emmett would have a *fit* if he knew I was looking at him like this. He was *so* independent, especially after the polio. He always wanted to show me he could take care of himself. He even told me that he could bathe himself. At six. So young. He didn't need me to do that for him anymore. How hard that was for me, to suffer in silence, to give him his space and pray to God that he was getting everything clean.[108]

For the briefest moment, in her visual performance of wake work, Mamie stood not alone but with her son. She "caught [her]self," but only in the sense that she was all caught up in the relationship she had developed with her son, mothering and contending, even in death, with the wishes of the boy who, at six, started asking for privacy. What Mamie saw, then, she saw *with* Emmett. Even though he was dead. Even though, by every modern reckoning of the material world, from the differentiation between animate and inanimate matter to the differentiation between the human and nonhuman, he presently lacked anything that might entitle matter to consideration of this kind. Even though he was already going the way of the nonhuman and presently wanted for all of that human's qualifying and entitling distinctions. Call it bipedalism, call it the soul, call it language, call it reason, or call it, considering the specificity of this impossible ethical exchange between a mother and her son, the "face." It was an *immaculate perception*, though perhaps one that ultimately better resembled Mary's grief-stricken vision of Jesus on the cross than the good news about the son she was carrying or the original Catholic sense of Mary's "immaculate conception."

As Mamie's only son, who carried the instrument of his torture, resurfaced on the third day, was martyred for a movement, and even transformed the fisherman who discovered him into a fisher of men, the frequent analogization of Emmett Till and Jesus is well-warranted. But an analogization between Mamie and Mary, I propose, can be equally illuminating with respect to the significance and meaning of what Mamie saw. However, this requires some interrogation of the historical confusion between the original sense of Mary's "immaculate conception" in Catholic theology, which refers to Mary's own conception when "she was preserved by God from the taint of original sin," and what some might dismiss as its mistaken Protestant afterlife as a reference instead to "Mary's conception of Jesus through the power of the Holy Spirit."[109] My own sense of the resonance between Mary and Mamie, in what I am labeling Mamie's immaculate perception, riffs on this latter sense, which, however mistaken, arguably possesses its own theological import, especially to the extent that it may be recognized as a distinctly black idea. The shifting connotation of "immaculate" in Mary's immaculate conception, from the original and literal sense of "spotlessly clean" or "pure" to the mistaken sense of inexplicable or miraculous, accords with a black historical experience that finds less solace perhaps in Mary's purity than "the way out of no way" that God made for this mother and her son. Furthermore, we might also ask: What is spotlessness to the spot of the modern world? Perhaps those whose "only sin," as Louis Armstrong famously sang, "is in [their] skin," or whose dictionaries tell them, as Spike Lee captures in *Malcolm X*, that "black" means "soiled with dirt," need a better word than an immaculateness that promises to wash them "*white* as snow."[110] Consider, on the one hand, the theological cover that ideas of purity have historically provided for whiteness, which arguably reaches its apex in the visual hegemony of a blond-haired, blue-eyed Jesus and Mary with the good hair. Consider, on the other hand, the harm that this Manichean theologic has historically visited upon black people in general, and black women in particular. This is the context in which we need to appreciate the theological necessity of James Cone's pioneering contention that "Jesus is Black" and Amey Victoria Adkins-Jones's equally illuminating claim that Mary is too.[111] Black theology's revelation of what Kelly Brown Douglas has surveyed as "the Black Christ" contemplates not the spotlessness of this "sunbaked Hebrew," as James Baldwin reminds us, but rather his nail-scarred hands and wounded side, which the black church's chanting, moaning, and intoning have made sacred.[112] Following the literal meaning of *immaculate*, then, we might alternatively recognize black theology's revelation of Jesus as a *maculate* perception. The disclosure of a stained, spotted, and suffering Christ, who is black not in the racially essentialist sense that would merely invert the implicit whiteness of a blond-haired, blue-eyed Jesus, who, at least as revealed in the historical exploits of his followers, not only came down from the cross of life but then proceeded to crucify the earth. Rather, Jesus has been discovered to be black in the sense of his social alignment with the oppressed as one who, scripture tells us, assumed "the *position* of a slave."[113] The same "position," in fact, that Frank Wilderson asks us to "assume" in *Afropessimism*.[114] Relative to discourses of immaculateness, the salutary power of this maculate perception of Jesus, who will bear his wounds into eternity and whose blemishes and spots are consequently the stuff of heaven, is clear for black worshippers living in an antiblack world. It also yields an illuminating analogy for what Mamie saw, which, if immaculate in the sense of witnessing an impossible moment of sociality, was also a maculate perception in the sense that she refused to have the body retouched. Emmett, too, comes to us "in the position of a slave," a socially dead inhabitant of the deep still bearing the stains of his submersion in the Tallahatchie. What Mamie saw, in the impossible social moment she shared with her son and in her refusal to allow him to be retouched, was an im/maculate perception.

This brief detour into black Christology and Mariology further informs a third sense in which Mamie's "stand alone" nevertheless exemplifies a radical sociality. It's the answered prayer that Mamie arguably received from an on-time God, whom she had asked to "*take* my soul" and "*show* me what . . . to do":

> When I got up to that casket, and looked over in there, something happened to me that is akin to *getting religion*. I have seen people shout. I

> have seen them jerk. I have seen them lose control of themselves and be very happy. And then again I've seen them very sad.
>
> But it hit me from the head and the feet at the same time. And it met in the middle and *straightened me up*. I looked at my arms because it felt that every bone had turned to steel. I wanted to know was the change physical, was it noticeable. Then after examining myself, I looked in the casket again, and I said, "Oh my God!"[115]

If, according to Zora Neale Hurston, black Pentecostal shouting "is a survival of the African 'possession' by the gods," then perhaps Mamie's experience of "getting religion" indexes her own possession.[116] It's the answer to her prayer for the Lord to take her soul and, more, to ultimately show her what she had already "seen" in innumerable black Pentecostal worship services: "people shout," "jerk," "lose control," and get "very happy." In *Blackpentecostal Breath* (2016), Ashon Crawley otherwise thinks this choreography of moving and moved flesh under the rubric of "twentieth century Blackpentecostal shouting," whose unregulated movement, through aversion, comes to mark "the dividing line between white bodies and the complex modes of fleshly disembodiment that are called blackness" within western philosophical and theological traditions.[117]

Indeed, spiritual possession of this sort has long been held in contempt and suspicion by a western philosophical tradition that otherwise valorizes self-possession and the ability, against all external stimuli, to keep it together. One significant case in point related to this discussion of "getting religion" is Sigmund Freud's famous disavowal of the "oceanic feeling," which he defines, following Romain Rolland, as a "feeling as of something limitless, unbounded," and a sense of "being one with the external world as a whole." While Rolland understood this "oceanic feeling" to be the "true source of religious sentiments," Freud otherwise dismissed the feeling as a pathological holdover of the infant's inability to differentiate itself from other people and things.[118] Thus, in Freud's estimation, "getting religion" constitutes a pathological failure of the self to hold the corporeal line distinguishing itself from the external world, as Milam and his folks may otherwise be recognized to model so capably in the way that they *stand*. That is, ten toes down and in full possession of all their "rights," including the right to stand their ground. Taking Milam's stand as an archetype of white embodiment, Mamie's "stand alone," by contrast, yields an instance of what Crawley has alternatively described as black "fleshly disembodiment." Even as a stand, it enacts not Milam's exclusionary rootedness but, however subtly, movement. And not even autonomous movement but a movement instead that "hit [her] from the head and the feet at the same time. And it met in the middle and straightened [her] up." Lacking a discrete author, this nonautonomous movement visits upon the autonomous individual its own undoing. And does so at the very height of the stand-your-ground subject's bodily performance of ontological separation: the two-footed interface with the planet that is this individual's posture of least contingency.

As glimpsed in whiteness's stand and blackness's ongoing inhabitation of the deep, the dividing line between white embodiment and black "fleshly disembodiment" prompts further consideration of the "oceanic feeling" as a possible origin for religious sentiment. Although the "oceanic feeling" can conceivably be experienced anywhere, it is perhaps no surprise that, as perhaps humanity's best analog for "something limitless," the ocean specifically serves this nominal function. What is surprising, however, is the conspicuous absence of any discussion of the literal ocean in either Rolland's or Freud's commentary on the "oceanic feeling." Whether avowed or disavowed, then, even the "oceanic feeling" is paradoxically guilty of the West's prevailing terracentrism. Moreover, the human experience of the ocean that serves as the material referent for this feeling is not homogenous. Rather, as a specifically modern phenomenon available to a critical mass of humanity in the transatlantic wake of Christopher Columbus, it diverges sharply along racial lines—giving rise to whiteness as stand-your-ground subjectivity, on the one hand, and blackness as the ongoing inhabitation of the deep, on the other.[119] As an origin for religious sentiment, any "oceanic feeling" experienced from within an avowal of whiteness's "stand" bespeaks a historically shallow encounter with the ocean experienced from the relative safety of the shore or from the deck of a ship with certain knowledge of reaching the shore. In this case, the shore or deck maintains either a stable outlet from or the possibility of realizing some ontological resolution beyond this "feeling as of something limitless, unbounded," ghettoizing its "one[ness] with the external world" as exceptional rather than mundane. However, in the case of the black religion that Mamie got, a radically different historical experience of the ocean is at stake: not the "oceanic feeling" of the shore or deck but the *deep feeling* otherwise given in the middle passing Africans' unrelenting "feeling of, feeling for" the ocean and their shipmates.[120]

In addition to what Hurston registers as an African survival of "possession by the gods," I propose that we might also understand shouting, and New World black religious practice more broadly, as an African seizure upon the *deep feeling* of Middle Passage. This feeling not merely of exceptional union with but of irrevocable immersion in the external world. This is to suggest an understanding of New World black religious expression not only as a matter of the retention of so-called "Africanisms" but also as something actively informed by the lived experience of New World blackness, including a novel and unrelenting experience of Earth as Ocean. Put another way, what the bush burning but not consumed is to Judaism the Africans underwater but not dead may be to the New World black religious practice elaborated in the wake of the deep feeling of a global ocean, from which all life derives. Perhaps it's this deep feeling that animates every *barco de iaôs*, a group of initiates into the Afro-Brazilian religion Candomblé that, in a manner suggestive of the well-documented shipmate relationship of Middle Passage, are called by the Portuguese word for boat. Or that animates the veneration of Iemanjá and Olokun (the deities of the ocean and its depths respectively) in Candomblé, and the veneration of their analogues throughout the Yoruba religious diaspora.[121] Or that animates spirituals such as "Deep River" or "The Old Ship of Zion." Or the distinctly black practice of the ritual of baptism that King imagined steadied protesters before the fire hoses in Alabama during his mountaintop speech: "Bull Connor next would say, 'Turn the fire hoses on.' And as I said to you the other night, Bull Connor didn't know history. He knew a kind of physics that somehow didn't relate to the transphysics that we knew about. And that was the fact that there was a certain kind of fire that no water could put out. And we went before the fire hoses; we had known water. If we were Baptist or some other denomination, we had been immersed. If we were Methodist, and some others, we had been sprinkled, but we knew water."[122] Indeed, it has been the sustained contention of this book that the African Diaspora harbors a profound knowledge of water. And if in "Deep Imagination" I argued that this knowledge finds expression in the ongoing aesthetic exploits of a "material imagination" devoted to water, here we might otherwise understand this aquatic knowledge to find religious expression in not just an oceanic but a deep feeling. This feeling yields perhaps another way of thinking about the "social" that, according to Crawley, "Blackpentecostal shouting creates" even when performed, as in the case of Mamie's "stand alone," by an "individual shouter." Crawley writes, "Blackpentecostal shouting creates a social and though it can be performed alone, it is the being together with others at the moment of such performance that is privileged. The individual shouter creates social form by mixing in an irreducibly already available individual styling. It makes the kids laugh and learn. It makes the elders happy to see spiritual change. This feeling of joy disperses through the congregation."[123] If the black Pentecostal shouting of even one shouter can "create a social," in the manner Crawley describes, Mamie's "stand alone," which was like a shout, like getting religion, created a social movement. What if the religion that straightened Mamie up was the same

FIGURE 6.2. Civil rights protesters in Birmingham, Alabama, sprayed by police with a high-pressure water hose, May 1963. Photo: Charles Moore.

religion that stood protesters up before the fire hoses (figures 6.2 and 6.3)? What if, when Mamie got religion before Emmett Till's casket, when she straightened up and shouted "Oh, my God," she created "a social form"? A stand, not against or separate from the world but in radical consent to remain in and open to the world. A stand, like Mary's before the cross of Christ, where Jesus's mother learned that she had more sons than she carried and the disciple whom Jesus loved more mothers than carried him. So Mamie's deep vision was also the occasion for a radical recalibration of the social. "*Woman, behold your sons. The sufferers to whom you belong as much as the boy going the way of the more-than-human as you mother and care for me still.* And to the would-be disciples of this deep vision, *behold your mother's look, and go and do likewise.*" A stand that, in this way, was also a consent not to be a single being. And what if, by opening the casket, instigating the photograph, and traveling the country speaking her eye, Mamie invited "the world," this time like Jesus, to *come and see* too?

FIGURE 6.3. Civil rights protesters in Birmingham, Alabama, defiantly standing before a high-pressure water hose. Bob Adelman, *No Man Is an Island, Kelly Ingram Park, Birmingham, Alabama*, 1963.

VI. face (v)

Today, we who file past the exhibition of Emmett's original casket in the National Museum of African American History and Culture do so, as often as we do, in remembrance and extension of the open-casket public funeral services that were held in Chicago from September 2 to September 5, 1955. This four-day mass witnessing event began with a Friday evening viewing in the chapel of A. A. Rayner Funeral Home, hours after Mamie's "first look," and continued at the Roberts Temple Church of God in Christ with a Saturday funeral and two additional days of viewing, "to let everyone have a chance to see Emmett."[124] Over four days, as many as 100,000 people are estimated to have seen, in the flesh, what Mamie saw. And "every fifth person or so" showed signs of having caught Mamie's religion by "falling out" and "fainting" when they saw what Mamie saw.[125] On the day I joined this foundering cloud of witnesses, standing before Emmett's casket in the museum, I better understood Mamie's own description of how she felt upon receiving her son back from Mississippi in a crate. "*At that moment, there was nothing in the world but that giant crate. Death to me was so much larger than life.*"[126] So death also seemed to me as I beheld the original casket in which Emmett was buried. And suddenly I found myself grateful for whoever's curatorial vision had discerned that a single church pew should be placed before the casket for those filing by. When I sat down to gather myself, a stranger approached from behind and laid a hand on my shoulder. Then, I let go.

The witness I bore to Emmett that day, the witness I am trying to bear in this chapter, is all bound up with that pew, which, unlike individual chairs, is shared and, thus, implies and founds a social. It is all bound up, too, with that hand on my shoulder. It is a beholding that extends from being held in and by the testimony of this growing cloud of witnesses to what Levinas might and might not describe as the ethical discourse of Emmett's faceless face. Whatever I see in the broken face of Emmett Till, especially beyond a death that can seem "so much larger than life," I see with the help of others. Consciously or not, this is the only way anyone ever really looks at Emmett, insofar as the hand on all our shoulders is Mamie's. We see what, and because, she saw first.

If what Mamie saw and the public engagement with what she saw was indeed the "Big Bang" of the Civil Rights Movement, then it yields a compelling example of what Sharon Sliwinski has described as the "richly illustrated" history of the struggle for human rights more generally. In her book *Human Rights in Camera*, she writes: "The long struggle for universal human rights is a story of atrocious events and courageous campaigners, but it is also a lively aesthetic scene full of pictorial images and fascinated spectators. Social justice campaigns almost always involve passionate political speeches and exhausting political reform, but they also almost always involve the circulation of visual images and animated, emotional discussions about the experience of viewing them. The history of human rights—and the history of their abuse—is a richly illustrated one."[127] Thus, Sliwinski calls special attention to the visual register of the human rights struggle and—in a history otherwise dominated by accounts of atrocities, activism, and reform—invites our further attunement to an equally significant "aesthetic scene," involving the passionate engagement of spectators with visual images. Sliwinski's analytic is perhaps especially suited to a consideration of the US Civil Rights Movement, which is popularly imagined to have begun with the shared experience of viewing Emmett Till. If, as she argues, "the circulation of representations of distant events creates a virtual community between spectators," then I'm interested, here, in the specific "virtual community" hailed by what Mamie saw in an elaboration of civil rights *movement*.[128] To write of civil rights movement in the minuscule is my attempt to get at something both less and, in some ways, more than what history has come to formalize as the Civil Rights Movement. Namely, the thread of Mamie's religion that I see running through the canon of that movement's significant events and reforms. Although distinct from and minor relative to the dominant perception of the Civil Rights Movement as primarily a struggle for political recognition, the expression of civil rights movement, which I detect in the ongoing witness to Emmett Till, can also be recognized to persist beyond the movement's formal end.

For Sliwinski, "aesthetic scenes" like those that unfold in the ongoing viewing of Emmett's unmade and unrecognizable face are historically a crucial location where the "ideal of a human subject naturally endowed with dignity and rights" becomes literally visible through its violation and "by virtue of spectator's passionate engagement with pictures."[129] The logic being that pictures of an aggrieved human subject possess an unaccountable, but nonetheless discernible, ability to stoke the imagination and desire for a world where such atrocities do not exist. In many respects, the photograph of Emmett Till works precisely in this way, picturing the violation of a human subject at the citadel of its most privileged synecdoche: the face, whose individual and idiosyncratic expression is precisely where the individual self makes itself most "self-evident." Yet if in this way "our shared ideas about the constitution of the human subject leans on aesthetic encounters," then what we might describe, after Rizvana Bradley, as the "anteaesthetics" of what Mamie saw can otherwise be understood to rally a virtual community not around the ideal of the liberal human subject, to whose "rights" we've already seen Milam lay violent claim, but around the irreducible relations that are this subject's undoing. Whether in the photograph of an unmade, no longer recognizably human subject, or the unmade witnesses to that unmaking, I want to think about the "virtual community" hailed by what Mamie saw and how it might be understood to locate not the recognition of our shared human rights but our collective performance of an ecological *rite.* A ritual enactment of black ecological life that is an expression of the ceremony Sylvia Wynter would have us find.[130]

Either side of the "aesthetic scene" of Emmett Till's extended viewing—both the representations and the witness's engagement with those representations—reveals an aesthetic that in several important ways interrupts our thinking about the individual human subject. Like the pew placed before Emmett's casket in the National Museum of African American History and Culture, the aesthetic scene constituted by Emmett Till's ongoing viewing yields an aesthetics of sociality, not in the sense of a social collection of individuals but in that of a social that unsettles the very notion of the individual as such. That is, a social that is social all the way down. We see this, for instance, in Mamie's characterization of the subject of the enduring witness to Emmett Till as an irreducible "we." One whose collective witness exceeds the moment of looking as Gordon's "something-to-be-done." In her memoir, Mamie writes: "I knew that if they walked by that casket, if people opened the pages of *Jet* magazine and the *Chicago Defender*, if other people could see it with their own eyes, then together we might find a way to express what we had seen. It was important to do that, I thought, to help people recognize the horrible problems we were facing in the South."[131] Thus, Emmett hails a "we" that "together" not only sees but also, just as we have come to distinguish the witness from the spectator, commits itself to the future expression of what we've seen. The seeming individuals constituting this "we," in their vulnerability to getting Mamie's religion, nevertheless experience a radically destabilized relationship to their individual subjectivity. Aesthetically speaking, "falling out" or "fainting" is hardly the subject's strongest look. If Milam had to stand atop the bluff to see Emmett's hypothetical descent, and if the stand is otherwise the consummate expression of the individual human subject, these mourners were given instead to foundering. They could no more stand their ground than they could stand the sight of the ruin of Emmett's face. They paid their attention at the steep price of their very selves.

An aesthetics of sociality also defined the public engagement with Mamie's speeches about what she saw during her NAACP speaking tour. Since the aesthetic arrangement of a speech typically features a speaker who talks and an audience that listens, it is telling that Mamie instead characterizes her speeches as a "dialogue":

> There was just too much sorrow for one person to endure, too much pain for one person to absorb, too much anger for one person to express. So the crowds helped me get through it. They listened as I talked about Emmett and his trip and the brutal murder and the horrible injustice that I had suffered, that black people were suffering every day in so many ways. We connected. I talked, they listened. But, in a way, it was a *dialogue*. Just by being there, they were saying something to me. Something very important. They were saying that people cared about what had happened. That's what I needed to know, especially after spending a week at the Sumner trial, where it didn't seem that people cared at all. I am so thankful for the crowds that turned out to listen to me, and to communicate with me in the process.[132]

What happened to Emmett was not only "too much"—sorrow to endure, pain to absorb, anger to express—but too much "for *one person*." Yet if Mamie has already described the witness to Emmett in terms of an irreducible "we" that "might find a way to express what we had seen," perhaps it is no surprise that, when the time for expression came, it took the form of a "dialogue." The crowds that turned out to listen to Mamie tell about what she saw also spoke. They spoke a better word than the willful misrecognition of Emmett during a trial, in which Emmett's murderers took absurd cover behind the inscrutable fruit of their own violence. In opposition to such painful "oversight," the crowds communicated a balm of care. What was too much for one person they helped to shoulder. Yet the very fact that life can yield burdens of this sort is perhaps its own clue that one person is not a viable unit of life. Maybe, to echo Black Mary's rebuke of Citizen's declaration of self-sufficiency in *Gem of the Ocean* ("I got me. That's all there is."), one person "ain't never gonna be enough."[133]

The social aesthetic evident in our passionate engagement with representations of Emmett, from the open-casket funeral to the photograph, also inheres in the aesthetics of the representations themselves and the problem that Emmett's faceless face is for the thought of liberal subjectivity. Although I've chosen not to reproduce the photograph, perhaps a more fruitful way to discern the aesthetics of what Mamie saw is to look carefully at how she, like King, *voiced* her vision. That is, how Emmett specifically came to be represented in Mamie's repeated articulations of what she saw, beginning with her testimony during the murder trial: "I looked at the face very carefully. I looked at the ears, and the forehead, and the hairline, and also the hair; and I looked at the nose and the lips, and the chin. I just looked at it all over very thoroughly. And I was able to find out that it was my boy. And I knew definitely that it was my boy beyond a shadow of a doubt."[134] On the witness stand, Mamie detailed not only what but how she saw. "Carefully" and "thoroughly" she cataloged each part of Emmett's broken face, and in this way, she "was able to find out that it was my boy." Still, in the courtroom, Mamie elaborated her vision in a scopic field where whiteness not only exclusively possessed "the right to look" but also defined the terms and limits of viable vision. What the court privileged was not Mamie's epistemologically weak *finding out* but "medical" and "scientific" *recognition*, even as it judged that Emmett was beyond such recognition. Moreover, this impenetrable veil was drawn precisely over Emmett's face, which was the overwhelming focus of the testimony solicited to establish his unrecognizability in a way that otherwise reflected the face's privileged status in operations of recognition. More than any other part of his body, it was Emmett's unrecognizable face that was on trial as the undeveloped negative of the face's aesthetic and ethical renown.

However, after having to detail what she saw in a courtroom where black looking was inadmissible, Mamie found numerous occasions to rehearse her look in more affirming contexts, including her speaking tour with the NAACP, multiple documentaries, and, finally, her memoir. Although no two recountings of her look were identical, like the first, each conformed to the basic pattern of a careful and thorough inventory of Emmett's body. Due to this basic pattern, Mamie's repeated narration of what she saw resembles the literary *blazon*, a poetic form—made popular by Petrarch and used extensively by Elizabethan poets—that catalogs a beloved's (traditionally a woman's) physical features or attributes through a series of comparisons usually drawn from nature. A familiar example that further indexes the aesthetic primacy of the face is found in the tenth stanza of Edmund Spenser's *Epithalamion*:

Her goodly eyes like sapphires shining bright,
Her forehead ivory white,
Her cheeks like apples which the sun hath rudded,
Her lips like cherries charming men to bite.

As a celebration of transcendent beauty, the blazon is perhaps an unlikely vehicle to facilitate what we have otherwise described as Mamie's maculate perception. Yet in many ways, the form's basic convention as a catalog resonates with the characterization of her looking that Mamie offers in her memoir: "I had started out doing this item analysis with the kind of detachment a forensic doctor might have, but I wasn't a forensic doctor. I was Emmett's mother and I was overwhelmed by a mother's anguish and I continued tracking Emmett through his night of torture. Step by step, as methodically as his killers had mutilated my baby, I was putting him back together again, but only to identify the body." Mamie was not a doctor. She lacked a doctor's detachment and, we know from the trial, his recourse to medical and scientific language. But faced with the broken body of her beloved, the blazon of her "item analysis" held out to her a means of re-membering a son returned to her in pieces. Not only in the sense of an exercise of memory but also in the sense of literally "putting him back together again." In this way, Mamie's "item analysis," although performed out of necessity and under a different set of pressures, can also appear to mimic how the blazon's piecemeal attention typically serves to illuminate an idealized whole. The way, for instance, that the itemization of the face in Thomas Campion's "There Is a Garden in Her Face" ultimately illuminates the whole of the beloved's face as a garden. But for Mamie, under the circumstances, putting her son "back together again" was precisely not to re-create or recuperate an idealized whole "but only to identify the body."[135] That is, only to confirm her irretrievable loss and so, somehow, make peace with the pieces.

If Mamie's careful cataloging of the broken face of her son can be read as a blazon, in other ways her appropriation of the form is all wrong. First, her "item analysis" inverts the blazon's typical pattern of a man describing a woman with a mother describing her son. And second, it almost entirely omits the use of simile or comparison, employing, in its stead, a brutal realism. So Mamie can be recognized to have gathered her son's broken face on October 29, 1955, at Bethel AME Church in Baltimore, Maryland, during her NAACP speaking tour. At the conclusion of a significantly more elaborate catalog than she was able to voice under the constraints of the witness stand, Mamie finally detailed how she

> stopped then, and put all of these pieces together, and it wasn't exactly an easy job. But after I took them one by one, I said that's Emmett's nose, the bottom part here, you couldn't mistake that. And I said, that's his forehead, because it was very prominent. And I looked at his one eye over here, that was bulging out. His eyes were very light in color, and I said that certainly is his eye. And then I looked over here where it seemed that the right eye had been picked out with a nut picker, so I couldn't really go by that.
>
> I decided to examine his ears because he had very large ears, larger than an ordinary person. That's when I found out that part of the ear was gone, and the entire back of the head had been knocked out.[136]

If, as some feminist critiques of the blazon have argued, the form's catalog of lofty comparisons can yield a playground for the male gaze that objectifies and abstracts women into transcendent objects of male sexual desire, Mamie's appropriation of the blazon, by contrast, refuses the simile's launchpad into transcendence.[137] Instead, her "item analysis" is relentlessly, even exorbitantly, *fleshly* and is offered in an expression not of sexual desire but of maternal care. This fleshly regard for the face contrasts sharply with the face's familiar function as the site of the human's imagined transcendence, whether aesthetically, by housing eyes said to be the windows of the soul, or philosophically, in the sense that, for Levinas, the Other "shows himself in expression, in the face, and comes from on high."[138] Furthermore, Mamie can be recognized to stay with the flesh in still another way. Not only does she refuse the simile's escape valve, but her re-membering of this broken flesh is not a stable thing of the past. When, for instance, Mamie says to the crowd gathered at Bethel AME, this "bottom part *here*," or "his one eye over *here*," or "then I looked over *here*," where exactly do we understand this repeated "here" to be? As much as it may be located in A. A. Rayner Funeral Home, is it not also here in Bethel AME Church and everywhere and -when else she speaks this look? Does she not, in this way, stay with Emmett's broken body by insisting it into the present, "here" and now? So Mamie can be recognized not only to remember a past look but also to reanimate and relive her deep vision in the present.

Third, Mamie's appropriation of the blazon is also all wrong in the sense that her rehearsals of what she saw progressively come to attend to the wrong parts of the body, at least with regard to the blazon's aesthetic conventions, if not the established estimations of aesthetics more broadly. After the trial and speaking tour, Mamie's rehearsals of what she saw began to diverge significantly from previous accounts focusing exclusively on Emmett's face. In her interview for the documentary *The Murder of Emmett Till* (2003), for example, Mamie begins narrating her look by recalling how she decided to "start at his feet and work my way up, maybe gathering strength as I went."[139] And in her memoir, she begins the account of what she saw similarly: "Quickly I diverted my eyes down to his feet. That's how I needed to handle it. I decided that I would examine him from his feet to his head. I knew I could do it that way. I needed to do it that way. I just could not bear to examine his face. Not yet. I would have to get my courage back, let it build up again slowly as I moved back up his body to his head."[140] Mamie's decision to begin her inventory of the broken body of her son feet first—which, incidentally, is how his haunted body was discovered in the Tallahatchie—decenters the aesthetic and ethical primacy of the face. Not through neglect. These later narrations of her look are more, not less, thorough, and in the memoir span several pages. Rather, Mamie decenters the face through a profound expansion and democratization of her regard, which she lavishes on every part of Emmett's body equally. Thus, her memoir proceeds to detail how:

> I looked at the feet first and they were familiar, and then the ankles. I knew those ankles because I had been so glad to see that they weren't like mine. I'd always thought of my ankles as rather fat in the back. Bo's were always shaped so nicely, so slender, so well tapered. I had always admired the shape of his little ankles, and I had always wished mine were like his. I examined him very carefully, the way a mother might check a newborn. Just to be sure. I felt them, so cold, so hard now. In the back where the tendon runs to the heel, I could put my finger in there and feel the indentation. Not like mine, round without that dip. Then I came on up the leg. How strong his legs had become. I recalled how worried I had been when he was stricken with polio. There weren't many people who had come back from polio the way Bo had, but he had been such a

> strong little boy, so full of life, so determined. And his knees. I paused at the knees. They weren't knobby knees, they were nice, fat, round knees and rather flat. And they were *my* knees. I would know them anywhere. How the doctors had frightened me so, when Bo was born, and his knee had gotten tangled in the umbilical cord and had become so swollen. . . . He wasn't crippled for life, not crippled at all, the way they said he would be. I moved on up a little farther and stopped at his private area. Just long enough, really, to see that everything was still there. That had been one of the terrible rumors that had spread—that Emmett had been castrated. I was relieved for a moment before I caught myself. Oh, my God. Emmett would have a *fit* if he knew I was looking at him like this. . . . As I continued moving on up, I wondered how I had become so intimately aware of all the details of Emmett's body. It was as if I had just always known them, the way only a mother can know her child—by heart. . . . I noticed that none of Emmett's body was scarred. It was bloated, the skin was loose, but there were no scars, no signs of violence anywhere. Until I got to his chin.[141]

Because of the exorbitant attention that Mamie pays to each part of Emmett's body—feet, ankles, knees, legs, midsection—and not just his face, this expression of her "item analysis" perhaps better resembles the *contreblazon*. This form inverts the traditional blazon either by cataloging the wrong, which is to say the less traditionally aesthetic, parts of the body or, as in the famous Shakespearean sonnet "My mistress' eyes are *nothing* like the sun," negating them entirely.[142] Here, Mamie's "item analysis" resembles the contreblazon in the former sense, and its attention is wrong not only because it attends to body parts that are not traditionally aesthetic but also because it begins feet first and, thus, displaces the typical primacy of the face in operations of human recognition and ethical regard.

Still, I wonder about another possible implication of Mamie's decision to begin her maternal regard with Emmett's feet and work her way up. About how, specifically, this order of operations could help her get her "courage back" and gather "strength," and about the especially pregnant pause she takes at Emmett's midsection. I've already discussed the impossible social exchange that Mamie and Emmett share in this moment. How Mamie "catches herself," but precisely in relation, and not the composure or self-possession that is typically meant by that formulation. I wonder why this ethical exchange takes place here, when, for Levinas, ethics otherwise finds its preeminent expression in "the face of the Other." According to Levinas, the Other opposes

> to the force that strikes him not a force of resistance, but the very unforeseeableness of his reaction. He thus opposes to me not a greater force, an energy assessable and consequently presenting itself as though it were part of a whole, but the very transcendence of his being by relation to that whole; not some superlative of power, but precisely the infinity of his transcendence. This infinity, stronger than murder, already resists us in his face, is his face, is the primordial expression, is the first word: "you shall not commit murder." The infinite paralyses power by its infinite resistance to murder, which, firm and insurmountable, gleams in the face of the Other, in the total nudity of his defenseless eyes, in the nudity of the absolute openness of the Transcendent. There is here a relation not with a very great resistance, but with something absolutely other: the resistance of what has no resistance—the ethical resistance.[143]

What Levinas calls "the face of the Other" essentially refers not to an enfleshed or embodied phenomenon but rather to the transcendent fact of the Other's absolute alterity. That is, the sheer fact that the Other is other and not me; thus, by "the very unforeseeableness of [their] reaction," it introduces a question to my power, to whatever I can do, that can never go unasked, no matter how I choose to answer. Even if like a stop sign I choose to ignore it, I nevertheless know that I have done so and thus, by some measure, have already stopped, however imperceptibly. It's in this way that the Other poses to me an ethical resistance against which there is no resistance. Yet even if such ethical resistance comes from "on high," it is telling that it nevertheless finds material expression precisely in the Other's face. It, and not any other body part, "gleams." Its "defenseless eyes" open onto "infinity" as the preeminent expression of the Other's ethical resistance. Perhaps we experience something like this encounter with absolute alterity, which is for Levinas the primordial expression of ethics, when we come face-to-face with the photograph of Emmett Till. Such a reading of the aesthetic scene that is our ongoing viewing of Emmett would certainly account for how engagement with Emmett and the photograph could inspire a struggle for human and civil rights. But if Mamie's moment of ethical regard is otherwise located at Emmett's midsection, and we ultimately see *what she saw*, then perhaps those among us who have caught Mamie's religion are learning to heed the ethical discourse of another, wrong part.

Maybe it's the fact that Mamie "examined him very carefully, the way a mother might check a newborn," or the passing mention of how "his knee had gotten tangled in the umbilical cord," but presuming Mamie's "item analysis" was as thorough as she claimed, I can't help but consider what else she likely saw while pausing at Emmett's midsection and remaining faithful to his desire that she not look at his "private area." I'm thinking about Emmett's navel. Mamie's catalog does not mention it explicitly, although the multiple vignettes onto which her catalog lets out imply its life-giving work and labor. Nor is the navel an especially aesthetic body part. Expressionless, featureless, it holds no muses on retainer. It does not gleam. Still, the navel is not entirely without its bards. In his novel *The Known World* (2003), Edward P. Jones imagines the navel's circle as the feeblest shield against slavery's "natal alienation," which facilitates Stamford's attempt to remember his parents' names:

> He closed his eyes and took his parents in his hands and put them all about the plantation where he had last seen them. . . . He left off for a moment to touch his navel and that told him that he had once been somebody's baby boy, been a part of a real live woman who had been with a real man. . . . In his mind, Stamford took up his parents again and put them in front of the master's big house, he put them in front of the master and the mistress, he put them in front of the master's children . . . he put them in the fields, he put them in the sky, and at last he put them before the cemetery where there were no names. And that was it: His mother's name was June, and so he opened his right hand and let her go. His father's name did not come to him, try as he might to put him all about the plantation. Maybe God had slipped just that one time. Stamford slept, and just before dawn he awoke and said into the darkness, "Colter."[144]

So, we might imagine that the navel also facilitated Mamie's struggle to remember her son. Telling her, as it told Stamford, that she had once been somebody's "Mom," as Emmett addressed her for the last time in a letter mailed from Mississippi: "Dear Mom," written in a beautiful cursive hand. Telling her that she had been a part of a real live boy and, in this way, granting her strength and courage to bear his broken face. The navel also preoccupies Paule Marshall in her novel *Praisesong for the Widow* when a young Avey Johnson stands at the 125th Street pier in New York City amid a large group of black Harlemites waiting to board the Hudson River Day Line:

> Boat rides up the Hudson! Sometimes, standing with her family amid the growing crowds on the pier, waiting for the *Robert Fulton* to heave into sight, she would have the same strange sensation as when she stood beside her great-aunt outside the church in Tatem, watching the elderly folk inside perform the Ring Shout. As more people arrived to throng the

area beside the river and the cool morning air warmed to the greetings and talk, she would feel what seemed to be hundreds of slender threads streaming out from her navel and from the place where her heart was to enter those around her. And the threads went out *not only to people she recognized* from the neighborhood but to those she didn't know as well, such as the roomers just up from the South and the small group of West Indians whose off accent called to mind Gullah talk and who it was said were as passionate about their rice as her father. . . .

Then it would seem to her that she had it all wrong and the threads didn't come from her, but from them, from everyone on the pier, including the rowdies, issuing out of their navels and hearts to stream into her as she stood there holding the bag containing the paper plates and cups, napkins and tablecloth which she was in charge of. She visualized the threads as being silken, like those used in the embroidery on a summer dress, and of a hundred different colors. And although they were thin to the point of invisibility, they felt as strong entering her as the lifelines of woven hemp that trailed out into the water at Coney Island. If she cared to she could dog-paddle (she couldn't swim) out to where the Hudson was deepest and not worry. The moment she began to founder those on shore would simply pull on the silken threads and haul her in.[145]

Perhaps the threads streaming from and into Avey's navel, establishing her connection even to people she did not recognize, also have a word not just for Mamie but for all of us who have looked upon Emmett's unrecognizable face and seen what she saw. As the site of mutual and indiscriminate relation, the navel does not fuss over recognition as a prerequisite for relation. What "primordial expression" of ethics might this long-retired mooring of the umbilical cord, which, at the first, connected Mamie to a son she could not see, let alone recognize, have had to say to Mamie? To us?

If Levinas imagines the ethical discourse of the face as a transcendent "Thou shall not kill," perhaps feeling our help from Jones and Marshall, we can similarly elaborate a discourse of the navel and its fleshly rejoinder to the face's gleaming revelation of absolute alterity. Namely, that these differences, as Denise Ferreira da Silva has helped us understand, do not entail separations.[146] We are not quite the individuals, or the presumptive social field of I's and Others, that we think we are. And we have the scars to prove it. Since we are all caught up and catching ourselves in relations we cannot always see, perhaps the navel's word to us is "Bear life!" Never mind Giorgio Agamben's theorization of "bare life" in *Homo Sacer* or the impulse to name whatever it is we are so long as we are alive or even thereafter.

Just carry, behold, care for, regard, bear life! Whatever it looks like and however unrecognizably it presents. Consent to the irreducible relations that give us, the pieces that we are of one another. The relations that were a ground unto Avey and to middle passing Africans, even in the deep end. The nothing but relation that any of us have to stand on.

Pausing at Emmett's midsection, who knows but that Mamie became the pupil of the ethical discourse of the navel, whose first words are "Thou shalt carry," "Thou shalt bear." And even if we cannot be sure that she did, we can. And do, in the sense that, according to Roland Barthes, the very nature of the photograph can be understood to induce this kind of labor: "From a real body, which was there, proceed radiations which ultimately touch me, who am here; the duration of the transmission is insignificant; the photograph of the missing being, as [Susan] Sontag says, will touch me like the delayed rays of a star. A sort of umbilical cord links the body of the photographed thing to my gaze: light, though impalpable, is here a carnal medium, a skin I share with anyone who has been photographed."[147] If a "sort of umbilical cord" indeed links the viewer to "the body of the photographed thing," then perhaps a better characterization of the "aesthetic scene" that defines our engagement with the photograph of Emmett Till is not the Levinasian face-to-face and however it may be understood to locate the thought of the liberal individual's human or civil rights, but Avey and her innumerable threads. If "our shared ideas about the constitution of the human subject leans on aesthetic encounters," then our encounter with what Mamie saw gestures instead to the irreducible relations from which we attempt to abstract such a subject, even in the interest of its protection. Yet Avey is our witness that there is also protection enough in the entanglement whose jeopardy we are much more adept at imagining. And if we are to truly be the pupils of what Mamie saw, then we must take our cue from the fact that, in putting her son back together, in what may be her strongest divergence from the blazon, Mamie labors not to reconstitute a whole but rather to come to terms with and consent to her loss. She writes in her memoir, "It was Emmett. I knew it the way a mother knows every part of herself. Especially her child. I had examined every part of him I had ever loved, every part of him I had nurtured and helped to mend. I *looked deeply* at that entire body for something, anything that would help me find my son. Finally, I found him. And lost him."[148] The individual will not hold. And it simply will not do, it has not done, to try, even in the interest of its care, to hold on to it as if it would. And we need not, should not, wait for death to give up this ghost. We can, however, hold on to, be held by, and tend to the justice and flourishing of all our relations. In this way, we can do as Mamie declared we should do, in the absence of a face to recognize:

"People had to *face* my son and realize just how twisted, how distorted, how terrifying, race hatred could be. How it had menaced my son during his last, tortured hours on earth. How it continued to stalk us all. Which is why people also had to face themselves. They would have to see their own responsibility in pushing for an end to this evil."[149] With the photograph of Emmett Till, then, Mamie transforms *face* from a noun into a verb. In the absence of a face to recognize, people had instead not only to "*face* her son" (and with him, I argue, the inhabitants of the deep) but also to face their own responsibility for ending such violence, which, in some estimations of the scale of antiblackness, is commensurate with ending the world. And by forcing us to face the antiblack world, the photograph of Emmett Till sends us away as witnesses.

Still, over and over again, what was remarked of Till's face was not just its unrecognizability but, more specifically, that it was no longer recognizably "human." "The body," Mamie writes, "didn't even appear human. I remember thinking it looked like something from outer space."[150] But if here the extent of the disfiguration of Till's alien face captures and exposes, in Mamie's words, "just how twisted, how distorted, how terrifying, race hatred could be," in another image of a black boy who was weighed in the water, albeit under dramatically different circumstances, this unrecognizability is rather the occasion to imagine what Moten has encouraged us to imagine as our "unrecognizable existence." Especially as that existence would need to be imagined on a blue planet.

VII. inter/face

When I first saw images of *Vicissitudes* online, I, too, mistook the children underwater for a monument to Middle Passage (see plate 3). It was an easy mistake to make. Little better historically accounts for the uncanny sight of human beings on the ocean floor than the slave ships hemorrhaging human cargo during the transatlantic slave trade. It also doesn't help that the twenty-six children that comprise the underwater sculpture were submerged just off the coast of Grenada, one of the British Caribbean's most significant disembarkation points during the slave trade and whose majority-black population today consists overwhelmingly of the descendants of slaves. Nor that the ring of reinforced cement behind the children's hands, structuring them in a circle, strongly resembles manacles. Nor that one of the two children who lend their bodies to the sculpture is a black boy. This black boy (plate 4). With so many red herrings, who could blame those who viewed and shared images of the sculpture for the misinterpretation—that this ring of children solemnly holding hands at the bottom of the sea monumentalizes the "inhabitants of the deep"—that took hold online?

In the wake of *Vicissitudes'* online reception, however, Jason deCaires Taylor issued this clarification on his personal website: "It was never my intention to have any connection to the Middle passage." Instead, the sculpture was intended as a living "collaboration with nature": "By using low carbon, pH neutral materials designed to be colonised, the surrounding environment transforms the artworks. Each sculpture is effectively an artificial reef that provides new habitat spaces for a variety of marine life whilst drawing tourists away from natural, fragile areas. The works, which are assimilated by the sea, send a message of regeneration and hope at a time of significant threats to our marine world."[151] If the intended meaning of *Vicissitudes* can be lost in the underwater alchemy of historical associations with Middle Passage, this is significantly less the case in later images of the sculpture, after they have spent a significant time underwater (plate 5). Notably, these later images rarely, if ever, feature in posts commemorating Middle Passage, in no small part because the children in them are no longer recognizably human. According to Elizabeth DeLoughrey, "The two children whose features have been so precisely captured in sculpture are continually transformed into a more-than-human future. Looking over the changes in the children's faces over the past few years, one can see that the . . . human component . . . has been reconfigured. The face in particular, *which functions as the synecdoche for the human*, is no longer recognizable, and the creatures inhabiting the face, eyes, mouth, or other facial features seem to signify a terrifying multispecies being akin to the futurity of science fiction."[152] Still, I'd like to take seriously the black mis/interpretive community that the earliest images of *Vicissitudes* continues to hail, as recently as Juneteenth 2022, when the image made its rounds on social media with the tagline "For those who chose the sea." Indeed, this misinterpretation of the sculpture has proven so intractable that it's outlasted even the artist's clarification, which has subsequently been removed from his website.

Yet by way of conclusion, I'd like to question what it would mean to bear witness to the inhabitants of the deep as much in this last, unrecognizably human, image as in the earlier one. Such was my ethical commitment when I encountered the black coral boy of *Vicissitudes* on a dive in August 2023, in a somewhat unorthodox face-to-face (plate 6). What would it mean to not fail to also behold the inhabitants of the deep in this more-than-human image, in which we behold, in Deborah Bird Rose's words, not the face but the interface?[153] Not the synecdoche of the human, or more the individual human subject but, at the very site where that subject is most reified, "a place of interaction" expressing the testament of all our irreducible relations. Indeed, what are we, and what is our existence, but interaction, inside and out? What we may struggle to apprehend in the painful photograph of Emmett Till perhaps we can more readily apprehend in the close-up of this inter/face, which pictures the submerged more-than-human future and inheritance of not just Emmett's but every face. Or have kisses taught us nothing? Every face is an inter/face. And when we persevere in our witness to the inhabitants of the deep, even when faced with the unrecognizable, more-than-human face of the black boy from *Vicissitudes*, we not only dispense with the sort of shallow historical thinking that overlooks the deep roots of the climate crisis in slavery and colonization, but we also bear witness to the sort of irreducibly ecological life to which the inhabitants of the deep yielded in their interaction with a blue planet. Such existence may not be recognizable, but it is livable. And on this blue planet, it's the only life we've got.

Epilogue

ANKLE DEEP

PERHAPS I SHOULD HAVE KNOWN that setting out to write a book about the deep would require me to get my feet wet.

In some ways, I did know. Throughout the writing of this book, I openly courted the ocean, somehow feeling that I could not write about Middle Passage in good faith without experiencing the "landless realm of the deep ocean" for myself.[1] While on a research Fulbright in Salvador da Bahia, Brazil, in 2011, I developed a notion to apprentice myself to a group of local fishermen in the historic neighborhood of Rio Vermelho. To my surprise, the fisherman entertained my unusual request, though not without first issuing stern warnings about seasickness. Feeling somehow called by the ocean, like Avey Johnson in *Praisesong for the Widow*, I believed this calling sufficient to do for me what they strongly insisted Dramamine would. If I had remembered Avey's own bouts with seasickness in that novel, I might have reconsidered. Or maybe I abstained out of some unconscious obligation to or earnest remembrance of those who had no Dramamine when they ventured into this river without a middle or shore. Whatever my reasons, I realized the seriousness of my folly the moment the land "vanished on both sides" of our crude boat and I spent most of my first fishing expedition leaning over the side, depositing into the ocean's already considerable volume.[2] I had the opportunity to release a more honorable gift to the ocean during the Festa de Iemanjá, held annually in Rio Vermelho on February 2, and waited on the beach beside countless others, including my newfound fishermen friends, to see if Iemanjá would accept our offerings.

Notwithstanding these significant overtures, I knew that my courtship of the deep called for a greater depth of intimacy than a beach or a boat could accommodate. Here, too, again like Avey, I dragged my feet, waiting until nearly the end of writing this book to finally become a certified scuba diver. The motivation to take up scuba diving first emerged when I came across images of Jason deCaires Taylor's underwater sculpture *Vicissitudes* in graduate school and, like so many others, mistook the ring of children on the ocean floor for a memorial to Middle Passage. Since then, I felt a strong desire to visit in person the sculpture referenced in "Deep Vision." But with few personal precedents for black scuba divers and what I rightly suspected could be a cost-prohibitive hobby, it was August 2023 before I finally found my way to the Molinere Underwater Sculpture Park off the coast of Grenada. It was on this same research trip, in preparation for my visit with *Vicissitudes*, that I finally earned my diving certification with the help, to my surprise and delight, of a black scuba diving instructor. That I've managed to get licensed to dive but not yet to drive is an irony my family and friends never miss an opportunity to remind me of. I'm going about this licensing thing all backward, they say. Or maybe not. Blue as our planet is, perhaps we humans ought to prioritize learning how to navigate the ocean. Perhaps, soon, we'll have no choice.

As of this writing, I have dived as deep as sixty feet below the Atlantic Ocean, with plans to dive deeper. Yet nowhere on God's blue planet have I been deeper than when visiting the grave of Emmett Till in Burr Oak Cemetery outside of Chicago. If the deep is indeed, as this book argues, a formation that exceeds not only the ocean but at times also water itself, then it's entirely plausible that the deep could be found in a cemetery. Why not, if we've already seen Bigger Thomas inhabit the deep in a jail cell, or Todd Clifton on a New York City sidewalk, or Citizen Barlow in Aunt Ester's parlor—all without a single drop of water in sight? Yet this is not quite the sense in which I encountered my deepest deep at Burr Oak Cemetery. On the occasion of my visit to Emmett Till's grave, the deep had more than a merely symbolic presence. Allow me, then, to detail the unusual circumstances of the deep's *physical* manifestation in the middle of a cemetery on dry land.

I had come to Chicago on a kind of pilgrimage. Years earlier I tried visiting Till's grave during the 2019 Modern Language Association conference. But after visiting the site of the funeral, Roberts Temple Church of God in Christ, and staying longer than I had intended, I ran out of time before my flight home. In

April 2022, I finally returned to fulfill my obligation and pay my respects to this premature ancestor. After checking into my hotel, I headed to the hotel bar to do some writing. I find a good cocktail can sometimes make writing easier or me braver. While I was seated at the bar, a salesman approached and began to pitch his rum to the bartender. The rum's name: *Equiano*. Typically, I'm loath to speak to people I don't know. But because I was writing sentences about the rum's namesake at that very moment, I feared saying nothing might piss God off. The way Shug Avery suspects we do whenever we walk past the color purple without taking notice.[3] I don't know if Equiano ever found its way onto the shelves of the hotel bar. But it did supply a toast between two strangers to the success of their Equiano-inspired ventures.

As senseless and hopeless as the world can often seem, moments like this chance encounter at a hotel bar conspire to renew my precarious conviction that the work we do really does matter somehow. That continuing to elaborate the strange meaning of being black matters and that, however antiblack the world, it is a labor backed and supported by life and a God who sees, as a slave girl named Hagar discovered while fleeing her masters.[4] The next day, after a night of heavy rainfall, my partner and I set out for Burr Oak Cemetery in an Uber, sensing that the gravity of our visit to Till's grave might require ceremony to hold us in the care and love of this God who sees. I have the good fortune of being partnered to a minister, who is quite proficient in finding ceremony; during an otherwise quiet and meditative ride, I asked her to choose a scripture to read aloud when the time came.[5]

I don't know what I was expecting. The Burr Oak Cemetery is a cemetery like any other cemetery—unremarkable and in a bit of disrepair. There was absolutely nothing to suggest that the fourteen-year-old martyr of the Civil Rights Movement had been laid to rest here. Not even a plaque. Without any signage or direction, I considered Equiano's still yet-to-be-discovered grave and Alice Walker's struggle to find the neglected grave of Zora Neale Hurston.[6] How remembrance is a struggle and a fight against history's will to forget. How, without this hard, difficult, and often lonely work, our ancestors teeter on the edge of oblivion. How the overgrowth of the earth isn't to blame for this. How the Earth, despite spinning and revolving through space at incredible speeds, has never dropped a single one. Looking out upon waves of the dead cresting in orderly rows of headstones and anticipating futility, we approached the cemetery's small administration building to ask for help. We spoke to a woman through an opaque window who explained that there were efforts underway to have the cemetery recognized as a historical landmark. The status would provide additional resources for the cemetery's upkeep and the creation of infrastructure that would better aid visitors in locating Till's grave. In the cemetery's present, historically unmarked state, however, the woman could only direct us to a crudely drawn map posted on the window. Hardly precise but enough to help us gain our bearings in the sea of the dead.

When we reached the place about where we thought the grave should be, we still struggled to find it. Our efforts were not helped by the nature of Till's headstone, which, I knew from pictures, is horizontal rather than vertical and was thus obscured by the uncut grass. After repeatedly searching the general area, I almost despaired of ever finding Emmett. Then I saw it: a small area of the cemetery grounds nearby completely submerged in water, which had yet to evaporate from the previous night's rainfall. The small island of water held the perfect reflection of a sky too clear to have ever known rain, much like the ocean can sometimes appear to evaporate into the sky all at once, transforming boats into birds. From where I stood, I couldn't make out what lay beneath the water's surface.

It can't be. Can it?

To be sure, I would have to get closer and start swimming my ground. So I made like Moses, took off my shoes and socks, rolled up my pants, and waded out into what I had already begun to suspect might be holy ground. Chicago in April has a stubborn memory of winter. The water was ice cold and the grass slick like seaweed beneath my bare feet. Like the fisherman who discovered Emmett's body in the Tallahatchie River, when I looked down at one of the submerged headstones, I saw this text looking back at me through the water:

EMMETT L. TILL
IN LOVING MEMORY
JULY 25, 1941–AUG 28, 1955

As I stood in ankle-deep water before the grave of this dear ancestor and inhabitant of the deep, it was all I could do to remain upright (plates 7 and 8). Then my partner, standing nearby and sensing the moment, began reading aloud the scripture she had chosen back in the car:

> In visions God brought me into the land of Israel and put me down on a very high mountain; on it, toward the south, it seemed that a city was being built. That is where God took me, and there in front of me was a man whose appearance was like bronze. He had a flax cord and a measuring rod in his hand, and he stood in the gateway. The man said to me, "Human being, look with your eyes, hear with your ears, and pay attention to all

the things I am showing you; because the reason you were brought here is so that I could show them to you. Tell everything you see to the house of Israel."[7]

Then he brought me back to the entrance of the house, and I saw water flowing eastward from under the threshold of the house, for the house faced east. The water flowed down from under the right side of the house, south of the altar. Next he led me out through the north gate and took me around outside to the outer gate, by way of the east gate, where I saw water trickling from the south side. With a line in his hand the man went out toward the east and measured a thousand cubits [one-third of a mile] and had me wade across the stream; *the water came up to my ankles*. He measured another thousand and had me wade through the water, which reached my knees. He measured another thousand and had me wade through water up to my waist. Finally he measured a thousand, and it was a river I couldn't cross on foot, because the water was so deep one would have to swim across; it was a river that could not be waded through. He asked me, "human being, have you seen this?" Then, guiding me, he got me back to the river bank. After being returned, I saw on the bank of the river a great number of trees on the one side and on the other side. He said to me, "this water flows toward the eastern region and continues down the 'Aravah. When it enters the sea, the sea of stagnant water, [the Dead Sea,] its water will become fresh. When this happens, swarms of all kinds of living creatures will be able to live in it wherever the stream flows; so that there will be a vast number of fish; for this water is flowing there, so that, wherever the river goes, everything will be restored and able to live."[8]

After she finished reading, we stood together in holy silence, feeling a slave girl beside a spring in the desert was on to something when she named God as she did. There was no sermon. So I'll resist offering one here. Except to ask, as each chapter of this book strains to imagine: What would it mean for the "human being" to consent to inhabit the deep? A world where all life flourishes awaits our answer.

When we turned to leave, for reasons I'm still not sure of, I reached down, cupped a handful of water, and poured it over my head.

Acknowledgments
DEEP GRATITUDE

Let *us* make . . .
—GENESIS 1:26 (KJV)

Strange, really—to have written my first book and never felt less like an author. I do not mean this self-deprecatingly or as an expression of self-doubt. It's just that the name you find on this book's cover quite literally only scratches the surface.

I had a speech impediment as a kid. Though *impediment*, it strikes me today, isn't quite the right word. My speech was not impeded so much as I spoke too much, too quickly, and too fast to be intelligible. Speech for me was like the gushing fire hydrants we jailbroke in lieu of access to public pools and, as far as I knew, just as fun. Even when I finally learned to discipline my runaway mouth and speak "correctly," I became an unconfident speaker and learned to make a refuge of silence. Perhaps to compensate for my speech difficulties, I remember deciding at a very young age that writing would be my salvation. I was in grade school at a private PWI, and in lieu of speaking up in class, I decided I would prove myself to my teachers (and myself) through my writing. But this seemingly innocuous decision also meant that I could not receive any help. It wasn't just my awareness that the black kid was in some ways expected to need help. It was that I needed my writing to validate me. And how could it, if it was not mine?

Today, I wish so much more for my grade-school self than this fantasy of authorship. I wish him (I wish myself) enough poetic sensibility to know author*ship* as a literal ship. A boat I'm in with others, just as the "inhabitants of the deep" were in the same boat. At present, the manifest of this ship is missing many names besides my own. Allow me, then, to acknowledge my shipmates.

There are ideas and sentences in this book that are as old as my years as an undergraduate at the University of Pennsylvania. Thank you, Herman Beavers, for teaching me that arguments, and not just sentences, can be beautiful. Thank you, Salamishah Tillet, for the refuge of your office hours and for treating me like I had a PhD long before I did. Thank you, too, to the Mellon Mays Undergraduate Fellowship and my cohort: Joshua Bennett, Alysia Harris, Petal Samuels, Lyric Saunders, Brandi Waters, and Rhaisa Williams.

When I think back on my time in graduate school at Duke University English, I still don't know how I got over. Between crippling anxiety, mounting incompletes, and dictating my qualifying exams with two broken hands after a bad bike accident, there were many times when I doubted that I would. Thank you, Priscilla Wald; your Theories of Nature and the Human seminar invigorated my thinking about water and oceans. Thank you, Nathaniel Mackey, for cultivating and affirming my poetic voice, even when it meant taking a little more time on my papers (read: an incomplete or two). Thank you, Maurice Wallace, for wearing both your hats: for your lectures and your sermons, for your mentorship and your prayers. Thank you, Fred Moten, for inviting me out to California and gathering me the summer before I went on the job market. You saw so much in me and my work that I couldn't. Thank you also to Ashon Crawley, Allison Curseen, and Damien-Adia Marassa. When I arrived at Duke, you all showed me such kindness and hospitality, and so much of how I've come to understand the everyday of black study derives from your friendship and example.

To all my colleagues in African and African Diaspora studies and English at Boston College, thank you. So much of what this book has become is indebted to your intellectual companionship and mentorship. Special thanks to Min Hyoung Song for helping me conceive of this project as a book and reading the first draft of the manuscript in its entirety. Thank you also to Laura Tanner and Angela Aards for reading and commenting on multiple chapter drafts. Thank you, Rhonda Fredericks, for your impeccable style, friendship, and encouragement when life is lifing. Thank you, Régine Jean Charles, for opening your home to me and inviting me to your church and for all of your prayers. Thank you, Kyrah Malika Daniels, for your themed parties. Thank you, Amey Victoria Adkins-Jones, for being my roommate and putting up with my coffee grinder in the mornings. And thanks, once again, to the big homie, Allison Curseen. From Durham to Boston and beyond, I got you and I know you got me.

Thank you to all of my new colleagues in Black studies and English at Yale University. Special shout-out to Elleza Kelley and Ernest Mitchell, who teach me every day that black study is friendship as much as it is anything else. I'm so glad we're in the same boat. Thank you, also, to Daphne Brooks, Hester Blum, Erica Edwards, Steve Mentz, and Kevin Quashie for reading and responding to an early draft of the manuscript. Thank you to Braxton Shelley, who has read and offered feedback on more drafts of this book than anyone, and without whose intellectual and spiritual friendship this book simply doesn't get done. Finally, thank you to my editors at Duke University Press, Ken Wissoker and Lisa Lawley, for your thoughtful consideration of the manuscript and for helping to shepherd it to completion.

The writing of this book has also been a lesson in ecology for me: that nothing exists apart from the conditions and contexts that make it possible. In addition to the people who have helped me along the way, the writing and research that led to the creation of this book have also received generous support from the Mellon Mays Undergraduate Fellowship, the Fulbright Program, the Harrington Faculty Fellowship at the University of Texas at Austin, the Career Enhancement Fellowship from the Institute for Citizens and Scholars (thank you, Evie Shockley, for serving as my mentor), the Race, Indigeneity, and Transnational Migration Faculty Fellowship at Yale, and the Frederick W. Hilles Publication Fund at Yale. Thank you.

The most important word in this book is *deep*, and I reserve my deepest gratitude for my family. Thank you to my siblings, Amanda, Anita, Joshua, and Maria, and my oldest niece, Amaya, who's been grandfathered into the original party of five. I love you with my whole heart, even though you clown me for spending all this time in school just to become an *assistant* professor. To my stepmother, Pamela Howard, thank you for your steak dinners and praying me through so many challenging seasons. To my mother, Zoraida Decos, thank you for giving me life and for the beauty your gardening brought to our lives as children. You taught me how to wonder at the ground and at the mystery of growth. To my father, Michael Howard: I think I write because you write. All those journals you keep taught me that writing could be a way to move through life. There isn't a sentence I write without you and your example. I hope you find your care for language reflected in these pages. I hope this book honors you.

And finally, to my wife and best friend, Cami Alese King: Long before any of these words find their way to a page, they take their first breaths in conversation with you. Thank you for being a safe space to stammer. Thank you for being home.

Notes

PROLOGUE. THE BLUENESS OF BLACKNESS

1. Equiano, *Interesting Narrative*, 38.
2. Washington, *Up from Slavery* (emphasis added).
3. Bryer and Hartig, *Conversations with August Wilson*, 253.
4. The problem with beginnings, as with history, is that we make them up. Not that they are wholly fictional, but they are the product of decisions and emphases we rarely cop to fully. Both the origins of African Diaspora literature and the African Diaspora could reasonably be located elsewhere than Equiano's 1789 narrative and the experience of Middle Passage to which the beginning of that narrative bears witness. With respect to African American literature specifically, Phillis Wheatley's earlier *Poems on Various Subjects, Religious and Moral* (1773) makes for a more logical starting place. Yet, beside this study's interest in the black literary tradition's animation by the "deep," I choose to begin my account of African Diaspora literature with Equiano (however much the scope of this study leans African American), due to his geographic indeterminacy and the fact that his narrative also marks a beginning for the Caribbean and black British literary traditions. If black literature has several possible beginnings, so too does Africa's diaspora, which precedes the transatlantic slave trade just as it continues in its wake. Consider, e.g., Ivan Van Sertima's *They Came Before Columbus* (1976), which surveys archaeological evidence of African migration to the New World before the slave trade. Or consider the African origins of our species, such that Africa's diaspora, in some respects, may even be recognized as humanity itself. Still, I choose to begin my account of Africa's diaspora with Middle Passage because of its scale and role in the globalization of race and racial ideology. And because Middle Passage wrought a world that is still with us.

5. The archival evidence in question is a baptismal record and a ship manifest, which list Equiano's birthplace as South Carolina. See Carretta, *Equiano, the African*.

6. Carretta, *Equiano, the African*, xiv–xv (emphasis added). For a powerful rebuttal of Carretta's argument, see Cathy Davidson's "Olaudah Equiano, Written by Himself." There she illuminates how Carretta's interpretation of his archival findings fails to grapple sufficiently with the fundamental ways in which "indeterminacy" is a constitutive condition of eighteenth-century black life and experience. Davidson's sense of the precariousness and indeterminacy of eighteenth-century black life leads her to other possible explanations for why Equiano might have felt compelled to strategically claim South Carolinian birth, which, in her estimation, are far more plausible than the possibility that he invented his African nativity.

7. In a convention familiar to the genre of the slave narrative, *The Interesting Narrative* was published with the signatures of numerous white men vouching for the authenticity of Equiano's story. And notwithstanding the conflicting evidence specifically surrounding Equiano's nativity, Carretta also comments on what he perceives as the otherwise remarkable historical consistency and verifiability of Equiano's narrative.

8. The problem of "authenticity" is a central problematic in the study of slave narratives, due to their subjection to varying levels of mediation. In his introduction to *The Oxford Handbook of the African American Slave Narrative*, John Ernest writes: "Many early book-length narratives were published specifically to promote the anti-slavery cause, and their authenticity was questioned so frequently—often, because white readers didn't believe that black Americans were capable of writing their own life stories—that the phrase 'written by himself' or 'written by herself' became a regular feature of these publications." Ernest proceeds to quote James Olney's important article "'I Was Born': Slave Narratives, Their Status as Autobiography and as Literature." In that article, Olney observes that "unlike autobiography in general the narratives are all trained on one and the same objective reality, they have a coherent and defined audience, and have behind them and guiding them an organized group of 'sponsors,' and they are possessed of very specific motives, intentions, and uses understood by narrators, sponsors, and audiences alike: to reveal the truth of slavery and so to bring about its abolition." Following Olney, and due to the political conditions under which the narratives were produced, Ernest asks, "What 'truth of slavery' could one hope to find from such resources beyond the views that guided them in the first place?" Ernest, *Oxford Handbook of the African American Slave Narrative*, 6; Olney, "'I Was Born,'" 52.

9. Trevor Burnard argues this in a special issue of the journal *Historically Speaking* dedicated to the controversy surrounding Carretta's discovery. See Burnard, "Goodbye, Equiano, the African," 11.

10. Hartman, *Lose Your Mother*, 101.

11. Burnard, "Goodbye, Equiano, the African," 11 (emphasis added).

12. Gumbs, *Undrowned*, 1–2.

13. Following M. NourbeSe Philip's mandate in *Zong!* to "defend the dead" (26), Christina Sharpe asks in her book *In the Wake*, "What does it mean to defend the dead? To tend to the Black dead and dying: to tend to the Black person, to Black people, always living in the push toward our death?" (10).

14. For a survey of the historiography of the transatlantic slave trade, and the fierce debates around the uses and limitations of quantitative analysis, see Domingues da Silva and Misevich, "Atlantic Slavery and the Slave Trade."

15. Brand, *Land to Light On*, 46.

16. Rather than saying goodbye to Equiano or recuperating the narrative's authenticity as a launching pad unto some high place, this book gets down by choosing instead to wade deeper into the indeterminacy of the narrative's disputed beginnings as a means of interrogating the indeterminacy of the beginnings of blackness more broadly. Such indeterminacy—what we cannot know for certain—need not be the slave narrative's or blackness's cross to bear. Not unless we adopt Jesus's orientation to the cross by actually taking it up and heading somewhere good, somewhere beyond the mere abjection of the slave ship that may or may not have saluted Equiano in the beginning. Instead, such indeterminacy can be the occasion of a deep interrogation of the Human, and of the nature of human life on Earth. All we do not and cannot know—like Frederick Douglass's lack of any accurate knowledge of his birthday beyond seasonal designations like "cherry time" or "planting time" given in his narrative—may just as well occasion our interrogation of the "genre of the human" predicated on individual rather than collective reckonings of time as signal black abjection. And, in the mode of Sylvia Wynter, a profound interrogation of the assumptions and ideologies of western humanism is precisely how this book aims to get down. See Douglass's *Narrative* (13) and Wynter's "Unsettling the Coloniality of Being/Power/Truth/Freedom" (269).

17. Equiano, *Interesting Narrative*, 38 (emphasis added).

18. Interestingly, Tiffany Lethabo King makes the opposite point in *The Black Shoals*, where she argues that conceptions of blackness in black studies can tend to overemphasize the ocean, at the expense of the development of a robust analytic for the land. But as my argument proceeds to detail, through a consideration of Omise'eke Natasha Tinsley's "Black Atlantic, Queer Atlantic," this apparent emphasis on the ocean can itself overlook the materiality of the sea.

19. Wilderson, *Red, White, and Black*, xi. Wilderson's mandate has also been taken up by Christina Sharpe and Fred Moten, respectively, in *In the Wake* and *The Universal Machine*.

20. Patterson, *Slavery and Social Death*, 38.

21. Hartman, *Lose Your Mother*, 6.

22. Wilderson, *Red, White, and Black*, 337.

23. Gilroy, *Black Atlantic*; Benítez-Rojo, *Repeating Island*.

24. Tinsley, "Black Atlantic, Queer Atlantic," 197 (emphasis added).

25. Tinsley, "Black Atlantic, Queer Atlantic," 199.

26. Brayton, *Shakespeare's Ocean*, 23.

27. Melville, *Moby-Dick*, 214.

28. Literary scholar Hester Blum proposes the term *oceanic studies* in her article "The Prospect of Oceanic Studies." And literary scholar Steve Mentz proposes the term *blue humanities* in his book *An Introduction to the Blue Humanities*.

29. Dan Brayton proposes the phrase *terrestrial bias* in *Shakespeare's Ocean*, 15–42. Marcus Rediker discusses his term *terracentrism* in his interview with Jeffrey Williams; Rediker, "History Below Deck," 563.

30. Mentz, *Introduction to the Blue Humanities*.

31. Pip is a black cabin boy aboard the *Pequod* who nearly drowns during a whale chase in Herman Melville's novel *Moby-Dick*.

With my use of the majuscule *Human* and minuscule *human*, I intend here and henceforth, first, the dominant, normative, and global standard-bearing genre of the Human arguably indexed by whiteness and, second, the human as such, which makes no analogous claims to normativity or global standardization.

32. Gen. 1:1–2 (New King James Version).

33. Fanon, *Black Skin, White Masks*, 89.

34. R. Wright, *Native Son*, 255.

35. Gen. 2:7 (NKJV). Emphasis in both quotes added.

36. See Patterson, *Slavery and Social Death*; Wilderson, *Red, White, and Black*, 11.

37. The racial geography yielded by Wright's rewriting of the Genesis narrative effectively maps the color line onto the geographic binary of land and sea. And this cosmology is made physically manifest in what remain—in the wake of Middle Passage and white settler colonialism—humanity's racially uneven claims to the ground. Long after the historical tenure of the transatlantic slave trade, water persists in the black literary imagination as an index of the groundlessness of black being in ways not only precipitated but subsequently haunted by the "ancient waters" of Middle Passage.

38. Wilderson, *Red, White, and Black*, 37, 38.

39. See Keller, *Face of the Deep*.

40. M. Wright, *Physics of Blackness*, 14.

41. M. Wright, *Physics of Blackness*, 7–8.

42. M. Wright, *Physics of Blackness*, 26.

43. M. Wright, *Physics of Blackness*, 5.

44. M. Wright, *Physics of Blackness*, 5, 12, 25.

45. M. Wright, *Physics of Blackness*, 23.

46. Quoted in Sensbach, "Beyond Equiano" (2006), 12.

47. Sensbach, "Beyond Equiano" (2008), 108 (emphasis added).

48. Hartman, "Venus in Two Acts," 11.

49. On the distinction between the antiblack world and the Earth, see Howard, "To See the Earth Before the End of the Antiblack World."

50. Carretta, *Equiano, the African*, xvii.

51. On the concept of "Africanisms," see, Herskovits, *The Myth of the Negro Past*, 1–32. Equiano, *Interesting Narrative*, 38.

52. In *Slavery and Social Death*, Orlando Patterson outlines what he identifies as the "constituent elements" of slavery. Afropessimism also uses this phrasing in its delineation, after Patterson, of the "constituent elements" of social death, which include gratuitous violence, general dishonor, and natal alienation. See Patterson, *Slavery and Social Death*, 1–16; Wilderson, *Afropessimism*, 14.

Here, in my thinking on black ecological life, I am riffing on Stefano Harney and Fred Moten's reflections on "black social life" in their essay "Michael Brown." They write, "How can we survive genocide? We can only address this question by studying how we have survived genocide. In the interest of imagining what exists, there is an image of Michael Brown we must refuse in favor of another image we don't have. One is a lie, the other unavailable. If we refuse to show the image of a lonely body, of the outline of the space that body simultaneously took and left, we do so in order to imagine jurisgenerative black social life walking down the middle of the street—*for a minute, but only for a minute, unpoliced, another city gathers, dancing.* We know it's there, and here, and real; we know what we can't have happens all the time" (81, emphasis added).

53. Here, I am riffing on a line from the title poem of Ed Roberson's collection *To See the Earth Before the End of the World*: "People are grabbing at the chance to see / the Earth before the end of the world" (3).

54. Wright, Native Son, 255 (emphasis added).

55. "Well I'll be damned.... It didn't even hurt. Wait'll I tell Nel." Morrison, *Sula*, 149.

56. Coogler, *Black Panther.*

57. Equiano, *Interesting Narrative*, 41 (emphasis added).

INTRODUCTION. THE DEEP

1. Rev. 7:9 (New King James Version).

2. Trans-Atlantic Slave Trade Database, Slave Voyages, accessed October 2, 2024, https://www.slavevoyages.org/voyage/database.

3. Here I riff on Saidiya Hartman's often-cited method of "critical fabulation." See Hartman, "Venus in Two Acts," 11–12.

4. Equiano, *Interesting Narrative*, 41.

5. Lucille Clifton, "won't you celebrate with me," Poetry Foundation, accessed October 15, 2024, https://www.poetryfoundation.org/poems/50974/wont-you-celebrate-with-me.

6. Equiano, *Interesting Narrative*, 41 (emphasis added).

7. Equiano, *Interesting Narrative*, 39 (emphasis added).

8. The notion of "gratuitous violence" derives from Orlando Patterson's classic definition of slavery as the "permanent, violent domination of natally alienated and generally dishonored persons." The influential school of black thought known as Afropessimism locates in this definition three constitutive elements of not just slavery but blackness, including "natal alienation, general dishonor, and gratuitous violence." See Patterson, *Slavery and Social Death*, 13; Wilderson, *Red, White, and Black*, 17.

9. Glissant's oceanic salute is quoted from the first of *Les Chants de Maldoror (*1868) by Isidore Ducasse/Comte de Lautréamont. See Glissant, *Poetics of Relation*, 7. I am grateful to Ernest Mitchell for pointing out to me that Glissant "greets the ocean with the informal *tu,* which is reserved for children, friends, and God. There's a familiarity and intimacy to the greeting which makes sense for Glissant, born in a coastal town of Martinique, notably different from the sensibility of Equiano who . . . was raised in the interior and was encountering the ocean for the first time." Edward Mitchell, pers. comm., May 23, 2024.

10. As pioneering examples of what might be labeled *black ecocriticism*, I want to acknowledge Kimberly Ruffin's *Black on Earth: African American Ecoliterary Traditions* (2010) and Anissa Janine Wardi's *Water and African American Memory: An Ecocritical Perspective* (2011).

As a framing of black study, I appreciate the simplicity of what Fred Moten has described as "the devotional practice that is given in recitation of the sentence 'blackness is x.'" *Blackness is an ongoing inhabitation of the deep* is my own contribution to this great cloud of witnesses. See Moten, *Black and Blur*, vii.

11. Philip, *Zong!*, 3.

12. Douglass, *Narrative*, 48.

13. Douglass, *Narrative*, 57.

14. Douglass, *Narrative*, 48.

15. Douglass, *Narrative*, 48.

16. In Dungy, *Black Nature*, vii.

17. T. Walker, "Sailing to Freedom," 18.

18. Douglass, *Narrative*, 48.

19. Douglass, *Narrative*, 48–49.

20. Douglass, *Narrative*, 49.

21. Douglass, *Heroic Slave*, 246.

22. Douglass, *Self-Made Men*, 5–6.

23. Ferreira da Silva, "On Difference Without Separability."

24. Bibb, *Life and Adventures*, 28–29 (emphasis added).

25. Bibb, *Life and Adventures*, 29–30.

26. Bibb to Douglass, March 7, 1849, Frederick Douglass Papers Project, accessed October 1, 2024, https://frederickdouglasspapersproject.com/s/digitaledition/item/6311.

27. Douglass's rendezvous with the Chesapeake in particular recalls the familiar practice of *petit marronage*.

28. Brathwaite, "Caribbean Man," 90.

29. Equiano's narrative ultimately argues for the abolition of the transatlantic slave trade by proposing the alternative prosperity that would come from the world's regard of Africa as a global trading partner. Moreover, Equiano himself secures his manumission through trading.

30. Douglass, *Narrative*, 53.

31. Douglass, *Narrative*, 49 (emphasis added).

32. Stepto, *From Behind the Veil*, 167.

33. Stepto refers to Douglass's *Narrative* in particular as "the paradigmatic narrative of ascent." See Stepto, *From Behind the Veil*, 66.

34. Equiano, *Interesting Narrative*, 40.

35. Stepto, *From Behind the Veil*, 67. For another pioneering study of black longitudinal migration, see Griffin, *"Who Set You Flowin'?"*

36. Stepto, *From Behind the Veil*, 167.

37. Stepto, *From Behind the Veil*, 66. To a limited degree, Stepto also cites Solomon Northup's *Twelve Years a Slave* and Booker T. Washington's *Up from Slavery* as examples of immersion narratives that, while they center southern migrations, otherwise lack the form's complementary emphasis on tribal/cultural literacy.

38. I borrow the phrase "plan of living" from *Invisible Man*, where Ralph Ellison writes, "The mind that has conceived a plan of living must never lose sight of the chaos against which that pattern was conceived." I employ this phrase throughout this book to refer alternately to western humanism's and modernity's "plan of living," to speak to how humanity, or at least the reigning regime or genre of the Human, has organized life on Earth, often against the grain of life itself. And given the ocean's aesthetic and epistemic association with chaos, I argue that the ocean is the chaos that modernity has forgot and against which it has conceived its plan of living to the exclusion of all alternatives. See Ellison, *Invisible Man*, 580.

39. Stepto, *From Behind the Veil*, 167.

40. August Wilson's *Gem of the Ocean* is particularly exemplary of this connection between blackness's inhabitation of the deep and its facilitation of a parallel cultural

immersion. The ritualistic journey to the "City of Bones" at the center of the play literally immerses the play's protagonist, Citizen Barlow, in his cultural heritage in ways that actively empower and inform his struggle for freedom.

41. Hartman, *Lose Your Mother*, 101–9.

42. Paule Marshall's *Praisesong for the Widow* and August Wilson's *Gem of the Ocean* are two examples of texts that embody the submersion narrative in their entirety.

43. Emphasis added.

44. Emphasis added.

45. Brown, *Otis Redding*, 134.

46. Wright, *Native Son*, 255; Patterson, *Slavery and Social Death*, 5.

47. Emphasis added. I riff here on the language of Farah Jasmine Griffin's classic study, "*Who Set You Flowin'?*": *The African-American Migration Narrative*.

48. I am indebted to Christina Sharpe's discussion of the left-to-die boat in *In the Wake: On Blackness and Being*. See Sharpe, *In the Wake*, 58–59, 107. The "loophole of retreat" derives from Harriet Jacobs's narrative, *Incidents in the Life of a Slave Girl*. During the seven years she lived in the crawlspace, Jacobs used this "loophole of retreat" to look after and at her children, among other things. The term has since become generally symbolic, for numerous artists and black studies scholars, of how black people—and black women in particular—create space and possibility within experiences of confinement. T. Walker, "Introduction," 1.

49. See Rediker, *Freedom Ship*; T. Walker, "Sailing to Freedom," 18.

50. Bachelard, *Water and Dreams*, 3.

51. Bachelard, *Water and Dreams*, 11–12.

52. Walker, *Color Purple*, 198; Wynter, "Novel and History," 99.

53. René Descartes in *Discourse on Method* quoted in Wynter, "Black Metamorphosis," 19.

54. Wynter, "Black Metamorphosis," 1.

55. Wynter, "Novel and History," 99.

56. Wynter, "Black Metamorphosis," 18, 17; Spillers, "Mama's Baby, Papa's Maybe," 68.

57. Glissant describes the hold of the slave ship in "The Open Boat" as "a womb, a womb abyss." He writes, "This boat is your womb, a matrix, and yet it expels you. This boat: pregnant with as many dead as living under the sentence of death." In her unpublished manuscript, "Black Metamorphosis," Wynter identifies New World blacks as "the native[s] of that area of experience that we term the New World." See Glissant, *Poetics of Relation*, 6; Wynter, "Black Metamorphosis," 1.

58. Wynter, "Novel and History," 99.

59. On the shoals, see King, *Black Shoals*, 4. Tinsley writes, for instance, that "diving into this water stands to transform African diaspora scholarship in ways as surprising as Equiano's first glimpse of the sea"; see Tinsley, "Black Atlantic, Queer Atlantic," 197. Wynter, "Novel and History," 99.

60. Ellison, *Invisible Man*, 580; Borgese quoted in DeLoughrey, "Submarine Futures of the Anthropocene," 37.

61. In a way that captures the universal naivete of humanity's first large-scale encounter with the deep sea, Arnold Guyot characterizes the Atlantic as an "unknown" and "dreaded" ocean in his mythologization of Europe's early modern encounter with the Atlantic. See Guyot, *Earth and Man*, 233.

62. McKittrick, *Demonic Grounds*, 132–33.
63. Melville, *Moby-Dick*, 142, 380 (emphasis added).
64. On "terracentrism," see Rediker, "Hydrarchy and Terracentrism."
65. Wilderson, *Red, White, and Black*, 35–53.
66. Melville, *Moby-Dick*, 308 (emphasis added).
67. Philip, *Zong!*, 195.
68. Wilson, *Gem of the Ocean*, 52.
69. Till-Mobley and Benson, *Death of Innocence*, 129.
70. Huie, "Shocking Story," 207 (emphasis added).
71. A. Walker, *Sent by Earth*, 27.

CHAPTER 1. DEEP HUMANITIES

1. Moten, *Universal Machine*, 199.

2. "Uncover your origins" tagline from Ancestry, accessed December 1, 2019, ancestry.com. *Tehom* is ancient Hebrew for the deep and appears in Genesis as the primordial ocean of the Jewish and Christian creation narrative. Olokun is the deity and personification of the primordial sea in the Yoruba creation story. See Genesis 1:2 (New King James Version) and Marrero, "Olokun en África y en Cuba."

3. Roberson, *Voices Cast Out*, 93 (emphasis added).

4. Moten, *Universal Machine*, 199.

5. "1964, March 29—Malcolm X—We didn't land on Plymouth Rock—Closed Captioned," posted November 3, 2014, by Captioning for Everyone, YouTube, 3:44, https://www.youtube.com/watch?v=3Aq2Zoi8D6A&ab_channel=CaptioningforEveryone.

6. Tocqueville, *Democracy in America*, 30.

7. Everett, *James*, 95.

8. Douglass, *Narrative*, 5; Ellison, *Invisible Man*, 436.

9. Huie, "Shocking Story."

10. This phrase repeats across the media coverage of Sandra Bland's death. See "Questions Still Swirling Around the Death of Sandra Bland," *New York Times*, July 24, 2015, https://www.nytimes.com/interactive/2015/07/24/us/sandra-bland-questions-about-her-death.html; Jamelle Bouie, "Blame the Police," *Slate*, July 22, 2015, https://slate.com/news-and-politics/2015/07/sandra-blands-arrest-and-death-are-a-national-scandal-brian-encinia-and-the-police-are-to-blame.html.

11. Roberson, *Voices Cast Out*, 36.

12. Trans-Atlantic Slave Trade Database, Slave Voyages, accessed October 2, 2024, https://www.slavevoyages.org/voyage/database.

13. Coogler, *Black Panther*.

14. Wilderson, *Red, White, and Black*, 37, 38.

15. Crawley, "Otherwise Possibility."

16. On stand-your-ground law, see Douglas, *Stand Your Ground*.

17. Brand, *Land to Light On*, 47.

18. Ellison, *Invisible Man*, 438, 441.

19. "So far, these effects have largely been caused by only 25% of the world population." Crutzen, "Geology of Mankind."

20. Hurston, "How It Feels to Be Colored Me," 175.

21. A. Walker, *In Search of Our Mother's Gardens*, 346.

22. Gilroy, *Black Atlantic*, 4.

23. Smallwood, *Saltwater Slavery*, 126.

24. Mintz and Price, *Birth of African-American Culture*, 84.

25. Lewis and Maslin, *Human Planet*, 166.

26. Crosby, *Columbian Exchange*.

27. Lewis and Maslin, *Human Planet*, 10–11.

28. Thoreau, "Walking" (emphasis added).

29. Thoreau, "Walking" (emphasis added).

30. Thoreau, "Walking."

31. Thoreau, "Walking."

32. Thoreau, "Walking."

33. McKittrick, *Demonic Grounds*, 132–33.

34. Outka, *Race and Nature*, 11.

35. Outka, *Race and Nature*, 16–17. This feeling of overwhelm, common to the sublime and to trauma, also resembles Sigmund Freud's "oceanic feeling," which likewise not only associates the ocean with the infinite but creates a similar state of confusion between subject and world.

36. Outka, *Race and Nature*, 17.

37. Outka, *Race and Nature*, 16.

38. Quoted in Outka, *Race and Nature*, 20.

39. Outka, *Race and Nature*, 23.

40. Outka, *Race and Nature*, 25.

41. Outka, *Race and Nature*, 25.

42. Fanon, *Black Skin, White Masks*, 89.

43. Douglass, *Narrative*, 37 (emphasis added).

44. Ferreira da Silva, "On Difference Without Separability."

45. Outka, *Race and Nature*, 15–16.

46. Outka, *Race and Nature*, 14.

47. Outka, *Race and Nature*, 201–5.

48. In a way reflective of a general anxiety marking early modern rhetoric surrounding the ocean, Arnold Guyot characterizes the Atlantic as an "unknown" and "dreaded" ocean in his mythologization of Europe's initial encounter with the Atlantic and subsequent colonization of the New World. Later in this chapter, I consider the passage in question, which Thoreau also quotes extensively in "Walking," in greater depth. See Guyot, *Earth and Man*, 233.

49. Guyot, *Earth and Man*, 233 (emphasis added). Thoreau also quotes this passage in "Walking."

50. Smallwood, *Saltwater Slavery*, 124.

51. A reviewer of an earlier draft of this chapter helpfully pointed out that "the Portuguese had been in the Atlantic since the Middle Ages (and perhaps earlier) and all over the Atlantic coast of West Africa by the mid fifteenth century." Likewise, as Kevin Dawson illuminates in *Undercurrents of Power*, West Africans living on the Atlantic maintained a vibrant and substantial "aquatic culture," which included the ocean and which preexisted European contact. Indeed, Europeans and Africans were not uniformly unfamiliar with the Atlantic. But this knowledge, I argue, pertained mostly to a knowledge of the Atlantic

as a *margin* or *barrier*, as Guyot and Thoreau refer to it, respectively. My specific claim, then, is that all early modern humans were largely, if not entirely, unfamiliar with what Smallwood calls the "landless realm of the *deep* ocean." Smallwood, *Saltwater Slavery*, 124.

52. Guyot, *Earth and Man*, 233.

53. Smallwood, *Saltwater Slavery*, 131 (emphasis added).

54. Smallwood, *Saltwater Slavery*, 129.

55. Guyot, *Earth and Man*, 233.

56. Lewis and Maslin, *Human Planet*, 174.

57. Furthermore, that the yield of agriculture here is not food but "treasures" and "wealth" betrays the historical shift from subsistence farming to monoculture farming in a market economy infamous for its ecological harm and thus the transplantation to the New World of the same extractive land practices that presumably exhausted the soil of the Old. Guyot obscures the ecological harm of these practices in his rehearsal of yet another familiar ideology of white settler colonialism in his reference to the "inexhaustible fertility" of the New World. In contrast, the OWM is otherwise said to have "tilled the *impoverished* soil" of Europe. Thus, not only is the New World rhetorically made available to limitless extraction, but the ecological violence of that extraction is also obscured in the Old through its transformation into a defect of the soil itself. In his gloss of the OWM's long and teeming repose in "Walking," however, Thoreau gives the lie to this obfuscation by writing instead that the OWM "exhausted the rich soil of Europe," thus attributing the poor quality of Europe's soil to exhaustive land practices rather than to the soil itself. See Guyot, *Earth and Man*, 231–32; Thoreau, "Walking."

58. Guyot, *Earth and Man*, 228–29.

59. Guyot, *Earth and Man*, 233 (emphasis added).

60. Thoreau, "Walking."

61. Before the transatlantic confrontation of hemispheres of humanity previously separated for millennia, such encapsulating knowledge claims about the earth or the human species were not only not yet possible but, for most of the global human community, also unnecessary and unimportant. It's not until the historical onset of white settler colonialism that it becomes both possible and necessary for some humans to speak a totalizing word for both the planet and the species.

62. Rousseau, *Inquiry*, 11.

63. Rousseau, *Inquiry*, 12 (emphasis added).

64. Ellison, *Invisible Man*, 580.

65. In Dungy, *Black Nature*, 57.

66. Rousseau, *Inquiry*, 13 (emphasis added).

67. Douglas, *Stand Your Ground*, xiii.

68. Adam Howard, "Defense: Zimmerman 'Not Guilty of Anything but Protecting His Own Life,'" *Grio*, July 12, 2013, https://thegrio.com/2013/07/12/defense-zimmerman-not-guilty-of-anything-but-protecting-his-own-life.

69. Charles Mills quotes Edward Said as contending that by 1914, "Europe held a grand total of roughly 85% of the earth as colonies, protectorates, dependencies, dominions, and commonwealths." See Mills, *Racial Contract*, 29.

70. Rediker, "Hydrarchy and Terracentrism"; Rediker, "Motley Crew for Our Times?"; Brayton, *Shakespeare's Ocean*.

71. Wynter, "Ceremony Must Be Found," 19.

72. Worster, *Nature's Economy*, 58–59.

73. Guyot, *Earth and Man*, 22–23.

74. Toepfer, "'Organization,'" 24.

75. Guyot Hall is named in honor of Arnold Guyot, Princeton's first professor of geology and geography. This, however, is scheduled to change as early as 2025, when the environmental sciences are to be moved to a new building and Guyot Hall is to be renamed Schmitt Hall.

76. Guyot, *Earth and Man*, 22.

77. Ferreira da Silva, "On Difference Without Separability."

78. Guyot, *Earth and Man*, 29.

79. Thoreau, "Walking."

80. The wilderness was whites-only not in the sense that nonwhites were always formally barred or absent from the wilderness but rather in the sense that any nonwhite presence or relation to the wilderness still had to negotiate the general and exclusive land claims of the unfolding enterprise of white settler colonialism. For the American Indian, this meant the possibility of expropriation, while for the black American this meant (the possibility of) being reduced to property too.

81. A recent example of the tendency I describe is the controversy surrounding the publication of an "all-white" photograph of prominent young climate activists, including Greta Thunberg, which deliberately cropped out the Ugandan climate activist Vanessa Nakate. See Kenya Evelyn, "Outrage at Whites-Only Image as Ugandan Climate Activist Cropped from Photo," *Guardian*, January 25, 2020, https://www.theguardian.com/world/2020/jan/24/whites-only-photo-uganda-climate-activist-vanessa-nakate.

82. Thoreau, "Walking."

83. Thoreau illuminates the significance of the "art of Walking" by analyzing the etymology of the verb *to saunter*. He writes:

> I have met with but one or two persons in the course of my life who understood the art of Walking, that is, of taking walks—who had a genius, so to speak, for *sauntering*, which word is beautifully derived "from idle people who roved about the country, in the Middle Ages, and asked charity, under pretense of going *a la SainteTerre*," to the Holy Land, till the children exclaimed, "There goes a *Sainte-Terrer*," a Saunterer, a Holy-Lander. They who never go to the Holy Land in their walks, as they pretend, are indeed mere idlers and vagabonds; but they who do go there are saunterers in the good sense, such as I mean. Some, however, would derive the word from *sans terre* without land or a home, which, therefore, in the good sense, will mean, having no particular home, but equally at home everywhere.

84. Of course, the same goes for women, whose capacities as landowners were also restricted during colonization. And along with whiteness, the maleness of landowners is also not incidental to this emerging dominant relation to land.

85. Thoreau, "Walking."

86. Thoreau, "Walking."

87. Leopold, *Sand County Almanac*, 239.

88. Leopold, *Sand County Almanac*, 204.

89. Leopold, *Sand County Almanac*, 238–39.

90. Leopold, *Sand County Almanac*, 239.

91. Douglass, *Narrative*, 49.

92. Leopold begins his chapter on the land ethic with the example of Odysseus's lynching of twelve slave girls. He writes, "This hanging involved no question of propriety. The girls were property. The disposal of property was then, as now, a matter of expediency, not of right and wrong." Leopold, *Sand County Almanac*, 237.

93. Smallwood, *Saltwater Slavery*, 126.

94. Equiano, *Interesting Narrative*, 38. Although I attend to Equiano's account of his experience of Middle Passage as if it is indeed biographical, I am aware of Vincent Carretta's *Equiano, the African* and the now widely accepted possibility that Equiano was actually born in South Carolina and that his account of his personal experience of Middle Passage is fictional. But this possibility only strengthens the essential claim I am making in this chapter, as Equiano's effort to craft a believable and faithful account of Middle Passage suggests that this oceanic encounter was common enough among Middle Passage survivors for Equiano to both know and reproduce it.

95. Dawson, *Undercurrents of Power*, 2.

96. Smallwood, *Saltwater Slavery*, 131.

97. Hurston, *Barracoon*, 55.

98. Glissant, *Poetics of Relation*, 7.

99. Jefferson, *Notes on the State*, 155.

100. Smallwood, *Saltwater Slavery*, 125.

101. Glissant, *Poetics of Relation*, 7.

102. Mentz, "Blue Humanities," 69; Blum, "Prospect of Oceanic Studies."

103. DeLoughrey, "Submarine Futures of the Anthropocene," 32.

104. Brayton, *Shakespeare's Ocean*, 15.

105. Burch and Sekula, *Forgotten Space*. I learned of this documentary through Christina Sharpe's *In the Wake*, which offers an illuminating analysis.

106. Patterson, *Slavery and Social Death*, 5.

107. Wilderson, *Red, White, and Black*, 37.

108. Wilderson, *Red, White, and Black*, 11.

109. Fanon, *Black Skin, White Masks*, 117.

110. Wilderson, *Red, White, and Black*, 38.

111. Roberson, "We Must Be Careful," 4. Throughout this book I employ Roberson's use of capitalization when referring to "the Earth," in the sense of planet Earth, as distinct from "the world," in the sense of human worldings, which are socially and culturally constructed.

112. Fanon, *Black Skin, White Masks*, 82–83.

113. Tinsley, "Black Atlantic, Queer Atlantic," 199.

114. Bachelard, *Water and Dreams*, 3.

115. Brand, *Map to the Door of No Return*, 6.

116. Philip, *Zong!*, 195.

117. Equiano, *Interesting Narrative*, 39; Bachelard, *Water and Dreams*, 2–3; Brand, *Map to the Door of No Return*, 11.

118. Equiano, *Interesting Narrative*, 41.

119. Alexis Pauline Gumbs, in *Undrowned*, also troubles the distinction between those who drowned and those who survived by pointing to the planetary scale of breathing despite unbreathable conditions and atmospheres.

120. Bachelard, *Water and Dreams*, 3.

CHAPTER 2. DEEP STUDY

1. Melville, *Moby-Dick*, 314.

2. Melville, *Moby-Dick*, 380.

3. Melville, *Moby-Dick*, 100, 142 (emphasis added).

4. I am thinking here with Denise Ferreira da Silva's helpful formulation of "difference without separability." If difference is otherness in the minuscule, we might take what she describes as "separability" as Otherness in the majuscule.

5. Du Bois, *Souls of Black Folk*, 15.

6. See Lee and Bean, "America's Changing Color Lines."

7. Crenshaw, "Mapping the Margins."

8. Wilderson, *Red, White, and Black*.

9. I elaborate this point elsewhere; Howard, "To See the Earth Before the End of the Antiblack World." Indeed, with the advent of the Anthropocene, we are now said to inhabit a profoundly human planet. See Lewis and Maslin, *Human Planet*.

10. Wilderson, *Afropessimism*, 192, 219.

11. Although I find Wilderson's argument about the category of the non-Human to be quite persuasive, I do wonder if the category isn't a bit more complex and promiscuous than his outline allows. Natives have also historically been relegated, albeit less consistently and with less of a global consensus, to the category of the non-Human. Thus, it would also seem that at least to some extent, in addition to land, civil society derives confirmation of Humanity from the figure of the native. Similarly, I wonder whether man, as a synecdoche for the Human, doesn't get confirmation of maleness in a somewhat analogous way. Like the Black, women also don't appear to be in possession of anything exterior to themselves that civil society wants besides confirmation of human/male existence and a shot at perpetuity. I still buy the distinctiveness of antiblackness but wonder if this complexity holds the possibility for coalition and solidarity.

12. Wilderson, *Red, White, and Black*, 11.

13. Patterson, *Slavery and Social Death*, 5.

14. Wilderson, *Afropessimism*, 15.

15. Leopold, *Sand County Almanac*, 240.

16. Leopold, *Sand County Almanac*, 239.

17. Buell, *Environmental Imagination*, 2.

18. Buell, *Environmental Imagination*, 3.

19. Cohen, "Ecology's Rainbow," xx.

20. Buell, foreword to Cohen, *Prismatic Ecology*, ix.

21. Cohen, "Ecology's Rainbow," xvi.

22. Cohen, "Ecology's Rainbow," xx.

23. Brayton, *Shakespeare's Ocean*, 18 (emphasis added).

24. Brayton, *Shakespeare's Ocean*, 20. Brayton is careful not to be overly critical of Leopold on this point, given the significance and spirit of his contributions to environmental thought. And while I agree with Brayton that, at least on this point, the spirit rather than the letter of Leopold's work should be honored, on other accounts, like the land ethic's erasure of black and native suffering, I believe Leopold merits significant criticism.

25. Brayton, *Shakespeare's Ocean*, 22.

26. Brayton, *Shakespeare's Ocean*, 23–24, 39[AA], 39.

27. Quoted in Brayton, *Shakespeare's Ocean*, 15. For the original image of "The Road to Homo Sapiens," see Howell, *Early Man*, 44–45. For online access to "The Road to Homo Sapiens" and various iterations of "The March of Progress," see Conniff and Giller, "Iconic. Almost by Accident," https://www.yalealumnimagazine.com/articles/3977-march-of-progress.

28. Mentz, *Introduction to the Blue Humanities*, 17, 19.

29. Blum, "Prospect of Oceanic Studies," 671; Blum, "Terraqueous Planet," 26.

30. Buell, *Future of Environmental Criticism*, vi.

31. Wilderson, *Afropessimism*, 228.

32. Wilderson, *Red, White, and Black*, 37.

33. "Our flesh and energies are instrumentalized for postcolonial, immigrant, feminist, LGBTQ, transgender, and workers' agendas," not "authorized by Black agendas predicated on Black ethical dilemmas." Wilderson, *Afropessimism*, 15.

34. Leopold, *Sand County Almanac*, 201.

35. Leopold, *Sand County Almanac*, 203.

36. Patterson, *Slavery and Social Death*, 5; Leopold, *Sand County Almanac*, 239.

37. Outka, *Race and Nature*, 2.

38. Outka, *Race and Nature*, 10–11.

39. Zakiyyah Iman Jackson takes up this question brilliantly in her book *Becoming Human*, in which she not only critiques this mechanism of black subjugation but helps us to question the human organization of life according to a hierarchical "scale of being" in the first place. See also Bennett, *Being Property Once Myself*.

40. Mills, *Racial Contract*, 29.

41. Brand, *Map to the Door of No Return*, 31.

42. W. H. Auden, quoted in Brayton, *Shakespeare's Ocean*, 23.

43. Melville, *Moby-Dick*, 214 (emphasis added).

44. Quoted in Wynter, "1492," 23 (emphasis added).

45. Wilderson, *Afropessimism*, 224.

46. T. King, *Black Shoals*, 207.

47. Spillers, "Mama's Baby, Papa's Maybe," 72.

48. Mentz, *Introduction to the Blue Humanities*, xv.

49. On Shakespeare's ocean, see Brayton, *Shakespeare's Ocean*; Mentz, *At the Bottom*.

50. Find below a more exhaustive list of Melville's bibliography, a mere cursory look at which is sufficient to reveal his enduring preoccupation with the ocean.

Typee: A Peep at Polynesian Life (1846)
Omoo: A Narrative of Adventures in the South Seas (1847)
Mardi: And a Voyage Thither (1849)
Redburn: His First Voyage (1849)
White-Jacket; or, The World in a Man-of-War (1850)
Moby-Dick; or, The Whale (1851)
Pierre; or, The Ambiguities (1852)
"Isle of the Cross" (1853 unpublished, and now lost)
"Bartleby, the Scrivener" (1853) (short story)
The Encantadas, or Enchanted Isles (1854) (novella)
Benito Cereno (1855) (novella)

Israel Potter: His Fifty Years of Exile (1855)
The Confidence-Man: His Masquerade (1857)
Battle-Pieces and Aspects of the War (1866) (poetry collection)
Clarel: A Poem and Pilgrimage in the Holy Land (1876) (epic poem)
John Marr and Other Sailors (1888) (poetry collection)
Timoleon (1891) (poetry collection)
Billy Budd, Sailor (An Inside Narrative) (1891, unfinished; published posthumously in 1924; authoritative edition in 1962)

51. Melville, *Moby-Dick*, 16.
52. Brayton, *Shakespeare's Ocean*, 23.
53. Melville, *Moby-Dick*, 91, 92.
54. Melville, *Moby-Dick*, 164.
55. Melville, *Moby-Dick*, 214 (emphasis added).
56. Brayton, *Shakespeare's Ocean*, 22.
57. Brayton, *Shakespeare's Ocean*, 23.
58. Melville, *Moby-Dick*, 214.
59. Hobbes, *Leviathan*, 64.
60. Melville, *Moby-Dick*, 215.
61. As quoted in Brayton, *Shakespeare's Ocean*, 23–24.
62. Keller, *Face of the Deep*, xvi.
63. Keller, *Face of the Deep*, 7.
64. Heise, *Sense of Place and Sense of Planet*.
65. Melville, *Moby-Dick*, 214.
66. Gen. 1:9–10 (New King James Version; emphasis added).
67. Kalyan Ray, "Himalayan Study Springs Ocean Water Surprise," *Deccan Herald* (Karnataka), July 25, 2023, https://www.deccanherald.com/science/himalayan-study-springs-ocean-water-surprise-1240773.html; Craig Robert Martin, "How Were the Himalayas Formed? Rocks Tell a New Story," *Print*, November 8, 2020, https://theprint.in/environment/how-were-the-himalayas-formed-rocks-tell-a-new-story/539090.
68. T. King, *Black Shoals*.
69. I borrow this phrase from Ursula K. Heise, who deploys it in *Sense of Place and Sense of Planet*.
70. Guyot, *Earth and Man*, 21.
71. Fields and Fields, *Racecraft*, 22.
72. Lewis and Maslin, *Human Planet*, 4.
73. Fields and Fields, *Racecraft*, 22.
74. Lewis and Maslin, *Human Planet*, 166.
75. See map in Lewis and Maslin, *Human Planet*, 162–63.
76. Of course, sea-level rise has already claimed enough islands to destabilize the notion of geographic permanence altogether.
77. Rev. 21:1 (NKJV).
78. *Oxford English Dictionary*, "aboriginally (adv.), sense 1," accessed July 2023, https://doi.org/10.1093/OED/4380802813.
79. Melville, *Moby-Dick*, 21, 172, 100, 349, 182.
80. Melville, *Moby-Dick*, 16.

81. Melville, *Moby-Dick*, 214, 16.

82. Equiano, *Interesting Narrative*, 38.

83. Melville, *Moby-Dick*, 214.

84. Curseen, *Minor Moves*.

85. Nations being the exclusive formation that they are, the United Nations may even be an oxymoron.

86. Melville, *Moby-Dick*, 103.

87. Melville, *Moby-Dick*, 103.

88. Melville, *Moby-Dick*, 130.

89. Thoreau, "Walking."

90. Melville, *Moby-Dick*, 101.

91. Melville, *Moby-Dick*, 102.

92. These episodes are recounted in chapters 78 and 74, respectively, in Melville, *Moby-Dick*.

93. Melville, *Moby-Dick*, 123, 101, 123, 176.

94. Melville, *Moby-Dick*, 405, 406.

95. Melville, *Moby-Dick*, 383.

96. Spillers, "Mama's Baby, Papa's Maybe," 67.

97. Melville, *Moby-Dick*, 101.

98. Melville, *Moby-Dick*, 139.

99. Melville, *Moby-Dick*, 140.

100. Melville, *Moby-Dick*, 140.

101. Melville, *Moby-Dick*, 143–44.

102. Melville, *Moby-Dick*, 101.

103. Melville, *Moby-Dick*, 306.

104. The novel never explicitly specifies Pip's slave or free status, but the prevailing reading of Pip is as a free African American sailor. However, being born in Alabama, as his original designation as a "Poor Alabama Boy" seems to suggest, would almost certainly make Pip a slave during the time when *Moby-Dick* is believed to be set (the 1830s or 1840s). Alternatively, being born in Tolland County, Connecticut, would almost certainly make Pip free. After Connecticut passed a gradual abolition act in 1784, slavery wasn't completely outlawed until 1848. Still, the 1830 census lists only twenty-five slaves in Connecticut. Moreover, Pip technically could not have been the literal slave of any of his crewmates because slavery was legally abolished in Massachusetts in the early 1780s, and the *Pequod* is a Nantucket whaler. See Melville, *Moby-Dick*, chap. 27, Melville Electronic Library, https://melville.electroniclibrary.org/editions/versions-of-moby-dick/27-knights-and-squires.

105. Melville, *Moby-Dick*, 101.

106. Melville, *Moby-Dick*, 306.

107. Of course, I have in mind here the iconic antilynching flag that was flown outside the New York City office of the NAACP from 1920–38. See "This Flag Helped End Lynching in the U.S.," PBS, January 23, 2025, https://www.pbs.org/wgbh/americanexperience/features/flag-helped-end-lynching-us/.

108. Curseen, *Minor Moves*.

109. Melville, *Moby-Dick*, 307 (emphasis added).

110. Patterson, *Slavery and Social Death*, 5.

111. Melville, *Moby-Dick*, 307 (emphasis added).

112. Melville, *Moby-Dick*, 307.
113. Melville, *Moby-Dick*, 308.
114. Spillers, "Mama's Baby, Papa's Maybe," 67.
115. Melville, *Moby-Dick*, 308 (emphasis added).
116. Gen. 1:2 (NKJV).
117. Quoted in Moten, *In the Break*, 30.
118. Melville, *Moby-Dick*, 344.
119. Melville, *Moby-Dick*, 305–6.
120. Melville, *Moby-Dick*, 307.

CHAPTER 3. DEEP VOICE

1. PADI, *Open Water Diver Manual*, 81–82.
2. Wilson, *Gem of the Ocean*, 53.
3. Philip, *Zong!*, 3.
4. Philip, *Zong!*, 189 (emphasis added).
5. Philip, *Zong!*, 195.
6. Ellison, *Invisible Man*, 440.
7. Ellison, *Invisible Man*, 251.
8. R. Wright, *Native Son*, 95.
9. Wilson, *Gem of the Ocean*, 60.
10. Du Bois, *Souls of Black Folk*, 7.
11. Douglass, *Narrative*, 20 (emphasis added).
12. Du Bois, *Souls of Black Folk*, 169.
13. Du Bois, *Souls of Black Folk*, 167.
14. Quoted in Du Bois, *Souls of Black Folk*, 7. For an image of Arthur Symons's epigraph to Du Bois's "Of Our Spiritual Strivings," including musical notation, see W. E. B. Du Bois, *The Souls of Black Folk*, Project Gutenberg, accessed July 9, 2025, https://www.gutenberg.org/files/408/408-h/408-h.htm#chap01.
15. Du Bois, *Souls of Black Folk*, 170 (emphasis added).
16. Smallwood, *Saltwater Slavery*, 124.
17. Glissant, *Poetics of Relation*, 6.
18. Bachelard, *Water and Dreams*, 3.
19. Roberson, *Voices Cast Out*, 36 (emphasis added).
20. Douglass, *Narrative*, 16.
21. Fanon, *Black Skin, White Masks*, 105, 117.
22. Huie, "Shocking Story," 207.
23. Roberson, *Voices Cast Out*, 36.
24. Equiano, *Interesting Narrative*, 39.
25. Douglass, *Narrative*, 48.
26. Walcott, "The Sea Is History," in *Selected Poems*, 137.
27. Benjamin, "On the Concept of History."
28. Spillers, "Mama's Baby, Papa's Maybe," 68 (emphasis added).
29. Glissant theorizes Middle Passage as a threefold encounter with what he terms the "abyss." First, there is the encounter of the enslaved with the slave ship's hold, which he

theorizes as a "womb-abyss," that is not only "pregnant with as many dead as living under the sentence of death" but which also "generates the clamor of your protests" and "produces all the coming unanimity." Glissant's subsequent conceptions of the "abyss," however, extend beyond the hold to the ocean and the "abyss" physically expressed by its depth and breath. That is, first, the vertical "depths of the sea," which never fail to bring to mind the inhabitants of the deep and their "scarcely corroded balls and chains," and second, the abyss of memory, figured by the ocean's breadth, as "the reverse image of all that had been left behind." Thus, "the entire ocean, the entire sea . . . make one vast beginning, *but* a beginning whose time is marked by the balls and chains gone green." Glissant, *Poetics of Relation*, 6, 7.

30. Wilderson, *Red, White, and Black*, 37, 38.

31. Sharpe, *In the Wake*, 3.

32. Moten, *Universal Machine*, 199.

33. Glissant, *Poetics of Relation*, 7.

34. Spillers, "Mama's Baby, Papa's Maybe," 72.

35. See Wilderson, *Afropessimism*; Wilderson, *Red, White, and Black*; and Sexton, "Social Life of Social Death."

36. Wilderson, *Red, White, and Black*, 11.

37. Moten, *Universal Machine*, 199.

38. Wilderson, *Red, White, and Black*, 11.

39. Fanon, *Black Skin, White Masks*, 105.

40. Fanon, *Black Skin, White Masks*, 116–17.

41. Fanon, *Black Skin, White Masks*, 92.

42. On nausea, see Fanon, *Black Skin, White Masks*, 92, 96; on vertigo, see Glissant, *Poetics of Relation*, 5.

43. Fanon, *Black Skin, White Masks*, 92.

44. Fanon, *Black Skin, White Masks*, xii.

45. Du Bois, *Souls of Black Folk*, 13.

46. Ellison, *Invisible Man*, 576.

47. Lewis and Maslin, *Human Planet*, 4.

48. Roberson, *To See the Earth*, 4.

49. Oxford English Dictionary, s.v. "problem (n.)," December 2024, https://doi.org/10.1093/OED/8217366941.

50. Du Bois, *Souls of Black Folk*, 14 (emphasis added).

51. Sexton, "Social Life of Social Death," 6–7.

52. Brand, *Land to Light On*, 48.

53. Du Bois, *Souls of Black Folk*, 13 (emphasis added).

54. Sartre, *Being and Nothingness*, 231.

55. Sartre, *Being and Nothingness*, 232.

CHAPTER 4. DEEP IMAGINATION

1. Ellison, *Invisible Man*, 7–8 (emphasis original).

2. Ellison, *Invisible Man*, 12, 8.

3. Bachelard, *Water and Dreams*, 3.

4. Marshall, *Praisesong for the Widow*, 39.

5. Marshall, *Praisesong for the Widow*, 40, 42 (emphasis original).

6. Stepto, *From Behind the Veil*, 167.

7. Marshall, *Praisesong for the Widow*, 34.

8. Marshall, *Praisesong for the Widow*, 42.

9. These lines, while adapted to reflect the analogous place of water in Aunt Cuney's sermon, are inspired by and derived from the sermon concerning the "Blackness of Blackness" in the prologue of Ellison's *Invisible Man*:

> "Brothers and sisters, my text this morning is the 'Blackness of Blackness.'"
>
> And a congregation of voices answered: "That blackness is most black, brother, most black . . ."
>
> "In the beginning . . ."
> "At the very start," they cried.
> ". . . there was blackness . . ."
> "Preach it . . ."
> ". . . and the sun . . ."
> "The sun, Lawd . . ."
> ". . . was bloody red . . ."
> "Red . . ."
> "Now black is . . ." the preacher shouted.
> "Bloody . . ."
> "I said black is . . ." "Preach it, brother . . ."
> "an' black ain't . . ."
> "Red, Lawd, red: He said it's red!"
> "Amen, brother . . ."
> "Black will git you . . ."
> "Yes, it will . . ."
> "Yes it will . . ."
> ". . . an' black won't . . ."
> "Naw, it won't!"
> "It do . . ."
> "It do, Lawd . . ."
> ". . . an' it don't."
> "Halleluiah . . ."
> ". . . It'll put you, glory, glory, Oh my Lawd, in the WHALE'S BELLY."
> "Preach it, dear brother . . ."
> ". . . an' make you tempt . . ."
> "Good God a-mighty!"
> "Old Aunt Nelly!"
> "Black will make you . . ."
> "Black . . ."
> ". . . or black will un-make you."
> "Ain't it the truth, Lawd?" (9–10)

10. Marshall, *Praisesong for the Widow*, 37.

11. Marshall, *Praisesong for the Widow*, 38–39 (emphasis added).
12. Marshall, *Praisesong for the Widow*, 42.
13. Marshall, *Praisesong for the Widow*, 34.
14. Marshall, *Praisesong for the Widow*, 42.
15. The famous passage to which I am alluding here reads as follows:

> I shall then suggest that ideology "acts" or "functions" in such a way that it "recruits" subjects among the individuals (it recruits them all), or "transforms" the individuals into subjects (it transforms them all) by that very precise operation which I have called *interpellation* or hailing, and which can be imagined along the lines of the most commonplace everyday police (or other) hailing: "Hey, you there!"
>
> Assuming that the theoretical scene I have imagined takes place in the street, the hailed individual will turn round. By this mere one-hundred-and-eighty-degree physical conversion, he becomes a *subject*. Why? Because he has recognized that the hail was "really" addressed to him, and that "it was *really him* who was hailed" (and not someone else). Experience shows that the practical telecommunication of hailings is such that they hardly ever miss their man: verbal call or whistle, the one hailed always recognizes that it is really him who is being hailed. And yet it is a strange phenomenon, and one which cannot be explained solely by "guilt feelings," despite the large numbers who "have something on their consciences." Althusser, "Ideology and Ideological State Apparatuses," 174.

16. Ellison, *Invisible Man*, 12–13.
17. Quoted in Powell, "Summoning the Ancestors," 257.
18. Powell, "Summoning the Ancestors," 254.
19. Powell, "Summoning the Ancestors," 258.
20. Powell, "Summoning the Ancestors," 268.
21. Powell, "Summoning the Ancestors," 264.
22. Dash, *Daughters of the Dust* (1991).
23. See Kaplan, "Souls at the Crossroads," 524n17. See also Dash, *Daughters of the Dust* (1992).
24. Marshall, *Praisesong for the Widow*, 39–40.
25. Marshall, *Praisesong for the Widow*, 44.
26. Marshall, *Praisesong for the Widow*, 39–40.
27. Marshall, *Praisesong for the Widow*, 39.
28. Cone, *Cross and the Lynching Tree*, 95 (emphasis added).
29. Cone, *Cross and the Lynching Tree*, 2.
30. Ellison, *Invisible Man*, 4–5.
31. R. Wright, *Native Son*, 95.
32. Du Bois, *Souls of Black Folk*, 170 (emphasis added).
33. Moten, "Notes on Passage," 55.
34. Du Bois, *Souls of Black Folk*, 7.
35. Sexton, "Social Life of Social Death," 7.
36. Philip, *Zong!*, 189.
37. Marshall, *Praisesong for the Widow*, 39.

38. Here, I am thinking specifically of the critique of racial essentialism and narrowly drawn definitions of blackness in the work of Evie Shockley and Michelle Wright. See Shockley, *Renegade Poetics*; and M. Wright, *Physics of Blackness*.

39. Roberson, "Structure, Then the Music," 763.

40. Marshall, *Praisesong for the Widow*, 256.

41. Bachelard, *Water and Dreams*, 3 (emphasis added to "material imagination").

42. Bachelard, *Water and Dreams*, 3.

43. Baldwin, "Sonny's Blues," 46.

44. Baldwin, "Sonny's Blues," 47.

45. Baldwin, "Sonny's Blues," 45 (emphasis added).

46. Shockley argues that we should understand the modifier *black* to describe aesthetic decisions motivated by the "subjectivity of the African American writer—that is, the subjectivity produced by the *experience* of identifying or being interpolated as 'black' in the U.S.—actively working out a poetics in the context of a racist society." See her discussion of "black aesthetics" in Shockley, *Renegade Poetics*, 9.

47. Marshall, *Praisesong for the Widow*, 37–38 (emphasis added).

48. Equiano, *Interesting Narrative*, 38–39 (emphasis added).

49. Gen. 1:2 (King James Version).

50. Keller, *Face of the Deep*, 3–24.

51. See Houston Baker's discussion of the trope of the mask in Baker, *Modernism and the Harlem Renaissance*.

52. Tocqueville, *Democracy in America*, 30.

53. Here, I riff on a line from Ed Roberson's poem "To See the Earth Before the End of the World."

54. Equiano, *Interesting Narrative*, 39 (emphasis added).

55. Equiano, *Interesting Narrative*, 41.

56. I specifically have in mind the ongoing theoretical debate in black studies between "Afropessimism" and "black optimism" but leave off the prefixes in favor of the more general terms of optimism and pessimism to call attention to the ways in which the tradition has always wrestled with the suffering and joy inhering in the lived experience of blackness.

57. Bachelard, *Water and Dreams*, 8.

58. Smallwood, *Saltwater Slavery*, 124.

CHAPTER 5. DEEP LIFE

1. "Walking," the essay that yielded a significant mantra of the US environmentalist movement—"In Wilderness is the preservation of the World"—opens this way.

2. Thoreau, "Walking."

3. Equiano, *Interesting Narrative*, 41 (emphasis added).

4. Wilson, *Gem of the Ocean*, 81.

5. Wilson, *Gem of the Ocean*, 85.

6. Wilson, *Gem of the Ocean*, 57.

7. Wilson, *Gem of the Ocean*, 82.

8. These words were spoken by Stephon Clark's grandmother in the wake of his death. Sacramento Bee, "Stephon Clarks' Grandmother Recounts the Night He Was Shot by

Sacramento Police," YouTube, March 25, 2018, 6:25, https://www.youtube.com/watch?v=C4A3JVonK6k&t=301s.

9. Wilson, *Gem of the Ocean*, 85.

10. Roberson, *Voices Cast Out*, 36.

11. Wilson, *Gem of the Ocean*, 53, 65.

12. *Oxford English Dictionary*, "so (adv., conj.)," accessed September 2023, https://doi.org/10.1093/OED/1889545529.

13. *Oxford English Dictionary*, "therefore (adv., n.)," accessed September 2024, https://doi.org/10.1093/OED/4109030633.

14. Sharpe, *In the Wake*, 17; McKay, *Harlem Shadows*, 53.

15. Wilderson, *Red, White, and Black*, 37, 38.

16. Thoreau, "Walking."

17. Sharpe, *In the Wake*, 17.

18. Roberson, *To See the Earth*, 12.

19. Thurman, *Meditations of the Heart*, 142.

20. Wilderson in Hartman, "Position of the Unthought," 187; Thoreau, "Walking."

21. *Oxford English Dictionary*, "so."

22. The plays are also known as the Pittsburgh cycle. Bryer and Hartig, *Conversations with August Wilson*, xvii–xxii. The plays in the cycle are:

1900s *Gem of the Ocean* (2003)
1910s *Joe Turner's Come and Gone* (1986)
1920s *Ma Rainey's Black Bottom* (1984)
1930s *The Piano Lesson* (1987)
1940s *Seven Guitars* (1995)
1950s *Fences* (1985)
1960s *Two Trains Running* (1990)
1970s *Jitney* (1982)
1980s *King Hedley II* (1999)
1990s *Radio Golf* (2005)

23. Wilson, "American Histories."

24. Rashad, "Riding the Waves of History."

25. Wilson, *Gem of the Ocean*, 11.

26. Bryer and Hartig, *Conversations with August Wilson*, 253, 210.

27. Bryer and Hartig, *Conversations with August Wilson*, 105–6.

28. Wilson, *Joe Turner's Come and Gone*, 32.

29. Wilson, "American Histories"; Bryer and Hartig, *Conversations with August Wilson*, 116, 255.

30. Bryer and Hartig, *Conversations with August Wilson*, 239.

31. Philip, *Zong!*, 189.

32. R. Wright, *Native Son*, 253.

33. Spillers, "Mama's Baby, Papa's Maybe," 68.

34. Hartman, *Lose Your Mother*.

35. Glissant, *Poetics of Relation*, 6 (emphasis added).

36. Wilderson, *Red, White, and Black*, 37, 38.

37. Moten, *Universal Machine*, 199.
38. Wilson, *Gem of the Ocean*, 60.
39. Wilson, *Gem of the Ocean*, 31.
40. Wilson, *Gem of the Ocean*, 38.
41. Bryer and Hartig, *Conversations with August Wilson*, 104–5.
42. Du Bois, *Souls of Black Folk*, 3.
43. Wilson, *Gem of the Ocean*, 33.
44. Ellison, *Invisible Man*, 456.
45. Bryer and Hartig, *Conversations with August Wilson*, 6 (emphasis added).
46. Wilson, *Gem of the Ocean*, 37 (emphasis added).
47. Bryer and Hartig, *Conversations with August Wilson*, 75 (emphasis added).
48. Bryer and Hartig, *Conversations with August Wilson*, 104–5 (emphasis added).
49. Wilson, *Gem of the Ocean*, 45.
50. Wilson, *Gem of the Ocean*, 21.
51. On the ocean being positioned outside the world, see Brayton, *Shakespeare's Ocean*, 23.
52. Wilderson, *Afropessimism*, 42.
53. Wilderson, *Afropessimism*, 103.
54. Bryer and Hartig, *Conversations with August Wilson*, 68.
55. Wilson, *Gem of the Ocean*, 70.
56. Howard, "To See the Earth."
57. Bryer and Hartig, *Conversations with August Wilson*, 106.
58. "A tanned skin is something more than respectable, and perhaps olive is a fitter color than white for a man—a denizen of the woods." Thoreau, "Walking."
59. Wynter, "*PROUD FLESH* Inter/views," 24.
60. Du Bois, *Souls of Black Folk*, 13.
61. Du Bois, *Souls of Black Folk*, 13.
62. Wilson, *Gem of the Ocean*, 69–70 (emphasis added).
63. Wilson, *Gem of the Ocean*, 21.
64. Wilson, *Gem of the Ocean*, 43.
65. Wilson, *Gem of the Ocean*, 66.
66. On the shipmate relationship, see Tinsley, "Black Atlantic, Queer Atlantic," 192, 198.
67. Wilson, *Gem of the Ocean*, 65.
68. Wilson, *Gem of the Ocean*, 52–53.
69. Wilson, *Gem of the Ocean*, 52; Rowell quoted in Andersen, *Planetary Pynchon*, 181.
70. On terracentrism, see Rediker, "History Below Deck," 563; on terrestrial bias, see Brayton, *Shakespeare's Ocean*, 15–42.
71. Wilson, *Gem of the Ocean*, 69.
72. Wilson, *Gem of the Ocean*, 65.
73. Wilson, *Gem of the Ocean*, 53.
74. Wilson, *Gem of the Ocean*, 67.

CHAPTER 6. DEEP VISION

1. *Oxford English Dictionary*, "witness (n.)," accessed June 2024, https://doi.org/10.1093/OED/2374883376.

2. Spillers, "Mama's Baby, Papa's Maybe," 67.

3. Brand, *Land to Light On*, 46.

4. Sharpe, *In the Wake*, 102–34.

5. Hartman, *Scenes of Subjection*, 3–14.

6. See Smiley N. Pool's photo from Hurricane Katrina in Diane Wanek, "History Through Pulitzer: 'Hurricane Katrina,'" Durham Museum, September 5, 2020, https://durhammuseum.org/history-through-pulitzer-hurricane-katrina. For the left-to-die boat, see "The Left-to-Die Boat," Forensic Architecture, accessed October 11, 2024, https://forensic-architecture.org/investigation/the-left-to-die-boat; Heller et al., *Forensic Oceanography*.

7. Fanon, *Black Skin, White Masks*, 90.

8. Equiano, *Interesting Narrative*, 40 (emphasis added).

9. Hartman, *Scenes of Subjection*, 19.

10. As progressive works of visual media, both *The Slave Ship* and *Amistad* arguably aspire to enlist witnesses of this sort. In particular, Turner's *The Slave Ship*, whose 1840 exhibition at the Royal Academy of Arts coincided with the World Anti-Slavery Convention in London, arguably asks future political action of its would-be witnesses. See Manderson, "Bodies in the Water." But aside from their spectacularity, *The Slave Ship* and *Amistad* further work to obscure the nature of black suffering by subscribing their would-be witnesses to either the narrow emancipatory ambitions of the British abolitionist movement, in the case of the former, or, in the case of the latter, celebrating the ultimate capacity of the law to bestow and protect freedom. In this way, both visualizations imagine black suffering as capable of being fully redressed by the state and the law, and so mystify the nature of a "social death" from which neither has proven capable of recalling us who are called black any more than that second woman's scream can be sounded out so clearly underwater.

11. Griffin, *If You Can't Be Free*.

12. Kelley, "Ordinary Allurements."

13. Glissant, *Poetics of Relation*, 190.

14. For a powerful and pioneering example of work at this particular intersection, see T. King, *Black Shoals*.

15. Matt. 6:23 (New International Version).

16. Levinas, *Totality and Infinity*, 199.

17. Sharpe, *In the Wake*, 19.

18. Moten, *Black and Blur*, 234.

19. Hampton, *Eyes on the Prize*.

20. Alexander, "'Can You Be Black?'"

21. Jacobs, *Incidents in the Life*, 173, 224.

22. Cone, *Cross and the Lynching Tree*.

23. Isa. 52:14 (King James Version).

24. Were I a theologian, I might also ask: Why does it matter that Jesus, to whom Emmett, in his martyrdom and as Mamie Till-Mobley's only son, is often likened, assumed this formless form on the cross?

25. "Nation Horrified."

26. The dimensions of the magazine's pages were 5 1/8 × 7 3/8 inches.

27. Philip, *Zong!*, 189.

28. The first six photographs included in the photo-essay before the concluding seventh close-up are, in the order in which they appear: the mother-son portrait of Mamie and Emmett; the cotton-gin fan; two of Emmett's cousins, Simeon and Maurice Wright; Emmett's great-uncle Rev. Moses Wright (mistakenly identified as Emmett's grandfather); and finally, a side-by-side pairing of a photograph of Mamie Till-Mobley's "first look" at her son in the casket and a straight-on photograph of Emmett's upper torso and face.

29. While there are multiple photographs of Emmett's face (which also appears in the fifth and sixth photographs in "Nation Horrified"), it is to this photograph in particular, which is the most pronounced in the article and among the most reproduced, that I refer when I speak of "the photograph of Emmett Till."

30. "Nation Horrified," 9.

31. Moten, *In the Break*, 192–211.

32. Fanon, *Black Skin, White Masks*, xii; Wilderson, *Red, White, and Black*, 11.

33. Huie, "Shocking Story," 207 (emphasis added).

34. Sharpe, *In the Wake*, 7 (emphasis added).

35. Foucault, "Of Other Spaces," 23.

36. Till-Mobley and Benso, *Death of Innocence*, 134.

37. See Whitaker, "Case Study in Southern Justice," 67 (emphasis added).

38. Myrdal, *American Dilemma*, 587 (emphasis added).

39. *Oxford English Dictionary*, "plane (n.^{3}, sense 1.a)," accessed July 2023, https://doi.org/10.1093/OED/1061391985.

40. Packard, *American Nightmare*, 165.

41. Faulkner, "On Fear," 32.

42. Mamie Till, in Nelson, *Murder of Emmett Till.*

43. J. W. Milam and Roy Bryant trial transcript, 1955, 206, recovered and transcribed by the FBI in May 2005, Davis Houck Papers, Emmett Till Archives, Florida State University Digital Library, https://repository.lib.fsu.edu/islandora/object/fsu%3A390158 (emphasis added).

44. Fanon, *Black Skin, White Masks*, 8.

45. Carter, *Anarchy of Black Religion*, 17.

46. Carter, *Anarchy of Black Religion*, 7.

47. Huie, "Shocking Story," 206.

48. Huie, "Shocking Story," 208.

49. Fanon, *Black Skin, White Masks*, 8.

50. Till-Mobley and Benson, *Death of Innocence*, 129.

51. On Emmett's foot, see Till-Mobley and Benson, *Death of Innocence*, 177.

52. Gordon, *Ghostly Matters*, xvi.

53. Along with indigenous genocide and dispossession.

54. Gordon, *Ghostly Matters*, xvi.

55. Moten, *In the Break*, 195.

56. Goldsby, "High and Low Tech of It," 255.

57. Goldsby, "High and Low Tech of It," 248.

58. Goldsby, "High and Low Tech of It," 254.

59. For a sample of international news coverage, limited to Europe, see the list below, excerpted from "The Murder of Emmett Till," American Experience, accessed October 10, 2022, https://www.pbs.org/wgbh/americanexperience/features/till-timeline.

September 2, 1955

- In Belgium, the newspaper *Le Drapeau Rouge* (the Red Flag) publishes a brief article titled: "Racism in the USA: A Young Black Is Lynched in Mississippi."

September 20, 1955

- The French daily newspaper *Le Monde* runs an article reporting that the American public is following the Till case "with passionate attention."

September 26, 1955

- In Belgium, two left-wing newspapers publish articles on the acquittal. *Le Peuple*, the daily Belgian Socialist newspaper, calls the acquittal "a judicial scandal in the United States." *Le Drapeau Rouge* (the Red Flag) publishes: "Killing a black person isn't a crime in the home of the Yankees: The white killers of young Emmett Till are acquitted!"
- In France, *L'Aurore* newspaper publishes: "The Scandalous Acquittal in Sumner" and the daily newspaper *Le Figaro* adds: "The Shame of the Sumner Jury."

September 27, 1955

- The French daily newspaper *Le Monde* runs an article: "The Sumner Trial Marks, Perhaps, an Opening of Consciousness."

September 28, 1955

- In Germany, the newspaper *Freies Volk* publishes: "The Life of a Negro Isn't Worth a Whistle."
- In France, the French Communist Party newspaper *L'Humanité* writes: "After the Mockery of Justice in Mississippi: Emotion in Paris."

October 22, 1955

- The American Jewish Committee in New York releases a report urging Congress to bolster Federal Civil Rights legislation in light of the Till case. Their report includes quotes from newspapers in six European countries expressing shock and outrage after the Till verdict.

60. David Halberstam quoted in Goldsby, "High and Low Tech of It," 258, 255.

61. "Nation Horrified."

62. Goldsby, "High and Low Tech of It," 251.

63. David Halberstam quoted in Goldsby, "High and Low Tech of It," 259.

64. "The Murder of Emmett Till," American Experience, accessed January 1, 2025, https://www.pbs.org/wgbh/americanexperience/features/till-timeline.

65. Charles Diggs Jr., quoted in Rubin, "Reflections on the Death," 48.

66. Robinson, *Black Marxism*.

67. Till-Mobley and Benson, *Death of Innocence*, xii.

68. On the allusion to *tehom* in Wright, see this book's prologue.

69. Sharpe, *In the Wake*.

70. Till-Mobley and Benson, *Death of Innocence*, 139.

71. I'm thankful to musicologist Braxton Shelley, who, fittingly, helped me hear the resonances of Mamie's *let*.

72. Hartman, *Lose Your Mother*, 167–68.

73. M. King, *Call to Conscience*, 223.

74. IBW 21st, "Martin Luther King's Last Speech: I've Been to the Mountaintop," YouTube, April 2, 2018, 3:27, https://www.youtube.com/watch?v=zgVrlx68v-o&ab_channel=IBW21st.

75. Wallace, *King's Vibrato*.

76. Num. 27:12–23; Heb. 10:37; James 5:7–12; Rev. 1:7–8 (KJV).

77. Mirzoeff, *Right to Look*, 26.

78. Till-Mobley and Benson, *Death of Innocence*, 139.

79. Till-Mobley and Benson, *Death of Innocence*, 129.

80. Till-Mobley and Benson, *Death of Innocence*, 131.

81. "The Trial of J. W. Milam and Roy Bryant," American Experience, accessed October 1, 2022, https://www.pbs.org/wgbh/americanexperience/features/emmett-trial-jw-milam-and-roy-bryant.

82. Whitaker, "Case Study in Southern Justice," 155; Mirzoeff, *Right to Look*.

83. Quoted in Metress, *Lynching of Emmett Till*, 65.

84. Till-Mobley and Benson, *Death of Innocence*, 159.

85. Milam and Bryant trial transcript, 49.

86. Milam and Bryant trial transcript, 44.

87. Milam and Bryant trial transcript, 34.

88. Mirzoeff, *Right to Look*, 1.

89. Mirzoeff, *Right to Look*, 2.

90. Rediker, *Slave Ship*, 234.

91. Rediker, *Slave Ship*, 235; Glissant, *Poetics of Relation*, 6.

92. Richard Rubin, "The Ghosts of Emmett Till," *New York Times Magazine*, July 31, 2005, https://www.nytimes.com/2005/07/31/magazine/the-ghosts-of-emmett-till.html; Milam and Bryant trial transcript, 298.

93. Milam and Bryant trial transcript, 299–300.

94. Foucault, *Birth of the Clinic*, 114.

95. Milam and Bryant trial transcript, 297–98.

96. Milam and Bryant trial transcript, 289–90.

97. Till-Bradley, "I Want You to Know," 1:144.

98. Baucom, *Specters of the Atlantic*, 180.

99. Wilderson, *Red, White, and Black*, 11.

100. Baucom, *Specters of the Atlantic*, 207.

101. Here, I am riffing on Fred Moten's riff on Édouard Glissant's phrase, which Moten takes as the title for his book trilogy, *consent not to be a single being*. Glissant in Diawara, "One World in Relation," 5.

102. Huie, "Shocking Story," 207.

103. Till-Mobley and Benson, *Death of Innocence*, 131.

104. Till-Mobley and Benson, *Death of Innocence*, 132.

105. Till-Mobley and Benson, *Death of Innocence*, 132.

106. Till-Mobley and Benson, *Death of Innocence*, 134.

107. Sharpe, *In the Wake*, 17.

108. Till-Mobley and Benson, *Death of Innocence*, 135 (emphasis original).

109. *Oxford English Dictionary*, "Immaculate Conception (n., sense 1–2)," accessed July 2023, https://doi.org/10.1093/OED/1026496365.

110. Lyric from the well-known hymn "Jesus Paid It All." In context: "Sin had left a crimson stain, he washed it white as snow." Elvina M. Hall and John T. Grape, first published as "Fullness in Christ," in Theodore E. Perkins, *Sabbath Carols: A New Collection of Music and Hymns* (New York: Brown and Perkins, 1868), 93.

111. Cone, *God of the Oppressed*; Adkins-Jones, *Immaculate Misconceptions*.

112. Douglas, *Black Christ*.

113. Phil. 2:7 (New Revised Standard Version).

114. Wilderson, *Afropessimism*, 103.

115. Till-Bradley, "I Want You to Know," 136 (emphasis added).

116. Hurston, *Sanctified Church*, 88.

117. Crawley, *Blackpentecostal Breath*, 28.

118. Freud, *Civilization and Its Discontents*, 64.

119. See chapter 1, "Deep Humanities," where I elaborate this argument more fully.

120. Tinsley, "Black Atlantic, Queer Atlantic," 199.

121. Matory, *Black Atlantic Religion*, 238. In the original Yoruba context, Iemanjá is the goddess of a freshwater river, and is interestingly recast as the goddess of the sea in the New World. The New World veneration of Iemanjá, then, may be reflective of the cosmological labor of incorporating the deep ocean into the Yoruba cosmology. See Matory, *Black Atlantic Religion*, 22. Relative to Iemanjá, there are few studies on the New World veneration of Olokun. For a comparative study of Olokun in Africa and Cuba, see Marrero, "Olokun en África y en Cuba." For more information on Olokun in traditional Yoroba, see Elugbaju and Raheem, *Myth, Ritual, and Visible Expressions of Ọbàtálá and Olókun,* 103–216.

122. M. King, *Call to Conscience*, 212.

123. Crawley, *Blackpentecostal Breath*, 106.

124. Till-Mobley and Benson, *Death of Innocence*, 141.

125. Till-Mobley and Benson, *Death of Innocence*, 141–42.

126. Till-Mobley and Benson, *Death of Innocence*, 132.

127. Sliwinski, *Human Rights in Camera*, 4.

128. Sliwinski, *Human Rights in Camera*, 5.

129. Sliwinski, *Human Rights in Camera*, 9.

130. Sliwinski, *Human Rights in Camera*, 5; Bradley, *Anteaesthetics*. See Wynter, "The Ceremony Must Be Found."

131. Till-Mobley and Benson, *Death of Innocence*, 139.

132. Till-Mobley and Benson, *Death of Innocence*, 195 (emphasis added).

133. Wilson, *Gem of the Ocean*, 42.

134. Milam and Bryant trial transcript, 186.

135. Spenser, *Epithalamion*, https://www.poetryfoundation.org/poems/45191/epithalamion-56d22497d00d4; Till-Mobley and Benson, *Death of Innocence*, 135; Campion, "There Is a Garden in Her Face," https://www.poetryfoundation.org/poems/43871/there-is-a-garden-in-her-face.

136. Till-Bradley, "I Want You to Know," 137.

137. Vickers, "'Blazon of Sweet Beauty's Best.'"
138. Levinas, *Totality and Infinity*, 203.
139. In Nelson, *Murder of Emmett Till.*
140. Till-Mobley and Benson, *Death of Innocence*, 134.
141. Till-Mobley and Benson, *Death of Innocence*, 134–35 (emphasis original).
142. Emphasis added to sonnet title.
143. Levinas, *Totality and Infinity*, 199.
144. Jones, *Known World*, 192–93.
145. Marshall, *Praisesong for the Widow*, 190–91 (emphasis added).
146. Ferreira da Silva, "On Difference Without Separability."
147. Barthes, *Camera Lucida*, 80–81.
148. Till-Mobley and Benson, *Death of Innocence*, 136 (emphasis added).
149. Till-Mobley and Benson, *Death of Innocence*, 142.
150. Till-Mobley and Benson, *Death of Innocence*, 134.
151. "Home," Jason deCaires Taylor (website), accessed September 15, 2023, https://underwatersculpture.com.
152. DeLoughrey, "Submarine Futures of the Anthropocene," 41.
153. Quoted in DeLoughrey, "Submarine Futures of the Anthropocene," 41.

EPILOGUE. ANKLE DEEP

1. Smallwood, *Saltwater Slavery*, 124.
2. Here I allude to a passage from Édouard Glissant's "The Open Boat" that I have referenced throughout this book: "The banks of the river have vanished on both sides of the boat. What kind of river, then, has no middle? Is nothing there but straight ahead? Is this boat sailing into eternity toward the edges of a nonworld that no ancestor will haunt?" See Glissant, *Poetics of Relation*, 7.
3. A. Walker, *Color Purple*, 195.
4. Gen. 16:13 (New King James Version).
5. For this sense of significance in finding ceremony, I am indebted to Sylvia Wynter's essay "The Ceremony Must Be Found: After Humanism."
6. A. Walker, *In Search of Our Mothers' Gardens*, 93–116.
7. Ezek. 40:2–4 (Complete Jewish Bible).
8. Ezek. 47:1–9 (CJB).

Bibliography

Adkins-Jones, Amey Victoria. *Immaculate Misconceptions: A Black Mariology*. Oxford, UK: Oxford University Press, 2025.

Agamben, Giorgio. *Homo Sacer: Sovereign Power and Bare Life*. Stanford, CA: Stanford University Press, 1998.

Alexander, Elizabeth. "'Can You Be Black and Look at This?': Reading the Rodney King Video(s)." *Public Culture* 7, no. 1 (1994): 77–94. https://doi.org/10.1215/08992363-7-1-77.

Althusser, Louis. "Ideology and Ideological State Apparatuses (Notes Towards an Investigation)." In *Lenin and Philosophy, and Other Essays*, 121–76. Translated by Ben Brewster. New York: Monthly Review, 1971.

Andersen, Tore Rye. *Planetary Pynchon: History, Modernity, and the Anthropocene*. Cambridge: Cambridge University Press, 2023.

Bachelard, Gaston. *Water and Dreams: An Essay on the Imagination of Matter*. Translated by Edith R. Farrell. Dallas: Pegasus Foundation, 1999.

Baker, Houston A., Jr. *Modernism and the Harlem Renaissance*. Chicago: University of Chicago Press, 1987.

Baldwin, James. "Sonny's Blues." In *The Jazz Fiction Anthology*, edited by Sascha Feinstein and David Rife, 17–48. Bloomington: Indiana University Press, 2009.

Barthes, Roland. *Camera Lucida: Reflections on Photography*. Translated by Richard Howard. New York: Hill and Wang, 1982.

Baucom, Ian. *Specters of the Atlantic: Finance Capital, Slavery, and the Philosophy of History*. Durham, NC: Duke University Press, 2005.

Benítez-Rojo, Antonio. *The Repeating Island: The Caribbean and the Postmodern Perspective*. Durham, NC: Duke University Press, 1997.

Benjamin, Walter. "On the Concept of History." Translated by Dennis Redmond. 1940. Marxists Internet Archive. Accessed December 1, 2024. https://www.marxists.org/reference/archive/benjamin/1940/history.htm.

Bennett, Joshua. *Being Property Once Myself: Blackness and the End of Man*. Cambridge, MA: Harvard University Press, 2020.

Bibb, Henry. *The Life and Adventures of Henry Bibb: An American Slave*. Madison: University of Wisconsin Press, 2001. Originally published in 1849.

Blum, Hester. "The Prospect of Oceanic Studies." *PMLA* 125, no. 3 (2010): 670–77. https://www.jstor.org/stable/25704464.

Blum, Hester. "Terraqueous Planet." In *The Planetary Turn: Relationality and Geoaesthetics in the Twenty-First Century*, edited by Amy J. Elias and Christian Mararu, 25–36. Evanston, IL: Northwestern University Press, 2015.

Bradley, Rizvana. *Anteaesthetics: Black Aesthesis and the Critique of Form*. Stanford, CA: Stanford University Press, 2023.

Brand, Dionne. *Land to Light On*. Toronto, ON: McClelland and Stewart, 1997.

Brand, Dionne. *A Map to the Door of No Return: Notes to Belonging*. Toronto, ON: Vintage Canada, 2002.

Brathwaite, Edward Kamau. "Caribbean Man in Space and Time." *Small Axe* 25, no. 3 (2021): 90–104. https://doi.org/10.1215/07990537-9583432.

Brayton, Daniel. *Shakespeare's Ocean: An Ecocritical Exploration*. Charlottesville: University of Virginia Press, 2012.

Brown, Geoff. *Otis Redding: Try a Little Tenderness*. Edinburgh: Canongate, 2002.

Bryer, Jackson R., and Mary C. Hartig, eds. *Conversations with August Wilson*. Jackson: University Press of Mississippi, 2006.

Buell, Lawrence. *The Environmental Imagination: Thoreau, Nature Writing, and the Formation of American Culture*. Cambridge, MA: Harvard University Press, 1995.

Buell, Lawrence. Foreword to *Prismatic Ecology: Ecotheory Beyond Green*, edited by Jeffrey Jerome Cohen, ix–xii. Minneapolis: University of Minnesota Press, 2014.

Buell, Lawrence. *The Future of Environmental Criticism: Environmental Crisis and Literary Imagination*. New York: John Wiley and Sons, 2009.

Burch, Noël, and Allan Sekula, dirs. *The Forgotten Space*. Vienna: Wildart Film, 2010.

Burnard, Trevor. "Goodbye, Equiano, the African." *Historically Speaking* 7, no. 3 (2006): 10–11. https://doi.org/10.1353/hsp.2006.0076.

Carretta, Vincent. *Equiano, the African: Biography of a Self-Made Man*. Athens: University of Georgia Press, 2005.

Carter, J. Kameron. *The Anarchy of Black Religion: A Mystic Song*. Durham, NC: Duke University Press, 2023.

Cohen, Jeffrey Jerome. "Ecology's Rainbow." Introduction to *Prismatic Ecology: Ecotheory Beyond Green*, edited by Jeffrey Jerome Cohen, xv–xxxvi. Minneapolis: University of Minnesota Press, 2014.

Cone, James H. *The Cross and the Lynching Tree*. Maryknoll, NY: Orbis Books, 2011.

Cone, James H. *God of the Oppressed*. New York: HarperCollins, 1975.

Conniff, Richard, and Geoffrey Giller. "Iconic. Almost by Accident." Nov.–Dec. 2024. https://www.yalealumnimagazine.com/articles/3977-march-of-progress.

Coogler, Ryan, dir. *Black Panther*. Burbank, CA: Marvel Studios, 2018. DVD.

Crawley, Ashon T. *Blackpentecostal Breath: The Aesthetics of Possibility*. New York: Fordham University Press, 2017.

Crawley, Ashon. "Otherwise Possibility." *Southern Cultures* 28, no. 2 (2022): 18–29. https://dx.doi.org/10.1353/scu.2022.0013.

Crenshaw, Kimberlé. "Mapping the Margins: Intersectionality, Identity Politics, and Violence Against Women of Color." *Stanford Law Review* 43, no. 6 (1991): 1241–99. https://www.jstor.org/stable/1229039.

Crosby, Alfred W. *The Columbian Exchange: Biological and Cultural Consequences of 1492*. Westport, CT: Greenwood, 2003.

Crutzen, Paul J. "Geology of Mankind." *Nature* 415, no. 6867 (2002): 23. https://www.nature.com/articles/415023a.

Curseen, Allison. *Minor Moves: Unruly Readings and Black Girl Performance in Antebellum Narratives*. Chapel Hill: University of North Carolina Press, forthcoming.

Dash, Julie, dir. *Daughters of the Dust*. New York: Kino International, 1991.

Dash, Julie. *Daughters of the Dust: The Making of an African American Woman's Film*. New York: New Press, 1992.

Davidson, Cathy N. "Olaudah Equiano, Written by Himself." *NOVEL: A Forum on Fiction* 40, no. 1–2 (2006): 18–51. http://www.jstor.org/stable/40267683.

Dawson, Kevin. *Undercurrents of Power: Aquatic Culture in the African Diaspora*. Philadelphia: University of Pennsylvania Press, 2018.

DeLoughrey, Elizabeth. "Submarine Futures of the Anthropocene." *Comparative Literature* 69, no. 1 (2017): 32–44. https://www.jstor.org/stable/44211319.

Diawara, Manthia. "One World in Relation: Édouard Glissant in Conversation with Manthia Diawara." *Nka: Journal of Contemporary African Art* 2011, no. 28 (Spring 2011): 4–19. https://doi.org/10.1215/10757163-1266639.

Domingues da Silva, Daniel B., and Philip Misevich. "Atlantic Slavery and the Slave Trade: History and Historiography." In *Oxford Research Encyclopedia of African History*. Oxford University Press. Article published November 20, 2018. https://doi.org/10.1093/acrefore/9780190277734.013.371.

Douglas, Kelly Brown. *The Black Christ*. 25th anniversary ed. Maryknoll, NY: Orbis Books, 2021.

Douglas, Kelly Brown. *Stand Your Ground: Black Bodies and the Justice of God*. Maryknoll, NY: Orbis Books, 2015.

Douglass, Frederick. *The Heroic Slave*. In *Frederick Douglass: Selected Speeches and Writings*, edited by Philip S. Foner. Chicago: Lawrence Hill Books, 1999. Originally published in 1852.

Douglass, Frederick. *Narrative of the Life of Frederick Douglass, an American Slave, Written by Himself*. 2nd ed. Edited by William L. Andrews and William S. McFeely. New York: W. W. Norton, 2016. Originally published in 1845.

Douglass, Frederick. *Self-Made Men: Address Before the Students of the Indian Industrial School, Carlisle, Pa.* Carlisle, PA: Indian Print, 1893. https://carlisleindian.dickinson.edu/index.php/publications/frederick-douglass-speech-self-made-men-1893.

Du Bois, W. E. B. *The Souls of Black Folk*. Edited by Brent Hayes Edwards. New York: Oxford University Press, 2009. Originally published in 1903.

Dungy, Camille T., ed. *Black Nature: Four Centuries of African American Nature Poetry*. Athens: University of Georgia Press, 2009.

Ellison, Ralph. *Invisible Man*. New York: Vintage International, 1995. Originally published in 1952.

Equiano, Olaudah. *The Interesting Narrative of the Life of Olaudah Equiano, or Gustavus Vassa, the African, Written by Himself*. Edited by Werner Sollors. New York: W. W. Norton, 2001. Originally published in 1789.

Ernest, John. Introduction to *The Oxford Handbook of the African American Slave Narrative*, edited by John Ernest, 2–18. New York: Oxford University Press, 2014.

Everett, Percival. *James*. New York: Doubleday, 2024.

Fanon, Frantz. *Black Skin, White Masks*. Translated by Richard Philcox. New York: Grove, 2008. Originally published in 1952.

Faulkner, William. "On Fear: The South in Labor." *Harper's Magazine*, June 1956, 29–34.

Ferreira da Silva, Denise. "On Difference Without Separability." In *Catalogo: 32nd bienal de São Paulo—incerteza viva*, edited by Jochen Volz and Júlia Rebouças, 57–65. São Paulo: Fundação Bienal de São Paulo, 2016. Exhibition catalog.

Fields, Karen E., and Barbara J. Fields. *Racecraft: The Soul of Inequality in American Life*. New York: Verso, 2012.

Foucault, Michel. *Birth of the Clinic: An Archaeology of Medical Perception*. Translated by A. M. Sheridan. New York: Vintage Books, 1994.

Foucault, Michel. "Of Other Spaces." Translated by Jay Miskowiec. *Diacritics* 16, no. 1 (1986): 22–27. https://www.jstor.org/stable/464648.

Freud, Sigmund. *Civilization and Its Discontents*. In *The Standard Edition of the Complete Psychological Works of Sigmund Freud*, vol. 21, *1927–1931: The Future of an Illusion, Civilization and Its Discontents*, edited and translated by James Strachey. London: Hogarth Press and the Institute of Psycho-Analysis, 1961.

Gilroy, Paul. *The Black Atlantic: Modernity and Double Consciousness*. Cambridge, MA: Harvard University Press, 1993.

Glissant, Édouard. *Poetics of Relation*. Translated by Betsy Wing. Ann Arbor: University of Michigan Press, 1997.

Goldsby, Jacqueline. "The High and Low Tech of It: The Meaning of Lynching and the Death of Emmett Till." *Yale Journal of Criticism* 9, no. 2 (1996): 245–82. https://doi.org/10.1353/yale.1996.0016.

Gordon, Avery F. *Ghostly Matters: Haunting and the Sociological Imagination*. Minneapolis: University of Minnesota Press, 2008.

Griffin, Farah Jasmine. *If You Can't Be Free, Be a Mystery: In Search of Billie Holiday*. New York: Ballantine Books, 2001.

Griffin, Farah Jasmine. *"Who Set You Flowin'?": The African-American Migration Narrative*. New York: Oxford University Press, 1995.

Gumbs, Alexis Pauline. *Undrowned: Black Feminist Lessons from Marine Mammals*. Chico, CA: AK Press, 2020.

Guyot, Arnold. *The Earth and Man: Lectures on Comparative Physical Geography, in Its Relation to the History of Mankind*. Translated by C. C. Felton. Boston: Gould and Lincoln, 1858.

Hampton, Henry, prod. *Eyes on the Prize: America's Civil Rights Movement.* Part 1. Alexandria, VA: PBS Video, 2006. DVD. First aired 1987.

Harney, Stefano, and Fred Moten. "Michael Brown." *boundary 2* 42, no. 4 (2015): 81–87. https://doi.org/10.1215/01903659-3156141.

Hartman, Saidiya. *Lose Your Mother: A Journey Along the Atlantic Slave Route.* New York: Farrar, Straus and Giroux, 2008.

Hartman, Saidiya. "The Position of the Unthought." Interview by Frank B. Wilderson III. *Qui Parle* 13, no. 2 (2003): 183–201. https://doi.org/10.1215/quiparle.13.2.183.

Hartman, Saidiya. *Scenes of Subjection: Terror, Slavery, and Self-Making in Nineteenth-Century America.* New York: Oxford University Press, 1997.

Hartman, Saidiya. "Venus in Two Acts." *Small Axe* 12, no. 2 (2008): 1–14. https://doi.org/10.1215/-12-2-1.

Heise, Ursula K. *Sense of Place and Sense of Planet: The Environmental Imagination of the Global.* New York: Oxford University Press, 2008.

Heller, Charles, Lorenzo Pezzani, and Situ Studio. *Forensic Oceanography: Report on the "Left-to-Die Boat."* London: Centre for Research Architecture, Goldsmiths, University of London, 2012. https://www.fidh.org/IMG/pdf/fo-report.pdf.

Herskovits, Melville J. *The Myth of the Negro Past.* New York: Harper, 1941.

Hobbes, Thomas. *Leviathan; or, The Matter, Form and Power of a Commonwealth, Ecclesiastical and Civil.* London: George Routledge and Sons, 1886.

Howard, Jonathan. "To See the Earth Before the End of the Antiblack World." *Souls: A Critical Journal of Black Politics, Culture, and Society* 22, no. 2–4 (2020): 292–314. https://doi.org/10.1080/10999949.2021.2003622.

Howell, F. Clark. *Early Man.* New York: Time-Life Books, 1968.

Huie, William Bradford. "The Shocking Story of Approved Killing in Mississippi." In Metress, *Lynching of Emmett Till*, 200–208.

Hurston, Zora Neale. *Barracoon: The Story of the Last "Black Cargo."* New York: HarperCollins, 2018.

Hurston, Zora Neale. "How It Feels to Be Colored Me." In *You Don't Know Us Negroes and Other Essays*, edited by Henry Louis Gates Jr. and Genevieve West, 174–78. New York: Amistad HarperCollins, 2022.

Hurston, Zora Neale. *The Sanctified Church.* Berkeley, CA: Marlowe, 1981.

Jackson, Zakiyyah Iman. *Becoming Human: Matter and Meaning in an Antiblack World.* New York: New York University Press, 2020.

Jacobs, Harriet. *Incidents in the Life of a Slave Girl, Written by Herself.* Edited by L. Maria Child. Boston, 1861.

Jefferson, Thomas. *Notes on the State of Virginia.* Richmond, VA: J. W. Randolph, 1853.

Jones, Edward P. *The Known World.* New York: Amistad, 2003.

Kaplan, Sara Clarke. "Souls at the Crossroads, Africans on the Water: The Politics of Diasporic Melancholia." *Callaloo* 30, no. 2 (2007): 511–26. https://www.jstor.org/stable/30129761.

Keller, Catherine. *Face of the Deep: A Theology of Becoming.* New York: Routledge, 2003.

Kelley, Elleza. "Ordinary Allurements: Christina Sharpe's Reading Lessons." *Yale Review* 111, no. 2 (2023). https://yalereview.org/article/elleza-kelley-ordinary-allurements.

King, Martin Luther, Jr. *A Call to Conscience: The Landmark Speeches of Dr. Martin Luther King, Jr.* Edited by Clayborne Carson and Kris Shepard. New York: Intellectual Properties Management in association with Warner Books, 2001.

King, Tiffany Lethabo. *The Black Shoals: Offshore Formations of Black and Native Studies.* Durham, NC: Duke University Press, 2019.

Lee, Jennifer, and Frank D. Bean. "America's Changing Color Lines: Immigration, Race/Ethnicity, and Multiracial Identification." *Annual Review of Sociology* 30 (2004): 221–42. http://www.jstor.org/stable/29737692.

Leopold, Aldo. *A Sand County Almanac, and Sketches Here and There.* New York: Oxford University Press, 1989.

Levinas, Emmanuel. *Totality and Infinity: An Essay on Exteriority.* Translated by Alphonso Lingis. Dordrecht: Kluwer, 1979.

Lewis, Simon L., and Mark A. Maslin. *The Human Planet: How We Created the Anthropocene.* New Haven, CT: Yale University Press, 2018.

Manderson, Desmond. "Bodies in the Water: On Reading Images More Sensibly." *Law and Literature* 27, no. 2 (2015): 279–93. https://www.jstor.org/stable/26770753.

Marrero, Roberto Garcés. "Olokun en África y en Cuba: Cosmología Afrocubana y Tradición Oral." *Polish Journal of the Arts and Culture* (New Series) 15 (2022): 85–101.

Marshall, Paule. *Praisesong for the Widow.* New York: Putnam's, 1983.

Matory, J. Lorand. *Black Atlantic Religion: Tradition, Transnationalism, and Matriarchy in the Afro-Brazilian Candomblé.* Princeton, NJ: Princeton University Press, 2005.

McKay, Claude. *Harlem Shadows: The Poems of Claude McKay.* New York: Harcourt, Brace, 1922.

McKittrick, Katherine. *Demonic Grounds: Black Women and the Cartographies of Struggle.* Minneapolis: University of Minnesota Press, 2006.

Melville, Herman. *Moby-Dick; or, The Whale.* 3rd ed. Edited by Hershel Parker. New York: W. W. Norton, 2017. Originally published in 1851.

Mentz, Steve. *At the Bottom of Shakespeare's Ocean.* London: Continuum, 2009.

Mentz, Steve. "Blue Humanities." In *Posthuman Glossary*, edited by Rosi Braidotti and Maria Hlavajova, 69–72. London: Bloomsbury Academic, 2018.

Mentz, Steve. *An Introduction to the Blue Humanities.* New York: Taylor and Francis, 2023.

Metress, Christopher, ed. *The Lynching of Emmett Till: A Documentary Narrative.* Charlottesville: University of Virginia Press, 2002.

Mills, Charles W. *The Racial Contract.* Ithaca, NY: Cornell University Press, 1997.

Mintz, Sidney W., and Richard Price. *The Birth of African-American Culture: An Anthropological Perspective.* Boston: Beacon, 1992.

Mirzoeff, Nicholas. *The Right to Look: A Counterhistory of Visuality.* Durham, NC: Duke University Press, 2011.

Morrison, Toni. *Sula.* New York: Vintage, 2004.

Moten, Fred. *Black and Blur.* Durham, NC: Duke University Press, 2017.

Moten, Fred. *In the Break: The Aesthetics of the Black Radical Tradition.* Minneapolis: University of Minnesota Press, 2003.

Moten, Fred. "Notes on Passage (the New International of Sovereign Feelings)." *Palimpsest: A Journal on Women, Gender, and the Black International* 3, no. 1 (2014): 51–74. https://doi.org/10.1353/pal.2014.0010.

Moten, Fred. *The Universal Machine*. Durham, NC: Duke University Press, 2018.
Myrdal, Gunnar. *An American Dilemma: The Negro Problem and Modern Democracy*, vol. 2. New York: Routledge, 1996.
"Nation Horrified by Murder of Kidnaped Chicago Youth." *Jet*, September 15, 1955, 6–9. https://books.google.com/books?id=57EDAAAAMBAJ&printsec=frontcover&source=gbs_ge_summary_r&cad=0#v=onepage&q&f=false.
Nelson, Stanley, dir. *The Murder of Emmett Till*. Boston: WGBH Educational Foundation, 2003.
Olney, James. "'I Was Born': Slave Narratives, Their Status as Autobiography and as Literature." *Callaloo*, no. 20 (Winter 1984): 46–73. https://doi.org/10.2307/2930678.
Outka, Paul. *Race and Nature from Transcendentalism to the Harlem Renaissance*. New York: Palgrave Macmillan, 2008.
Packard, Jerrold M. *American Nightmare: The History of Jim Crow*. New York: St. Martin's Griffin, 2002.
Patterson, Orlando. *Slavery and Social Death: A Comparative Study*. Cambridge, MA: Harvard University Press, 1982.
Philip, M. NourbeSe. *Zong!* Middletown, CT: Wesleyan University Press, 2008.
Powell, Timothy. "Summoning the Ancestors: The Flying Africans' Story and Its Enduring Legacy." In *African American Life in the Georgia Lowcountry: The Atlantic World and the Gullah Geechee*, edited by Philip Morgan, 253–82. Athens: University of Georgia Press, 2010.
Professional Association of Diving Instructors (PADI). *Open Water Diver Manual*. Rancho Santa Margarita, CA: PADI, 2010.
Raheem, Oluwafunminiyi Wasiu, and Ayowole S. Elugbaju. *Myth, Ritual, and Visible Expressions of Ọbàtálá and Olókun*. Lanham, MD: Lexington Books, 2025.
Rashad, Phylicia. "Riding the Waves of History: 'The Gem of the Ocean.'" *American Theatre*, October 1, 2007. https://www.americantheatre.org/2007/10/01/riding-the-waves-of-history-the-gem-of-the-ocean.
Rediker, Marcus. *Freedom Ship: The Uncharted History of Escaping Slavery by Sea*. New York: Viking, 2025.
Rediker, Marcus. "History Below Deck." Interview by Jeffrey J. Williams. *symploke* 28, no. 1–2 (2020): 547–66. https://doi.org/10.5250/symploke.28.1-2.0547.
Rediker, Marcus. "Hydrarchy and Terracentrism." In *Hydrarchy*, edited by Anna Colin and Mia Jankowicz, 10–18. Cairo: Contemporary Image Collective, 2012.
Rediker, Marcus. "A Motley Crew for Our Times? Multiracial Mobs, History from Below and the Memory of Struggle." Interview. *Radical Philosophy*, no. 207 (Spring 2020): 93–100. https://www.radicalphilosophy.com/interview/a-motley-crew-for-our-times.
Rediker, Marcus. *The Slave Ship: A Human History*. New York: Viking, 2007.
Roberson, Ed. "The Structure, Then the Music." Interview by Randall Horton. *Callaloo* 33, no. 3 (2010): 762–69. https://www.jstor.org/stable/40962667.
Roberson, Ed. *To See the Earth Before the End of the World*. Middletown, CT: Wesleyan University Press, 2017.
Roberson, Ed. *Voices Cast Out to Talk Us In*. Iowa City: University of Iowa Press, 1995.
Roberson, Ed. "We Must Be Careful." In Dungy, *Black Nature*, 3–5.
Robinson, Cedric J. *Black Marxism: The Making of the Black Radical Tradition*. Chapel Hill: University of North Carolina Press, 2000.

Rousseau, Jean-Jacques. *An Inquiry into the Nature of the Social Contract, or Principles of Political Right. Translated from the French*. Manchester, UK: A. Heywood, 1840. Originally published in 1762.

Rubin, Anne Sarah. "Reflections on the Death of Emmett Till." *Southern Cultures* 2, no. 1 (1995): 45–66. https://www.jstor.org/stable/26235389.

Ruffin, Kimberly N. *Black on Earth: African American Ecoliterary Traditions*. Athens: University of Georgia Press, 2010.

Sartre, Jean-Paul. *Being and Nothingness: An Essay in Phenomenological Ontology*. New York: Citadel Press, 2001.

Sensbach, Jon. "Beyond Equiano." *Historically Speaking* 7, no. 3 (2006): 12–13. https://doi.org/10.1353/hsp.2006.0079.

Sensbach, Jon. "Beyond Equiano." In *Recent Themes in the History of Africa and the Atlantic World: Historians in Conversation*, edited by Donald A. Yerxa, 106–10. Columbia: University of South Carolina Press, 2008.

Sexton, Jared. "The Social Life of Social Death: On Afro-Pessimism and Black Optimism." *InTensions*, no. 5 (2011): 1–47. https://doi.org/10.25071/1913-5874/37359.

Sharpe, Christina. *In the Wake: On Blackness and Being*. Durham, NC: Duke University Press, 2016.

Shockley, Evie. *Renegade Poetics: Black Aesthetics and Formal Innovation in African American Poetry*. Iowa City: University of Iowa Press, 2011.

Sliwinski, Sharon. *Human Rights in Camera*. Chicago: University of Chicago Press, 2011.

Smallwood, Stephanie E. *Saltwater Slavery: A Middle Passage from Africa to American Diaspora*. Cambridge, MA: Harvard University Press, 2007.

Solomon, Rivers. *The Deep*. New York: Saga Press, 2019.

Spillers, Hortense J. "Mama's Baby, Papa's Maybe: An American Grammar Book." *Diacritics* 17, no. 2 (1987): 64–81. https://www.jstor.org/stable/464747.

Stepto, Robert B. *From Behind the Veil: A Study of Afro-American Narrative*. 2nd ed. Urbana: University of Illinois Press, 1991.

Thoreau, Henry David. "Walking." *Atlantic*, June 1862. https://www.theatlantic.com/magazine/archive/1862/06/walking/304674.

Thurman, Howard. *Meditations of the Heart*. Boston: Beacon, 2023.

Till-Bradley, Mamie. "I Want You to Know What They Did to My Boy." In *Rhetoric, Religion, and the Civil Rights Movement, 1954–1965*, edited by Davis W. Houck and David E. Dixon, 1:131–44. Waco, TX: Baylor University Press, 2006.

Till-Mobley, Mamie, and Christopher Benson. *Death of Innocence: The Story of the Hate Crime That Changed America*. New York: Random House, 2003.

Tinsley, Omise'eke Natasha. "Black Atlantic, Queer Atlantic: Queer Imaginings of the Middle Passage." *GLQ: A Journal of Lesbian and Gay Studies* 14, no. 2–3 (2008): 191–215. https://doi.org/10.1215/10642684-2007-030.

Tocqueville, Alexis de. *Democracy in America*, vol. 1. Edited by Francis Bowen. Translated by Henry Reeve. New York: Century, 1898. Originally published in 1835.

Toepfer, Georg. "'Organization': Its Conceptual History and Its Relationship to Other Fundamental Biological Concepts." In *Organization in Biology*, edited by Matteo Mossio, 23–40. Cham: Springer, 2024.

Van Sertima, Ivan. *They Came Before Columbus: The African Presence in Ancient America*. New York: Random House, 1976.

Vickers, Nancy J. "'The Blazon of Sweet Beauty's Best': Shakespeare's Lucrece." In *Shakespeare and the Question of Theory*, edited by Geoffrey H. Hartoman and Patricia Parker, 95–115. London: Routledge, 1985.

Walcott, Derek. *Selected Poems*. Edited by Edward Baugh. New York: Farrar, Straus and Giroux, 2007.

Walker, Alice. *The Color Purple*. 1982. Reprint, New York: Penguin, 2019.

Walker, Alice. *In Search of Our Mothers' Gardens: Womanist Prose*. San Diego: Harcourt Brace Jovanovich, 1983.

Walker, Alice. *Sent by Earth: A Message from the Grandmother Spirit*. New York: Seven Stories, 2001.

Walker, Timothy D. "Introduction." In *Sailing to Freedom: Maritime Dimensions of the Underground Railroad*, edited by Timothy D. Walker, 1–13. Amherst: University of Massachusetts Press, 2021.

Walker, Timothy D. "Sailing to Freedom: Maritime Dimensions of the Underground Railroad." In *Sailing to Freedom: Maritime Dimensions of the Underground Railroad*, edited by Timothy D. Walker, 14–35. Amherst: University of Massachusetts Press, 2021.

Wallace, Maurice O. *King's Vibrato: Modernism, Blackness, and the Sonic Life of Martin Luther King Jr*. Durham, NC: Duke University Press, 2022.

Wardi, Anissa J. *Water and African American Memory: An Ecocritical Perspective*. Gainesville: University Press of Florida, 2016.

Washington, Booker T. *Up from Slavery: An Autobiography*. Garden City, NY: Doubleday, 1901.

Whitaker, Hugh Stephen. "A Case Study in Southern Justice: The Emmett Till Case." Master's thesis, Florida State University, 1963. http://purl.fcla.edu/fsu/etd-05272004-140932.

Wilderson, Frank B., III. *Afropessimism*. New York: Liveright, 2020.

Wilderson, Frank B., III. *Red, White, and Black: Cinema and the Structure of US Antagonisms*. Durham, NC: Duke University Press, 2010.

Wilson, August. "American Histories: Chasing Dreams and Nightmares; Sailing the Stream of Black Culture." *New York Times*, April 23, 2000. https://www.nytimes.com/2000/04/23/arts/american-histories-chasing-dreams-and-nightmares-sailing-the-stream-of.html.

Wilson, August. *Gem of the Ocean*. New York: Theatre Communications Group, 2006.

Wilson, August. *Joe Turner's Come and Gone*. New York: Plume, 1988.

Worster, Donald. *Nature's Economy: A History of Ecological Ideas*. 2nd ed. Cambridge: Cambridge University Press, 1994.

Wright, Michelle. *Physics of Blackness: Beyond the Middle Passage Epistemology*. Minneapolis: University of Minnesota Press, 2015.

Wright, Richard. *Native Son*. Perennial Classics ed. New York: Harper Perennial, 1966. Originally published in 1940.

Wynter, Sylvia. "Black Metamorphosis: New Natives in a New World." Unpublished manuscript. Institute of the Black World Papers. Schomburg Center for Research in Black Culture, New York.

Wynter, Sylvia. "The Ceremony Must Be Found: After Humanism." *boundary 2* 12/13, no. 3–1 (1984): 19–70. https://www.jstor.org/stable/302808.

Wynter, Sylvia. "1492: A New World View." In *Race, Discourse, and the Origin of the Americas: A New World View*, edited by Vera Lawrence Hyatt and Rex Nettleford, 5–57. Washington, DC: Smithsonian Institution Press, 1995.

Wynter, Sylvia. "Novel and History, Plot and Plantation." *Savacou*, no. 5 (1971): 95–102.

Wynter, Sylvia. "*PROUD FLESH* Inter/views: Sylvia Wynter." *PROUD FLESH: New Afrikan Journal of Culture, Politics and Consciousness*, no. 4 (2006): 1–35. https://www.africaknowledgeproject.org/index.php/proudflesh/article/view/202.

Wynter, Sylvia. "Unsettling the Coloniality of Being/Power/Truth/Freedom: Towards the Human, After Man, Its Overrepresentation—an Argument." *CR: The New Centennial Review* 3, no. 3 (2003): 257–337. https://doi.org/10.1353/ncr.2004.0015.

Index

Page references in *italics* indicate figures.